This is the most comprehensive, practical and useful guide to data strategy that I have come across. I have developed a few data strategies and would have found it easier and produced a better strategy if I had read Ian Wallis' book first. This is a book that is informed by deep, real-world experience of data strategy and the many change challenges involved. It has all the frameworks, tools and thinking you could need, laid out in a clear and readable way. For anyone involved in data or digital strategies it is a must read.

Tony Gosling, *Chief Digital Officer, RSBG UK Group*

Whether you are new to the area or just an old dog learning new tricks, this book offers vast experience, anecdotes and learnings from the front line for you to apply in the modern era of data. There is just so much to learn and revisit, e.g. on defensive vs offensive, dynamic data strategy, secret to success in R.A.V.E. – but most of all it's a journey not a destination.

Graeme McDermott, *Chief Data Officer, Tempcover*

Data Strategy: From definition to execution is an excellent resource for newbies to data strategy and more seasoned professionals alike. It provides a well-organised, clear approach to developing a data strategy through its complete life cycle, alongside the potential pitfalls of getting a strategy from paper into reality. The author's style is engaging and well thought out, clearly coming from a place of significant experience – if you're writing a data strategy (or if you're planning to) I heartily recommend this book, you're bound to learn something useful!

Jon Alvis, *Data Governance SME, Member of BSI AMT/004 Group (for ISO 8000)*

This really is everything you need to know about writing and delivering a data strategy! I found it filled with great analogies and stories from across the public and private sector. With the ten top things to remember at the end of every chapter, it really helped to summarise the key points. I particularly liked that it covered all the salient points of a data strategy, from control to exploitation, from strategy development to implementation and everything in between. A must read for those embarking on their data strategy journey!

Lisa Allen, *Vice Chair, DAMA UK*

Essential reading for anyone starting out on implementing, or reviewing a current data strategy. This book provides insights the author has gained from many years implementing data strategies across many enterprises. Providing a through exposition on the do's and don'ts, highlighting the importance of having a measurable implementation plan, and that the strategy needs to be linked to enterprise business goals. This is a valuable guide and a perfect antidote for those who operate in organisations where ignorance masquerades as knowledge!

Godfrey Morgan, *Head of Strategy and Governance, People Analytics and Insight, CPO, HMRC*

CW01497622

Ian Wallis has produced an excellent guide to crafting and executing a data strategy. It is eminently readable, always relatable but crucially entirely practical in its approach to enabling Data Strategists - whether that is your job title or not - to plan, produce and implement meaningful data strategies in any organisation. Ian guides the reader through the steps needed to get senior level buy in, tell the story of the strategy, ground the plan in reality and be positioned to secure backing and resource for the successful creation of a fully formed strategy. All with a view to see your business extract value from one of its greatest assets – data. The author's practical approach to implementation, his real life experiences, but only occasional references to what might be seen as technical speak, brings this thinking to life making this a very digestible guide. The thoughtful 'top ten takeaways' provide very handy references points and reminders at the end of each chapter, and his work is both an excellent standalone learning piece as well as a 'return to' check in guide. It's a great read and he knows his stuff.

Colin Grieves, *Managing Director,*
UK&I at Experian, Marketing Services

To be a leader in a sector and across multiple markets it is essential to have a functional data strategy. However, the line between success and failure in defining and implementing such strategy is becoming increasingly blurred due to the complexity of the topic. Data Strategy is your guide to avoid the noise and to focus on the areas that really can make a difference to setting up an operational and effective data strategy.

Dr Marzia Bolpagni, *Head of BIM International,*
Associate Director, Mace

Whether new to developing a data strategy or looking to enhance an existing one this book is an essential read. It offers unique insight to the author's extensive experience combined with relevant reference material to help direct personal research. I found the takeaway points at the end of each chapter particularly useful. It is helping to define an approach and make the challenge of updating the data strategy achievable.

Karen Alford FCCA, *FCRM Manager, Digital Asset Data and*
Information, Environment Agency

This guide on how to plan, craft and execute a data strategy is outstanding in its level of detail and completeness. The author weaves his extensive and varied experience as a data practitioner into the fabric of theory to create a wonderful, practical, 'how to' guide. He takes you through the early planning stages, points out the pitfalls to avoid, shares some highly useful tips (e.g. CLEAR) and shows you how to navigate the rocky waters to implementation and the measurement of value of your data strategy. Whether you are creating a data strategy for the first time or looking to be even better next time, this is a must read!

Glenn Waine, *VP/Head of Data Science and Analytics, Gale Partners*

I read this book cover-to-cover in one day. Why? It's the first to fully weave the fundamentals of strategy and cultural change into the 'technical' aspects of creating and executing on a well thought out data strategy. A must-read for all who desire tangible, long-term results from the use of data in decision-making throughout an enterprise. Masterfully written, Ian!

Lori L. Silverman, *CEO/Founder and Shift Strategist, Partners for Progress;*
Co-author, 'Business Storytelling for Dummies'

DATA STRATEGY

BCS, THE CHARTERED INSTITUTE FOR IT

BCS, The Chartered Institute for IT, is committed to making IT good for society. We use the power of our network to bring about positive, tangible change. We champion the global IT profession and the interests of individuals, engaged in that profession, for the benefit of all.

Exchanging IT expertise and knowledge
The Institute fosters links between experts from industry, academia and business to promote new thinking, education and knowledge sharing.

Supporting practitioners
Through continuing professional development and a series of respected IT qualifications, the Institute seeks to promote professional practice tuned to the demands of business. It provides practical support and information services to its members and volunteer communities around the world.

Setting standards and frameworks
The Institute collaborates with government, industry and relevant bodies to establish good working practices, codes of conduct, skills frameworks and common standards. It also offers a range of consultancy services to employers to help them adopt best practice.

Become a member
Over 70,000 people including students, teachers, professionals and practitioners enjoy the benefits of BCS membership. These include access to an international community, invitations to a roster of local and national events, career development tools and a quarterly thought-leadership magazine. Visit www.bcs.org/membership to find out more.

Further information
BCS, The Chartered Institute for IT,
3 Newbridge Square,
Swindon, SN1 1BY, United Kingdom.
T +44 (0) 1793 417 417
(Monday to Friday, 09:00 to 17:00 UK time)
www.bcs.org/contact
http://shop.bcs.org/

DATA STRATEGY
From definition to execution

Ian Wallis

bcs
The
Chartered
Institute
for IT

Published by BCS Learning and Development Ltd, a wholly owned subsidiary of BCS, The Chartered Institute for IT, 3 Newbridge Square, Swindon, SN1 1BY, UK.
www.bcs.org

Paperback ISBN: 978-1-78017-5416
PDF ISBN: 978-1-78017-5423
ePUB ISBN: 978-1-78017-5430

British Cataloguing in Publication Data.
A CIP catalogue record for this book is available at the British Library.

Publisher's acknowledgements
Reviewers: Mark Dodd and Katie Walsh
Publisher: Ian Borthwick
Commissioning editor: Rebecca Youé
Production manager: Florence Leroy
Project manager: Sunrise Setting Ltd
Copy-editor: Merle Read
Proofreader: Sarah Cook
Indexer: Fionbar Lyons
Cover design: Alex Wright
Cover image: istock/fbxx
Typeset by Lapiz Digital Services, Chennai, India.

CONTENTS

LIST OF FIGURES AND TABLES

AUTHOR

Ian is Managing Director of Data Strategists Ltd, which he formed in 2005. He has been a data and analytics professional for more than 30 years, working in 12 business sectors – both public and private. He has delivered some of the UK's largest data and analytics transformation programmes as well as a number of global programmes. His experience extends from data management – including delivering single customer view programmes for several organisations – to advanced analytics and insight to generate competitive advantage.

Ian has a strong focus on how to deliver strategy into execution to deliver value and building strong data, analytics and insight teams. He believes that wider business engagement is critical to achieve successful outcomes, with culture, information literacy and an agile approach to the data to analytics delivery cycle critical to success. He has forward deployed analytics 'translators' into customer groups for the last 20 years and strongly advocates taking a proactive approach to solve business problems.

He's a regular conference speaker, often presenting on the importance of ensuring data and analytics programmes are done with the organisation, and not to them, and delivering intelligence into the hands of those who need to make decisions to enable them to achieve real value as a result. He has also run numerous highly regarded workshops on defining and executing data strategies, which underpin this book.

ACKNOWLEDGEMENTS

I would like to thank a number of people, without whom this book would not have materialised.

First and foremost, my wife, Louise, who has lost evenings and weekends over the last year whilst I've researched and drafted this book and has kept me going to be able to share my experience with you. I am truly grateful for the love we have shared over the last thirty years and the support to be able to finally achieve the goal of completing the book. My father, Eric, has been a constant and positive conscience to me making progress and, after more than thirty years of my career in data, analytics and insight, may finally begin to understand what it is I do!

I would like to thank those who have provided helpful advice, comments and input along the way, especially the reviewers, including my former colleagues Godfrey Morgan, whose quote features in this book, and Tony Gosling, whose experience in consulting and digital has given valuable insight.

I would like to thank those who have contributed content and given permission for their work to be reproduced in this book. I have made new contacts along the way and hope I have positioned your work in a way that faithfully represents it in the context of data strategy. Many authors have provided valuable insights to help shape my thinking, along with numerous experiences through my career. I thank all who have contributed indirectly to the knowledge I have gained to provide the content in this book.

I have had support along the way from the team at BCS, and must call out Ian Borthwick, whose perseverance over more than a year to get me to commit to write this book showed his determination and enthusiasm to publish a book on data strategy through BCS! In turn, Ian and Rebecca Youé have been flexible and understanding in what has been a challenging year for many and which was not envisaged at the outset.

The last year has been one in which data, and its exploitation, has been at the forefront of guiding us through the coronavirus pandemic across the world. It has demonstrated the value of data, the potential for it to be misinterpreted, the power of being able to predict and the importance of having quality data. Data has probably never been more at the heart of our daily lives, and so I hope this book is timely in helping you navigate your way through how to structure data in your own organisations. I would also like to dedicate this book to the many people who sadly did not make it through the pandemic: for all the insight data enables, it is an aggregate that can often lose sight of individuals, and we forget this to our cost.

Ian Wallis
April 2021

ABBREVIATIONS

5W1H	who, what, when, where, why and how
AC	actual cost
AI	artificial intelligence
ALCOA	attributable, legible, contemporaneous, original, accurate
BDN	benefits dependency network
BI	business intelligence
CBER	Center for Biologics Evaluation and Research (part of FDA)
CDER	Center for Drug Evaluation and Research (part of FDA)
CDO	chief data officer
CEO	chief executive officer
CFO	chief financial (or finance) officer
CFTC	Commodity Futures Trading Commission (USA)
CIO	chief information officer
CLEAR	clarity, leadership, execution, agility, relevancy
DSDM	dynamic systems development method
EU	European Union
EV	earned value
EVM	earned value management
FBM	Fogg behaviour model
FCA	Financial Conduct Authority
FDA	Food and Drug Administration (USA)
GDPR	General Data Protection Regulation (EU legislation 2016/679)
HMRC	Her Majesty's Revenue and Customs (UK)
HR	human resources
ICO	Information Commissioner's Office (UK)
IFRS	International Financial Reporting Standards
IPO	initial public offering
ISO	International Organization for Standardization
IT	information technology
KAB	knowledge, attitude and behaviour

KAP	knowledge, attitude and practice
KPI	key performance indicator
MDM	master data management
MI	management information
ML	machine learning
NEP	National Enabling Programme
NSW	New South Wales (Australia)
OED	Open Exposure Data Standard
OKRs	objectives and key results
ORD	Open Results Data Standard
PDCA	plan – do – check – adjust/act
PESTLE	political, economic, sociological, technological, legal and environmental
PfMO	portfolio management office
PI	performance indicator
PMO	programme management office
PRIDE	purpose, relevance, inspiring, deliverable, enabling
PV	planned value
RACI	responsible, accountable, consulted, informed
RAID	risks, assumptions, issues and dependencies
RASCI	responsible, accountable, support, consulted, informed
RAVE	relevance, awareness, value, execution
ROI	return on investment
SME	subject matter expert
UK	United Kingdom
US	United States of America

1 INTRODUCTION: WHY IS A DATA STRATEGY RELEVANT TODAY?

'Business strategy is the battleplan for a better future.'

Patrick Dixon[1]

Strategy. For those of us who work in organisations in the 21st century, it is hard to imagine a world in which the term 'strategy' would not be heard. Yet the reality is that it is a relatively new concept for business. This is even more so when the term is applied to data, with a significant number of organisations lacking a data strategy despite it being ubiquitous as the means to conduct business: data is fundamental to drive operational activity, undertake financial transactions, engage with customers, deliver products and services, and operate the internal functions without which an organisation simply could not function.

The English term 'strategy' originates from the ancient Greek *strategos*, meaning the 'art of troop leader; office of general, command, generalship'. However, it was the Chinese who have often been regarded as the founders of the principle, with *The Art of War*, attributed to Sun Tzu and dated to the 5th century BCE, acclaimed as the pioneering work on military strategy. Remarkably, it was not until the 18th century that 'strategy' was translated into Western vernacular languages when it was used in its military form by Count Guibert in France and Claus von Clausewitz, the famous Prussian general.

The military use recognised strategy as the series of engagements that lead to winning the war, with tactics the activities that take place in the context of an engagement. The business use of strategy and tactics remain intertwined in much the same way today.

It was not until the 1960s that strategy became part of business language (see the timeline in the box), largely through academia finding its way into the growing sphere of management consulting, with strategy becoming a new revenue stream for these organisations who to that point had concentrated on organisational structure to derive income. It also led to consulting firms being formed which were focused on strategy alone – Boston Consulting Group being one which formed in 1963.

> **1954** Peter Drucker writes *The Practice of Management*, which becomes the foundation of business management for decades to come, introducing the concept of 'planned abandonment' – deciding what to stop doing, to successfully pursue what is new and highly promising – moving the concept of business strategy towards making decisions on how to achieve corporate goals. He also introduces the concept of management based on objectives.

---

[1] Patrick Dixon, *Building a Better Business: The Key to Future Marketing, Management and Motivation*. London: Profile Books, 2005.

1962 Alfred Chandler, in *Strategy and Structure: Chapters in the History of Industrial Enterprise*, declares: 'Strategy is the determination of the basic long-term goals of an enterprise, and the adoption of courses of action and the allocation of resources necessary for carrying out these goals.'

1965 Igor Ansoff, in *Corporate Strategy*, introduces the concept of gap analysis, identifying the difference between the current state and the desired future state, and introduces a number of 'gap reducing actions'.

1973 Peter Drucker addresses strategic planning as part of the management process in his book, *Management: Tasks, Responsibilities, Practices*: 'Strategic planning is the continuous process of making present entrepreneurial (risk-taking) decisions systematically and with the greatest knowledge of their futurity; organizing systematically the efforts needed to carry out these decisions; and measuring the results of these decisions against the expectations through organized, systematic feedback.'

1979 George Steiner, seen as a father figure in the emerging strategic planning arena, only defines strategy in the notes at the end of his book *Strategic Planning*, despite strategy running throughout it. He describes it as a way of referring to what one does to counter a competitor's actual or predicted moves, and acknowledges the diverse views as to how to define strategy.

1979/80 Michael Porter, initially in *Harvard Business Review* and subsequently in his book *Competitive Strategy*, defines strategy as the 'broad formula for how a business is going to compete, what its goals should be, and what policies will be needed to carry out those goals' and the 'combination of the ends (goals) for which the firm is striving and the means (policies) by which it is seeking to get there'. His 'five forces' become a standard model for competitive strategy.

1980 Benjamin Tregoe and John Zimmerman, in *Top Management Strategy*, describe strategy as 'the framework which guides those choices that determine the nature and direction of an organization'. They identify nine driving forces but insist that only one of these could be selected as the basis for the business strategy.

1981 Bruce Henderson, who founded BCG, advises in *The Concept of Strategy* that 'Strategy depends upon the ability to foresee future consequences of present initiatives.'

Since the 1960s, strategy has evolved but the balance between strategy and tactics remains. Today, strategy is a recognised business discipline in its own right, and there are a myriad of consulting firms offering strategic capabilities across every domain, sector and geographical location. It is surprising, therefore, that so many organisations are still unable to execute strategy effectively.

Henry Mintzberg was one of the first to call out the complexity[2] of defining a strategy and seeing it through to implementation almost three decades ago. Many had focused on the definition of a strategy, but there seemed to be an almost inherent assumption that the organisation would simply 'get on' with implementing it as if that was the easy part, which Mintzberg identified in linking the two. In the meantime, complexity in our organisations has increased dramatically, with multiple channels, globalisation, the velocity of activities and pace of constant change becoming just a few of the things our strategies have to adapt to, comprehend and incorporate.

1.1 DATA IS EVERYWHERE

A similar scenario, in terms of the evolution of awareness and focus within the business world, has taken place over the last 40 years or so with regard to data. The initial explosion of data volumes that arose as technology moved into the workplace and provided us with the means to conduct business on a global stage, message one another frequently, process large data sets in spreadsheets and communicate to our customers and employees at scale took us into a different business environment. Data became accessible to many, systems started to present opportunities for reuse rather than single purpose, and expectations grew about the speed at which decisions could be reached by using computer processing power rather than the limitation of our brains, paper and pen.

The world of data has changed beyond all recognition since the 1990s – it has been my career throughout that period and change has occurred at an unparalleled pace. Today, we take for granted having computer devices all around us – the latest mobile phones are more powerful than the laptop many of us use for daily tasks. Indeed, the smartphone is faster than a 1980s Cray-2 supercomputer and, more remarkably, faster than the computer on board the Orion spaceship NASA is testing for its mission to Mars.[3]

The world is a smaller place, with the internet in many ways removing geography altogether as a barrier or constraint. Something can happen the other side of the world and within seconds everyone can see it on social media as well as news sites. Through video conferencing, the office is less a fixed focal point and people operate from wherever suits them – as long as there is bandwidth and a willingness to work flexibly, it is possible to conduct business almost anywhere, at any time.

All of this consumes data, generates data and builds a rich landscape of data points that can tell a lot about an individual. Whilst cookies were invented in 1994 to aid with shopping and recording items of interest on the internet, they escalated to be able to build a browsing profile of an individual that became of particular interest to hackers, which alerted authorities to crack down on compliance and has led to a reluctance amongst some to surf the internet without resorting to virtual private network to access sites incognito. This demonstrates how the development of a technology enabler has led to a dramatic increase in data traffic – a website would typically have around 20

---

2 H. Mintzberg, *The Rise and Fall of Strategic Planning*. Hemel Hempstead: Prentice Hall, 1994.

3 S. Nunez, Your Phone Is Now More Powerful Than Your PC. 2020. https://insights.samsung.com/2020/08/07/your-phone-is-now-more-powerful-than-your-pc-2/.

cookies,[4] so in the course of a week the volume of cookies stored would be significant for an active user of the internet, unless there is active blocking or screening taking place – and introduced a whole new security risk that has led to a major industry forming to tackle cyber-security and provide products to mitigate the risk for individuals and organisations alike.

In a relatively short period of time, data volumes have exploded, making it harder to manage effectively and compliantly – the so-called rise of 'big data' that was coined in 2005. Multi-channel has often led to multi-systems and platforms, duplicating data and failing to join it up in a way that enables the organisation to understand it, manage it or exploit it. The race to maintain a competitive edge has led to inefficiencies that those organisations that started out as dot.com businesses have not had to wrestle with, such that the levels of service in established organisations can often be woefully behind their competitors. One major UK retailer was recently advertising a 3–5 day delivery time frame as its standard, when competitors such as Amazon were offering same or next day delivery.

In effect, data is now the battleground of every market, every sector, in virtually every place. It is no longer the prerogative of the large organisation to be smarter than those of more limited means. Every organisation has data, the means to be able to manipulate it have become more commoditised through developments such as cloud computing, and a start-up can be nimbler and more targeted than a large corporation that is grappling with legacy technologies – a culture that is still operating in a traditional way and a lead time to make change that is beyond the comprehension of its smaller rivals. If ever there was the time for a return to David defeating Goliath, this is it!

Yet, only a minority of organisations appear to have identified the need for a data strategy and very few have successfully developed and implemented one. If you have identified an interest or responsibility to do something in this sphere it makes you a relatively rare breed. If you are able to pull it off by convincing your organisation of the need for a data strategy, defining it and implementing it successfully, then you truly are in a scarce pool of data strategists.

This book combines practical experience, academic research and input from many other experts in their field to try to guide you through the process of identifying the need for a data strategy and the case for change that it necessitates, determining what it should include, defining the content and then executing it through a clear implementation plan to achieve a successful outcome. It is a guide, as each organisation is different in the sense of maturity and readiness, but is intended to provide sufficient insight for the road that lies before you to enable you to map out your own journey and navigate through the potential pitfalls on the way.

1.2 WHY IS GAINING AGREEMENT TO DEFINE AND EXECUTE A DATA STRATEGY SO DIFFICULT?

The logic for a data strategy might be clear to you – if not, then I am hoping to convince you by the end of this book of its merits! – but this is probably not the case for the vast majority of your colleagues in the organisation.

---

4   Cookie Checker: Is Your Website GDPR and CCPA Compliant? 2020. https://www.cookiebot.com/en/cookie-checker/.

In 2012 Cynthia Montgomery published a book anyone interested in strategy should know well as a great starting point to understand its purpose – *The Strategist*.[5] Montgomery ran the strategy unit at Harvard Business School and turned her insights from her oversubscribed course on strategy into the book. She states:

> Some ... find it extremely difficult to identify why their companies exist. Accustomed to describing their businesses by the industries they're in or the products they make, they can't distinguish them from competitors on anything beyond a superficial level. Nor have they spent much time thinking concretely about where they want their companies to be in ten years and the forces, internal and external, that will get them there.

> If leaders aren't clear about this, imagine the confusion in their businesses three or four levels lower. Yet, people throughout a business – in marketing, production, service, as well as near the top of the organization – must make decisions every day that could and should be based on some shared sense of what the company is trying to be and do. If they disagree about that, or simply don't understand it, how can they make consistent decisions that move the company forward? Similarly, how can leaders expect customers, providers of capital, or other stakeholders to understand what is really important about their companies if they themselves can't identify it? This is truly basic – there is no way a business can thrive until these questions are answered.

I have sought to highlight in this book, through many sources, how ineffective senior leaders often are across the world at strategy definition and execution, how frequently such programmes fail and the evidence as to why this happens. When considering what Montgomery has to say, just reflect on the fact that these were senior executives and company owners who had sought out her course and therefore had an appetite to learn. Yet clearly they were unprepared in terms of thought or evidence about strategy.

Bear in mind that Montgomery and others are talking about strategy as a whole, typically focused on corporate strategy, which is an essential component to any organisation – if you don't know where you're going, how do you know whether you're on the right path to get there, you might put it.

Data strategy is even less understood, so the chances of success can be further decreased, simply because you need organisation-wide commitment and buy-in to succeed. Data does not exist in a bubble; it is not the preserve of a function that can fix it for all, detached from touching everyone else. It is core to how you run the organisation, and without a focus on where you are heading, it is going to trip the organisation up at every turn – regulatory compliance; operational effectiveness; financial performance; customer and employee experience; essentially, the efficiency in managing virtually every activity in the organisation.

The key point to make is that you need to regard data as an asset. In the right state, data is one of the most valuable parts of your organisation. But data needs to maintain compliance, to be fit for purpose to avoid some potentially fatal decisions being made and to enable your organisation to function effectively. Then, it is truly an asset.

---

5   C.A. Montgomery, *The Strategist: Be the Leader Your Business Needs*. New York: HarperCollins, 2012.

There are many horror stories of data misuse that have got into the public domain (clearly, far more never make it outside the organisation). IBM has estimated that bad data costs US companies $3.1 trillion a year, equating to 12 per cent of revenue.[6] I have listed a few examples, just to show how simple it can be to misuse data and reach a conclusion that has major impacts on your organisation:

- The Mars Climate Orbiter, launched in 1999, was run on software, supplied by two different organisations, that failed to convert imperial measurements into metric, with the result that the thrusters fired at the wrong time – 105 miles closer to the planet than intended – which led to the craft disintegrating in the Martian atmosphere. The entire multimillion-dollar investment was lost. Numerous organisations have made the basic error of mixing the two measurement standards with often significant impact.

- The Enron scandal in 2001 was a result of data being provided to shareholders falsifying the true position, and a lack of controls prevented this from being identified.

- In 2012 an error in risk calculation led to the UK West Coast Mainline rail franchise tender process having to be suspended and compensation of £40 million being made to the bidders.

- The UK National Audit Office found that 375,000 people who should have been contacted by a call centre in 2020 to advise on shielding during the coronavirus pandemic could not be reached due to missing or inaccurate phone records. A further 126,000 people were contacted and advised to shield who did not need to do so.

There are many examples of data being at the heart of significant costs being incurred, businesses lost and reputations left in tatters. This is caused by poor data quality and errors that go unchecked through the many processes at work in the organisation encompassing data collection, utilisation and manipulation that underpin how it works. In addition, there are then the increasing scale and number of fines levied for data breaches and data protection failings that are becoming more commonplace. If this is not a cause for concern for your organisation, then it is either oblivious to the risk or has control of what eludes some of the biggest organisations across the world today.

1.3 DATA IS BECOMING READILY ACCESSIBLE

The coronavirus pandemic has brought data to the forefront of public consciousness. The plethora of data gathered has led to a surfeit of information, which has been both beneficial and confusing to navigate. The interpretation of the data has led to the rapid development of vaccines and impressive programmes to inoculate adult populations in many countries. There has been international cooperation and information sharing to enable knowledge of variants of the disease to be identified and traced to provide rapid testing and learning, so there is a continuous process of iteration and improvement in the way nations tackle the pandemic.

---

6   In T.C. Redman, Bad Data Costs the U.S. $3 Trillion Per Year. *Harvard Business Review*, 22 September 2016. https://hbr. org/2016/09/bad-data-costs-the-u-s-3-trillion-per-year.

Whilst this level of cooperation isn't necessarily new, it is one of the clearest examples in how data has been used globally to provide information, from an individual and aggregated basis, that has been turned into intelligence and is informing positions that national governments have taken. It is transforming expectations, with the UK government highlighting in its national data strategy[7] that there is a duty on it to do more, using data for the benefit of society and enabling a more integrated and rewarding experience in engaging with public services, whilst also protecting individuals from harm and treating them fairly, and also, potentially, extending to related private sector services.

Barriers to accessing data are becoming more recognisable as an issue and are being seen as a blocker to enabling the smarter use of data through technology and innovative propositions. Offsetting this is the concern over data privacy, the rights of the individual and the need to hold data, all aspects of an evolving and more clearly defined data protection regulatory landscape. The term 'responsible' is often incorporated into governance controls and legislation to try to strike the balance, but of course the challenge is finding an agreed position as to what constitutes 'responsible', especially when operating across national boundaries.

The technology landscape, too, is changing as the evolution of cloud computing becomes increasingly the norm for many organisations. The notion of the cloud is a way of describing an 'off-premise' solution to storing data, as it is still physically held in a location – often multiple locations – and so the regime in each nation in which the data is held needs to reflect the same safeguards as those countries to which it relates. This can lead to a tricky challenge of identifying backup systems in cloud computing, tracking how resilience impacts on storage, and other issues which need careful consideration and ongoing monitoring. The continuing dependency on maintaining public trust in organisations to manage their data safely and securely is also a major factor. This can be undermined very quickly; it only takes one major incident and the trust can be eroded.

The increasing prevalence of advanced capabilities in organisations, such as artificial intelligence (AI), is very data dependent and also data hungry. These applications require good quality data in large amounts to work to maximum effectiveness, so the investment in, and accessibility of, data is critical for success. This requires progress on data sharing and trust to be established in the first place, used as the basis from which to invest in the quality of the data in order to materialise the benefits of the advanced capabilities.

1.4 HOW DOES A DATA STRATEGY HELP?

By identifying the alignment of data-related activities – from the effective management of data through to its exploitation – you are putting in place a vision for how a critical asset in your organisation is going to support achieving corporate goals. Establishing common objectives in how the organisation will manage and exploit data is an essential step towards ensuring compliance, operational integrity and consistency in what underpins decision making. It provides a framework to enable the organisation to move

---

7   National Data Strategy, GOV.UK. www.gov.uk.

to managing data as an asset, recognising the need to invest to be able to turn it into something that generates value rather than simply consumes cost. Through the choices made and the focus given in the data strategy, the opportunities that will be available to the organisation to accelerate corporate goals and to realise benefits that might otherwise have been overlooked will be determined.

The vast majority of data in an organisation is not exploited, yet is obtained for some reason, whether historic or still relevant to the present. In itself, this is quite concerning. Regardless of its use, that data needs to be understood and maintained compliantly, and whilst estimates vary, the consensus seems to be that less than one percent of unstructured data is effectively catalogued and exploited in organisations today.[8] Aside from the potential that may be hidden in plain sight, how compliant is your retention of that data?

This doesn't just hold true for unstructured data either. Most organisations are regarded as exploiting less than half their structured data,[9] that which is held in systems and therefore is more accessible.

If you are focused on the goals set out in a corporate strategy, how do you know you are delivering these effectively if you overlook the majority of the data within the organisation? Any use of data is limited to 'that which we know' and may be missing real insights into performance, costs or opportunities through the failure to join up the data across the organisation to give a more informed view.

Many organisations start a data strategy from a need to get data into some sort of organised state in which it is feasible to demonstrate compliance. In my opinion, compliance should be a component of a data strategy, not the data strategy in itself. It is referred to in this book as balancing a defensive view with an offensive position, and it rarely works to focus solely on defence.

If this is where you find yourself, then it is likely your organisation has either been caught in the glare of a regulator or has suddenly become aware it may well be in that position soon. It is an opportunity to use compliance to pivot attention in the organisation to data, but I am passionate that this presents a window to expand it into so much more. Whilst you have executive attention, consider how the cost of compliance could also be pitched as the investment opportunity to deliver real value to the organisation – open eyes to the offensive opportunities that are virgin territory and hence a potential gold mine of revenue or other gains to be achieved.

This book explores both defence and offence as strategies. A data strategy should accommodate both – to use a military analogy, there is no point in an all-out attack and leaving your base unguarded. My advice is to seek to operationalise both approaches within your strategy and to seek out the sweet spot arising from the opportunity to devise a data strategy. Over time, the focus will shift, typically towards a more offensive strategy as the elements that form the foundations of good data management practice become embedded into your organisation's ways of working. There will be a need to revisit these,

---

8   L. DalleMule and T.H. Davenport, What's Your Data Strategy? *Harvard Business Review*, May–June 2017.

9   L. DalleMule and T.H. Davenport, What's Your Data Strategy? *Harvard Business Review*, May–June 2017.

as over time the discipline will waver and need reaffirming and re-establishing, but the value of a data strategy is most visible through the impact it can make in delivering the corporate strategy and raising awareness and expectations of 'the art of the possible'.

1.5 THE ROLE OF THIS BOOK

The intention in writing this book was to transfer more than 30 years of experience gained in data and analytics into some practical use for those who are faced with one of the most challenging – but most rewarding, if you get it right! – tasks: defining and executing a data strategy successfully. It is based on the knowledge I have amassed of nearly 20 organisations across a dozen sectors, along with the workshops I have run on this topic. I have seen tremendous change in the scale, opportunity and professionalism of the data and analytics community. It is my goal to use my experience to my utmost to help ensure that the current and next generation of data and analytics leaders are as well informed as possible to enable them to succeed.

I have covered the significant breadth of activity that is required to enable a data strategy to move through an extensive effort from identification, into definition, through execution to releasing benefits to the organisation. There are many different ways to tackle an undertaking of the scale of defining and executing a data strategy, especially in some of the larger organisations. It is a process which I have distilled into ten phases, though it is highly iterative: so do not be concerned if you find yourself oscillating back and forth so long as there is a purpose in so doing. These phases are summarised in Chapter 12: five for definition (positioning; readiness and scope; definition; route map; content, structure and alignment) and five for execution (communication, culture and change readiness; mobilisation and planning; delivery; flexibility; demonstrating value).

My hope is that you are able to use the framework, learn from the content and find a way to implement it within your own organisation. It is often a misconception that it is a technical task, for whilst there is a need to comprehend the technical aspects with sufficient depth of knowledge to lead this process, it is more about culture, stakeholder management, communications, leadership and strong programme management skills. These are often misrepresented as 'softer' skills, but as a practitioner I can certainly tell you there is nothing 'soft' about being able to marshal some of the biggest challenges anyone could face to drive change in your organisation.

If you believe the data strategy is an exercise to be done and then you move on, then this may not be the book, or the task, for you. This is about dedication, drive, perseverance and commitment to deliver change in an organisation based on a subject which is possibly not well understood. And yet it goes to the heart of the organisation, its people, processes and technology, influencing its ways of working in a way that will probably take you into every function to some degree. If you don't understand your organisation at the start, you will certainly know it well by the time you deliver the data strategy implementation, and almost certainly will have played a significant role in changing it in ways never comprehended when you embarked on your task.

I have sought to provide some useful reminders at the end of each chapter, primarily as something to reflect on rather than as a shortcut to the answer. Each chapter builds and takes you through the process from identifying the need for a data strategy to executing it in all its glory. My final chapter brings together some of those themes alongside some further observations.

I hope you find the book to be an informative, challenging but instructive guide to take you through the end-to-end process of delivering a data strategy. I have structured it to flow in such a way that I provide my experience and advice at the appropriate stage of the process. Every organisation is different: there will be parts which may not apply to yours and other instances that resonate loudly with what you are facing. However, remember that every organisation has data, and so every organisation should have a data strategy. You are not alone in dealing with this challenge and you are developing a rare skill, as data strategists are a relatively rare breed that will become more in demand in the future.

2 POSITIONING THE DATA STRATEGY

'Data is great, but strategy is better!'

Steven Sinofsky[1]

The rationale for a data strategy has been established in the previous chapter. The challenge now is how to position it within the organisation. The data strategy may be new, or it may be reworking a previous data strategy that promised a lot and achieved little, other than filling shelf space and gathering dust. Either way, the organisation is probably not yelling out for a data strategy. So how do you establish a need, build a level of interest, and then deliver something which will resonate with the wider organisation and therefore stand a fighting chance of transitioning from theory into practice?

This chapter will be based on a simple question, which then triggers a series of supplementary questions: why do you believe you need a data strategy? Is this something you have initiated – in which case, why? And, if so, how have you pitched it to others? Are they engaged? Do they understand what they will get? Or have they simply nodded their approval on the basis it won't impact them and it is perceived as a way to keep you engaged in anything other than interfering in their business?

If the data strategy has been commissioned by the executive board, what has triggered this and why now? Is there something topical, whether positive or negative, that has suddenly made the executives realise the need? What is their expectation of what is required and what impact do they expect it to have?

Prior to commencing the work on the data strategy, it is essential to establish the right environment. This involves:

- preparing your stakeholders with some appreciation of what is to come;
- being clear with stakeholders what you need from them to support you through data strategy definition and execution;
- being clear on the transformation it will drive as a result.

Anything less and you might as well start to clear shelf space for the latest edition of the data strategy to accompany its predecessors.

The fact that a data strategy has been commissioned does not necessarily reflect the organisational maturity to embrace having one. The work above goes some way to preparing the ground on this, but you should also steel yourself for a detached reality – the executive board gets it, wants it and has asked you to lead on defining it, but the rest of the organisation is not on the same page. In many cases, you will find a data strategy

---

1   Steven Sinofsky, Harvard Business School, 2013.

that flounders not from the lack of executive commitment, but because of the inability to get traction where it really matters, beyond the executive board and into the minds of managers and employees in your organisation. It may be a lack of communication, resistance to change or a number of other reasons, but your task will be to cut through this if you are to succeed.

This topic will be discussed at some length in this book, but bear in mind that there is a difference between executive buy-in and the need to mobilise the whole workforce if your data strategy is to have any likelihood of success.

What do I mean by data strategy?

I have found that the corporate lexicon has appropriated terms in the wider data and information arena that have become increasingly unhelpful. Take chief information officer (CIO) as an example. This was borne out of the widespread use of the term 'information technology', yet, perversely, the technology bit was dropped and information stuck, despite most CIOs having historically had little focus on information (in terms of the generation of it from data) or being the right person to lead on information across the organisation.

In the same vein, data strategy is often a misnomer for a much wider scope of coverage, but the lack of coherence in how we use the language has led to data strategy being perceived to cover data management activities all the way through to exploitation of data in the broadest sense. The occasional use of information strategy, intelligence strategy or even data exploitation strategy may differentiate, but the lack of a common definition on what we mean tends to lead to data strategy being used as a catch-all for the more widespread coverage such a document would typically include. Much of this is due to the generic use of the term 'data' to cover everything from its capture, management, governance through to reporting, analytics and insight.

2.1 TERMINOLOGY – SO WHAT IS A DATA STRATEGY?

For the purposes of this book, the term 'data strategy' is used in its widest sense, rather than confined to purely data collection, storage, governance and compliance – its management, if you like. It also encompasses its exploitation, which can take many forms, as data is there to help the organisation make effective decisions and deliver effective outcomes for its customers and its workforce. However, there is not universal acceptance of or agreement on the application of the term, and so you may find that there are subtle differences in what one organisation would expect in a data strategy to the next.

Depending on your organisation, you may feel the term 'data strategy' is limiting, constraining it to data in the narrowest sense and therefore perceive it to be an unsatisfactory term for something that covers a wider spectrum. From a purist point of view, the term 'data strategy' would seem to limit, but in reality data is a commonly used term that is often describing not only the data itself, but also its exploitation. I tend to suggest you go with the flow within the organisation, and if data is a term commonly used more widely then stick with it. You can define it up front, but it is far more important to have a term which stakeholders across the organisation are comfortable with, as they will provide the resources and support to turn delivery into success.

I am using 'data strategy' as an overarching term to describe a far broader set of capabilities from which sub-strategies can be developed to focus on particular facets of the strategy, such as management information (MI) and reporting; analytics, machine learning and AI; insight; and, of course, data management. The breadth of the definition of a data strategy being used in the context of this book encompasses all parts in the information ecosystem in Figure 2.1. In my opinion, the full range of end-to-end activity involving the transition from data collection to its exploitation and, ultimately, archiving and deletion in line with compliance is essential to regard as one integrated operating model and is therefore best coordinated as a single strategy. In terms of your own approach, as long as it is made absolutely clear at the start of the data strategy document as to the definition you are applying then any ambiguity is avoided, and the relevance of the scope of the definition is more an academic point than an obstacle to the value of the data strategy itself.

> I would argue that the first hurdle is successfully negotiated if the organisation has identified it has a need for a data strategy; the precise meaning and therefore the content can be agreed as the expectation is explored with the executives who have commissioned it.

Figure 2.1 The information ecosystem

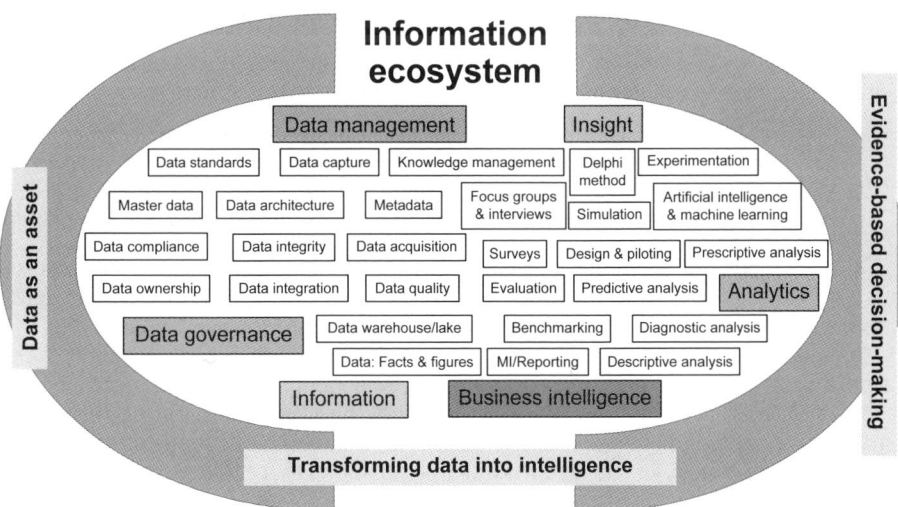

13

Figure 2.1 demonstrates the diversity of content in an information ecosystem. It starts with data management and governance setting the foundations to establish data and information as an asset, through to analytics and insight establishing the value from evidence-based decision making.

The data strategy should certainly cover the following from the ecosystem:

- Data management, as it is commonly termed, including structured and unstructured data, by which I mean:

  - data standards;
  - data architecture;
  - data governance and quality;
  - data integration and migration;
  - data acquisition;
  - data transformation and exchange (that is, with other parties, requiring typically a memorandum of understanding between both organisations);
  - data compliance – including regulations and any other legal constraints – and corporate data security;
  - data accessibility – providing appropriate access to the people who need it;
  - master data management – which systems hold the primary version of data, and which leads in to the systems strategy, in terms of rationalising (potentially part of technology debt) or acquiring systems.

- Data exploitation, which can be subdivided into:

  - reporting and the provision of MI, especially key performance indicators (KPIs), usually involving dashboards and other visualisation techniques;
  - analytics (descriptive, diagnostic, predictive and prescriptive), including the application of machine learning and AI (sometimes referred to as data science);
  - insight – the gathering of additional information and data through research activities to fill gaps in understanding or test out approaches, and the benchmarking and baselining of activities and performance to determine comparative performance with other organisations conducting similar activities;
  - knowledge management to garner real insight from a myriad of internal sources that are often unstructured and difficult to capture and/or harmonise to deliver coherent insight for the organisation in a structured form.

The data strategy will start the process of making people within your organisation recognise data as an asset (Figure 2.2). This may be happening for the first time – perhaps data has been overlooked and assumed to date, rather than managed as an asset class in its own right – or you may be in a position where there is a recognition of data and its importance to the organisation already. Either way, every organisation today is a data business of some sort, with a value attached to that data. If the organisation has not recognised this yet then it is a real opportunity to use the data strategy as the lever to make people realise that data is indeed an asset, it has value and this can diminish if it is not captured, managed, maintained and utilised correctly. If you can change the thinking of your organisation to reflect this, then you are truly on your way to reorientating your organisation to become a data business.

Figure 2.2 A perspective on the assets of an organisation

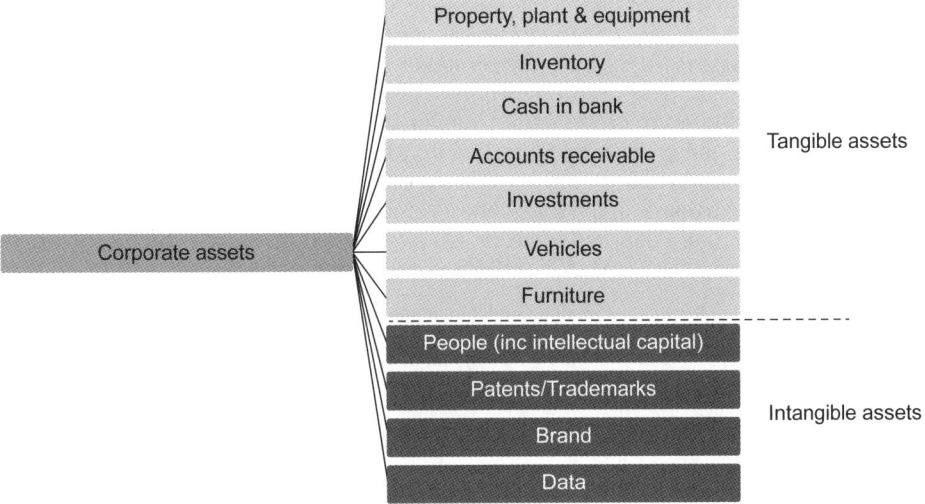

The accounting standards as to what constitutes an asset are very clear. The International Financial Reporting Standards (IFRS) definition states: 'an asset is a resource controlled by the enterprise as a result of past events and from which future economic benefits are expected to flow to the enterprise'.[2] Despite this being further classified into operating and non-operating assets, data is still not recognised, whilst people – the hearts, minds and resource that makes the organisation operational – are not considered other than through the conversion of their intellectual capital into specifics, such as patents, trademarks and the like.

Further, the IFRS state that an asset has three key properties: ownership, such that it can be turned into cash and cash equivalents; economic value, enabling it to be exchanged or sold; and resource, which can be used to generate future economic benefits. Clearly, data does not meet these directly, but with a little imagination it is feasible to argue that data can be sold, that it can certainly generate future economic benefits (otherwise many acquisitions would not hold water as viable transactions) and that an organisation 'owns' the data as an asset. Yet, despite this it is still not officially classed as an asset.

However, this shouldn't stop you managing it as you would any other precious enterprise asset.

---

2   International Financial Reporting Standards Foundation (IFRS), Conceptual Framework for Financial Reporting. 2018. https://www.ifrs.org/issued-standards/list-of-standards/conceptual-framework/.

For example, in the bankruptcy evaluation of Caesars Entertainment Group – the owner of Caesar's Palace in Las Vegas – the most valuable asset was not the physical resort or the land, it was the customer loyalty programme which consisted of 45 million members and was valued at $1 billion by creditors.[3]

Increasingly, as some of the world's biggest corporations do not come from traditional bricks and mortar institutions but are technology and data driven, the balance of assets will need to reflect the value of those assets which the financial regulators seem to struggle to incorporate into their strict definitions. In today's crowded marketplace, you need to be able to compete on many fronts – price, product, service, brand, delivery – and differentiating your organisation based upon the intelligence that effective exploitation of data can bring is an important way to build your customer base into one which delivers repeat business and increases profitability. In reality, every organisation needs to be a data business in the 21st century, and this necessitates treating data as a precious asset. If you are aspiring to be, or are already, a data business then you are in need of a data strategy to harness it and drive your organisation forward.

Do reflect that data strategy is pivotal to the activities of the organisation. It encompasses the trinity of people, process and technology, all of which are entirely data dependent as none of these operate without using data at their heart (Figure 2.3). Consider:

- what employees need to enable them to be empowered in decision making;
- how data enables a process to flow efficiently or otherwise, and how it can enable significant improvements through data capture, maintenance or enhancement;
- technology that works with the data, managing, presenting and manipulating it to enable the organisation to deliver its products and services to its customers in an optimised fashion.

Figure 2.3 The triumvirate of people, process and technology, enabled by data

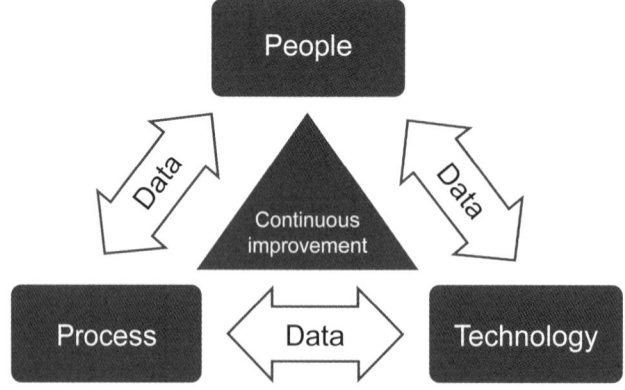

3   Reuters Events, Feeding the Machine: Lessons in Loyalty from Caesars Palace. 2015. https://www.reutersevents.com/travel/revenue-and-data-management/feeding-machine-lessons-loyalty-caesars-palace.

It isn't always practicable to deliver all three in a way that drives improvements across every one of these, and at times compromises have to be made, but it is useful in considering how the data strategy will make a positive impact, enabling the organisation to achieve its overall goals more efficiently and effectively.

2.1.1 Differentiating the data strategy

I would suggest that there is a difference between what I am loosely terming data strategy and other related strategies, such as a digital strategy, technology strategy or a compliance/risk strategy (I cover this in more detail in Chapter 6). The data strategy will feature in, and be dependent on, all of the above but will have this relationship with many other functional strategies within an organisation. This is key to ensure that the strategies all converge, and to recognise the dependencies between them and to keep them synchronised throughout to avoid divergence.

Each strategy within an organisation should be set out clearly in terms of its scope and remit, to ensure there is clarity as to how each of these dovetails with one another. Linkages should exist, recognising the interdependencies, and it should be easy for a reader of one strategy to forge links between separate strategies to connect these dependencies. The key to establish, within the definitions and scope, is the primacy of strategies on any particular topic. This will make it easier to track where dependencies sit and the key driver lies, otherwise it is difficult to keep the range of strategies synchronised. There should be a lead for each strategy within the organisation, and if there is any doubt about the scope of the data strategy, I would recommend engaging your counterparts on the other strategies to ensure there is clarity.

There could be a range of strategies within your organisation (see Figure 2.4), depending on the maturity and approach it takes. Typically, each functional area will have a strategy, and whilst there are some interdependencies at work, it is the cross-functional strategies such as data, digital and technology which are most likely to cut across the majority and therefore have these interdependencies. You will find, therefore, that the secondary strategies have relationships which the tertiary strategies may underpin with more detail.

In terms of the data strategy, it is most likely that this will enable a number of aspects of the other, secondary, strategies to be achieved as there will inevitably be a data angle, whether to aid new processes, decision making or the evidence and measurement to demonstrate a successful outcome.

2.2 THE RELEVANCE OF A DATA STRATEGY

The data strategy needs to provide a clear line of sight between the vision and purpose it is serving and how that fits in with the direction of the organisation and enables the delivery of the corporate strategy. It has to be relevant to all, and therefore accessible in its language and intent.

Figure 2.4 Multiple strategies enabling the corporate strategy to be delivered, with sub-strategies in support

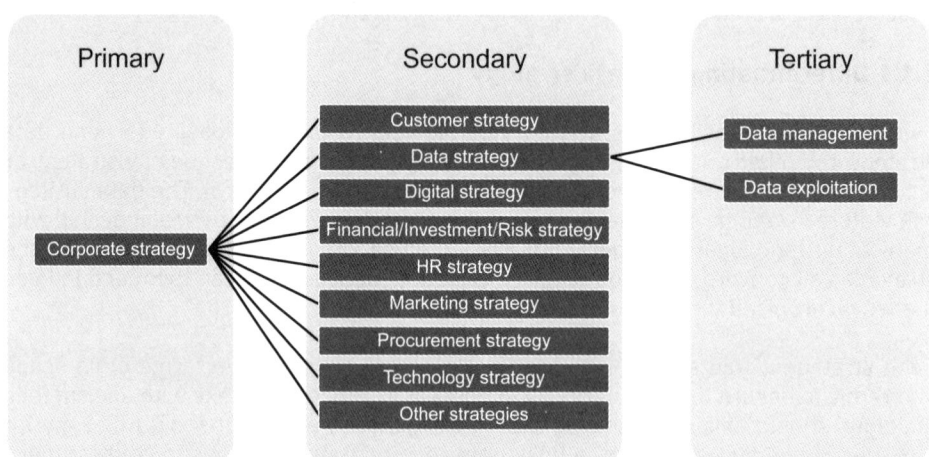

In theory, every organisation should start with a data strategy aligned to the corporate goals before embarking on collecting and acquiring data. In practice, this is rarely possible and the fast pace of events in new start-ups tends to preclude the breadth of thinking that would be needed in a data strategy within a year or two. However, the concept of the data strategy serving the corporate goals, as defined in the corporate strategy, is certainly one which is essential for delivering successful outcomes for every organisation.

In today's fast-moving world, data is growing exponentially – it is claimed that 90 per cent of the data available in the world today only became available in the last two years[4] and 2.5 quintillion bytes of data are produced every day.[5] By 2025, it is predicted that there will be 463 exabytes created daily globally.[6]

At one point, there was a view that data could be stored at low cost, which led to a mindset of 'let's keep it all'. However, the sheer scale of data at our fingertips in our organisations today and the growing overhead to keep acquiring and integrating it has made this more difficult to do in a meaningful way, and the regulatory frameworks have moved on to challenge the legitimate reasons for organisations retaining data if they cannot demonstrate a purpose related to its collection to do so. In addition, the

---

4   IBM, What Is Big Data? More than Volume, Velocity and Variety… 2017. https://developer.ibm.com/technologies/analytics/blogs/what-is-big-data-more-than-volume-velocity-and-variety/.

5   DOMO, Everyone on the Same Page, All the Time. 2018. https://www.domo.com/solution/everyone-on-the-same-page-all-the-time-5.

6   IDC Research/World Economic Forum, How Much Data Is Generated Each Day? 2019. https://www.weforum.org/agenda/2019/04/how-much-data-is-generated-each-day-cf4bddf29f/.

regulations are seeking to move organisations to anonymise data if possible, to remove the risk of identification beyond a period in which that identification can be justified, and making data retention based on an opt-in model rather than the onus on the person to opt out.

The data strategy may be prepared and thus nominally 'owned' by a specific function. In many cases, what is seen as the natural home for data is actually quite the wrong one – the IT function. There is a common misconception that the people who run systems in the organisation must also be the right people to fix the data. The IT function does deliver systems into the organisation, but it is people in the rest of the organisation who are predominantly the users of these systems and create and manage the data that resides within them. The default to IT is a sign that the organisation has not recognised that this is a team game, that data is the lifeblood of the organisation, and hence it has to be a corporate-wide initiative to fix what is largely an operational problem.

In many senses, the lack of awareness of the wider responsibilities for data are the reason why many CIOs fail to really get to grips with the data management issues in hand. In a survey commissioned by Dun & Bradstreet,[7] 45 per cent of respondents said it was challenging that data was in the domain of the IT function rather than the business. Without the wider organisation falling into line, there will be no change in attitude or increase in responsibility.

Ownership needs to reside in the senior leaders of the organisation who are setting the goals of the organisation and dependent on having the data to achieve them. Data strategies driven by the IT function tend to focus more insularly on the things it can have some influence over, such as data storage, security and retention – which are admirable in their own right, but a shadow of what a real data strategy needs to contain to drive an organisation forward.

The growth of the chief data officer (CDO) role in larger organisations provides a natural home for the definition and preparation of the data strategy, although this role is not common across small and medium-sized enterprises. However, it does not need to be a CDO – I have rarely worked in an organisation with a CDO, perhaps because someone is doing the role of a CDO but without the title (for instance, I have been a CDO in all but name in several organisations). The key is to have the right level of executive buy-in, so someone at the executive board level would be ideal.

It is essential that the data strategy has widespread acknowledgement and buy-in throughout the organisation. To achieve this, it is imperative to have stakeholder engagement throughout the process of formulating the data strategy. As with good analytics practice, there is a need to adopt the principles of Agile (discussed later in the book) and be prepared to plan – do – check – adjust/act (PDCA), which provides a reality check as to whether the data strategy is supporting and enabling the wider organisation and thereby has a chance of being adopted. All too often, organisations do not engage when devising a data strategy, only putting it to the test when in a final draft stage, by which time a lot of time and effort has been expended and a negative response is seen

---

[7] Dun & Bradstreet, The Past, Present and Future of Data. 2019. https://www.dnb.co.uk/perspectives/master-data/data-management-report.html.

to be a disaster. Get the feedback in early, co-create the data strategy and build a sense of momentum behind it within the organisation.

It is also important to regard the data strategy as a living document. Do not regard it as a masterpiece, never to be reviewed, amended or critiqued within the time frame it covers, but instead see it as a strategy that can flex to the changing demands of an organisation.

> In one of my assignments, I was shown a data strategy that was no longer in use and regarded as obsolete. It turned out the organisation had acquired another company and so the focus of the organisation shifted to integrate the new business, and hence the data strategy was not fit for purpose any more. No one seemed to think of reshaping the data strategy to keep it relevant, and it seemed as if there was an acceptance to move from a data strategy to a series of tactical decisions devoid of any overarching strategic direction.

2.3 ALIGNMENT WITHIN THE ORGANISATION

As discussed earlier in this book, the term 'strategy' was slow to make it into the business lexicon but it now seems ubiquitous. Every area of the organisation seems to have a strategy, so where does the data strategy fit?

The key for a successful data strategy is to align it clearly with the corporate strategy. The data strategy is a crucial enabler of the corporate strategy, and the data strategy should clearly call out those components that have a clear line of sight to delivering, or enabling, the corporate goals. If the data strategy does not align to the corporate goals it will be a much more challenging task to get the wider organisation to buy into it, not least because it will fail to have any resonance with the objectives of the organisational leaders and be regarded as optional at best.

If the data strategy does not align with the corporate strategy it is because the author of the data strategy either has missed the clear links that will be there or has a completely different agenda to the rest of the organisation. The former is alarming, but the latter is likely to lead to a parting of the ways between employee and employer! It is important to stay grounded in the drivers of success for the organisation as a whole and to frame the data strategy in that context.

> Of course, this presumes all the relevant strategies are in place, which may not be the case. It may be that there are operational plans being followed which are one-year proxies for a strategy, which is far from ideal but will need to be considered in the context of devising your data strategy. It may also be that other parts of the organisation are working on their strategies too, but are running behind yours. If this is the case it warrants additional effort to try to remain synchronised in the thinking and the management of dependencies and assumptions, but there is always the potential to diverge. There is also the possibility that the other

strategies are simply not well written, lacking sufficient clarity in that they are ambiguous or misaligned in their own thinking and as a result fail to support the corporate strategy goals.

I can only advise you to be bold – highlight the potential flaws in those strategies as you see them impacting on your data strategy and be prepared to help in any redrafting of those other strategies to ultimately lead to better alignment with your own.

Should the data strategy slavishly follow the corporate strategy? Despite my comments above, the answer is no. There should be a symbiotic relationship between the data and corporate strategies, otherwise the opportunities to do things differently that lead to better outcomes – and to be innovative in how the analytics and insight outputs are utilised, which in turn can lead to opportunities that might otherwise not be spotted – will not arise. Therefore, the data strategy has to be developed against the framework of the corporate strategy first and foremost, but not be constrained by it in its ambition to go beyond.

A challenge I set when devising a data strategy is to ask what value-add will it bring to move the organisation forward, and how recognisable will the difference be should the full scope of the data strategy be delivered. I believe that those responsible for devising the data strategy have to take the same level of accountability for realising the benefits within the data strategy as an executive board does with the corporate strategy. This also makes the task of translating it into practice a more 'real' activity, as the data strategy has to be capable of being implemented – both in terms of the clarity within the data strategy but also with regard to the feasibility.

This is all the more challenging if you are operating in an organisation that is perhaps limited in its adoption of the latest technology through either a conservative approach or a lack of budget to invest. Similarly, in an organisation that might be termed as 'data naive' it can be difficult to get traction, or at least to do so in the right places to make progress that can be embedded into the organisation. In both cases, strong leadership in data strategy can make a real difference to such organisations, but it needs absolute commitment from the executive board to get behind your strategy implementation. The board will need to recognise that some of the key deliverables will not reap immediate benefits or generate revenue, but are essential enablers and hence require prioritisation and investment.

If the data strategy is a key enabler of the corporate strategy, then it is important that those deliverables within the data strategy are clearly articulated and linked directly to the success of the organisation. It surprises me how often this gets overlooked when the data strategy is being devised, yet it is a compelling business case in itself to demonstrate the dependency for the wider organisation to be successful, and to ensure that the data, analytics and insight areas are at the heart of planning for those activities to be resourced and the right approach is defined.

The alignment with the corporate strategy is best achieved if, amongst the stakeholder group that is engaged from the outset, there is representation from the corporate strategy area. This raises the profile of the data strategy within the organisation, identifies the dependencies and enablers linking the data and corporate strategies, and enhances the credibility of the data strategy. This is especially important if you are developing the data strategy in your organisation for the first time – you want every opportunity to raise the profile of the work you are doing to ensure it has every chance of becoming embedded into the organisation.

2.4 A SUCCESSFUL DATA STRATEGY – MAKING IT CLEAR!

The case for a data strategy has been made, so what are the essentials to make it a success?

I recommend focusing on five key attributes that underpin the data strategy process and which you will likely want to refer to throughout the process of defining and developing the data strategy. They form the acronym 'CLEAR', which in itself is a useful reminder of what you are seeking to achieve in developing your data strategy.

2.4.1 Clarity

It is important to bear in mind the need for clarity throughout the process of developing a data strategy. This operates on many levels, as I shall explain, but it is an overarching discipline to follow from the very outset of this process.

The start of the data strategy definition process requires absolute clarity. It needs to align with the expectation you have created within the organisation as to what the data strategy will encapsulate, the impact you have outlined it will have on the wider organisation and the positioning of the data strategy within the organisation. It is essential to have commitment across the organisation to support and embrace the approach to developing the data strategy and to be clear on the demands you are placing on the organisation to peer review and comment as the data strategy takes shape.

The data strategy itself needs clarity in its communication, and this is where stakeholder engagement needs to be deliberately involved to provide active participation and reviewing of the document as it is developed. Part of this is also to ensure the data strategy is written in plain English (or whatever language it will be produced in), avoiding technical terms, ambiguity and acronyms and, most of all, keeping it simple. You may wish to consider the lexicon of terms used in relation to that recognised within your organisation, as it makes sense to write the strategy in a way which chimes with what your stakeholders would recognise and relate to.

It is important to remember that to engage senior stakeholders and staff outside the function largely responsible for delivering the data strategy, there is a need to keep the content short and clear; the document should not be an onerous read and should be focused on *what* the strategy aims to achieve rather than providing detail of *how* it will be delivered.

The use of terms which may seem commonplace to the author of a data strategy may not be clear to the reader. It will prove a major obstacle to the data strategy if the reader is unable to understand, simply because terminology has created a barrier. Therefore, it is essential that jargon is kept to a minimum: where it is felt that it is needed, the terms should be explained fully, with an annexe providing a list of all such terms used throughout the document.

2.4.2 Leadership

The data strategy is setting the stall out as to how the organisation's capability in the important area of data, analytics and insight will deliver change to the organisation over the period it covers. It must provide clarity, but, more to the point, it has to give leadership and direction.

The key to achieving this is to engage stakeholders from the outset. It may seem unusual to get those who may be outside the relevant areas of expertise involved so early, but it is about setting the context and thereby demonstrating that the data strategy is pivotal to achieve the corporate goals. Early engagement of stakeholders provides the opportunity to seek feedback, including how easy it is to digest and act upon what is in the data strategy. Whilst it may seem to increase the number of active participants at an early stage, it does save time in the long run and will make for a better end product. It is also a sign of maturity on the part of those who make a bold move to gain such early engagement, as it demonstrates strong leadership and conviction.

Data is, fundamentally, a strategic asset. As such, it has to be managed strategically in terms of the wider goals and aspirations of the organisation and delivered operationally through tactical activity that the organisation takes day to day. Recognising the person who can provide the right level of sponsorship amongst your stakeholders is key to the success of your data strategy – in terms of both its definition and its execution. A really effective leader in that sponsorship role will play a major part in your being established as the expert in defining and executing the data strategy. It is an essential partnership, part coaching, part challenging, and a key role in translating the data strategy into terminology to secure the investment, executive buy-in and resources needed.

Leadership needs to occur on two levels: firstly, it is about the demonstration of wider understanding to position the data strategy as a key corporate document, for all the reasons outlined above; secondly, it is the leadership role the data strategy itself may provide, resulting in a reset of the corporate ambition due to opportunities that the data strategy presents. This could lead to a rethink either in the ambition of the organisation (pace of delivery or extent of the change anticipated) or in the direction and priorities it has set, based upon the opportunities identified in the course of developing the data strategy; these may be compelling enough to be added in to the corporate strategy or lead to an amendment of the existing content.

The course of devising and developing the data strategy presents a good opportunity for the data, analytics and insight areas to showcase their capabilities. It takes those who may spend a large portion of their time operating in the background firmly into the foreground, and demonstrates how effectively they understand the wider organisation and its goals. Increasingly, there is recognition of the importance of having staff in the data, analytics and insight arena who are comfortable operating at senior levels and can hold their own in both the technical and corporate arena, able to act as intermediaries. This role is becoming one of the most important in the increasingly technical environment in which many analysts are operating. Helping the organisation articulate the business problem and having the wherewithal to define all of, or key parts of, that problem as a requirement takes skill and determination. It is also just as complex to structure the requirement in a way that gets the most effective output from the analyst.

The final form of leadership is fulfilled through consideration of the team that will be tasked with the implementation of the data strategy. Many data strategies have failed to make it through to implementation, often because they lack any guidance for the implementation team or are too theoretical and so gather dust on the shelf.

In the latter case, it is always a salutary lesson when I enter an organisation for the first time and am told that there isn't a data strategy, only to find a copy filed away and forgotten. I don't believe anyone writes a data strategy and expects it to fail to see action, but it is all too common an outcome.

It is important, therefore, to provide the leadership that enables the implementation team to see the purpose, vision and direction of the data strategy, and for it to be understood and an implementation plan made to translate it into action.

Figure 2.5 Engaging Leadership model Copyright © Real World Group.

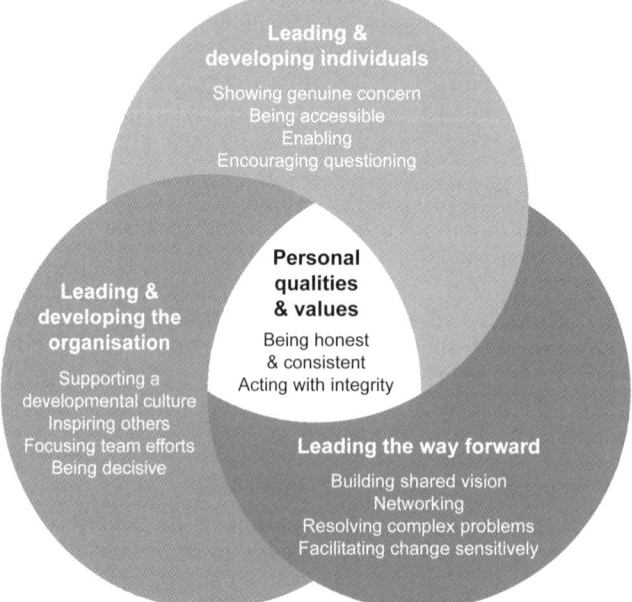

If you think of leadership styles that can be adopted, the process of leading the development of a data strategy plays into all of these in one way or another. This is well illustrated by the Engaging Leadership model by Alimo-Metcalfe and Alban-Metcalfe,[8] shown in Figure 2.5. Engaging Leadership is a highly validated model which consists of 14 scales or leadership aspects that are organised into the areas that can be seen in the diagram. Using these 14 scales as a framework, key aspects of effectively leading the development of a data strategy can be understood as follows:

- **Building shared vision** – in the process of compiling the data strategy, it is likely that inputs from colleagues and other individuals will be required. It is essential that the extent of the change envisaged through the delivery of the data strategy is understood to enable others to contribute to the data strategy: this will enrich the finished product. For example, engaging with the IT function as part of the process will enable that team to understand the direction the data strategy is taking and provide input to facilitate the change. This process is also likely to make people feel more motivated to bring the strategy to fruition, as they have been provided the opportunity to help shape how they feel things should be. It is also valuable as a means to work through what that would mean for staff across the organisation in advance of the data strategy being published.

- **Networking** – the importance of having a shared vision, as mentioned above, is a key factor in the success of the data strategy: an organisation-wide commitment to its delivery. The use of the behaviours included in this leadership scale, including using political skills to get buy-in and support from influential people within the organisation, as well as the leader utilising the networks they have across the entire organisation, will ensure there is buy-in to the data strategy and also help to bring more diverse views into its compilation.

- **Focusing team efforts** – the wider engagement outlined above builds organisational commitment to the execution of the data strategy and provides clarity on the part each function of the organisation needs to play for it to succeed. It can therefore be an effective enabler in aligning efforts across the organisation to a common purpose and give a sense of direction to those who need to execute it – as long as it is evident how the strategy translates into execution.

- **Inspiring others** – the process of taking the lead on developing the data strategy can, at times, feel onerous and challenging. The behaviours that are included in the 'Inspiring others' scale refer to gaining commitment to a project or cause through your own passion and determination (whether you are introverted or extroverted). It is important that the leader devising and developing the data strategy has a strong belief in it, clarity of purpose and direction, and that there is clarity of understanding and respect for the approach taken to produce the data strategy to engender a strong commitment amongst team members.

- **Acting with integrity and being honest and consistent** – the behaviours that are described under these scales are critical: the leader has to be the focal point and act with integrity and consistency throughout the process, willing to have difficult conversations or adapt to others' views as appropriate through honesty and staying true to the intent to deliver a data strategy that has been collectively developed.

---

8   Engaging Transformational Leadership. https://www.realworld-group.com/engaging-leadership.

2.4.3 Execution

I have mentioned the importance of thinking about the implementation, or execution, of the data strategy above. This is probably the least considered activity when creating any strategy, let alone a data strategy, often because it passes from those who operate in a stand-alone strategy function to either a separate operational group that implements strategy alongside the 'day job' or to a dedicated implementation team. It is clear that the less there is continuity in the process from strategy through to execution, the greater is the risk of the strategy failing to be implemented effectively.

The *Harvard Business Review* published an article by Ron Carucci in 2017 which goes to the heart of why strategies – of all varieties – fail to be executed.[9] It stated that research had identified that in the previous year 67 per cent of well-formulated strategies failed due to poor execution – two in three, which demonstrated there was clearly more chance of a strategy failing than it delivering. If this finding isn't stark enough, the article expanded on causes based on a ten-year longitudinal study into successful executives, undertaken by Carucci's firm (Navalent): 50 per cent were discovered to have failed within their first year having been unprepared for what faced them – as Carucci related from one interviewee, 'We fake it till we make it.'

Carucci identified a number of causes for such alarming failures in executive appointments and strategy execution:

- They lack depth in their competitive context.
- They are dishonest or naive about trade-offs.
- They leave old organizational designs in place.
- They can't handle the emotional toll.

In the article, Carucci referenced research undertaken by Bridges Business Consultancy[10] on an annual basis looking specifically at strategy execution amongst firms in Singapore and the USA. The first year Bridges conducted the survey, in 2002, 90 per cent of strategy implementations failed on the measure of achieving at least 50 per cent of the intended outcomes in the time set. In the 2012 survey, 80 per cent of business leaders felt their company was good at crafting strategy, but only 44 per cent saw similar capabilities in execution. Worse still, only 2 per cent believed the implementation would achieve 80–100 per cent of the objectives set. Perversely, the survey found business leaders spent more time on strategy implementation than crafting the strategy itself, and 96 per cent that thought that their bonuses should be tied to successful strategy implementation.

However, the disconnects don't end there. Seventy per cent of business leaders spent less than a day a month reviewing strategy, and those same leaders believed only 5 per cent of the employees of their organisations had a basic understanding of the company strategy. Middle management was seen as the biggest blocker to successful implementation at 56 per cent, rather than leaders or staff more broadly across the organisation.

---

9   R. Carucci, Executives Fail to Execute Strategy Because They're Too Internally Focused. *Harvard Business Review*, November 2017. https://hbr.org/2017/11/executives-fail-to-execute-strategy-because-theyre-too-internally-focused.

10 Bridges Business Consultancy Int Pte Ltd, Strategy Implementation Survey. 2012. www.bridgesconsultancy.com/research-case-study/research/.

The Bridges research in 2012 highlighted three key issues which still resonate today, especially for those who are about to embark on writing a data strategy:

1. ensuring staff members take or demonstrate different actions;
2. aligning implementation to the company's culture;
3. gaining people's support.

These three themes will be prevalent throughout this book, and I would recommend you keep them in mind at all times as a reminder to avoid slipping into one or more of these traps at any stage during the process of defining and executing the data strategy.

2.4.4 Agility

You are seeking to produce a data strategy at a time of complex and frequent change. The further the horizons are in the data strategy, the more the environment in which you operate is likely to change. This is not a point to constrain the ambitions you set, and the organisation may determine the period a strategy should cover, but simply to recognise there is a need for flexibility to be built in the longer the time frame of the data strategy. A year or two is relatively easy to visualise and contextualise in the wider organisation; three gives a more forward-looking, visionary feel to the data strategy; five or even ten years is shifting the balance significantly to a crystal ball being required to formulate a large part of the data strategy.

A key factor in devising the data strategy is to recognise that its implementation will require agility on many levels. The way in which it is framed will need to recognise that the organisational dynamics will determine where focus is applied and may mean the implementation resembles a yacht tacking from side to side, whilst remaining steadfast in getting to its final destination.

Even the compilation of the data strategy will require agility, as the knowledge and awareness of wider factors which play in to the way in which the strategy is positioned will go through constant change. This is part of everyday business: however, the challenge (and benefit, I might add) is that the wider stakeholder group that you need to engage with at the outset will bring a range of inputs and views to the team compiling the data strategy, some of which will appear contradictory or lacking sufficient detail to work with – it is beholden on you to demonstrate leadership by tasking those within the team to challenge these and seek clarification, so you can close down any factors which might lead to the strategy being devalued or the implementation being scuppered from the outset.

To stick with the yachting analogy, you need to have gathered all the inputs – maps, tide tables, weather forecasts, experience of the crew, fitness of the yacht itself to undertake the voyage, and of course continuously track these whilst afloat – before setting sail or, in this case, publishing the data strategy.

As you can see, there are a lot of moving parts in the preparation of a data strategy and it is essential to keep moving forward in its development phase. It will almost certainly not prove to be linear, but will require a lot of agility and flexibility, with sections revisited as more knowledge and inputs are captured to refine and inform it.

Once the implementation of the data strategy is under way, it will become apparent that the strategy has to be taken as guidance, but with sufficient scope to determine the means of executing it in the implementation phase. This highlights the important differentiation between a data strategy setting direction and the execution of it, which requires significant detail as to the who, what, when, where, why and how – variously referred to as the 5W1H, the Five Ws and How, or the Six Ws.

Figure 2.6 illustrates how to structure the use of the 5W1H methodology in practice, framing a series of questions to suit the nature of the question likely to be asked. In the case of data strategy, it most closely aligns with the approach for programme development, though at various times it may be worth adopting some of the other suggested approaches as you work through everything from checking evidence (akin to journalistic practices), removing barriers or solving problems you encounter, through to assigning tasks within the project itself.

In the implementation phase, there will be a need to recognise resource constraints as well as the wider organisational priorities determining the rate of progress. The data strategy should focus minds on the skills needed, not only in the specialist domains of data and analytics, but also in the wider organisation to be able to implement the strategy and realise the benefits. It is important to ensure the data strategy makes clear the skills gap and treats this as a key input in the successful implementation, as it is arguably more critical to have the right resource and commitment lined up than it is to focus on it as a technical deliverable. Therefore, some understanding of the readiness and maturity of the organisation is key in the process of defining the data strategy, as there is a compelling need to align these with the aspirations set out in the strategy.

The complexities of turning the data strategy into an executable plan are significant. As alluded to above, there are so many moving parts, along with significant shifts and challenges that will be encountered as the organisation progresses through the implementation period, that the need for agility will be critical. I discuss in Chapter 5 the difference between waymarkers and milestones, but the essence of the difference between a data strategy and its execution is in the goals each is seeking to achieve – the former is painting a picture of the future, setting direction and making reference to key points along the way, whilst the latter is taking the strategy and deconstructing it into a series of deliverables with clarity on the 5W1H to achieve the objectives of the strategy.

To use a further analogy, it is akin to preparing a sports team for an upcoming season, determining the right set of skills, tactics, outcomes and formations to be adopted and rehearsing them in a pre-season, prior to moving into the season proper, and having to adapt to the fortunes on the pitch each week to achieve what the team set out to deliver in its goals and objectives during the pre-season. As each match produces an end result there will be reflection, a refocusing if necessary, and a tweak to the formation to be used for the next match, but the intent remains the same. In other words, agility brings learning and adaptation, but doesn't lead to a shift in thinking or the abandonment of the original strategy, unless the outcomes are so severe it is no longer achievable.

2.4.5 Relevancy

I have touched on relevancy, in terms of staying true to the mission as set out in the data strategy, but also in terms of the need to engage widely with stakeholders and bring some of these into the team to help develop and refine the data strategy.

Figure 2.6 5W1H in practice Karen Cunningham (2019) 5W1H. Fox School of Business, Temple University https://digitalmarketing.temple.edu/kcunningham/2019/08/06/5w1h/.

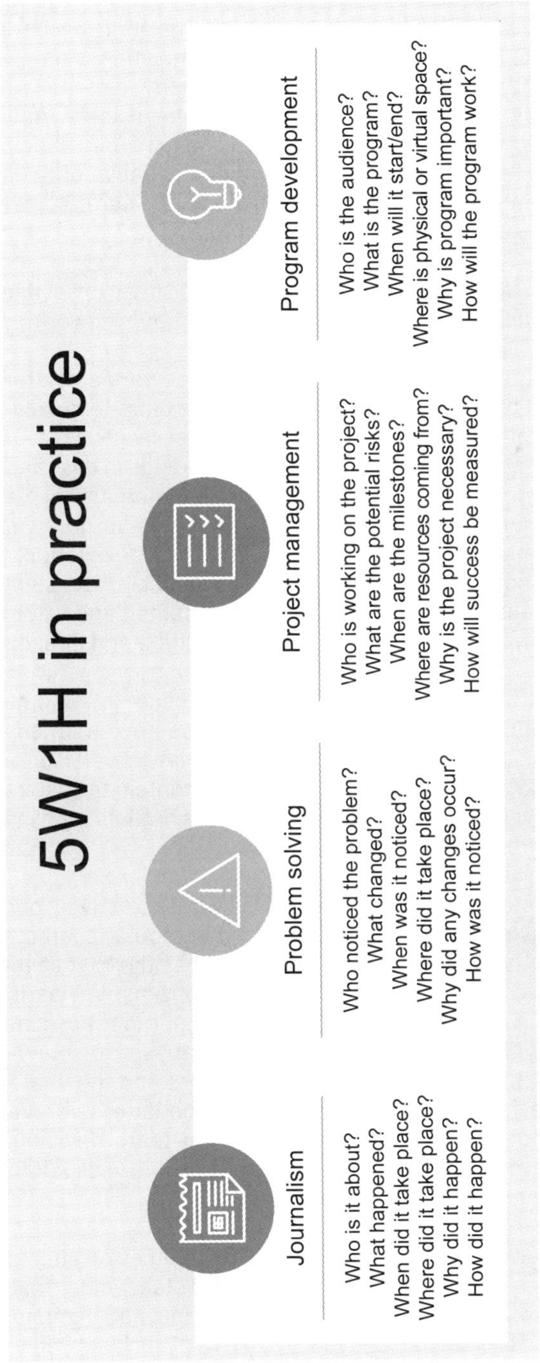

5W1H in practice

Journalism

Who is it about?
What happened?
When did it take place?
Where did it take place?
Why did it happen?
How did it happen?

Problem solving

Who noticed the problem?
What changed?
When was it noticed?
Where did it take place?
Why did any changes occur?
How was it noticed?

Project management

Who is working on the project?
What are the potential risks?
When are the milestones?
Where are resources coming from?
Why is the project necessary?
How will success be measured?

Program development

Who is the audience?
What is the program?
When will it start/end?
Where is physical or virtual space?
Why is program important?
How will the program work?

The key to remember is that the data strategy cannot operate via a siloed approach. Data, and its exploitation, sits at the heart of every business and is increasingly important as its capture becomes ever more complex as the channels through which it is made available and updated expand. The effectiveness of any organisation is now dominated by its efficient use of data, and this has been central to the demise of many household brand names in recent years that failed to recognise the need for a multi-channel experience, or were unable to adapt as more technically savvy organisations entered the market and changed the landscape for good. Any digitally native organisation will tell you that its lifeblood is data, and that a digital strategy is a core element for any organisation today, which makes data especially important.

It is the goal of those who are tasked with devising the data strategy to set it in a critical context to the ongoing existence and success of the organisation.

I have already mentioned the importance of getting a wide range of stakeholders involved from the outset, and bringing some of those into the team to develop the data strategy. This is essential as it brings a range of different perspectives, as well as an interesting challenge to the technical thinking that those with skills in data and analytics will have. Some of this may relate to terminology, understanding and explaining 'the art of the possible' (my favourite phrase) to those who may have no awareness or experience of what can be achieved and are therefore limited to the extent of what they can see on their somewhat shorter horizon. However, the blend of understanding what is possible, allied with the realism of how it could be implemented and drive benefit to the organisation, needs commitment from those outside the data and analytics space.

For this reason, engagement from the outset will grow the belief in the data strategy being attainable, and provide critical context of how it can be implemented to deliver the impact that is desired. This is what I mean by the term 'relevancy'. It is providing the contextual and credible to a data strategy that rightly should contain the aspirational – if the data strategy doesn't deliver a noticeable difference to the organisation in three, five or ten years' time then I would ask what it has achieved.

It is also essential that those stakeholder representatives who are actively participating in compiling the data strategy remain closely aligned and in regular contact with their home functions. There is nothing worse than the notion that those that the various functions have provided as conduits are seen to have 'gone native', as it destroys their credibility and with it the data strategy too. I would encourage those stakeholder representatives to check in with their functions on a regular basis, to sound out about the latest thinking, challenge preconceived notions of barriers and the 'that will never work' naysayers to provide evidence for their negativity; if the latter is proven to have firm foundations, this should be taken back to the project team devising the data strategy. There is no harm in road-testing the data strategy as it is in development, and it is far better to learn as you go than to fail in execution.

I discussed earlier in this chapter the interrelationships with other strategies, and the links between these can also be informed through an effective stakeholder management approach. The breadth of coverage of data means that it will inevitably impact on other strategies and vice versa, so it is essential that you are aware of such strategies either in development or already approved to ensure you are aligned. Using the stakeholders you have engaged through the data strategy will also enable you to identify the connections through their eyes as well as yours, which may help spot something in another strategy which would otherwise not have been so clear to you.

2.5 WHY IS A DATA STRATEGY IMPORTANT?

A data strategy is the opportunity to bring data, one of the most important assets your organisation has, to the fore and to drive the future direction of the organisation. This might seem to be a bold statement – after all, I have said that the data strategy is there to support the corporate strategy achieve its goals – but without clarity on the direction being taken with data in the organisation, it is likely to be much harder to achieve those corporate goals.

Data is the heart of how your organisation operates, linking people, process and technology around common goals, meaning much more can be achieved collectively than if those three operate without using data as the common reference point. Technology moves on quickly – often faster than organisations can keep up – and programmes are launched in many organisations without reference to the data. What is it telling us that we should consider before embarking on the programme? How will we use data to drive the programme? What insight do we want from our data to know whether we have delivered a successful outcome?

Organisations that want to exploit the potential of their data need a coherent way to ensure there is clarity on what is to be achieved, and this is where a data strategy comes in. What it often highlights, though, is that there is a lot of foundation work to be done to get the data into a state to exploit it fully, as fragmentation of data, poor data quality and missing or obsolete data are generally common barriers for all organisations. This in itself is useful, but can often feel like taking a giant stride backwards before being able to go forwards.

There is plenty of evidence of those organisations that are more forward-thinking in their approach to data making better decisions, which, in turn, lead to them outperforming their competitors. This isn't hidden away from everyone who isn't in the data profession; it is in well-known journals and newspapers – *The Economist*, *Forbes*, *New York Times*, *Harvard Business Review*, *Financial Times* to name a few – let alone the promotional materials released by management consulting and technology firms. However, data strategy is not yet commonplace in management thinking, nor are such strategies necessarily defined or executed (or both) well enough to make them effective. Even if you are relatively late to the data strategy party, it doesn't mean that you can't overtake those who arrived before you, let alone those who are still unaware there is a party to be joined.

I would close this chapter by stressing that more strategies fail than succeed, so do not think that this is easy; if it was, everyone would be doing it. I would suggest, though, that it is important that you go into defining a data strategy very aware of the pitfalls and what you need to do to try to avoid them.

2.6 TEN TO TAKE AWAY

Each chapter will conclude with ten key points to take into the next chapter.

These are the ten key take-away points to consider from this chapter as you go forward in your data strategy definition and execution journey.

1. There are a number of challenges in positioning the data strategy, especially if this is the first time your organisation has embarked on having one, and it is important you are able to comprehend the environment that led to it being commissioned.

2. Clarify what is understood by the desire to create a data strategy so there is common terminology to set expectations of what is to be delivered.

3. Identify who 'owns' the data strategy in your organisation, and ensure the expectations are clear and roles are defined.

4. Consider your stakeholder network – who you need to engage, influence and collaborate with to achieve the goal of defining your data strategy.

5. Look to include the management of data and the exploitation of it within the data strategy if possible – this links the investment in the foundations to the potential value generated to the wider organisation.

6. Focus on aligning to the corporate strategy. The data strategy is a key enabler to the corporate strategy, but could also present new opportunities to the organisation – consider how these might be introduced and integrated.

7. Remember the CLEAR principles – clarity, leadership, execution, agility and relevancy – in preparation for embarking on defining the data strategy. These are key to making sure you are prepared and have evaluated fully your starting point and the direction in which you are heading.

8. Ensure you are aligning people, process and technology. All require data in order to be effective, and the better the data, the more effective the organisation will be.

9. Test the data strategy as you define it, and use key links into stakeholder groups to get a sense of whether there is buy-in and a willingness to deliver – there is no point defining a data strategy no one wants to implement.

10. Data is an asset: position it in such a way that investment, quality and accessibility become understood in that context.

3   SETTING THE SCOPE OF THE DATA STRATEGY

'Strategy is about making choices, trade-offs; it's about deliberately choosing to be different.'

Michael Porter[1]

The previous chapter provided context on why you might embark on creating a data strategy, along with some of the key pointers to consider to ensure its success. The rest of the book will provide more detail on how you build on this, guiding you through the key considerations in developing the data strategy before you switch into implementation.

One of the challenges with developing a data strategy, particularly if this is the first time the organisation will have had one, is determining the scope. There are a number of reasons why an organisation embarks on developing a data strategy – a senior executive may have read of the benefits such a strategy has brought to other organisations, or recently joined from an organisation where a data strategy was in place and seen to have been of value; there may be an increased focus on data, whether due to compliance or opportunities having been identified to exploit it; or you may have been hired specifically to bring your experience in data or analytics into the organisation and therefore want to start with defining a data strategy. Of course, these are only a few reasons why a data strategy might be seen to be needed, but they give a sense of the diverse ways you might find your organisation seeking to embark on defining a data strategy for the first time.

Those organisations that have previously had a data strategy may be coming at this anew, determining whether there is a need to refresh what is in place or identifying that the data strategy hasn't delivered what was expected. This is not unusual as so many strategies fail to reach implementation, or stall at an early stage. Sometimes they fall into disrepute and it takes time for the organisation to feel it can embark on devising a strategy once more. In such cases, it is always useful to learn from past mistakes, but evidence shows that most strategies fail due to an inability to follow through into execution.

There are also organisations that simply do not recognise the strategy gap – they work in an operationally focused way, dealing with what lies ahead of them but failing to see what is a little way off but certainly heading their way. My analogy for this is being prepared for the next hurdle but failing to recognise it is a race involving ten to be navigated (as in the 110 metres hurdles in athletics) and falling over by the third one. There is a need for a strategy if you are to pace the stride to meet every hurdle in a pattern which suggests prior preparation and meticulous planning. Unsurprisingly, such organisations often find themselves in an endless cycle of restructuring, realigning and redefining their purpose and resource needs through a lack of strategy and planning.

---

1   Michael Porter, What Is Strategy? *Harvard Business Review*, November 1996.

The clarity on what constitutes a strategy is often lost for this type of organisation. Leaving the strategy process to the last quarter of a year, expecting it to be implemented in the following quarter, is destined to fail – a proper strategy is unlikely to go through the rigour of definition, design and approval in that time and so will drift into the very period it is intended to cover. In the meantime, the operational cycle has overtaken the strategy, with decisions having to be made which may, ultimately, fail to align to the strategic direction to be taken. In an instant, the strategy is obsolete through a lack of understanding and buy-in to it.

Ironically, this situation tends to give strategy a bad name, yet it is the execution of strategy as a concept in such organisations that is at fault. If you do not start with sufficient time to enable an effective strategy to be defined and all parties to be committed to its execution, it is rather like criticising the person who laid out the hurdles for your lack of training and preparation that led to you hitting that third hurdle.

There have been significant fines levied for breaches of regulations. Citigroup was fined £43.9 million in 2019 by the Bank of England's Prudential Regulation Authority for failings in its governance of regulatory reporting between 2014 and 2018.[2] Goldman Sachs and UBS have been fined £34.3 million[3] and £28 million[4] respectively for misreporting transactions. Perhaps most eye-watering in scale, Standard Chartered was fined $1.1 billion following allegations of bad anti-money-laundering practices and breaching sanctions by various American agencies and the UK's Financial Conduct Authority (FCA).[5] All of these had one common theme – poor data management practices that undermined the ability to conform to regulations.

Whatever the reason for your organisation to have determined that it needs a data strategy, the key is to have clarity on the scope of the data strategy and an awareness of what the organisation believes it requires, allied to an understanding of what the evidence suggests is needed. This is an important step to defining the scope of the data strategy; unless there is agreement from the outset then there is a high likelihood of failure due to neither party being clear on what a successful outcome looks like.

This chapter explores how scope is critical to developing a successful data strategy and what you need to ascertain to be sure you have clarity on scope as well as the reasoning behind the development of the data strategy.

---

2   Bank of England Prudential Regulation Authority, Final Notice, 26 November 2019. https://www.bankofengland.co.uk/-/media/boe/files/news/2019/november/pra-decision-notice-citigroup.pdf?la=en&hash=4030FC4D482DF4C330A367A7A1A97E4649FB2968.

3   FCA Fines Goldman Sachs International £34.3 million for Transaction Reporting Failures, 28 March 2019. https://www.fca.org.uk/news/press-releases/fca-fines-goldman-sachs-international-transaction-reporting-failures.

4   FCA Fines Goldman Sachs International £34.3 million for Transaction Reporting Failures, 28 March 2019. https://www.fca.org.uk/news/press-releases/fca-fines-goldman-sachs-international-transaction-reporting-failures.

5   Standard Chartered Fined $1.1bn for Money-Laundering and Sanctions Breaches, The Guardian, 9 April 2019. https://www.theguardian.com/business/2019/apr/09/standard-chartered-fined-money-laundering-sanctions-breaches.

3.1 WHAT IS YOUR GOAL IN DEVELOPING A DATA STRATEGY? THE IMPORTANCE OF CONTEXT

The data strategy needs to be carefully positioned within the organisation to ensure it has the profile to push the organisation towards being data-driven, and so that it is clearly visible how the data strategy is a critical enabler of all the other strategies across the organisation. As has been mentioned already, data is a common factor in the delivery of most activities, even if the organisation itself hasn't fully appreciated this to be the case; whether verbal, documented, captured in a system or tacit knowledge within the organisation, all of these form data and need a strategy to be able to provide cohesion, direction and purpose.

The counter to this perspective, of course, is that the organisation has operated effectively without a data strategy, so what difference will it make? There is a strong argument to say that if an organisation is not open to the concept of having a data strategy, then culturally it is probably a risk that even the most perfectly crafted data strategy will fail to make it through implementation, and therefore it is a futile exercise to devise one. However, I think this rational perspective is flawed unless it is explored further – let me explain.

If an organisation has never had a data strategy, then a resistance to having one is probably based on misconceptions: either a data strategy is seen to be irrelevant as the organisation has never had one, or seen the need for devising one; or resistance is based upon a perceived negative experience within the organisation or a previous experience elsewhere that senior executives have had. This may not even be specifically related to data – it may be a broader resistance to investing time in strategy. As this book will illustrate, strategy development and exploitation are littered with more failures than successes, and many senior executives are not effective in both the strategy definition and execution arena.

It is important to be able to surface these issues as the more you understand the rationale behind the resistance, the more you will be able to navigate a path to provide reassurance that you have listened, learnt and intend to act in a way that avoids the pitfalls put to you. Chapter 6 covers the importance of storytelling, but it is key to understand your stakeholders, their concerns and experiences, in order to build a compelling message that they will get behind.

If you are tasked with devising what should be in the data strategy, or have been given the task of writing one without any steer whatsoever, then do conduct some research within the organisation before determining the content. It will be critical to have people on board, and so consulting widely – canvassing opinion as to what issues people see, what constraints they have to operate within, how they could be more effective or efficient if only the right data of the appropriate quality was available – and investigating initiatives already under way which could be incorporated into the data strategy is key to making the end product recognisable to your audience such that they can align to it and help you deliver it. The context of the data strategy needs to be grounded in what your colleagues recognise as barriers or constraints to be both deliverable and also likely to succeed in driving change within the organisation.

Does a data strategy have a dependency upon an overall strategy for the organisation being in place? Whilst I would argue that a data strategy needs to align to the corporate strategy, if your organisation does not have a corporate strategy, or at least something clearly documented as such, then I would suggest there is still a compelling case to have a data strategy. This may seem contrary to the rationale I have set out elsewhere in this book, but let me illustrate through describing some of the corporate risks that a lack of a coherent approach to the management and exploitation of data can subject an organisation to.

In an environment in which data compliance and regulation is omnipresent, especially for organisations operating across borders or in mature markets such as the European Union, the minimum requirement is to be able to demonstrate that data management is compliant. To do this requires an understanding of the range of data sources within an organisation, how these are controlled, and how maintenance and retention routines are applied. These are foundation elements of a data strategy, and as such they mark the first steps to producing a data strategy.

The challenge of operating across borders that do not have clear guidance on how this is to be managed, nor reciprocal agreements in place, is perhaps becoming a more pressing issue. For instance, EU law is very clear on the risks of data being managed outside its jurisdiction due to different regimes, regulations and standards at play. Data containment – the physical constraints on where data is hosted geographically (including back-ups and other risks of data leakage) – is therefore critical for some organisations, as they need to be able to evidence no risk of data leakage across geographies despite being global enterprises. This tends to lead to constraints on how organisations might choose to work and, in an era in which cloud technology is becoming much more prevalent, rigour having to be applied to show data cannot escape via back-ups, test environments or other ways in which data could move outside of prescribed geographies. Once again, fines may be levied for transgressing data containment.

Analogous regulations apply to data privacy breaches, with some substantial fines being levied for failure to hold customer data suitably securely to prevent its unauthorised access via cyber attacks – in 2020 the UK Information Commissioner's Office (ICO) fined British Airways £183.9 million[6] and Marriott International £99 million[7] for data breaches. Data privacy is becoming more high profile and a concern for executives in large organisations around the world, with cyber attacks increasing. There is more detail on data privacy regulations in Chapter 6.

I would suggest that, for most organisations, it is well worth expanding on a review of data compliance (which all organisations should have undertaken to assure legal and regulatory controls are in place) to recognise how the data is utilised and exploited, and

---

6   Intention to Fine British Airways £183.39m under GDPR for Data Breach. https://ico.org.uk/about-the-ico/news-and-events/news-and-blogs/2019/07/ico-announces-intention-to-fine-british-airways/.

7   Intention to Fine Marriott International, Inc More than £99 million under GDPR for Data Breach. https://ico.org.uk/about-the-ico/news-and-events/news-and-blogs/2019/07/intention-to-fine-marriott-international-inc-more-than-99-million-under-gdpr-for-data-breach/.

to propose streamlining data sources where duplication occurs and to reduce rekeying of data. It is then only a short step further to devise a data strategy, which in turn provides a prompt to the wider organisation to think about what it is seeking to achieve, a reversal of approach to prompt corporate strategic thought based upon the potential opportunities to exploit data.

3.2 READINESS AND MATURITY OF THE ORGANISATION

The key to any successful strategy implementation is to understand the starting point in your organisation. Some organisations will be familiar with the concept of strategic planning and thinking, and may even have a highly structured process in how strategies are defined and approved within the organisation. This may not, however, be the same thing as being effective in deployment, and it is imperative to identify how successful the organisation has been in translating its current strategy – whether at a corporate level or divisional/functional level – into practice, embedding change into the organisation.

By contrast, there are organisations that are less structured at strategic thinking and work instead on a more operational basis, running from year to year in setting goals and defining targets. In certain instances such an approach can be a commendable one, for example in the crisis of rapid descent in a recession, where decisions need to be made quickly in a rapidly changing environment. However, these tend to be short-lived as the impact of such approaches is usually cost-driven and highly focused on retrenching to core activities, and are not sustainable for an organisation looking to thrive.

Alongside the readiness of the organisation to embark on a data strategy, there is also a question regarding its maturity to be able to do so effectively. This can best be explored and quantified using an assessment of the data maturity of the organisation, and Chapter 6 explores several models.

> The choice of model is less important than the adoption of it and the rigour with which it is applied. It is overly simplistic to say that they all do similar things, as whilst this is true it also ignores some interesting differences between them. However, in the overall challenge of getting data and its exploitation to the more sophisticated end of these models there is a lot to be said for picking a model and sticking with it, concentrating on what the model is identifying as the way to increase maturity, and ensuring resources and investment are secured to achieve this.

As highlighted above, a data strategy should, ideally, align to a corporate strategy. Therefore, the first challenge is to assess (a) whether the latter exists; (b) whether it is actively being implemented; and (c) how easily your intended data strategy can align to it. You should also find those responsible for defining and implementing the corporate strategy, and in a number of organisations these may be two distinct groups of people, possibly in completely different functions.

Let's work through these options in turn.

3.2.1 Lack of a corporate strategy, or failure to execute it effectively

If the organisation does not have a clear corporate strategy it may tell you a lot about the readiness of the organisation to embrace your plan to create and implement a data strategy. In some instances, it may be a case of having to approach the problem with an innovative solution, or alternatively being prepared to find senior stakeholders who are willing to support (ideally sponsor) why a data strategy makes sense for the organisation and be your champion at the top table.

If there seems to be little hope to engender the concept of embracing strategy into your organisation, and the maturity of the organisation is such that there is little understanding of why a data strategy should be the starting point for a change of direction, then look at alternative ways to tackle the problem. For instance, your organisation is likely to have some formal processes around risk management and mitigation strategies and, whether from a compliance angle or simply to minimise risk, tackling data issues will almost certainly assist and therefore gain support from the relevant executive owner. In addition, a data strategy is likely to have many audiences, but don't forget that those who are most likely to be the authors of it are also beneficiaries.

At its simplest level, a data strategy is a vision for where you want to be that helps the organisation achieve its overall goals more efficiently and effectively. As well as a number of key inputs required from the wider organisation there are a number which are self-driven and therefore can be instigated with minimal external input. For instance, most organisations are riddled with Excel spreadsheets containing data either taken from source systems or created/manipulated locally to add to the chaotic data landscape ('Excel – the Japanese knotweed of data', as my former colleague Godfrey Morgan used to say). Simply reviewing the key systems in the organisation to identify where data resides and cataloguing it is the starting point of a coherent approach to master data management, providing clarity on which sources of data are to be used (the master data), defining the metadata to underpin a common understanding of that data, and taking the first step to a data quality programme to improve quality and hence reliability.

Does a data strategy touch other teams, outside a data and analytics function? Yes, of course it does, but as a small project to drive greater coherence and compliance – as there is a fundamental principle here about being on the right side of the law, whether the General Data Protection Regulation (GDPR) or similar – it typically makes it easier to get buy-in from the likes of the architecture team in the IT function, legal professionals (or wherever accountability for compliance resides) and even the end users themselves, who may be relieved to be released from the burden of maintaining the Excel data sets that need regular feeds and maintenance. If it is possible to put a cost to all of this then it may appeal to the finance function, and often a chief financial officer (CFO) or finance director is a great ally if there are cost savings that can be achieved, compliance or regulatory fines that can be avoided or corporate risk that can be averted – after all, reputational damage can extend to limiting the careers of those serving on executive boards if they have failed to fulfil legal obligations in such situations.

Starting out on a data strategy without revealing it as a strategy may seem an odd approach to endorse, but in reality, the notion of a 'strategy' can sometimes slow progress rather than focus attention on the direction to be taken and forging a common set of goals. I have taken such an approach in several organisations, determining that the organisation's appetite for a strategy or highly structured process to get a strategy endorsed would thwart the progress it was intended to make. There is no harm in sharing the data strategy at a later point, especially as the organisation starts to see the value being realised in the approach you are taking and becomes curious as to whether there is a 'bigger plan', with colleagues looking to you because you seem to have an idea as to what the next project should be.

There are, of course, other areas that are liable to be in the data strategy that could be a good place to start to mobilise: for instance, resolving duplication and enhancing consistency in management reporting is a productive place where improvements can be made through greater control and governance. However, getting the data right has such profound benefits for wider activities it is often a good starting point. The current environment within the organisation, issues it faces, starting point for a data strategy to unfold and the ease to find willing volunteers are all likely to influence where opportunities lie.

If there is the potential to benefit from a senior stakeholder sponsoring your efforts to introduce a data strategy then I would always recommend pursuing that option. The key is to find the connection – what can you deliver that would benefit that stakeholder to enable them to spread, based on a practical example, the benefit to be achieved in the wider organisation if it were to similarly adopt the approach. It would be wise to guide your sponsor to where low-hanging fruit might be found, to be able to identify another area where there is either something that could be easily resolved or a blocker removed. This could even take the form of a two-pronged approach, in which your sponsor works at the board level to influence, whilst you work at levels below to get commitment in advance of any positive intent shown by the new business function or division.

The impact a committed sponsor can have is clear. It projects the benefits of a data strategy amongst a peer group with a level of authority you are likely to lack, simply due to the fact your sponsor will be a regular attendee on the board and known to their colleagues. The invitation you might get to address the board will always have more impact if it is set up by the sponsor, otherwise you are effectively 'cold calling' the board with something you may be passionate about but, in the short space of time you are given to do your pitch, may not be top of mind for those around the board table. Even the most sceptical board may give your sponsor some leeway to show the potential, along the lines of 'you're clearly enthused by the possibilities of this, even if we can't see it, so feel free to pursue on that project you've outlined where you see it having benefits'. By contrast, you may instead get a 'thanks, but it's not our priority just now'.

It should go without saying that you have to deliver for the credibility of your sponsor to remain intact. Do not overpromise and under-deliver, and ensure the activity you undertake is time bound so you are able to demonstrate progress. Although the data strategy may be intended for a period of years, if this is your first foray into delivering any of its content into the organisation be mindful you are being judged in weeks, not years. I will discuss adopting an Agile approach in Chapter 4, but remember to structure your first project into rapid phases so you can keep your sponsor engaged with clear signs of progress and, ideally, deliverables that amount to a real change that can, ideally, be quantified or, at worst, recognised.

Consider the feasibility of success in those early initiatives you are embarking on, as it is important to get a degree of momentum. Within the approach of PDCA enshrined in Agile, reflect on the attainability of the plan and the value it will deliver. There is little to be gained from a perfectly executed plan that is seen to deliver little, no matter how well it is done or how important it may be as a supporting activity to those higher-profile things to come later. Whilst it may sound a bit fatalistic, in reality your first three months will start to form opinions in the mind of your sponsor and other senior stakeholders; by six months the die will be cast and views will be shared amongst the group. Do not find you are failing to demonstrate meaningful progress. Communication is absolutely key, and I have devoted Chapter 7 to this topic to underline the importance of getting communication working for you in managing your stakeholders.

In pitching the rationale and compelling reasons for embarking on a data strategy to a potential sponsor in an organisation unfamiliar with the concept of having strategies – especially for a data strategy, since data is probably not 'owned' at an executive level and so lacks coherence in how it is managed in the organisation – it's probably best to start with a more modest goal. You probably need a series of interlocking projects, a programme, as the way to get started. This way, it keeps the vision, sets a number of deliverables as the goal, but focuses heavily on shorter-term objectives to be met to be regarded as a success. Once there is sufficient interest garnered in the path being followed, the concept of the data strategy can be introduced as the longer-term vision.

I have listed below a number of ways you could be embarking on a data strategy for the wrong reasons, and destined to fail. I've done so to try to illustrate the pitfalls of these, should you find yourself in this situation, so you can determine whether any of these apply to you and what it might mean. Through understanding the pitfalls, it may help you reorientate the positioning to a place which is more likely to lead to a successful outcome.

3.2.1.1 Strategy in name only

There are many organisations that invest time and effort in developing a strategy only for it to fail to make it to implementation – it becomes shelfware. The strategy may have been partly implemented, not as a strategic implementation, but simply because it made good sense to do so, and you should guard against finding fragments of the strategy and concluding it must have been implemented. I suggest that if you cannot draw a clear link between the strategy as you have discovered it and a coherent implementation, then it is reasonable to put it down to a coincidental link rather than a structured implementation programme.

If this situation describes your organisation, then you need to guard against falling into the same trap.

3.2.1.2 Strategy is owned by the strategy team

In some organisations the commitment to strategy is such that it has its own team, or even function. This might suggest that such an organisation is a strong advocate of defining and implementing strategy, but there is a common trap that occurs in such a situation, which I shall call the theorists dilemma. Often, the strategy team has been formed with the best of intentions, with the senior executives within the organisation being aware that there is a need for a strategy but not having the skills or the time to define one. The answer? To recruit and develop a strategy team to lead this important activity. The problem? It has instantly created a siloed approach in which strategy is a stand-alone function in the organisation.

The intent is fine but the execution has divorced it from the very people who need to define and implement the strategy and have the skin in the game to both make it realistic and enable it to be held to account. The strategy team sees its remit to devise the strategy; implementation is done elsewhere. The chasm grows, and hence the strategy becomes a theoretical construct that has divorced itself from the day-to-day activities of the organisation.

Does this mean that every organisation with a strategy team is doomed to fail? Clearly the answer is no, but the risk is high. The strategy team has to ensure it is not seen to be a theory team, divorced from the 'real world', and must be able to bridge the gap into implementation. It can do this by engaging the wider organisation every step of the way, facilitating the organisation to define the strategy, or seconding and rotating staff from across the organisation to spread a greater awareness of what purpose the strategy serves. Linking in with a recognised and effective governance group, such as a portfolio management group, within the organisation will also help provide the traction and visibility to the wider stakeholder network. Any or all of these approaches can be beneficial in bringing the strategy expertise closer to the organisation and making strategy implementation seamless from devising the strategy.

What does this mean for the data strategy? The approaches outlined above to overcome the strategy function being seen to be siloed are just as valid in the approach to defining the data strategy. Data permeates every part of the organisation, so it is essential that all are included to some degree in the construction and approval of the data strategy. The most common failures with data strategies are a lack of engagement, with too many people within the organisation being totally unaware the organisation even has a data strategy. In some cases, this includes staff within the data and analytics teams, who you might have thought would have been involved or consulted to some degree!

The next chapter talks in more detail about how to ensure engagement in defining and implementing the data strategy in your organisation, so I will merely state here that you can't engage enough.

3.2.1.3 Strategy is for an external audience
Some organisations are expected to map out a vision and some high-level objectives to satisfy external interests, whether these be shareholders or regulators. If the strategy process is heavily focused on meeting that expectation, it is a good indicator that the organisation is doing this because of external pressure rather than because an internal driver has set the direction. This isn't always the case, and in more enlightened organisations the benefit of setting a clear strategy makes the provision of the view to be shared with shareholders or regulators a much simpler exercise.

The challenge in being driven by the external expectation is that it urges a strong focus on meeting what is needed to satisfy that audience. Inevitably this is a particular view of the organisation, whether aligned to realising shareholder value or achieving/retaining compliance, and as such it does not provide an integrated view of the organisation to enable it to be used as a blueprint and then translated into an implementation plan. Data may be seen to be important as part of this exercise – certainly the focus on GDPR (and similar regulations in other jurisdictions) has led to an element of the data strategy related to compliance given an airing, though this may be a light touch given that many organisations would have been ill-prepared for the advent of GDPR, especially with unstructured data.

A data strategy is usually a key enabler for an organisation to enable value to be gained from its data, encompassing the whole lifecycle from capture to utilisation whilst doing so in a compliant manner. Any focus which is predominantly for an external audience is likely to be limited in scope and therefore of little use to anyone trying to promote the concept of a data strategy. If a strategy is seen within the organisation as 'something we do for others', then the likelihood is that this is not going to be fertile ground for the author of a data strategy.

In such cases, the approach described earlier, operating more covertly to deliver the data strategy via a series of small projects and hence focusing on the implementation as opposed to promoting the concept of a data strategy, may be your best route to making progress. Alternatively, if the external audience has a significant impact, there is the potential to use this to your advantage in pitching the strategy in such a way that it commits the organisation to something more than a minimalist solution to the immediate problem. For instance, if there are risks such as the potential for a serious data breach or a health and safety issue, then there could be the opportunity to go beyond remediation to identify a broader, more proactive approach.

3.2.1.4 Strategy has little credibility due to implementation failures

I have often said to those faced with defining a data strategy, 'Wait till you get to the implementation, if you think this part is hard!' I don't say this to diminish the challenge of getting a data strategy defined and approved; however, it is true that many strategies fail not because of their inherent weakness but because of the inability of the organisation to implement it successfully. This topic is discussed in more depth in Chapter 8.

If you are working in an organisation which is seen to be great on ideas but lacking the ability to execute them effectively, then this category is probably for you. The best strategy can be undermined by poor implementation, so I stress that every strategy needs to be defined with implementation in mind. If you are not thinking about how to implement it at every step of the way of the strategy definition process, then you are setting yourself up to fail. Even if you are not going to be part of the implementation team, why put the effort in to define the strategy if you cannot see a clear path to how it will be executed?

So how do you avoid being yet another statistic in the failed strategy count? The challenge is to learn from other failed attempts to implement a strategy and avoid the same pitfalls. However, many organisations don't like to publicise their failings or even conduct the sort of post-implementation or lessons learnt reviews that shed light on where things went wrong (I know of at least one organisation that dropped the term 'learnt' and instead called it 'lessons observed', given the same mistakes would still be repeated). Also, in all too many organisations, any lessons captured are stored away and never see the light of day; it is a tick-box exercise to conclude a process rather than one to facilitate improvement in future activities.

The best way to try to avoid such failure is to engage, engage, engage! Don't develop your data strategy in a vacuum: instead try to be as wide and all-encompassing as you can, and do your preparation in advance. Anticipate that you will receive a negative or, at best, lukewarm reception from some people in your organisation, especially amongst those you need to engage, influence and get involved, and have strategies in your mind as to how you will overcome this perception based upon experiencing past failures. Indeed, some of those with such experience may have been in your shoes, trying to lead change in the organisation: they may be really useful to learn from as you start on your own journey.

Chapter 4 talks about this in more detail, but in short, and as so often in life generally, the more preparatory work is done, the greater the likelihood of success.

3.2.2 Aligning to the corporate strategy

The organisation has a corporate strategy and is in the process of delivering against it, and you have been tasked with devising a data strategy. Sounds great, so what could possibly go wrong? Well, there are a number of potential issues which might scupper your brief to deliver a data strategy. In fact, you may be about to bring into sharp focus why the implementation of the corporate strategy isn't going as well as hoped, or may even be about to undershoot against expectation.

The corporate strategy sets out the blueprint of what the organisation is seeking to achieve over a given period, its key deliverables or programmes, and targets to achieve. Underpinning the strategy is an implementation plan which has distilled this into a series of activities and assigned responsibility and accountability across the organisation. The external impacts have been assessed as best as can be achieved in the absence of a crystal ball, and some assumptions about competitors, customers and your own capabilities have been integrated to give a rounded picture. This would be ideal if there wasn't a very big assumption built into much of the strategy – the accessibility, accuracy and therefore the reliance to be placed upon the data.

At one point in my career, I led a team which provided detailed data, analysis and insight on the markets the organisation operated in as an integral part of the planning process that fed into the strategic planning process. The team worked hard to consolidate a mass of information into a digestible synopsis of the market for each product range the organisation delivered, and gave the report to the relevant product manager for each of the product suites.

Two memorable events arose from that process. Firstly, one product manager skimmed through the extensive report and did his own calculations about the market (size, share, segments and so on), despite this being at the heart of the report provided. He presented his figures to the corporate executive board with predictions of the market share he should achieve over a five-year period and what was required to deliver this (investment, resources and so on). He was delighted to find his proposal accepted, and this was built into the overall objectives of the whole organisation as well as his own product area. But the figures he had worked from were completely inaccurate, based on flawed calculations, and not only had he committed to grow the entire market, but his own market share represented over 100 per cent of the current market size in certain segments: he had set himself, and the division he represented, up for a fall. Such was the nature of the process, with the group executive board looking at submissions across multiple areas, that it wasn't feasible for him to represent his calculations, this time using the data he had been provided in the first place. He had set himself an unachievable goal which couldn't be undone.

The second case, in the same organisation as part of the same strategic planning process, was the complete opposite – a whole product range was overlooked in another product manager's submission to the board. Here he managed to present a picture that represented all but one relatively discrete area of his division, somehow forgetting one specialist but significant area. This had some positives, in as much as he undercooked his overall numbers, but it also meant that the investment that area required to achieve good growth (as it was a part of the business that was growing faster than most) was not forthcoming. In addition, it meant that the targets for the management team in that area were non-existent, which was clearly something of a challenge! Once again, the data was there to be used, but in the haste to present a compelling story to the executive board the information was not utilised for the activity it was created specifically to support.

Whilst these are two specific examples of failure to utilise data that would have avoided rather significant mistakes, and as such not specifically strategy related, they do illustrate how poor decisions can be taken that become enshrined in a strategy despite being incompatible with the data (and the data strategy may highlight such issues through an inability to connect to the goals of the corporate strategy due to the data evidencing a gap between reality and what has been assumed within the corporate strategy).

The data strategy should be developed on the basis of the corporate strategy, as its goal is to enable the corporate strategy be delivered. If there are inconsistencies between the corporate strategy and data strategy these need to be addressed, so it is wise to engage those who are the architects and owners of the corporate strategy from the outset to develop the data strategy to be complementary. As soon as there are any points which seem to be at odds with the corporate strategy these should be explored and worked through.

If there is a compelling reason to revise the corporate strategy based upon something which has subsequently come to light in the development of the data strategy that looks like an opportunity that the organisation may wish to pursue, then this should be possible, and most importantly, needs to feed into the implementation plan for both the corporate and data strategies. Examples of such issues may be compliance constraints on being able to manage data in a way that was anticipated (for example, a company may acquire a competitor but be told it has to put a firewall between certain parts of the integrated new venture due to anti-competition regulatory constraints), or delays in system implementations preventing the delivery of insight to drive a new venture as soon as was anticipated.

On the whole, instances in which the data strategy is at odds with the corporate strategy should be few in number, but it is always worth checking and engaging those who constructed the corporate strategy from the outset. Indeed, it may be that the data strategy highlights opportunities which the corporate strategy had not anticipated, and so the corporate strategy can be enhanced to realise benefits which previously were not understood, for instance adoption of tools or techniques that enable an accelerated approach or opportunities for new product development. On the other hand, it could also flag a potentially significant failing in the corporate strategy and be pivotal in avoiding significant problems ahead for your organisation, such as a lack of awareness of data issues in a merger or acquisition that could unearth some significant corporate risks if not addressed urgently.

One final observation I want to make is to never assume that the published corporate strategy has actually succeeded in making it through into practical implementation. As this book will explain, the evidence that the majority of strategies do not succeed in implementation applies as much to the corporate strategy as to any other type of strategy you might find in your organisation. You may even find a reality gap between what the executive board believes to be the case and the practical situation on the ground – the board members may even be unaware of the existence of the corporate strategy if it hasn't been cascaded and explained in a way to engage them and relate it to what they do on a day-to-day basis.

Therefore, test your assumption that the corporate strategy is indeed in use to determine the direction of the organisation at every level of the workforce. It may be that there is a variant to the corporate strategy, a reality that manifests itself in the operational plans in various parts of the organisation, that is loosely aligned but is seeking to achieve a similar goal through different methods. If this describes the situation in your organisation, you are better off aligning to the practical reality of the 'unofficial' corporate strategy, as this is what the workforce is actually focused on delivering. Do continue to recognise the corporate strategy as documented, but don't make it a constraint on your ability to get successful engagement in defining and delivering the data strategy.

3.2.3 Why now?

Let's assume the organisation has a corporate strategy. The need for a data strategy may not have been identified previously, so why is it required now?

This is a question you may know the answer to, and could have been one of the key orchestrators in convincing the organisation of the merits in developing a data strategy. If not, then it is an opening question to ask the person tasking you with the responsibility. Understanding what has made a data strategy relevant at this point in time will give you a clear comprehension as to what those commissioning it believe it will deliver. Do understand, however, that there is every possibility that there may be a misapprehension as to what a data strategy is – it may have been mentioned in an article the executive has recently read, come up in conversation with a consultant or been highlighted at an industry conference by a competitor. There is a strong possibility that the original expectation is actually some way from what a data strategy entails, and therefore you need to check in regularly with your executive sponsor to inform on progress, clarify any outstanding issues and seek an ongoing mandate to proceed based on feedback.

There are three scenarios I will explore further (there are undoubtedly others) to provide advice to those who have just been briefed with the important task of devising a data strategy for the first time in the organisation.

3.2.3.1 'I've just heard that every organisation should have a data strategy, where's ours?'

The first scenario is the executive returning from a conference or some sort of training event who calls you into an office or fires off an email saying a data strategy is just what the organisation needs, everyone these days has one and you are the right person to do it. As already explained, it is important to use this first ever reference to a data strategy to get things straight. Assuming you have a notion of what a data strategy is (if not, you need to do a rapid bit of homework before having the follow-on conversation), you could even set out a loose framework of what you think a data strategy might entail and send this for comment in advance of the discussion.

If the pitch for the data strategy goes well, then you may have seized the initiative and be able to build confidence in your capability to deliver it, in which case you then need to maintain that confidence through building momentum and providing regular feedback. You will need to ensure you move quickly into identifying what resources you need, including those outside your control, and obtain access to those staff who have developed the corporate strategy. However, there is a lot of groundwork to be done and you will need to prepare your sponsor for this – if a rapid turnaround of the data strategy is expected, then you will have to either produce little more than a scoping document to give a flavour of the headlines to come in the final document or let your sponsor know that this is unrealistic, but do at least set out an outline of your approach to demonstrate the progress you will make and touch points to show what has been achieved.

If you can, ask your sponsor to provide access to other senior stakeholders to gain their insight as to the problems they face, the challenges in implementing the corporate strategy and the quality of information at their fingertips to make reliable decisions. Consulting widely at the outset gives you an opportunity to gather qualitative inputs that will help in prioritisation as you progress towards having the data strategy ready to go, such that the implementation plan becomes easier to devise based upon the early insight on how to get engagement amongst the senior stakeholders in your organisation. Do bear in mind that they too might have either little or no understanding as to what a data strategy is, so structure your questions generally rather than lead on the notion that everyone understands what a data strategy is. A senior stakeholder will not want to be embarrassed by questions on something they do not comprehend, and a short meeting may result to avoid their ignorance being revealed.

3.2.3.2 'Make me compliant!'

Another scenario is that there has been some sort of review, either external by a regulator or the ICO, or internal by the audit team, and this has highlighted the organisation's non-compliance with some form of regulation or practice that it should be following. Whilst the latter needs rectifying and will not go away – audit committees like to flex their independence by reminding senior executives that there are outstanding actions remaining, especially if chaired by non-executive chairs – the former may come with the threat of a forthcoming fine if rectification is not undertaken, or a fine regardless, as described at the start of this chapter. In extreme circumstances, it may mean dismissal or even prison for the senior accountable executive.

This tends to concentrate the mind, and if there are data issues at the heart of the transgression – as is invariably the case – then it is likely to lead to a programme of some sort to resolve the issue(s). It is an ideal opportunity to define the solution not as a compliance task, but instead as a means to instigate a wider review into data management – its capture, storage and exploitation – and pull it together in a data strategy.

How do you engineer the opportunity to take control and reorientate the requirement into a broader solution, one which requires a data strategy? It really depends on the situation, both in terms of the compliance issue and the appetite of the organisation. It may be seen as further delay to putting out a burning platform to embark on a data strategy at a time when the organisation is firmly in the spotlight, but there is just the opportunity to link several activities together to be able to demonstrate how a data strategy is both timely and a key enabler to solve the compliance issues for good.

The key is to get to grips with the problem at hand. What was the compliance issue and what brought it to light? Without knowing the problem you are unlikely to address the key issue that was core to the thinking of those instigating the data strategy. It isn't unusual to find that the compliance issue is symptomatic of something much broader that isn't working, and the issue has simply become the point at which the problem emerged into the spotlight.

Undertaking a root cause analysis or similar approach to get to the heart of the problem will almost certainly bring to the fore several more issues that need to be addressed. When these are added to other key issues that are probably simmering in the background that are relatively easy to uncover – systems migration/replacement programmes are often flawed through poor-quality data (more of this later), whilst inaccuracies in MI through manipulation of data in multiple departments producing different results is another issue – you are well on your way to being able to justify why a data strategy is needed.

Of course, it is a little more complex than presenting a ragtag bunch of issues to someone caught in the glare of negative publicity. These loose strands need to be woven together and presented in a coherent way, and a high-level plan should be sketched out to demonstrate how these can be resolved with the priority being the cause célèbre – the non-compliance issue which started this in the first place. You may discover that your key stakeholder doesn't comprehend the problem, but simply wants it to be solved, and quickly. I refer back to CLEAR from Chapter 2, especially relevancy, as focus and stakeholder engagement will be key here. Remember, the data strategy is actually solving a hot problem, and so there is a need to lead with the solution as an introduction to the wider strategy.

However, this is a great opportunity to paint the picture of how something that started out as a compliance headache can become something of significant benefit to the organisation as a whole, and that you are the person to take the lead on delivering it. Build the trust of the key stakeholder on this one and you have credibility to be recommending the progression with the data strategy as the right thing to do.

3.2.3.3 'We really need a data strategy'
A third scenario is to have an organisation at an appropriately mature stage, with an understanding and track record of successful strategic implementations under its belt,

that has realised it has an omission – a lack of a data strategy. In other words, the time has come to put this right, and it is over to you for delivery and alignment to the corporate strategy.

This might sound the ideal situation and in many respects it is, but there is likely a very structured approach to devising a strategy and the failure till now to spot the lack of a data strategy may suggest that those in the strategy space are not particularly familiar with what it entails. Therefore, it is important that you have sufficient latitude to be able to define the approach you need to take for this to succeed and avoid the pitfall of having a predetermined format and approach foisted upon you.

When developing a data strategy it is crucial to reach out to all parts of the organisation, get the right level of engagement and flex between a high-level vision and the detail of how data is to be managed – governance, standards, metadata, master systems, quality and so on – to ensure the key inputs enable the critical outputs to be delivered coherently. More so than many strategies, a data strategy covers all areas of an organisation: from comprehending the detailed activity and the baselined starting point, in order to ensure the route to successful implementation is feasible, to the visionary elements that comprehend, in the period covered by the data strategy, the art of the possible. It encapsulates people, process and technology, all of which are data-dependent to function.

One of the key artefacts to review will be the corporate strategy. How well can you align the data strategy to it? Will there need to be some rewriting of the corporate strategy to accommodate the data strategy? Could there be opportunities which the data strategy will introduce and need to be considered for inclusion in the corporate strategy? All of these points need careful consideration, as your organisation is relatively mature in its strategic thinking, and your task is to integrate and grow what is already in place rather than develop it in a silo. Engage those who have knowledge and experience of the corporate strategy, its content, drafting and key stakeholders, and it will save you significant time in your own process.

If the organisation is ready to embrace developing a data strategy, then the next chapter will guide you through the composition of the data strategy.

3.3 SETTING THE BOUNDARIES – UNDERSTANDING SCOPE AND THE RATIONALE

As demonstrated by the numerous examples of your starting point in defining a data strategy, the importance of having clarity as to the scope and the rationale for defining it is essential both for you, as the lead on it, but also for those you engage with going forward. If you are not able to provide that clarity and reasoning then it becomes challenging to get buy-in to the direction you are going, as it is highly likely every individual will have a slightly (or markedly, in some cases) different view as to the problem to be solved and the approach required.

There are challenges just in aligning others to a common understanding as to what a data strategy actually is, let alone why it is needed (as set out in Chapter 2). The way you approach developing the data strategy, from the moment you step forward to do so, is almost a strategy in its own right, as you will need to determine whom to involve, at what level and on what aspects, and how to ensure what you are doing continues to be visible to those who are not so directly involved. Having clarity behind the purpose and authority the data strategy carries is your first step before you seek to engage others. By all means refine and iterate to some degree, as this is a key way to draw your stakeholders in, but have a clearly defined scope and defensible terms of reference as to what you are tasked to achieve.

There is a lot of evidence in the public domain – through academic papers, conferences and books – that will enable you to understand why strategies fail, but these predominantly focus on the execution stage of the strategy, rather than the definition of the strategy itself. This may suggest that defining a strategy is the easy part, and I would tend to agree that the step beyond the strategy into execution itself is extremely challenging in most organisations.

Strategy, going back to its origins as the art of generalship or command, necessitates a general, or commander, without whom a strategy is likely to lack cohesion to see it through to being completed, agreed and ready for implementation. If there is a lack of clarity as to the long-term or overall goals in the organisation, then there is clearly a lack of strategic thinking to provide clarity of purpose. In such a situation, it is not unreasonable to conclude that without a driver of change any attempt to deliver a strategy is doomed to fail, not for the quality of the strategy itself, but the lack of understanding as to the why and the what, before even getting to the how, when and where, aided by the which (perhaps the most sophisticated, in terms of determining choices within the strategy).

Of course, if the strategy is never completed, or approved, it will not count amongst those that failed in implementation. The fact that data strategy definition may fail through a lack of effective leadership and sponsorship only increases the number that start but never make it through to successful implementation.

This matters in your task of defining a data strategy. I am making the point that there is an assumption in much of the literature that strategies lack implementation skills, communication or buy-in (amongst many others). However, a strategy that is well defined and employs effective stakeholder engagement and communication from the outset will avoid many of the pitfalls which perhaps only become readily apparent later in the process, when implementation stalls. As a result, getting the scope and the rationale for the data strategy agreed and communicated from the beginning is critical for success – not only in defining the data strategy but through the implementation stage too. Remember the 5W1H method from the preceding chapter: asking the same root questions (who, what, when, where, why and how) at least five times will enable you to explore the thinking to establish clarity and purpose as you embark on the challenge of developing a data strategy that will see it through to successful execution.

If probing highlights potential weaknesses in the scope or approach then call these out from the outset, as once you have started it can be hard to get a reset, and a failure to do so will formalise the brief to which you are working in such a way it may become impossible to deliver. The leader may also have to engage more widely before any change can be agreed, which will also lead to delay and doubts arising. Therefore, make sure your brief is coherent and has a clarity of purpose before you commit to taking responsibility for defining the data strategy. Changes will be needed along the way, but it is always easier to tack and adjust as you demonstrate progress than to appear stalled at the very beginning.

Do remember the point on terminology made in Chapter 2 that the term 'data strategy' can have very different meanings, so be clear on what your data strategy is focused on. Is it a full-spectrum review of the entire information cycle, including those items verging into a digital and technology landscape such as machine learning and AI, or more narrowly defined, restricted to selected elements of the information ecosystem (Figure 2.1)? Also, bear in mind the criticality of leadership in terms of the CLEAR approach. Effective stakeholder engagement at all levels will be essential.

It is also key to establish the type of output expected and the support you can look for from the wider organisation to ensure the process is collaborative throughout, and to have an understanding of how the strategy is approved and can then move into implementation. These represent your end goal, unless of course you are also seeing it through implementation.

Finally, this is your opportunity to revise the scope before you start work on defining the data strategy through engaging widely and ensuring all parties are agreed on the direction you are likely to head. Get a collective view on what they believe is needed – it is always easier to engage other stakeholders if their views have been sought and incorporated at the outset. If you are uneasy with the definition you have been given, the scope, timescale or the approach, then say so. It is essential that you get clarity and confirmation on these key points, as otherwise your progress will be hindered every step of the way, so articulate any concerns and reach agreement on how to deal with them from the start.

If you cannot reach agreement then it may be that this project is not one for you, but it may be a tough challenge to extricate yourself from it – be aware, the vast majority of strategies of all kinds fail to execute and realise benefits, and if this is 'your' project to lead you may wish to consider whether you are willing to commit to a project with a high propensity to fail to deliver all the benefits expected of it.

3.3.1 The role of sub-strategies in your data strategy approach

As the information lifecycle becomes ever more complex, with more channels, 'big data', AI, and an increasingly complex regulatory and compliance environment in which to operate, the scale of an all-encompassing data strategy becomes quite challenging. As a result, the data strategy can become encyclopaedic in size, trying to embrace every facet of the landscape and do justice to all to be considered within the data strategy.

The solution, which may seem both obvious but also a bit of a distraction from the issue, is to create the concept of sub-strategies within your data strategy.

> Sub-strategies strike an important balance between keeping the data strategy focused on the key goals over a given time frame and avoiding getting into too much detail, with the consequent danger of writing a data strategy so long it will not be read and so become consigned to the shelves forever.

The sections of the data strategy should align to the sub-strategies, if this is the approach you are seeking to take, which can help the difficult balancing act of keeping those who want to convey more information engaged whilst also making the data strategy an executive-level key document that is reviewed and approved at board level. Further, if you have stakeholders engaged in helping to shape the data strategy, operating as subject matter experts (SMEs) in various domains, what better than to empower them to take ownership of the sub-strategies and follow a similar path in creating these as has been employed in compiling the data strategy?

In this respect, it is quite feasible you could create sub-strategies focused on:

- data management, to include aspects such as data accessibility, security and compliance, master data management, data architecture, standards and quality, unstructured data, amongst others;

- MI/reporting, which can also be a driver to rationalise and focus on what KPIs are actually driving the organisation and are therefore needed to support decision making;

- analytics, including predictive analysis and moving the organisation up the value curve to exploit data more effectively by looking forward and preparing for change;

- insight, to encapsulate the gathering and exploitation of primary and secondary research and how it is managed and utilised in the decision-making process;

- advanced analytics/AI, increasingly an important area for all organisations, whether a consumer of such activity, a provider of services that utilise it or perhaps an organisation exploiting the technology.

These are commonly produced sub-strategies which underpin specific activities that will be incorporated in the data strategy.

There are others, not least the approach to data ethics, given this is often at the edge of compliance and may be driven by the balance between the efficacy of what is possible and the ethicality in what your organisation wants to be seen to be doing (often key to the brand perception). This can be a sub-strategy in its own right or a key aspect of the sub-strategies themselves, but it is almost certainly a growing area for consideration and likely to feature in some way in the overall data strategy.

The systems in your organisation – investment, implementation thereof, impact on data management and how the organisation interacts with and collects data – will inevitably feature in some way in the sub-strategies, though you would expect systems to be the focus of a technology strategy.

Readiness for the implementation of new systems is often overlooked from a data perspective, or is the poor relation, yet it is not an overstatement to say that we have systems simply to provide an effective means for the collection and exploitation of data, which is lost on many organisations that either assume data will continue as before or squeeze in some activity around data migration at the eleventh hour.

In addition, systems should be rationalised, wherever possible, driven by a master data management approach to ensure there is clarity on purpose and integrity of that data. This also extends to other related software tools, as many organisations have a proliferation of reporting tools, data visualisation software, even messaging capabilities and overlaps between social media platforms, intranets and collaboration tools, all of which come at a cost – and, inevitably, the more there are, the poorer the quality of data due to the higher cost of maintenance.

It is therefore important to recognise that there needs to be a link between the data and technology strategies, but this does not warrant picking out systems as a sub-strategy. Instead, as a key enabler, they should be referenced in the respective sub-strategies.

I advocate in this book the concept of a rolling view in defining the data strategy, rather than fixing an end date and then not considering how it needs to evolve until the latter stages of that period, when a new data strategy needs to be defined. In much the same way, sub-strategies should be live documents supporting the data strategy, and any significant changes would lead to a revision of either the sub-strategy or data strategy, depending on where that change is driven. I would also recommend staggering the release of sub-strategies, for whilst the data strategy is in flux it would be a significant distraction to try to author the many sub-strategies. Instead, have a rolling programme in updating and reviewing the sub-strategies, keeping these current but devoting time and resources in a revolving basis such that there is work always under way to keep the strategies at all levels moving forward and avoiding peaks and troughs of effort needing to be provided.

3.3.2 The impact that type of organisation has on a data strategy

It is a reasonable assertion to suggest that data is the same the world over, and so why would a data strategy vary from one type of organisation to another. It is less about the data itself, more the nature of the organisation driving the focus behind the collation and use of data to provide context, strategic purpose and, importantly, the culture of the organisation.

My career has given me experience of working across many sectors in organisations of varying size, stages of data maturity (even varying within an organisation) and organisational key drivers. I therefore have knowledge of working with data in a range of environments and an awareness that the experience of working with data and an ability to comprehend business challenges is the imperative more than deep specialist knowledge of the sector in which the organisation operates. After all, I am surrounded by colleagues who have this specialist domain expertise in abundance to learn from and adapt my expertise accordingly.

In my engagements with those who have been tasked with devising a data strategy, I am often asked whether domain expertise in the specific sector in which the organisation operates, allied to deep understanding of the organisation, is essential because of a fear that their situation is so unique there is no learning to be gained from others. I am also asked, less frequently, whether there is a standard template to devising a data strategy, a 'one size fits all' concept, that can simply be populated with information to generate a ready-made data strategy.

In reality, there is neither a need to be a deep expert in all matters an organisation undertakes to be able to devise a data strategy (certainly, in most large organisations, no one has the range of expertise and knowledge and so it is an unachievable goal) nor a simple template to provide a data strategy fit to drive an organisation forward due to the complexities and cultures that exist in each organisation.

This book attempts to guide you through the process and highlight the key steps along the way, but the discovery process will highlight what is specific to your organisation. In devising a data strategy, the key is to be able to communicate effectively across the organisation, comprehend the corporate strategy in terms of what it is seeking to achieve and the enablers necessary for it to do so, identify the current state of data across the information ecosystem in your organisation, and bring together stakeholders and specialist resources to help you craft the data strategy in a way that is easily translatable into implementation.

One of the obvious areas to highlight in terms of how organisations do have differing key drivers is the variation between those operating in the private sector compared to the public sector.

A private sector organisation is dealing with competition (mostly: some may be in monopolistic areas, which I will come to later); usually customers are able to come and go depending upon price, service or a combination of the two, and therefore the exploitation of data is seen to be a key differentiator from competitors through a range of actions (for instance, pricing, propositions, customer targeting).

In the mid 1990s Treacy and Wiersema[8] identified that there are broadly three generic competitive strategies:

- operational excellence, in which the organisation seeks to be as efficient as possible in its operational activities and reduce cost through automation of processes and activities such as just-in-time logistics;
- customer intimacy, providing a tailored range of services to the customer and using personalisation and a differentiated service offering to deliver to customer needs;
- product leadership, delivering a customer experience and brand recognition for innovation, product quality and being able to charge premium pricing in return.

Organisations must focus on which one they want to seek market leadership in and perform acceptably in the other two. Whilst this model is not exclusive to organisations in the private sector, the options are somewhat constrained for those operating in other markets.

---

8   Michael Treacy and Fred Wiersema, *The Discipline of Market Leaders: Choose Your Customers, Narrow Your Focus, Dominate Your Market.* Cambridge: Perseus Books, 1997.

To achieve operational excellence, the key driver is cost, as customers are not perceived to value choice. This fits most closely with mature markets where the output is commoditised, business volumes are high and hence cost leadership is essential. To succeed, organisations must be able to measure key processes and benchmark costs, not only their own but against known benchmarks competitors might be attaining, and to drive down cost through ever more effective and efficient processes. To deliver this, data has to be able to demonstrate performance but be readily available to support activities to drive cost initiatives. If your organisation is in this space then it has probably adopted process efficiency and quality control strategies (such as Six Sigma or total quality management), and the culture will be one driven by measures.

If customer intimacy is the goal, then there will be a focus on personalisation of the customer experience by delivering a service which has been customised to feel tailored to suit needs. This is likely to include bundling of services or products to provide a solution rather than the customer needing to identify what forms that solution for themselves. Clearly this is also data intensive as it needs significant amounts of customer data to anticipate needs and devise solutions which are likely to have a high success rate. Whilst the service is tailored, it isn't necessarily one driven by innovation or price, but its success is built on the anticipation of meeting needs as the customer has them, through existing products or services and presenting them in a personalised manner.

Finally, product leadership is absolute on being driven by product innovation and leadership. The products are seen to be one step ahead of the competition, driven by quality and branding that ties the customer in to that organisation's ethos of being first and hence superior to its rivals. It invests heavily in research and development, product engineering, marketing and hiring the brightest talent to drive innovation. It needs scale to do so effectively, which often necessitates expanding to markets beyond immediate geographic markets and acquiring organisations in their infancy that are seen to be on the cusp of developing products that are potential leaders of the future or opening up new, but related, markets to the organisation. Data is key to be able to provide collaborative working environments, accessing the latest knowledge within the organisation but also beyond, and to process large volumes of data to solve problems and drive innovation.

Whilst data drives each of these strategies, it is apparent that the drivers in each are quite different. Even though this model has been in place for nearly 25 years, the relevance of it to support those of us operating in a data strategy space remains. Comprehending where your organisation sits in this model will inform the priorities you need to focus on in defining the data strategy to align with the goals your organisation is seeking to achieve.

What does this mean for a public sector organisation? Well, for many, the notion of operational excellence is key to delivering high-quality services at low cost to ensure good use of taxpayer funds. The profit motive may not be as overarching as in the private sector, but this does not mean that the need to innovate is lacking – far from it. Public sector organisations have to be as smart as private sector organisations to fund change from within, and to ensure that talent and knowledge are accessible to maximise capabilities.

The challenge for organisations that are in less stable sectors, such as charities and other not-for-profit organisations, is the need to be effective across all three strategies within this model. With income less stable, continued delivery of projects which are seen to be of high importance to those providing funding has to be maintained to stay relevant and retain support. If this is not achieved, then those funding such organisations can fail to renew subscriptions or withdraw grants. As a result, operational excellence has to be the mantra, but customer intimacy is an equally important part of the organisational DNA.

This makes operating in such environments especially challenging, and innovation features strongly in the field of data and its exploitation. The need for a data strategy is particularly important for organisations operating in these sectors. It establishes clarity on how data can support the critically important activities to be delivered and how these can be achieved more effectively through better management and utilisation of data. It also provides a point of innovation, to establish new opportunities as well as significant improvements in the effectiveness of the ways of working through better insight.

In addition to the sector your organisation operates within, there are many other factors which will determine the nature of your data strategy and the approach to be taken in compiling it. For instance, an organisation operating in a regulated environment has to reflect the controls and constraints under which it operates, and ensure it stays compliant in its operations, which requires a strong hand through a coherent data strategy. In some markets, regulators publish their own data strategies and expect organisations within those markets to do likewise. In some instances, the justification for funding capital projects requires transparency in the data and analysis underpinning the rationale to gain approval from the regulator.

If the organisation is a monopoly, whether in full or part of its operations, much of the regulatory framework will likely apply. In such instances, a monopolistic organisation may be focused almost entirely by regulatory risk, hence the focus of a data strategy may be compliance-led. However, much like others operating in a strongly regulated environment, there is scope to drive greater operational excellence through better use of data.

The scale, ambition and resources of your organisation will have a bearing on the scale and scope of the data strategy you develop. In particular, resources will be critical enablers not just of the data strategy but also of determining the pace and scale of the implementation to achieve the ambition. There is more detail on the capability of resources, the maturity of the organisation and the importance these play in Chapter 6.

In setting the ambition of the data strategy, the complexity of the organisation and the legacy issues it faces will inevitably play a role in determining the scope. However, for a new start-up, the priorities are all based in the future. Their focus is on constructing the way in which the organisation intends to capture, use and manage data securely and effectively, and planning for the future when, for example, the need to upgrade systems and the exponential growth in data become critical issues.

An established organisation with a host of legacy systems and data quality issues is more likely to need to balance solving those issues with plotting a bold course for the future. The data strategy has to fit the organisation in which it will operate, and whilst the headings or chapters may be similar across data strategies (see Chapter 6 for more on content), the nature of the content is likely to differ significantly.

3.4 BALANCING CONTROL AND EXPLOITATION IN YOUR DATA STRATEGY

One of the key aspects of defining your data strategy is recognising the need to strike the right balance between implementing controls in your organisations versus exploiting data to generate insight and, potentially, competitive advantage. Of course, organisations tend to look at the return of an investment in committing to significant activities, and implementing a data strategy could easily be recognised as an investment. However, there is a delicate balance to be struck between investing in those things which are necessary to make the organisation compliant, better organised and decluttered (in terms of multiple data sets and conflicting reporting) and being able to generate insight and opportunities that may well change the dynamic of how well the organisation performs.

> It is all well and good to develop insight, but if it is built on poor-quality data the decisions may be as flawed as having not generated the insight at all (possibly more so – I often say that racing ahead to exploit data in really advanced ways whilst using poor-quality data gets you to the wrong answer faster than would otherwise have been the case).

Building the foundations, establishing control, is often the unseen value of a data strategy implementation. The foundations may not be visible to those who benefit from their having been put in place but they deliver more secure outcomes than would otherwise have been the case. Progress without the necessary foundations, and the whole edifice could easily come tumbling down. Investing in what you cannot see does not equate to those elements having less value – indeed, the value is in the assurance it gives to what is visible.

You may therefore find yourself drawn into defining a data strategy which is focused heavily on those elements which are largely about data exploitation. I tend to suggest that the balance between data management and exploitation is not about focusing exclusively on the control – the foundations – in your data strategy: in the vast majority of organisations you do need to present ways in which the data strategy can make a visible difference to your stakeholders to sustain their support and commitment to your programme. Identify 'quick wins' amongst the easy-to-improve exploitation tasks, some of which may be obvious at first glance.

These could include rationalising the disparate reporting activity into a more coherent and reliable set of reports issued once and used across all of the organisation, so that all decision-makers operate to the same set of information. You will be making small compromises in the integrity of approach, yet still releasing value to the organisation, albeit in a sub-optimal way until the foundations are in place to do this more effectively. However, in the meantime, you have succeeded in demonstrating some value, getting traction behind being able to deliver change and whetting the appetite of your stakeholders to deliver more.

3.5 TEN TO TAKE AWAY

Here are the summary ten key points to take away from this chapter.

1. Assess the readiness and maturity of the organisation at the outset.

2. Identify the key drivers for the commissioning of the data strategy and adopt the appropriate response to navigate your way through to deliver something of value to the organisation.

3. Consider the sponsorship of the data strategy – who is the key influencer, who is behind the data strategy, who has most to gain? Getting sponsorship right makes a substantial difference to your likelihood of success.

4. Review the scope and reset if appropriate before you make a start. Be clear on what is expected and the timeline to achieve it.

5. Most strategies fail, with many falling short in implementation. Consider how to avoid the common pitfalls that lead to failure and keep a focus on these as you progress through definition into execution.

6. Stakeholder engagement and communication will be key to avoid failure. Ensure you understand your starting point – what the stakeholders believe and expect of the data strategy, their commitment to it and how you maintain a dialogue.

7. Reflect on the structure of your data strategy, and the need to underpin it with more extensive sub-strategies to bring more detailed intentions out on specific strands of the data strategy.

8. Assess your organisation type – core strengths and positioning in the market (the types of organisation as defined by the three competitive strategies) – and align the data strategy to enhance the organisation in that organisational type.

9. Think about how you strike the balance between getting the foundations in place to support the exploitation of data, and the 'sell' of this to the organisation with your data strategy.

10. Don't discount quick wins to gain support through being opportunist. These may be imperfect in the longer term, but will build confidence and establish credibility if there is any doubt about the value a data strategy might bring to the organisation.

4　COMPOSING THE DATA STRATEGY

'Strategists who don't take time to think are just planners.'

Dr Max McKeown[1]

The success of a data strategy, as with every strategy, can be measured by the combination of a number of factors:

- **Relevance** – alignment to, and support for, the corporate strategy (or vision, if there isn't a strategy);
- **Awareness** – staff know it exists, and where to locate it;
- **Value** – in terms of both its usefulness and impact;
- **Execution** – the ease in being able to apply it to deliver a positive outcome.

Therefore, if you're an author of a successful data strategy in your organisation you may well have started the first corporate RAVE! As with any rave, it needs people to be willing to come along and give it a go and to be able to enjoy the experience to want to try it again. That's what you want to sense when your data strategy goes live. Sounds so easy, but it is often the point at which the data strategy flounders.

This chapter seeks to explain the importance of getting traction with your audience in composing your data strategy and, just as importantly, to understand what they may be seeking in order to get a ticket any way they can to join the rave. It aims to explore the role of your stakeholders, ranging from senior executives who need to endorse the strategy through to those who are the end users and will be key to whether the strategy becomes part of the fabric of the organisation in the way it operates.

The point has been made earlier in this book that a broad selection of inputs through consultation and involvement is necessary to prepare for success. This helps keeps the strategy grounded in language that is meaningful to the audience, based upon the knowledge and insights that those who know your stakeholders better than you do can provide. This simple step is so important and yet, so often, seen to be either too time-consuming ('we will need to explain every step of the way, and it will slow us down') or constraining ('we will only focus on the immediate problem, the strategy needs to be aspirational and our stakeholders don't have that understanding to add value').

Of course, there is a semblance of truth in those statements, but let me expose why they do not stand up to scrutiny. Firstly, it will take time, there will be a need to position and explain your data strategy, but if this isn't understood by those working alongside

---

1 M. McKeown, *The Strategy Book: How to Think and Act Strategically to Deliver Outstanding Results.* Harlow: Pearson Education, 2019.

you to develop the data strategy, what hope is there for other stakeholders to grasp the context, meaning and opportunity when they've been detached from the strategy process? Indeed, those who join you become valued for the challenge they are able to present, and the way it makes the strategy accessible to the wider audience through having been written to be widely understood. I will touch on this further shortly.

Secondly, the visionary constraint. It might sound obvious, but there is little point building complexity and visionary elements into the data strategy if the key stakeholders cannot relate to that material. Therefore, those who work alongside you in devising the data strategy are there to learn and to become the evangelists of the 'art of the possible' and the impact that could have on their respective business areas. Without the advanced 'sales party' – those who are trusted to speak the same language as the areas of the organisation they represent and can therefore position your vision to the key stakeholders – it becomes more difficult to bring stakeholders at all levels with you on why they should engage with the data strategy to adopt an approach which probably seems entirely alien to them.

It is often the balance of these two challenges, pushing ahead with the right level of ambition whilst recognising the need to bring all parties with you, that leads to a suitable compromise that can often yield a better result. Do bear in mind that at times it may feel you go slower to make faster progress, but try to avoid losing sight of the visionary aspects, as these are what keep giving that limited momentum a periodic jolt in the right direction.

4.1 THE IMPORTANCE OF ACCESSIBILITY

The term 'accessibility' has many applications, most of which are relevant to the context of data strategies. I will work through these in turn, but the key to this chapter is to remember, no matter how polished you believe the data strategy is, you are not the target audience and so not the person who determines whether it is deemed a success.

You must consider how you develop your communications approach to reflect the importance of accessibility and to ensure this is embodied in the communications plan you develop as part of the data strategy programme. There is more on communications in Chapter 7.

Clarity of purpose underpins the accessibility of your data strategy. I have covered the importance of clarity in earlier chapters, but make sure you have a clear understanding of the purpose of your data strategy, how it aligns to the wider corporate strategy and the expectations others might have in terms of what your output will look like. Do refer back to the CLEAR principles in Chapter 2, and use these as a barometer of how effectively you are using these five principles to make your data strategy accessible.

4.1.1 Key stakeholders

There is a need to recognise the stakeholders you are going to be dealing with and their respective roles, interests, diversity and motivations to enable you to progress. You cannot succeed without getting the right level of engagement across your organisation due to the participation the data strategy implementation will necessitate. If stakeholders do not feel they have been party to the data strategy definition, then they may well push back on the content regardless of how pertinent it is, simply through a lack of buy-in from the outset.

Even amongst the stakeholder groups identified below, there will be differences that you will need to distinguish and manage accordingly. The more sophisticated your understanding of the stakeholder groups, the more effective your communications are likely to be, and the greater the chances of success in defining and executing the data strategy.

4.1.1.1 Executive sponsor(s)

As discussed earlier, you need an executive sponsor to help drive the data strategy as a principle and to get engagement through the compilation and execution of it. This means your executive sponsor(s) will need to be briefed at various times on all aspects – think of the standard 5W1H question set applied to the rationale, composition and progress reporting of the data strategy along the way to appraise it in a manner that keeps it focused but comprehensive. The sponsor(s) will not necessarily want large amounts of detail, but enough to 'sell' the message and retain the levels of engagement at all stages – this is in your interest, as it makes your job in keeping resources assigned from other parts of the organisation easier to maintain.

Checking in from time to time with updates on progress and to share outputs will also enable the sponsor(s) to identify when the time is right to share more widely, and to review and adjust as needed based on peer review and feedback. Do utilise these opportunities to present based on outcomes, rather than the minutiae, in the sense of 'we can achieve *x* if we do *y*', as it gives a sense of purpose rather than being seen as a technical step.

The choice of executive sponsor, and their role and responsibilities, is set out in Chapter 7.

4.1.1.2 Senior executives

If the pitch is to be made to senior executives, which may follow on from the opportunity created by the executive sponsor(s), do ensure you focus on what the outcome will be and consider how best to make this as inclusive as possible. For instance, if this is a presentation to an executive board, think about the participants and balance the areas of greatest opportunity on which to focus, as well as reaching out to others around the table to make them feel involved and engaged. Consider the financial logic behind the data strategy. It will almost certainly get scrutiny on this basis as you are going to be tying up resources which could be deployed to revenue-generating opportunities elsewhere, so there has to be some logic behind an investment in the data strategy. Highlighting any competitive disadvantage you face – if you have evidence that competitors are exploiting their data more effectively – or the risks the organisation is carrying is a good way of illustrating the economic reality of why a data strategy makes sense.

Gather input from those working with you in devising the data strategy to get a feel for how best to communicate with their respective leaders, to learn what is front of mind at the point at which you are going to present and to appreciate the way in which they like to receive information. If it requires a bit of preparation, or a pre-meeting with some individuals ahead of the executive board meeting to provide further context, it is worth doing.

If you have the board supporting your work, then it makes it easier to retain the resources assigned to you, gives clarity on direction and keeps your executive sponsor(s) delighted at the perception of progress being made. Start with a poor first impression, or fail to hit the mark in terms of relevance, and it can be very difficult to win over key stakeholders going forward. Be prepared to lay out your pitch, but, if at all possible, you should be listening for a large part of this meeting, capturing key concerns, opportunities and priorities to be focused on in subsequent conversations.

4.1.2 The wider organisation

The data strategy has to resonate with the organisation at large to be translated into action. Therefore, it is important to think about the communications approach to engage the wider organisation at all stages, so that the emergence of a data strategy is not seen as a random event or out of the blue. Bear in mind that you should have representation from the wider organisation as part of your team, and you can use these virtual links back into the organisation to do 'show and tells' to present the work done so far and to get soundings back on the feasibility of realising the data strategy.

The range of knowledge, experience and comprehension of what a data strategy is will vary across the organisation, but start with the lowest common denominator as to the level of understanding to ensure you take all with you. As has been discussed earlier in this book, data strategies are often open to varying interpretations, even amongst practitioners in the field, so the risk of an extremely varied understanding across the entirety of the organisation will be high.

Work from the definition upwards, positioning it at all times in the 'what does it mean for me' outcomes-based focus to make it real. Your goal is to communicate a strategic vision that is clear, simple and logical, with sufficient emotional pull to get people engaged and wanting to follow. Test the approach on your own team, taking soundings from those who have come from the very teams you are seeking to engage, and be prepared to communicate in bite-sized chunks to avoid overcomplicating the message or overwhelming the audience.

It will be important to understand the lexicon in each and every part of the organisation, and the larger the organisation, the more fragmented that will be, typically split on the functional lines based on the structure of the organisation. Appreciate the acronyms in use, and avoid language that makes the strategy sound like an ivory-tower initiative from somewhere remote from those you are seeking to engage. After all, you want them to shoulder a significant proportion of the burden in delivering the data strategy in their everyday work. If they get it, you can build from there. Lose them from the start and it is a difficult to win them back.

4.1.2.1 Diversity

Do bear in mind that the organisation is inevitably diverse. It is likely that you can slice the audience in a number of ways – ethnicity, age, grade, location, function/department, profession, length of service; the list goes on. Each of these groups will also be diverse – simple demographics do not delineate us into convenient stovepipes – and whilst there may be some level of conformity (for example, all of the senior accountants may well have gone through the same qualification route), it is dangerous to think of any group as singular in thought or action.

Whilst this presents a challenge in how to engage broadly, it also presents a wonderful opportunity to build diverse thinking into the strategy; after all, a strategy is defining a vision which is largely about making a difference, so where better to begin than canvassing diverse opinions to get a rich set of inputs to the process. It also presents a need to segment and tailor communication and engagement in a way that suits the audience, so consider whether social media platforms, intranets, video briefings or other forms of communication are better than blasting a message in a single format – I'm sure we have all had many 'corporate' emails land in the inbox that we fully intend to read later but which never seem to make it to the top of the pile.

If you can, I would always recommend having a range of stakeholders who can provide a flavour of this diversity to enrich thinking and challenge preconceptions as you devise the strategy. Harvest the inputs of those who are not necessarily in the mainstream in their functions, who are often the problem solvers or creative thinkers, for these are the people who will challenge you and make your strategy far richer in return.

4.1.2.2 Inclusivity
The larger the organisation, the more diverse it may be in terms of having a broader spectrum of needs, especially when it comes to engaging with your colleagues and delivering effective communication. You are likely to find people, however, in all organisations who need support in being able to access information. You can assist this process and seek to engage by making your data strategy accessible to all. Whether this be accommodating personal needs to enable those individuals to play a part in the workforce, or providing materials in varying formats and/or languages, think about how your data strategy can be made to be as inclusive as possible. This is another form of diversity, but one which can be overlooked or given limited time.

If you want the data strategy to be truly inclusive, think through how to reach all communities within your organisation so it can be embraced by all. Remember, not all can access information in a way that you might be able to, and you should consider how you can make your communications as easy to access as possible to all groups within your organisation.

4.1.3 Third parties – partners and suppliers

The reality in many organisations today is that third parties play a critical role in managing systems, delivering operational activity and providing other services to your organisation. These organisations will also have to be informed, involved and motivated to help you deliver the data strategy, especially as it moves into implementation. This may have a contractual dimension to it which needs careful consideration; it may even incur significant cost, though if there is a 'win–win' in it for the partner or supplier organisation, then it may be in their interest to offset the cost, even considering investing their own funds to realise the benefit to their own organisation. It would be wise to keep such organisations engaged so there are no surprises and to enable them to plan ahead to be able to resource to assist your work.

4.1.4 External audiences

In some cases, the data strategy might be serving an audience far wider than your own organisation. If you work in a compliance/regulatory body, a government agency, a charity or some other organisation which is outward facing, then the data strategy may be an industry-wide directive or something which is setting the tone of how you expect others to operate or comply. This is a quite different dynamic to the development of a data strategy for use within an organisation, and usually has rounds of engagement and consultation that lead to drafting of the document before it is finally issued.

However, whilst there are differences, there are clearly similarities. The engagement and consultation processes are much the same, though you may well be working with specialists who have devised their own corporate data strategies and so might be more experienced in this field than you. If those individuals are willing and able to share their data strategies with you I would recommend you take them up on it, as it will give you an opportunity to understand the direction in which their organisation is headed, the maturity they have seemingly attained and the structure to the document with which they are familiar, and to compare and contrast the commonalities and differences across those organisations you are engaging to know how big a challenge you face in bringing coherence to an industry-wide data strategy.

If you are interacting with the public, rather than corporates, then the opportunity to engage is still there but has to be undertaken in a different way – questionnaires, focus groups, publishing drafts for comments – to gather feedback from interested parties. Unless the nature of your organisation is fundamentally different to any other, reach out to other public-facing organisations to learn from their experience in devising a data strategy that got sufficient interaction to give confidence it was in tune with wider expectations, putting it on a path to be successful. Take opportunities that the wider organisation may present to utilise those same information-gathering approaches where others are seeking opinions on topics that can accommodate asking some pertinent questions to support your work. Learn from the work others have undertaken in devising strategies to see what worked or failed to get engagement and useful information from the process.

Plain English!

There is a tendency to lapse into the use of jargon, acronyms and technical terms in strategies on the basis they are used every day. This applies to all organisations; indeed many of those I have worked at in my career are known for the acronym their name has become, and in some cases the acronym is so well known the full name of the organisation is probably forgotten.

In the data field, we are just as prone to turn simple things into complex terms or acronyms. Even data-related phrases which are commonplace are not necessarily universally understood by everyone in an organisation. For instance, what proportion of the workforce would give an accurate definition for terms such as metadata, business intelligence (BI) or insight? They are in everyday use but are assumed common vocabulary rather than tested as such.

Whilst I do not suggest abandoning terms which have become common vocabulary for our profession, I do recommend providing a simple glossary at the end of the data strategy document to try to iron out the meaning you are applying to these terms within the strategy. It may seem unnecessary, but if it ensures that time which might have been spent debating what a term means is directed to actually achieving something within the data strategy, then in my view that is time well spent.

Test, test and test again the language used throughout the data strategy with a mixed audience. Do not rely on those who have been assigned to help you construct the data strategy. As if by osmosis, they will become as oblivious to the use of the jargon in the data strategy as you are, so get others to sense-check it and, if there is any confusion or doubt, be prepared to change it. You do not want to find, some months down the line, that you and your team have been using vocabulary in one way to discover other stakeholders had a slightly different meaning, as this can lead to frustration, lack of progress and an undermining of the credibility of what you are trying to achieve. What can start out as a minor variation in interpretation can become a significant difference the longer it persists, and therefore harder to resolve, so try to ensure there is absolute clarity from the outset.

Explaining the jargon to the person who questions it is a natural reaction, but unless you are prepared to do that proactively every time someone reads it then change it the first time someone asks. You want the data strategy to be clear, understood and acted upon; don't put any barriers in the way which could lead to either inaction or a lack of coherence in the action taken.

4.2 DELIVER WITH PRIDE

I use yet another acronym to try to keep the evolving data strategy on track – PRIDE: purpose, relevance, inspiring, deliverable, enabling. This provides a useful way to consider the intent of the data strategy through its composition. Each component is described below.

4.2.1 Purpose

The purpose of creating a data strategy is apparently simple – to devise a data strategy to move the organisation forward in the broadest sense of data-related activities, whilst focusing on how this helps support the corporate strategy and vision.

This is not in doubt; however, there is a subtlety to this that purpose seeks to resolve, and that is more directly related to the delivery of the data strategy – what am I seeking to achieve as I deliver the data strategy, and how will I know I am delivering the purpose of the data strategy? The sense of purpose lies in the focus placed upon the transition to delivering, moving beyond the definition and the need for clarity into ensuring there is a purpose behind the data strategy, and compiling it in a way that gives it meaning.

We will explore this in further detail in Chapter 5, but to be clear here, the data strategy needs to be more than a theoretical exposition of how to manage and exploit data.

4.2.2 Relevance

The data strategy needs to be relevant to those who are intended to read it. This follows on from the accessibility section of this chapter. Unless there is an obvious link between the aim of the data strategy and the roles staff play across the organisation it will be seen to be rather theoretical and not relevant to the very people you are trying to engage. This is all too often a reason for data strategies stumbling between concept and execution.

Consult, engage, discuss but most of all listen to the challenges that staff across the organisation are only too willing to share with you, as these will give an insight into what those individuals are likely to be looking for in terms of direction. Why would you forgo the opportunity to do free research in scoping the key themes to address, and thereby targeting your audience with the answers they will be seeking? The more your strategy gives clarity to their specific challenges, the more the audience will read further and be willing to embark on the bolder strategic vision set out in the data strategy.

Gathering inputs will also enable you to test the frequency with which the same issues recur. This is a useful indicator to where some of the biggest problems might exist, as these are likely to cut across functional boundaries and therefore need more central coordination to bring respective parties together to hammer out the best solution for all concerned. You may discover organisational silos which are blocking progress, and if you can be the catalyst to bringing these together and forging a common understanding, then you are making progress as well as acting as a bridge between two groups who may not believe they have a common goal. If you can inspire curiosity in the data and its potential to enable improvements to be made, and get people engaged in working with you, it will make progress through implementation much easier.

Removing barriers will give your data strategy credibility, as well as demonstrating the value it can have in enabling focus to be put on the key targets across an organisation. It sounds relatively simple, even obvious, but do not discount the lack of cohesion and therefore traction that can be a blocker to solving some relatively straightforward things.

4.2.3 Inspiring

I described in earlier chapters how the data strategy needs to be an enabler of the corporate strategy, in terms of both providing a consistent thread through priorities as well as identifying those things that can raise the bar of the corporate strategy. The norm for many organisations, the larger the greater the likelihood, is for there to be a wealth of information flowing around in a largely unstructured form – emails, notes, conversations and notices via message boards and/or an intranet – such that the typical senior stakeholder becomes immune to reading it all. Your challenge, with a communication headed up as a data strategy and so unlikely to get most executives on the edge of their seat in anticipation, is to position it in a way which will capture their imagination.

I have already covered the need to get stakeholder buy-in throughout the research and compilation of the data strategy, and so long as you have followed this approach the awareness of a data strategy being in train should not come as a complete surprise. You should have your representatives from across the organisation participating in the process of information gathering, review and analysis leading to the delivery of the data strategy. Therefore, there are numerous links and opportunities to be exploited to communicate progress in readiness for the launch of the data strategy.

This is all well and good, but the essence of whether any of that engagement counts is how you position the data strategy with each and every stakeholder. A really effective data strategy should touch all staff in the organisation, and so be read by all to know what they should do when it comes to managing and exploiting data. We operate in a world which is driven by data: from the calendar function aligned to the email which tells you where you should be at a given moment of the working day, to the data we collect and utilise in our everyday activities, all of us are data providers and consumers. Yet many will say that data is 'not for them' or 'handled by those people [keeping it non-judgemental!] over there'.

This is the big ask in the process – make your data strategy inspiring!

Before considering the data strategy, let us consider the corporate strategy – is it inspiring? Has it had the impact it sought to achieve? Do people relate to it in their everyday work in the organisation? This might give you either positive steers on how to exploit the success of the corporate strategy in devising the data strategy, or it might lead you to take a very different path. Your research here will be highly informative of the route you take.

Whether the corporate strategy is your model or not, the data strategy you are developing needs to be inspiring, and by that, I mean it has to resonate with what people recognise as challenges or issues. It needs to demonstrate how these can be overcome in a way that is believable and has enough detail to give practical hints and advice. To make it feel real to staff it must focus on outcomes, what difference it will make and how it will deliver change to the organisation if implemented. Most importantly, the data strategy has to be something they want to get behind and make happen.

Do not get bogged down in the detail – that is the role of the implementation plan, which we will come to later in the book. Focus on the vision, the outcomes to be achieved and the impact the data strategy will have to realise the objectives in the corporate strategy. Make the storytelling behind the data strategy inspirational.

4.2.4 Deliverable

The strategy sets out the vision, where you intend to be in three, five or even ten years from now. It does not matter what the length of period is: the strategy is intended to lay out the big things to change and deliver to realise the goal. In so doing, the strategy sets waymarkers, points on the journey to be reached to keep the organisation on the path to achieve the desired outcomes as defined in the strategy.

In many respects, there are parallels in strategy design and execution with an analogy of an architect and a builder (for any strategy, but it certainly applies to a data strategy). The architect is the data strategist and the builder leads on the implementation, with the architect providing plans, dimensions, information on materials to be used, loads to be borne by walls within the structure and so on. By the time the architect has finished, there is a good understanding of what is to be achieved, the appearance at the end of the build phase and the space created through the provision of a series of rooms. This is your goal in defining the data strategy, to give clarity on what is to be done, what the organisation will have achieved and look like once the strategy has been delivered, and to provide a series of themes, or topics, within the strategy so it is a complete strategy, with all the rooms working together to provide the building that meets needs.

So where does that leave the builder?

The critical element in this process is to design with implementation in mind. Whilst you must avoid the trap of defining the implementation in too much detail, the waymarkers are intended to guide those who are tasked with executing the strategy to know how it should be achieved without having to guess. All too many strategies – of all varieties – fall down through a lack of forethought about how an implementation plan might be structured in order to achieve the strategy and failure to provide the clarity that is sought to guide the implementation process.

In this sense, the builder is tasked with following the plans set out by the architect, mindful that there may need to be some variation due to unforeseen or technical challenges. It is also likely that the environment may change, due to the organisation changing priorities or the structure of the organisation evolving in a way that might not have been foreseen. Much like minor planning changes required to revise permissions related to the architect's drawings, the strategy too needs to be reflective of such changes and be seen to be updated as necessary. As with a building, if there is a reason the design is no longer valid or relevant then there is little to be gained from ploughing on. Reassess, regroup and redraft to something that is more reflective of the demands of the organisation.

In much the same way as the builder follows the architect's drawings, the implementation team need to put the plan together to deliver the strategy. This is likely to be an overarching plan for most or all of the period the strategy covers, but with detail on the next year. The waymarkers turn into milestones, the themes into work strands or specific groups assigned responsibility for delivery, and the critical enabling deliverables – akin to load-bearing walls of the building – assigned appropriate significance to make them key deliverables on the critical path of the implementation plan.

Resources – skilled craftspeople and labourers – are hired or allocated to tasks within the implementation plan to deliver specifics, with oversight from the project leads (site managers) to ensure all is on track and appropriate to meet the objectives and hit the milestones. Project governance on the implementation is driven by a programme management office (PMO) or similar function in much the same way as the builder has a regular meeting with key delivery leads. Stakeholders are engaged and progress is signed off along the way – the implementation of the strategy as it reaches its milestones, the building as it meets building regulation standards to be approved to the next phase.

The key point of this part of PRIDE is to remember that the strategy will need to be delivered, possibly by others, and to avoid being drawn into the detail of implementation. However, it is important to recognise that the more clarity you provide to steer the execution of the strategy the more likely it is to succeed. Strike the right balance and the data strategy has a real chance of delivering the vision you set.

4.2.5 Enabling

The final, but essential, component on the path to success is to remember that the data strategy must achieve buy-in from the wider organisation if it is to have the impact you want. This brings us back to the start of the PRIDE acronym – purpose. If you have the context right in terms of setting the purpose, then you know what it is that you are seeking to achieve. Enabling is the flip side to the purpose question. It is aligning the data strategy to the specific activities that need to be achieved in order to deliver the corporate goals, which therefore makes it clear to all that this is a key enabling strategy for everyone to get behind to increase the likelihood of achieving the organisation's vision.

This requires all the components of PRIDE to be woven together, such that each component builds on the others to create momentum and absolute buy-in to what have become integral components of the wider organisation strategy. However, to be truly enabling, it must be feasible to measure the effectiveness of the data strategy, and to do this requires objectivity in the corporate strategy to show how delivering the data strategy has had an impact.

You may find that a lack of objectivity in the corporate strategy to enable the measurement of the data strategy contribution is the Achilles heel of being able to achieve PRIDE, but if you reach this point and are able to demonstrate the need for measurement in achieving the corporate strategy, then you have not only delivered a ready-to-go data strategy but have also made the organisation aware of a weakness in its strategy development. If the organisation remedies the omission of the measures around the implementation of the corporate strategy then you have the data strategy ready as a key enabler.

4.3 THE ACID TEST

If you are embarking on devising a data strategy it is imperative to avoid doing so in a silo. It is critical to seek independent review and feedback from an audience representative of the wider organisation to ensure the data strategy achieves the PRIDE objective. It is, therefore, essential to follow an Agile process to develop the data strategy, involving iterations until such time as there is confidence that the data strategy has relevance.

There are many excellent texts out there on Agile methodologies, and I don't intend to give an extensive review of the various approaches and their merits in this book. If you are interested to know more about Agile – its various approaches, techniques and ways of adapting to a range of situations – there are several texts listed in the bibliography at the end of this book.

So, what do I mean by the acid test in this context? To succeed, the data strategy needs to become embedded as part of the culture of the organisation. This is evidenced by the organisation becoming more data-focused, information literate and confident in using evidence to make decisions, which in turn delivers benefits that can be directly linked back to the data strategy. This must be underpinned by the organisation being compliant with regulations and operating within legal frameworks. It follows, therefore, that the data strategy has one overarching measure of success – the acid test, if you like – to demonstrate how deep its impact has been: has it embedded itself into the ways in which the organisation functions and made a difference?

The measure of success, it may seem, is entirely back-end loaded, by which I mean: how do you know you are on the road to success until some time has passed after the delivery of the data strategy? This is an entirely reasonable question, but you can make things easier for yourself by taking the right steps along the way as you create the data strategy – laying the foundations for success, if you like.

The five components of PRIDE outlined above aim to create the right conditions for success. Engagement is paramount in delivering these at every step of the way. Whether a working group of representatives from different parts of the organisation is brought together to help shape the data strategy, a looser federation of interested parties is engaged along the way to contribute and review, or a show-and-tell approach is adopted to review and revise the data strategy in its drafting to ensure it has buy-in, getting inputs from throughout your organisation is essential for success. These are likely to be the people within your organisation who have to bring the data strategy to life, so what better approach than to engage them fully in the process of its shaping, drafting and delivery in order to give it every chance of being adopted into day-to-day business activity?

It is essential that you ensure there is a clear link in the organisation between accountability and responsibility. It is one thing to have all parties on board with the data strategy, but some individuals in your organisation will need to hold clear accountability for driving it through delivery, whilst others will be responsible for whatever is needed to make change a reality. Without this, change will never materialise. The authority also needs to reside with both those who are accountable or responsible, as without authority it becomes difficult to have the means to deliver the right outcomes.

There is at least one further critical set of stakeholders to have on board, and that is those who, almost certainly at a relatively senior level in your organisation, are able to sign off on the data strategy. Where this responsibility rests varies, depending on the organisation's size, type and/or maturity of its operation.

In some organisations there is a dedicated strategy and planning function that drives the approach to strategy definition and adoption, which will need to participate and be on board with whatever direction your data strategy sets. Without the support of this function, you are never going to get your data strategy recognised, let alone adopted, and it should be a key stakeholder throughout the process. This group will have the means to steer your data strategy through whatever channels it needs to follow to be adopted, and it is likely to have the means to hold the organisation to account in its delivery.

Strategy may be driven by each functional director within your organisation, and as such brought to the top table as a deliverable of that function that needs wider support and engagement in its implementation. In such a scenario, it is probable that the relevant director is your sponsor, and therefore they have a clear line of communication through the development of the data strategy. Certainly, it would be wise to engage regularly with your sponsor to keep them apprised of progress, wider business engagement and any areas where assistance or advice would be helpful.

There may not be a focal point in your organisation, which may reflect a lack of maturity of strategy development or strong operational focus. If this is the case, look at how any previous attempts to deliver a strategy within the organisation have progressed for insight as to how you might best succeed in delivering your own data strategy. Find those functions that are most likely to have had cause to develop a strategy – such as human resources (HR), finance, operations (especially in terms of investment strategies for the workforce and/or plant and equipment to support the direction the organisation is taking) and technology (relating IT investment to strategic imperatives and choosing to disinvest in areas not seen as core, for example) – and approach colleagues in similar posts in those functions to see if they have experienced devising a strategy or been party to inputting into another strategy. Learn from what they say and try to see what the characteristics are behind success and failure. Plot a course accordingly, and engage those who seem to share your vision whom you meet along the way – there is more likelihood of traction if there is a groundswell of positivity across the organisation.

If your organisation is small, maybe centred on a single entrepreneur, it may be that the organisation has largely lived on short-term horizons out of necessity and/or been opportunist in growing from an idea into a more structured organisation, moving to formalise its way of operating. This is when governance, strategy and planning tend to come to the fore, and may be needed to secure additional funding, clarity of communication and direction, and possibly the introduction of a more formal board structure to provide governance, control and the delivery of a phase of expansion. Whether for internal purposes or for securing external support in the form of additional funding or assurance to other stakeholders (for example, compliance, governance or recruitment of senior-level staff to buy in to the direction of the organisation), this is a tremendous opportunity to set out the stall for data strategy and ensure it is more than simply a tick in the box.

Increasingly there is a focus on data strategy, both for ensuring compliance and for future revenue growth/cost efficiencies through the better exploitation of data, so this is an ideal time to promote the importance of a data strategy within your organisation. Getting stakeholder buy-in within the organisation is still critical, and likely needs the entrepreneur behind the organisation to be fully engaged and passionate about the role it can play in delivering an outcome that individual is seeking: so be bold, seek support early and have your case well prepared as to why this is towards the top of the list of things to invest time and effort in.

In an organisation that operates in a not-for-profit arena, the case for having your data strategy supported by the senior leaders of that organisation is just as compelling. It is likely that funds are limited and levers might seem to be more constrained than in other organisations, but arguably the impact of an effective data strategy can be all the greater for those reasons. There is a real opportunity to devise ways to make the organisation smarter through the better use of data, identify ways to exploit data which may utilise the experience of other organisations that are more advanced (and therefore deliver an impact quicker, by learning from their mistakes and successes to reduce time to deliver), and put the consumer of the service or product that the organisation delivers at the heart of the thinking and focus of delivery of the organisation.

It may be that the data strategy is an opportunity to give your organisation a refresh, and could be incorporated into wider communications, whether solely internal or also for external promotion. However, it is essential to pitch the data strategy as integral to the way the organisation will operate in the future and get engagement at the level of the chief executive officer (CEO) and/or senior stakeholders (possibly even non-executives, if there are such representatives on the board), as you are likely to be seeking time and resources to deliver the data strategy in an organisation which is not endowed with plenty of either.

Whatever is the right approach for you, the critical point in the work you put in to devising the data strategy is having the right level of challenge and support through the process. It is often left till too late to engage at the right level, or to ensure that the 'rules of the game' are fully understood and that the trajectory on which you are on to define the data strategy is going to align with the wider organisational way of operating, and therefore be adopted by the key stakeholders in your organisation.

In terms of developing the data strategy, it is entirely up to you whether you focus on sections of it to iterate and improve, thereby delivering in blocks, or work across the data strategy as a whole, possibly splitting out sections of it to working groups to develop and bring together via a coordinating group. Either way, there should be a common thread running through the data strategy, and so the iterations will also involve ensuring there is alignment and consistency in its approach, timelines and deliverables.

You will need to have one or more colleagues who are able to proofread the document as it takes shape who have enough understanding to spot inconsistencies and a process to realign the discrepancies appropriately. Alternatively this might be a task you take on personally, given this is your strategy to define and deliver, but if so, you will preferably delegate the initial drafting of elements or sections of the data strategy to others under your direction. This may not be practicable, simply through a lack of resources, in which case it takes a great deal of discipline to be able to detach from the detail and read it objectively as a stakeholder being asked to approve and/or implement the data strategy.

It is important to set timelines for completion of the tasks in the data strategy so there is an understanding of the pace and priority inherent within it. Defining a data strategy is a mix of art and science, in so much as some of the outcomes can be scoped and tightly defined in terms of timescales, whilst others require a level of intuition about likely adoption rates and shifts in behaviours, which are notoriously difficult to forecast due to so many outside influences being key to success. Do reflect, however, that whilst there is a tendency to be absolute in terms of deliverables and timings, this is something to be determined at the implementation stage, and the data strategy should focus on setting the direction and establishing the waymarkers to be achieved.

Do not fall into the trap of being too prescriptive – you do not know what lies ahead, and the more you bind those who have to implement the data strategy, the less useful it becomes in an evolving world. Do determine timelines, using broad statements to establish the waymarker and the likely state you are describing. Set a baseline to ensure there is a common understanding of the current situation, as this provides context to the future state you are seeking to describe and aids measurement through the clarity of difference that you are defining to be achieved.

Provide all of these essential elements to a data strategy in a simple, easily digestible manner and your critical stakeholders will be clear on the objectives you are setting before them and the implications of signing up the organisation to implement the data strategy. Ambiguity leads to paralysis, which in turn makes the data strategy meaningless and future efforts to implement a data strategy all the harder.

4.4 TEN TO TAKE AWAY

The key points from this chapter are:

1. To get traction, remember it is about a RAVE. Without relevance, awareness, value and execution, the data strategy is incomplete and so will be lacking an essential component for a successful outcome.

2. Keep your data strategy simple – avoid too much detail, but ensure it is clearly defined and jargon-free.

3. The data strategy needs to be accessible – in all ways – to meet the needs and expectations of diverse stakeholders, which requires a good understanding of their needs and to maintain a dialogue.

4. Define waymarkers to set the direction of travel and goals to be achieved.

5. Keep it grounded, clearly focused on the delivery of the corporate strategy (or organisational goals, in the absence of a strategy).

6. Make it clear why the data strategy matters, what is required to execute it and the impact it will have to position it appropriately in your organisation.

7. Deliver with PRIDE, but be prepared for challenges along the way – inevitably, there will be events and outcomes that are unforeseen that you will need to deal with.

8. The goal is to embed the data strategy into the organisation, having an impact on the future direction the organisation takes and delivering value. Ensure that there is an approach to cascade the data strategy to relevant personnel throughout the organisation to establish clarity of understanding.

9. Understand the sign-off process within your organisation and engage with this process early to ensure that there are no barriers to overcome as you complete the data strategy. Keeping this group onside is critical to being able to move into execution.

10. Establish the baseline that the data strategy is starting from and avoid being prescriptive about its execution. This is to guide an implementation plan, and the baseline will be essential for measurement in the implementation stage.

5 CREATING A ROUTE MAP – AIM HIGH, PLAN DEEP!

'A good plan is like a road map: it shows the final destination and usually the best way to get there.'

H. Stanley Judd[1]

In previous chapters I have covered the importance of timelines, waymarkers and articulating realistic goals as the critical focal points to have constantly in your mind whilst defining a data strategy. This is not just because these represent good practice in any major undertaking that needs a plan. In my experience, strategies have failed to be adopted or implemented, or have simply stalled, because these aspects were not thought through extensively enough in the preparatory stages and through the defining of the data strategy.

In many cases, those who define the data strategy and those who are tasked with implementing it may be two completely different sets of people. This might seem odd, but it can arise for a number of perfectly rational reasons. The timescale of pulling together a data strategy may be long, it might be driven by someone with a particular skillset or level of knowledge and experience, or it might be seen to be an activity which sits in different parts of an organisation. As a result, whether through individuals moving on, either within the organisation or leaving it altogether, retirement, how roles are tightly defined or the use of consultant or contractor resources to help drive the data strategy definition, the end-to-end process of data strategy definition can pass through many hands before getting to see the light of approval and moving into implementation.

It is worth reflecting on what this means. A data strategy needs to be owned corporately, not individually, to avoid the risk of work becoming lost or misunderstood as it passes through different hands, and so has to have the appropriate rigour in place to mitigate such risks.

Just as importantly, senior stakeholders are likely to change in the time it takes to get the concept of a data strategy agreed and it being ready for approval. This includes the sponsor, who may be the main advocate and why the data strategy is being pursued in the first place, and so the risk of such a change must be factored in to the thinking to minimise the risk of change.

Why do I explain this at a point in the book focused on creating a route map? Simply because your route begins from the very start, the first discussions that take place on why the organisation is interested in having a data strategy and what that means in reality. Documenting the starting point, the assumptions, the key stakeholders, and the time and resources available to deliver the data strategy is one of the most important

---

1 H.S. Judd, *How to Play Golf the Easy Way*. New York: Harper & Row, 1980.

tasks you undertake to ensure continuity is maintained in the subsequent phases through to implementation.

It is easy to reflect in hindsight what the starting point of the data strategy looked like, but the lens through which you look back is never quite the same as the one which gives greater clarity in real time. The lineage that links the concept of the data strategy through to its implementation will be invaluable to:

- future groups of people who are tasked with coordinating and communicating it through delivery;
- stakeholders to provide a common understanding of intent;
- those tasked with implementing various elements of it to provide what it was seeking to achieve.

Reality might dictate that this too evolves; nothing stays static and so the initial thinking might be at best only partly relevant as time moves on. However, capturing how thinking is evolving, and reflecting on the drivers behind why change has occurred, keeps all parties aligned and focused on what is to be achieved, when and why.

The purpose of this chapter, therefore, is to set out some key steps to be undertaken as you embark on planning the stages of the data strategy. There will be a series of deliverables and an assumption of progress to be made, given the data strategy will be time limited, whether to three, five, ten or any other number of years. The role of the data strategy is to illustrate a likely path to achieving data goals and to ensure there is linkage between it and the corporate strategy in terms of timing.

5.1 VISIONARY MEETS REALISM – HOW TO KEEP IT GROUNDED

I have previously made the point that there are two common failures with data strategies that lead to their becoming either shelfware or forgotten, and that is a lack of realism, or practical application to the current starting point, in terms of what it lays out as the vision to be delivered through the data strategy, and a lack of keeping it simple, or grounded in that reality.

It seems obvious to state that a data strategy must be followed by an implementation plan, which may set out the first year or longer, but if it is in any way unclear as to what is to be achieved, the implementation plan lacks a clear picture of where it needs to head or the pace at which it needs to progress. I have seen two polar opposites in this situation: the data strategy so aloof that it is far from clear as to what is to be achieved, where the organisation is starting from or any concept of steps along a continuum; and the data strategy that is so steeped in the detail, and devoid of the vision to set out the what, why and when over the longer time frame, that is has become an implementation plan and not a strategy at all.

These scenarios may seem avoidable, but it is remarkably common to find efforts to define a data strategy drifting one way or the other and, once on the wrong track, the drift increases and it becomes impossible to correct it. It is often the culture of the organisation too that determines such outcomes. There is a tendency for highly operationally focused organisations to want to get into the detail and fail to see the merits in something as visionary as a strategy. On the other hand, those organisations that are steeped in a culture of strategy and policy are more comfortable exploring the possibilities and therefore likely to be focused on a more theoretical perspective that can sometimes be a little detached from the practicalities of implementation.

These descriptions are extremes, and most organisations will fall somewhere in between on the spectrum, but it is worth considering what sort of organisation you are defining a data strategy within to spot any risks of being steered one way or the other.

If I return to the CLEAR principles outlined in Chapter 2, 'execution' is at the centre of the acronym, which is a neat reminder that it is important not to leave consideration of implementation until the end – it is at the heart of being CLEAR. As you develop the data strategy, utilising Agile to develop it iteratively, bear in mind the question 'How would I approach executing this?' If the answer is in any way unclear, ambiguous or simply too complex to comprehend, then a further iteration or two is likely required. A data strategy which is unclear as to how it can be executed is of no value whatsoever, and brings the concept into disrepute for the next person who is tasked with reviving the notion of creating a data strategy in that organisation.

So, what would an effective data strategy in terms of realism and being grounded entail? I recommend setting out clearly at the start a summary of what the data strategy is for, how it is to be utilised and how it will be measured (in terms of success). This introduction sets the scene for what follows, and as long as these clear principles are kept in mind when the data strategy is reviewed, then the reader should be on the same wavelength as the author.

The next step is to set out the structure of the data strategy, which is covered in more detail in the next chapter. For the moment, the structure has to aid the reader by having a logical flow to it, one which will translate effectively into a plan, coherent and cohesive in linking the key deliverables in the data strategy in an easy to understand manner that interlinks with all other relevant parts of the strategy. At no time should the reader have to interpret dependencies and associations within the data strategy – it is your job to provide the clarity of a meaningful narrative from start to finish within it.

The data strategy itself has to be clear in terms of content, providing definition if there is any doubt as to the interpretation that the reader may place upon any of it (a key challenge in the iterative shaping of the data strategy is to test out meaning and understanding, to iron out any risk of inconsistencies or lack of understanding in the drafting process). It must provide parameters, guides within which the individual or team responsible for its delivery into an implementation plan can have a consistent understanding of what is to be done, by when, for the bigger objectives along the way – the waymarkers that signal the way to delivering the vision of the data strategy.

If, at the end of drafting the data strategy, it is not clear to someone outside the close-knit group who have worked on defining and drafting it how to turn it into an implementation plan, then the process has failed. No matter how positive the reviews of the data strategy itself, the sense of achievement of having completed it, the praise that has been given following its presentation, an inability to execute the data strategy is failure. There is little to be gained from having a tick in the box only to see the data strategy fail to leave the starting blocks.

Therefore, find someone with deep implementation expertise and co-opt them onto your review group, but use them very sparingly. Bear in mind that you don't want them to go rogue and become too close to the subject to continue to provide implementation objectivity. Once you have finished final reviews of sections or elements of the data strategy, invite the implementation expert in and let them seek to interpret what is required of them without prompting – the more you influence their thinking, the more it undermines the capability of the data strategy to stand for itself. If they need clarification, guidance or further descriptions, or simply do not understand whole sections of it, take it at face value and work with it. Remember, keeping it simple and comprehensible is a key guide in this process, and your expert's feedback is invaluable in sharpening up that particular premise.

5.2 WHAT ARE YOUR TIMESCALES?

It continues to amaze me that many strategies – not just data strategies – seem to overlook any concept of timing in terms of the deliverables that are in scope. There may be some broad statement about the timescales being a three-, five- or ten-year strategy, with seldom any variation on these three options. That is not to say that these are wrong, but they are the commonly chosen periods despite the world seemingly changing at an ever faster pace. I am always bemused by a strategy for a decade and question the validity of its assumptions, given that we seem to move into a recession or similar major disruptive event roughly every ten years, and fast-moving technology is one of the biggest disruptors to major organisations operating in traditional sectors. But does a ten-year strategy reflect this fast-moving dynamic effectively? I'd suggest not, but that's another debate.

There are also far too many instances of organisations that leave devising a strategy to beyond the last minute and then start the period it is intended to cover with a 'best endeavours' attitude that morphs into an implementation plan of sorts, with the strategy never quite catching up. Unsurprisingly, this approach is destined to fail, typically quickly, on occasion before the strategy has even been completed. However, it is not uncommon for the lack of a strategy to be determined to be the cause of the problem, rather than the lack of planning. Do not find yourself falling into this trap.

The question remains of how long your data strategy should be, and it is a valid one. If you have a choice, I support keeping it to three years (see below). If you do not, then you have to align with corporate guidance that determines how long strategies should be for, though of course if this is the first time your organisation has had a data strategy you may need to work in line with the strategic cycle in play. In other words, your organisation may choose to work to a five-year planning cycle and have set periods defined for those five years that all strategies align to.

If you are delivering your data strategy in the midst of one of these periods you may need to fall into line: for example a five-year strategy might be 2021–2026, yet you are not going to complete yours till 2022. In such an instance, you might have to cover the period to 2026, thus delivering a data strategy which is for no more than four years in the first instance till you can realign with the usual planning cycle in 2026. In some cases, the standard rule in an organisation may be to have strategies of a fixed period – say five years – but not anchored by a fixed planning cycle.

Whatever the case in your organisation, it is important to know what the situation is before embarking on defining your data strategy. There is little to be gained developing a three-year strategy only to find it had to cover five years when presented.

I am a keen advocate of a principle of rolling strategies, which unfortunately seem to be relatively rare in the arena of planning cycles and fixed periods. I often recommend developing a three-year data strategy which is then a rolling strategy, learning from the experience gained in year one, monitoring its effectiveness against waymarkers within the data strategy and shaping what would have been year four as the 'new' year three.

One of the challenges in this approach is the rigour required to assess progress and provide confidence that the remaining two years of data strategy are still as valid before appending a new year three. However, I see this as a useful calibration between the implementation plan – which is usually developed on a yearly cycle – and the data strategy, to test the ambition of the data strategy: was it realistic, did unforeseen obstacles prevent progress, how robust was the thinking on dependencies and the assumptions made at the outset?

By using this iterative approach to continue to run with a three-year rolling data strategy, continuity is maintained, a view can be taken as to whether the data strategy is ambitious enough or overreaching in its goals, and the fourth year is incorporated at a lower risk than starting afresh with a new three-year plan at the end of the current data strategy. It is also less time-consuming to do this, both for the area of the organisation leading on it but also for those who contribute to its compilation in one way or another.

What differentiates it being right to set a course for a longer time frame from instances where a shorter time frame would be more appropriate?

In sectors where there is long-term stability, a need for major investment which takes long planning cycles and less volatility in the market, there is a case to be made to plan over longer-term horizons. This might be the case in major infrastructure environments such as the nuclear, rail or road industries for instance. In these sectors, it is easier to plan due to stability, based on the knowledge that there is an expectation that major change tends to take significant time to achieve. This may be less pertinent to a data strategy but, conversely, if funding is available to make a significant transition (should that be appropriate) it enables a long-term view to be taken on the breadth of what can be achieved.

Shorter timescales are more appropriate for highly volatile sectors, which may be due to the impact of technology, new entrants (many of which may, due to the rapid evolution of technology, trade solely as online businesses in an otherwise bricks and mortar sector), the pace of product evolution and the volatility in the market itself (at a time of recession or other economic upheaval, planning for the long term might seem fanciful if survival in the short term is the priority). Reasoning for shorter timescales could be a combination of all of these factors, of course. However, the pace of change is growing, the role of technology in our businesses is increasing (AI is a significant factor for many organisations at the moment and in the near future), and adjusting to change requires agility and adaptability on a scale not previously seen.

Where your organisation sits on the strategy timescale may even be changing, as there is a recognition that the 'old' ways of operating are no longer relevant to a faster-moving world. It could be that the data strategy is a catalyst to bring change to the thinking of your organisation, and I would certainly recommend putting a greater focus into the first three years of your data strategy simply because most strategies will become less relevant as we move beyond that period.

If you can get the first three years close to being reflective of reality, then you are truly a master at defining and delivering a data strategy. Revisiting the strategy for the years beyond the first three is both likely and responsible, as no sensible organisation would sign off on a strategy longer than three years and not conduct some sort of review ahead of year four. Such uncritical faith in the author having correctly predicted the outcomes not only of the organisation's own performance but also the dynamic of the market would be entirely misplaced.

5.3 WAYMARKERS RATHER THAN MILESTONES

I would hope that you have got the principle that there is a difference between a data strategy and an implementation plan by this stage. You will also have seen that I use the term 'waymarkers' rather than 'milestones', a term you may have heard more commonly.

If you wonder why I have used waymarkers to refer to points at a future time when you would expect the organisation to have achieved various elements outlined in the data strategy, it is because these are descriptors of what the organisation should look like, from a data perspective, rather than a specific deliverable.

The data strategy is intentionally a guide, a portrayal of what the journey the reader is about to embark on looks like, with some clear pointers and descriptors of things to be achieved along the way. It is a mix of the tangible and intangible, describing clear and measurable things to be achieved during implementation, but also outlining what this means for the culture of the organisation, the nature of changes to be implemented and how this move to a more data-led way of working will operate.

Waymarkers are intended to indicate key moments in time, points at which the organisation will look and/or feel different, and to provide an outline of what has been achieved at that point to recognise the extent of the change achieved. They thus bring together the physical and measurable activities, which in an implementation plan would be recognisable as milestones, and link with the intangible to show how the organisation has evolved to exploit these and other things which have successfully moved the organisation forward in its wider goals.

It is important to recognise that milestones are different from waymarkers and have a critical role to play in ensuring the implementation of the data strategy is on track as per the implementation plan. They are complementary to, and essential for, waymarkers to be delivered, for without milestones in the implementation plan there would almost certainly be an inability to trace what has been achieved in terms of the data strategy.

As I said earlier, the data strategy has to be measurable, and it is via the waymarkers that this is achieved. The waymarkers are an informed crystal ball into the future, outlining to the best knowledge available when the data strategy was defined what the organisation is expected to look like through the lens of the data strategy. Their purpose is to provide clarity of what the combination of tangible and intangible brings, how that morphs into one joined-up view (as reality is a combination of the two) and sets a sense of purpose in defining the implementation plan through a richer picture of what is to be achieved. They set the context, define the pace and broaden the implementation from a purely tangibly driven plan into one which has the wider scope of delivering cultural change and wider organisational impact embedded within it.

Rather like the stars by which a ship might navigate, the waymarkers appear periodically and are used to ensure the course remains consistent with achieving arrival at the intended destination. The navigator does not discount using landmarks along the way to assist where possible, and can correlate between land and stars even if both are not visible at the same time. However, the data strategy acts as the night sky, a reliable indicator for the navigator to use the stars as waymarkers on the journey but still with the ability to adjust and adapt should tides and currents dictate slightly different tactics in navigating to the same end destination.

5.4 PLANNING FOR SUCCESS

It has been stressed throughout the book that the implementation of the data strategy stands apart as a discrete phase of the overall process, yet it is essential that the data strategy is devised and defined with the execution of it in mind. Failure to do so will run the risk of the data strategy failing to be fit for purpose and the effort in defining it having been wasted.

I mentioned earlier in this chapter that I would strongly recommend having someone with a strong implementation background involved as a slightly detached critical friend of the data strategy drafting process. This objectivity is really important to ensure that the transition from data strategy to implementation plan is as simple and coherent as possible, avoiding ambiguity that can lead to divergence and drift from the original intent simply through misunderstanding. In many ways, it is the transition from an approved data strategy into implementation that carries the biggest risk, though for those engaged in the data strategy drafting process there is a tendency to focus on the approval itself as the end goal and the major hurdle.

The first step to aid the planning process is the clarity of the baseline position within the organisation. I have explained the importance of this elsewhere, but to reiterate: if there is a lack of understanding of what the starting point is, then there is almost certainly a risk of assumptions being made which later are found to be incorrect and a flawed understanding of the landscape in which the plan needs to function – this is especially true when it comes to the intangible elements that the plan needs to capture, such as the cultural shift that may form part of the data strategy.

All too often, data strategies focus on the end goal and miss the importance of establishing a common understanding of the baseline. This is essential in order to get agreement across the organisation on the scale of the task to be undertaken and the measures to be put in place.

Once there is a clear understanding of the baseline, and appropriate measurement in place to capture the starting position, it is feasible to begin to define the objectives within the data strategy and set out the waymarkers. In the same manner, taking the baseline and defined measures, the planning team can set out the goals and milestones for the period of the implementation plan, which is likely to be a twelve-month plan with a less detailed view beyond, possibly to reflect the length of period that the data strategy encompasses. These activities are separate, though an effective data strategy definition process takes account of the task of implementing it to make the translation from strategy to execution a relatively easy one.

The data strategy will be a multi-year strategy, as outlined in this chapter. As such, it needs to provide a balanced view of that period, identifying how the layers of activity in the years in question build to deliver a more advanced organisation in terms of data and its exploitation and compliance. It is a common trap to focus heavily on the more immediate period of the strategy, say the first year, and be less detailed on subsequent years. This is a risk simply because those involved with defining the data strategy will almost certainly be more familiar with the shorter-term view and less confident in defining the activities in the years beyond.

The reason I highlight this is that, with a multi-year strategy, there is a need to assure those who are signing off on the data strategy that the vision beyond what would form an immediate delivery plan will support the corporate strategy and deliver longer-term benefits. This is where the data strategy waymarkers demonstrate the outcomes in a descriptive and engaging way to secure the investment needed to underpin the whole implementation programme. If there is an imbalance towards the short term, it suggests that those closest to the data strategy do not have the vision themselves; this would lead to a more short-term view of investing for the year ahead through the usual budget round and planning process rather than committing to a longer-term strategy.

In addition, a lack of detail for subsequent years makes the task of implementation much harder. If the data strategy in year one already resembles an implementation plan, but years two and beyond are so lacking in detail to be vague and uncertain, then the risk is that the implementation plan for those years is either lacking or determines the strategy: in other words, the plan is the strategy due to the absence of detail and meaningful waymarkers.

The longer the period the data strategy covers, the harder it is to determine the emerging landscape due to both external influencers and internal factors. However, the waymarkers simply need to define a picture of the time in question, and the key changes from one period to another, to make it evident as to what has to be achieved – tangible and intangible – from one point in time to the next one. Therefore, be prepared to define the detail in terms of significant outcomes the further out you go, especially beyond three years, but paint the picture with sufficient detail that those who come to implement it can see how it has evolved from the previous waymarker and the contributory elements that have enabled progress to be made. Also, don't be afraid to make the waymarkers more spaced out as you move through the years – years one and two are likely to be quarterly, year three may be quarterly or half-yearly, and years four and beyond are almost certainly half-yearly moving to annually.

5.5 PRESENTING THE ROUTE MAP

The route map can take a number of forms, from a simple timeline with a series of boxes against the relevant points in time to explain the key outputs expected to have been delivered by that point, through a complex project plan format that displays interconnections between deliverables to show how these come together. No particular format is right or wrong; as with so much in the strategy space, what your organisation is used to and comfortable in relating to is likely to be influential. There is no point in making it too complicated when the essence of the route map is to keep it simple and high level – remember this is the data strategy, not the implementation plan.

The choice of style may also be one of personal preference – what you feel comfortable with, as you are likely to be at the forefront of presenting it to a wide range of stakeholders. There is also the limitation of the tools available, though this is becoming less challenging as tools become much easier to access via cloud-based platforms such as Office 365, Google Workspace and Apple iWork.

Whilst I do not want to limit your enthusiasm, or artistic flair, the most common ways of presenting a route map are as follows.

- **Gantt chart** – named after Henry Gantt, who designed it in the early years of the last century, this method has become a standard for project schedules and milestone tracking to this day. A standard bar chart, it is easy to create, is readily accessible to most audiences who will also be familiar with this form of presentation and can convey a lot of information relatively easily. Downsides of a Gantt chart include its oversimplification, and it is more challenging for the strategy implementation when complexities in resource management, dependency tracking and the need to operate at sub-task level can make operating via a Gantt chart more of a limitation than a help.

- **Flow diagram** – often portrayed as a journey map – a visualisation that shows how actions against a timeline lead to outcomes, often with a narrative of what each of those points on the journey look like. It works well visually, as it is in keeping with the concept of a route map, but it can be challenging to see how the strands come together, or to track any dependencies along the way. It can also be seen as prescriptive, presenting one route only and suggesting there is no alternative, when the data strategy route map is intended to be indicative of, rather than constraining, the implementation.

- **Radial grid** – often referred to as a sun ray diagram – this starts out with a common topic or a vision, which could be the data strategy in this instance, or the end state following the implementation of the data strategy, and then has branches radiating out that contain deliverables over a timeline, showing a level of building on each other. It can be challenging to comprehend the necessity of delivering all of the items in the sun ray versus the impact if there is a delay, as the grid does not illustrate the dependencies between the radials very effectively. However, it is a constructive way to convey a volume of information in a clear and defined approach that is generally easy to follow.

- **Projectmap** – a recent development which has been devised by an Israeli start-up called Proggio.[2] This tool is focused on revolutionising the project management space, replacing the need for Gantt charts by presenting a highly visual representation of your project that enables dependencies to be tracked and reporting to be delivered from within the tool. It can also be presented as a Kanban board (a visual depiction of work at all stages of the process using cards to represent tasks and activities) for use in Agile delivery, and it integrates with Jira, for those organisations that use this tool to manage tasks and epics also in Agile delivery.

Remember that the purpose of the route map is twofold: it needs to inform the key stakeholders who need to buy in to the data strategy and have an appreciation for what it is going to deliver, whilst understanding what is required to make this happen; and it must be a guide to the implementation team who have to turn the waymarkers in your data strategy into a plan that can be executed in a way that remains true to the goals, and therefore the value, outlined in the data strategy.

5.6 TEN TO TAKE AWAY

To summarise, key points from this chapter:

1. Design the data strategy with implementation in mind. Think about how you would act if you were to be given the data strategy and asked to implement it – would it be clear in terms of the baseline, direction, outcomes and what success looks like? Use a critical friend to challenge.

2. Test understanding through an independent reviewer to ensure the data strategy is clear and achievable. It is valuable to have an external party to those defining it to provide friendly challenge to the content.

3. A timeline is essential in your data strategy. Without this, the implementation is challenging, as expectations of pace and any perceived flow of activities are unclear.

4. Consider a rolling strategy, enabling the learning from the period covered and the evolving nature of the organisation to be reflected in adding a subsequent year on an annual basis.

5. Set waymarkers rather than milestones. Guide the execution: it is not a straightjacket. The data strategy must avoid becoming an implementation plan.

6. Ensure the data strategy is measurable and that this can be reflected in the implementation plan. The baseline must be clearly articulated, so there is a clear understanding of what has been measured to retain consistency into execution.

7. Waymarkers may be uneven in both their content and frequency in the data strategy. This is inevitable, so do not create them unnecessarily as it is understandable that the clarity of detail is probably greater earlier in the period the data strategy covers and at a higher level the further out it goes.

---

2   https://www.proggio.com/.

8. However, balance out the data strategy to avoid it looking like a year one implementation plan with a strategy bolted on for subsequent years. It needs to be consistent in being a strategy.

9. Reflect on how best to provide a route map, utilising approaches which are known to have worked in similar situations. Familiarity removes a potential barrier that something novel might create. The purpose of the route map is to convey visually what the data strategy will provide, so you want it to be easy to reach agreement.

10. The route map must be able to convince key stakeholders that this is what they want and expect to be able to reach agreement. Make it easy for them to comprehend what they will be getting.

6   CONTENT, STRUCTURE AND ALIGNMENT

'Good strategy requires leaders who are willing and able to say no to a wide variety of actions and interests. Strategy is at least as much about what an organization does not do as it is about what it does.'

Richard Rumelt[1]

We have reached the point in the book to start considering how you are going to write the strategy. What should it contain? What shouldn't I include? How do I strike a balance between being too verbose but providing the clarity to make it understood to others? What's the right level for a data strategy to be set at, and how do I know if I have got it right if this is the first time my organisation has seen a data strategy?

There are so many questions. Worse still, the answer to a number of them is the dreaded two-word response – it depends.

The intent of this chapter is to guide you through the process. It is not intended to deliver a templated data strategy – even if such a thing could be developed, it almost certainly would not fit your organisation, whether in terms of content, style, scale or fit with audience – nor a definitive list of contents. What it will provide is an indication of what should be considered for inclusion and in what level of detail, how to structure the data strategy to link the key themes together and act as a reminder of the importance of strategic alignment with other strategies within your organisation.

The key is to link the three activities of people capability, delivery across the information ecosystem and organisational maturity (Figure 6.1) together across the data strategy. This will be explored further in this chapter.

There are many points to bear in mind at this juncture, some of which have been covered in the preceding chapters:

- Who is the audience for the data strategy, and what are the various perspectives through which this document will be viewed?

- What level of detail is appropriate to ensure all who read it are engaged, whilst striking a balance between the risk of being too high level to be meaningful or too detailed to retain the reader's interest?

- How do I keep it grounded such that it is clear in its intent to define implementation plans that are true to the goals of the data strategy?

- How ambitious do I want to appear, and how specific should the waymarkers be to give enough guidance to make the ambition seem realistic?

- How do I give relevancy to the data strategy, such that the end destination is seen as one which delivers corporate goals and is realistic in the expectations set?

---

1   R. Rumelt, *Good Strategy, Bad Strategy: The Difference and Why It Matters.* London: Profile Books, 2012.

Figure 6.1 Linking the triumvirate of people capability, information delivery and organisational maturity

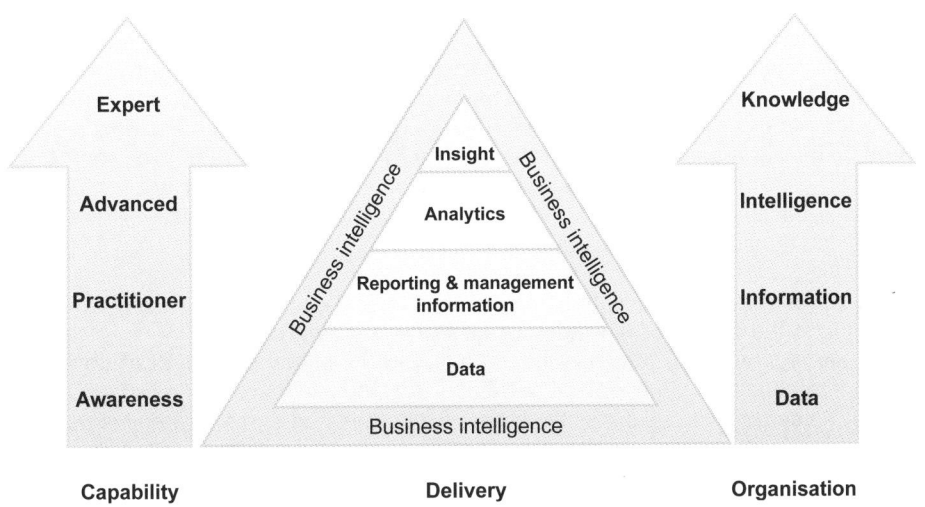

If you have clarity on these five questions then you are well placed to begin the process of defining the data strategy. If you are clear on fewer than three, then it suggests there is more work to be done, and more groundwork to be covered, before you are confident you are going to be heading on the right track. Anywhere in between and it suggests you have enough to make a start, whilst being conscious of the need to clarify those which are ambiguous as you go, ideally as early as you can.

6.1 APPROACH TO DEFINING THE CONTENT

Where to start? This is the conundrum many who have had to determine where to begin their data strategy have wrestled with and spent many anxious hours wondering whether their first foray into drafting it is on the right track. Clearly, this is a very personal challenge. Some relish getting to the stage of putting thoughts into words, feeling the rush of satisfaction at finally getting visible evidence of progress before them. Others find the information gathering, analysis and discussion the easiest part of the process, and find putting it into words particularly difficult and may make several abortive efforts before getting it finally under way.

In truth, there isn't a right or wrong way; our personal traits lead each of us to approach this in our own way that best suits us.

Two methods that I have observed to be really effective involve a collective approach. In the first, one person takes the lead as author, and others play different parts – depending on the numbers available to you to assist, one can act as the researcher, feeding key inputs as the author progresses, and both can challenge one another to determine whether the strategy is following a logical thread, with a third person acting as a reviewer of the first raw draft, tweaking and tightening sections as it takes shape. A fourth person can then review either the whole document or large parts of it with the detachment of having sat apart from the drafting process.

The second approach is similar to the first, but involves a more collaborative authoring approach, in which there is a team-based approach to writing sections – possibly relatively short elements of the document, such as a couple of paragraphs – and there is an editor who commissions and then reviews those elements as they come together to ensure they link, and smooths out the idiosyncratic writing styles of each contributor. Again, someone should review the final copy and sense-check for clarity, continuity and coherence, based upon a level of understanding of what the data strategy is seeking to achieve and the audience it is targeting.

Of course, you may be faced with having to draft the data strategy entirely on your own, either due to the size of organisation or lack of wider awareness of its importance. In such cases, you will be acting as judge and jury of the document you draft unless you can get someone with an impartial perspective from elsewhere in the organisation to provide the sense check – possibly someone who has had some strategy experience, either in your organisation or elsewhere, or who is familiar with presenting documents to senior stakeholders and knows what style tends to work and, just as importantly, what will jar.

I have mentioned Agile as a recommended approach to developing your data strategy, deploying iterative stages to progress things and set expectations of what is likely to be achieved within short windows of time. The benefit of this approach is the focus it provides on targeting specifics rather than being faced with the task of grappling with the whole document. This involves breaking down the data strategy based on your intended structure – we shall cover this shortly – and making it discrete, so there is a logical start, middle and end to the Agile sprint you construct.

Just remember, throughout the drafting process you can more easily shorten a document than extend it. Whilst the latter is feasible, it often involves more of a rewrite than a precis, and so is more time-consuming and challenging. Therefore, if you have succeeded in getting a flow going then it is easier to run with it, knowing it is too detailed, and trim once finished.

Finally, if you are ready to start to commit words to paper (or whatever software takes your fancy), do refer back to Chapter 2 on CLEAR. As a prompt to make sure you are focused on what is needed to make your data strategy a success, this section is an important reminder and should be used as a yardstick to ensure you are on the right path.

6.2 DETERMINING THE CONTENT

I do not want to be too specific in terms of specifying the content of your data strategy – to some extent, it depends on the nature and maturity of your organisation, the audience, and whether you are the first to define a data strategy or are following tracks laid before by others. It also depends on the sophistication of the strategy activity as a function within your organisation, which we touched on in an earlier chapter.

In general, it is important to reflect on the data needs that you can identify within the corporate strategy that should be reflected in the data strategy. As a minimum, you would expect to ensure these are fully covered and aligned appropriately.

There are some key elements you would expect to find in a data strategy:

- a strong data management vision;
- a coherent business case to support investment (even if that is just resources within the organisation, these still come at a cost);
- some guiding principles, values and alignment to the corporate vision;
- clearly articulated goals related to data;
- evaluation criteria and metrics to track success;
- clarity on the data strategy programme vision to be delivered;
- clarity of roles and responsibilities.

My recommendation is to contain the data strategy within 12–20 pages, and to focus on the high-level direction setting whilst providing waymarkers as a guide to drive the expected pace in the implementation phase. There are many data strategies out there which overshoot on this – one I had a workshop group review recently was in excess of 70 pages in length. Do not underestimate the challenge of writing something shorter but more focused. The French mathematician Blaise Pascal famously wrote, 'I have made this longer than usual because I have not had time to make it shorter.'[2] There is an art to being concise, complete and accurate, but it is unlikely your first iteration will succeed in this goal. The target of 20 pages will take time, effort and constant revision and is likely, therefore, to start out as a much larger document before being trimmed back to the recommended size.

I tend to think a data strategy should have an executive summary, with the goal to condense in about a page the key content of the document. It is a challenge to achieve, but it must set:

- context – why a data strategy, what is its alignment to the corporate strategy, why now and what it is seeking to achieve;
- scope – be clear on what is to be delivered, by when and how;
- what is required to deliver it – resources, dependencies, sponsorship, accountabilities;
- when it will be achieved – waymarker headlines only;
- the value it is expected to deliver.

This needs to be written tightly, avoiding flowery language and being absolutely clear on all points.

---

2   Blaise Pascal, *Lettres Provinciales*, 1657.

In terms of the rest of the document, I would expect the waymarkers to be displayed graphically along a timeline, perhaps a page or two, that can be referenced through the data strategy with the evaluation criteria and roles, responsibilities and accountability taking another page or so. The bulk of the content will be discussing data management and data exploitation in the context of a vision set out at the start of the data strategy – potentially over a couple of pages, to include reference to the business case or rationale for why a data strategy is required by the organisation – which is clearly aligned to the corporate strategy. As mentioned earlier, do consider the use of diagrams wherever possible, as these can convey a large amount of information succinctly and also help those who are more comfortable receiving information in a pictorial form than blocks of text.

There are some core topics I would recommend you consider in defining your own data strategy content, detailed below.

6.2.1 Purpose

Chapter 4 introduced 'purpose' as the first term of the PRIDE acronym. It is an essential component in stating your remit in defining a data strategy and therefore should be the opening statement of your data strategy. You need to be able to set the context of the data strategy, outlining any restrictions or constraints in the scope it covers, the context in which it sits (for instance, is this supporting key deliverables within the corporate strategy, or other documents which should be read in conjunction with the data strategy to provide the entire context?) and the time period it covers.

It is worth reflecting on a few key pointers when establishing purpose. Organisations typically want a data strategy to achieve a number of important goals, which may include some of the following (if not, it is still worth bearing these in mind when defining the purpose of your data strategy):

- Manage data securely, compliantly and consistently, which is critical to the organisation's success in minimising risk.

- Establish a credible approach to move the organisation to be insight-led, utilising data at the heart of the way it operates, to improve the quality of decisions made.

- Drive innovation and recognise data as an asset which can deliver value.

- Embrace digital opportunities, which require a more effective approach to data management and exploitation.

- Plan for future trends and be prepared for them to maximise opportunity and mitigate risk.

- Use data to establish competitive advantage in a sustainable and innovative way.

6.2.2 Introduction

It is likely that you will need to define the data strategy – what it contains, and just as importantly, what it does not. This is particularly important if this is the first time your organisation has had a data strategy; setting it in terms that the organisation comprehends is essential for it to be understood, contextualised and adopted.

This is the point at which you need to articulate what is meant by 'data' in the context of a data strategy. Most organisations use the term data strategy to mean the whole host of information requirements, not just those specific to data. I shall, therefore, refer to data strategy to cover the spectrum of data, information and the exploitation of data in the following sections. I recommend that you follow a similar course in scoping the breadth of the data strategy for your organisation.

It would be usual, rather like a book, to acknowledge those who contributed to the data strategy, recognising their contribution but also, by implication, the wide reach the data strategy has had in its compilation and the breadth of inputs it has incorporated. There should be recognition of the sponsor and the author(s), and remember to include the publication date. I strongly advise the inclusion of a recommendation regarding the review cycle and process (for instance, which governance board within the organisation 'signs off' on the data strategy and how it is commissioned). Whilst the recommendation may not be adopted, it does provide a prompt to the organisation to determine the appropriate review cycle and process following the adoption of the data strategy.

6.2.3 Data management

The first section of your data strategy usually covers data management. Before I go further, let me define what I mean by data management.

The challenge of defining the approach to data in a strategy document entitled 'data strategy' is how you refer to the data elements of it if the scope of the data strategy embraces all aspects of information (see Chapter 3 for further elaboration on scope). I am using the term 'data management' to encompass the full range of data-specific activities, which I shall cover below, and which are all related as elements of the management of data. The term often has specific meanings to some, so for those individuals I am taking liberties in how I use 'data management', but this is the challenge with the taxonomy in this field; it has evolved and so the terminology has morphed into having numerous meanings.

There are many frameworks available to define the data management spectrum. Two of the most established and commonly used are provided by DAMA and the CMMI (Capability Maturity Model Integration) Institute – the latter had been collaborating with the EDM Council but ceased to partner on the approach in 2014, with each having their own data maturity models as a result – which I will cover further in this section. There are numerous others, some of which I will also reference to highlight areas that are potentially of interest to explore further should you wish to depart from either the DAMA or CMMI frameworks.

I have added the Accenture data maturity model as I think it is helpful to demonstrate the transition from an ad hoc type of approach to what is termed an 'industrial' level as maturity develops across five key themes. The sequential nature of the flow is perhaps not to be seen literally, as it is feasible (and often desirable) to be making progress on multiple points simultaneously, but is indicative of a growing level of data management sophistication.

I do not intend to go into too much detail on each section of data management, simply because there are many publications available which cover this topic extensively. Remember, too, that this is a data strategy, so keep your content in this section relevant to the audience you are seeking to engage – it is not a research document or solely for data management professionals to digest.

6.2.3.1 Data maturity assessment

The starting point of a data strategy should be an assessment of where you are starting from as an organisation, and this applies in particular with the maturity of the organisation related to data management. There are many data maturity assessment methodologies out there, but most are variants of one another, typically with 5–6 levels and 20–25 categories on which to score current performance. The main variance tends to be based on the level of detail within criteria; some of the outlying criteria may differ, but as to be expected, the core components tend to be relatively common (for instance, data architecture, data governance, data quality, design and standards).

The benefit of establishing a baseline is the opportunity it gives to set realistic expectations of where you are seeking to reach within the time frame of the data strategy and the steps required to get there. This will enable you to establish a common understanding of your starting position, clearly articulated as to the basis on which this judgement has been reached and with reference to specifics within your organisation that provide meaningful context, and to therefore outline the approach needed to progress. Organisations with a low level of data maturity often have a lack of trust in the data and are not exploiting it fully for that reason. By contrast, those with a higher level of data maturity will be demonstrating how important data is to the organisation through their use of it in evidence-led decision making, with trust and transparency underpinning this approach, and will be more confident in their direction setting.

This provides a point on which to ground what follows in the data management section of your data strategy, which is why I usually advocate starting with this, rather than, as some data strategies choose, to end with it to summarise. I think it has more influence as a contextual scene setter that can gain audience attention, rather than making the risky assumption that the reader has made it to the end of the section, fully cognisant of how it comes together in the data maturity assessment.

The data maturity assessment should be used throughout the period the data strategy covers to drive coherent actions focused on how to enhance the maturity whilst embedding such changes in the organisation. It is an important baseline, enabling the organisation to have a standardised and agreed methodology for measurement. The assessment can be used as a barometer of progress to ensure those things it has committed to achieve are being supported and, where appropriate, funded to enable progress.

There are a number of data maturity assessment models available to use, two of which are shown in Figures 6.2 and 6.3. These are some of the more commonly used versions, but most consulting firms have devised variations that they will offer and provide consulting services to deliver. There are also maturity models which are specific to data governance (see Figure 6.4), as well as BI and analytics.

6.2.3.2 Data and its purpose

It is worth making a definitive statement within your data strategy about the relevance of data to your organisation. This might sound obvious, but treating data as an asset within your organisation is more likely to move the discussion towards a recognition that, as with any asset, it needs managing and funding to maintain it at its highest

Figure 6.2 Data management maturity model CMMI ©2014 All rights reserved. Used with permission.

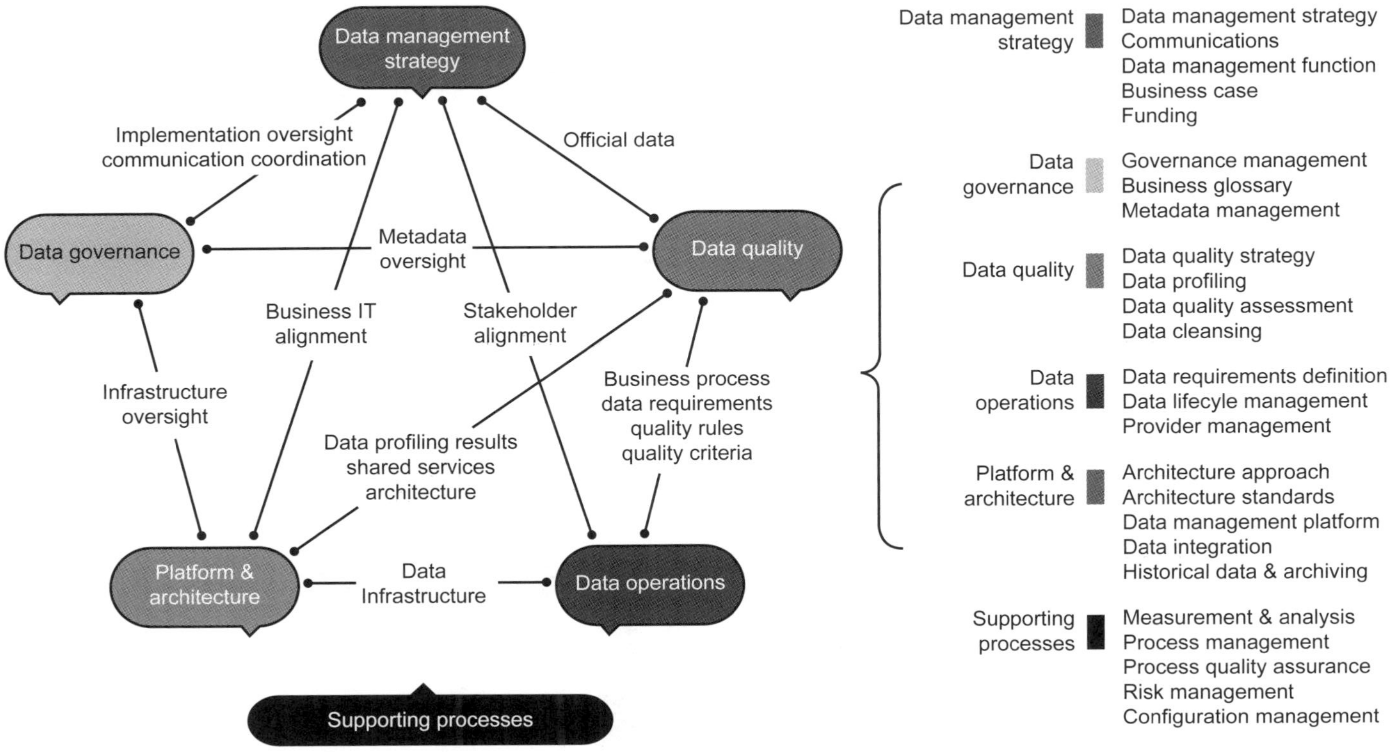

Figure 6.3 Data maturity model Copyright © 2018 Accenture

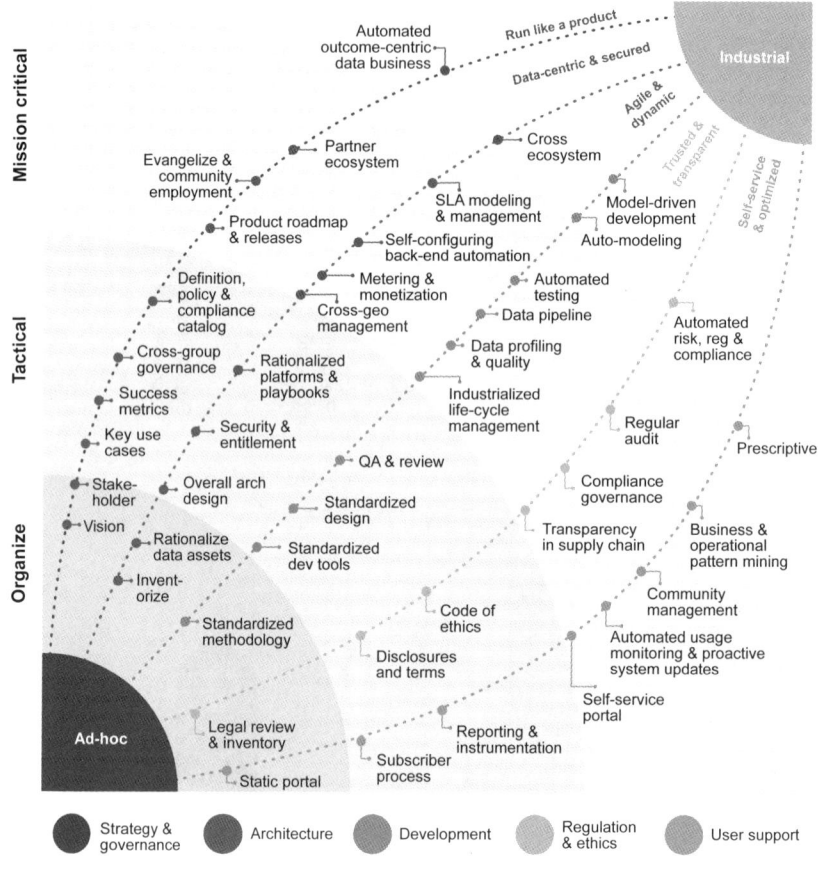

level of quality. If your organisation aspires to be information- and insight-led, then the quality of the data is aligned directly to the value its use will deliver in its processes and decision making.

This leads on to the concept of being 'fit for purpose'. Not all organisations have necessarily the understanding to know what fit for purpose amounts to, and therefore how good data needs to be. There is a balance to be struck with data quality. There is an investment required to make it highly performant for the organisation and it must be considered in the context that not all data is equal in its importance. As a result, investing time and resources in data quality is potentially a trade-off between the need for accuracy, precision and timeliness versus the data being good enough for decisions to be made. Of course, this has to reflect the need to be compliant and so it is a complex matrix that leads to determining what fit for purpose data amounts to, whilst remaining secure, safe and compliant.

Defining purpose also provides a way to set out the stall of the data strategy in any pitch for resources and/or funding. If there is broad agreement as to what constitutes fit for purpose, the data maturity assessment will provide a path to achieving this and highlight what needs to be addressed. This can be a useful springboard to a business case to deliver the operational activities that underpin the implementation of the data strategy.

6.2.3.3 Data governance

The data strategy needs to explain the approach to data across the spectrum of activities within what is collectively known as data governance. As the term suggests, the governance of data is focused on the end-to-end management of data and typically consists of common themes based on data architecture, data modelling and design, data security, master data management, data standards, data quality and the key aspects of how that is managed collectively, whether through operational data stores or data warehouses, or in document and content management systems.

There are numerous ways in which data governance is typically characterised, but one of the most established is the DAMA wheel. The definition DAMA uses to describe data governance is a more encompassing version to some, and this is where the terms data management and data governance can sometimes be interchangeable. For instance, DAMA would go so far as to suggest a data strategy is part of data governance, and perhaps in a narrower definition solely focused on data management this might have some merit, but in the rather broader (or some might say looser) definition of data strategy encompassing the exploitation of data then this doesn't hold true – data governance would typically be part of the data strategy.

The key difference between the DAMA wheel and the CMMI Institute model is that the former is based on knowledge, the latter on process. This leads to a slightly different focus, in which DAMA has 11 top level domains compared to just five in the CMMI model (six, if you include supporting processes), though there is a greater level of granularity in the latter with 20 process areas and five supporting areas underpinning the five categories of the model.

In practice, both models give a view on how to progress maturity, and so it is as much a question of preference as to whether you wish to base the maturity assessment on knowledge, process, competency (IBM model fits this approach) or business capability (DCAM model). The Accenture model is in some ways a blend, also has five key dimensions underpinning the approach, but is more extensive than some of the others in its reach into data exploitation.

It doesn't matter to me how you define data governance or data management – they are labels which, as we have seen, have different definitions in common use in well-established reference guides that are there to enable the implementation, and ongoing delivery, of data governance and management activities. What is key is to ensure there is a common understanding as to the terminology used within your own organisation, and the data strategy presents an important opportunity to establish the terminology you would like to see adopted going forward. Therefore, ensure you seize the moment to be clear on your definitions, both in the appropriate parts of the document and the glossary, which is going to be the authoritative list of definitions used in this data strategy and a handy reference guide to establishing the lexicon in the organisation.

Figure 6.4 The DAMA wheel Copyright © 2017 DAMA International.

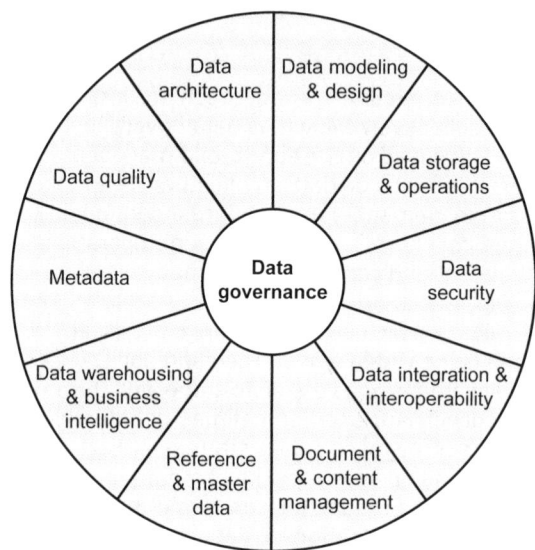

Rather like the DAMA wheel, the Gartner data governance maturity model[3] implies that data governance spans the full range of data management activities. It talks to information as early as level one on its multi-level approach, identifying this as the stage where the value of information is recognised and an enterprise information management strategy is required (for which the term 'data strategy' can be used so interchangeably!).

So, what place does data governance have within the data strategy?

Regardless of how wide you wish to make the definition, the need to establish principles of controls and standards is essential to make progress in the wider context of a data strategy. The definition may change, but the same principles apply.

Common data standards are essential to effective data governance and are the lynchpin of your data management capability. Data must be structured in a way that sources are known, defined, secure but accessible as needed to utilise it effectively. Data quality is the essential standard by which you certify that the data is reliable to use or highlight deficiencies. This applies to data whether in recognised systems or in any other means of storing it and is pivotal to your data strategy.

I have applied a kitemark approach to make the quality of data visible to all, in order to flag any MI or reporting issued to illustrate the reliability and veracity of the data within the report – green meaning the data is of high quality and decisions

3   K. Taylor, Data Governance Maturity Models Explained. https://www.hitechnectar.com/blogs/data-governance-maturity-models-explained/.

can be made with confidence; amber indicating it is broadly of acceptable quality, but there are issues and so it is good enough for indicative purposes but not accurate; red to demonstrate that the quality is limited and therefore only broad-brush decisions should be made if absolutely necessary, due to the risk of error.

The data maturity assessment will flush out where the gaps lie in your organisation's data governance, as well as other aspects of data management and its exploitation. The challenge is to align the organisation to put bandwidth and funding, if required, into resolving these gaps. The data strategy must set out clearly how this is to be approached, defining waymarkers to be achieved that align with the expected rate of progress that is at the heart of the data strategy.

How this looks for your organisation will entirely depend on its maturity and appetite to drive change. Much of this is cultural, behavioural and, sadly in many organisations, seen to be either someone else's problem or a burden being imposed on staff who are already busy. Assigning data owners and stewards, and setting quality standards with their input, is an essential first step to getting the corrective steps in place.

The compliance lever is always an option to get movement in the data governance arena. Personally, I tend to think this is a blunt instrument as there are usually plenty of positive reasons to improve data integrity and quality within an organisation. In a private sector organisation there are almost certainly revenue-generating opportunities to be had from knowing your customer better, or efficiencies to be gained by removing duplication of effort and/or making data more readily available. Those organisations outside the private sector can focus on efficiencies and effectiveness, especially in providing services of a higher quality at a lower cost by getting it right first time and presenting the whole picture to those in customer-facing roles.

That is not to say that the compliance angle is not important, as it most certainly is – just look at the scale of the fines levied to those companies highlighted in Chapter 3 to consider how your own organisation might be affected. Whether hefty fines or increased pressure to comply are a realistic risk, there is little to be gained from teetering on the edge of compliance as it is usually more expensive to fix retrospectively than to be compliant in operating today, not least as the time to resolve issues may be prohibitively expensive due to the scale and complexity involved. Better to be ahead of the curve, operating compliantly and maintaining a level which is affordable that ensures the organisation is both safe and legal.

In many organisations, data governance initiatives start by addressing specific tactical issues to get a level of traction and the potential for recognition if such initiatives can assist in solving them. This may, initially, constrain the scope of the data governance activity (for instance, to a specific function or project), but it could also enable it to be delivered more deeply through having something to focus on, thereby delivering more value and increasing the evidence on which it is judged to have succeeded.

As evidence grows of its success and awareness increases, so the data governance initiative can expand its scope and use the success as a case study to demonstrate the approach taken. This will enable the breadth of activity within data governance to be delivered, as the opportunities that lie ahead require more elements of data governance to be deployed. As a result, data standards, data quality and consistency in master data management will start to take hold in the organisation.

There are many fine texts out there on the topic of data governance, along with frameworks and models which can be used to measure the current state and track progress (further details in the bibliography of this book). Use these, as they are effective in providing clarity and cohesion across the organisation on what is needed – don't forget, data governance may not be the most exciting topic for many senior stakeholders to discuss at any length, so make it easy by making it accessible to them.

6.2.3.3.1 Data integrity The integrity of data is an area which typically forms part of the data governance activity. It is often used interchangeably with data quality, but this is perhaps a misunderstanding of the breadth of what data integrity encompasses. There are various definitions of data integrity and various sources which are available. Below are some of those most commonly referenced.

Good Manufacturing Practice/US Food and Drug Administration (FDA) 21 CFR Parts 210–12 – ALCOA – is used in the pharmaceutical industry and, as this is a regulated sector, requires evidence of compliance to the data integrity principles (subsequently expanded to ALCOA Plus with four additional criteria).[4] Some of the definitions are specific to the nature of the sector:

- Attributable – data should clearly demonstrate who observed and recorded it, when it was observed and recorded, and who it is about.

- Legible – data should be easy to understand, recorded permanently and original entries should be preserved.

- Contemporaneous – data should be recorded as it was observed, and at the time it was executed.

- Original – source data should be accessible and preserved in its original form.

- Accurate – data should be free from errors and conform with the protocol.

The Dodd–Frank Wall Street Reform and Consumer Protection Act CFTC 1.73 – an act passed in 2010 to increase accountability and transparency in the light of the financial crisis of 2008 – expects financial organisations to maintain data integrity, enforced by a variety of rules and regulations across multiple jurisdictions. This particularly requires a data integrity focus on the following:[5]

- Entity and Referential Integrity: Trusted identification and relationships exist between tables. Knowing that the structure is being maintained and also improved as a firm continues to grow.

---

4 U.S. Department of Health and Human Services, Food and Drug Administration, Center for Drug Evaluation and Research (CDER), Center for Biologics Evaluation and Research (CBER), Center for Veterinary Medicine (CVM), Pharmaceutical Quality/Manufacturing Standards (CGMP) Data Integrity and Compliance With CGMP Guidance for Industry. Draft Guidance. 2016. https://www.fda.gov/media/97005/download.

5 T. Kauzlarich, D. Wertheimer and J. Heigel, Data Integrity's Central Role in Financial Compliance: Maintaining Regulatory Compliance with Dodd-Frank Rule 1.73. Sagence, May 2014.

- Context of Data: Bad feeds and/or points of data will be addressed, corrected, documented, and communicated to required stakeholders.

- Incomplete Data: This causes disruptions amongst consumers and will need to be actioned by the team. Could be a bad file from a vendor or a failed process internally, but it will be easier to identify and investigate with a team that is centralised and understands the firm's entire data sets and their uses.

- Timeliness of Data: Files and processes will need to be run seamlessly to have the proper information flow through the organisation.

- Changing Environments: As system and software changes are made, attention will need to be placed on the impact of the data. The team will be responsible for ensuring that everything is cut over properly and seamlessly.

Generally, data integrity has a focus on the end-to-end lifecycle of data, wider than data quality, albeit that plays a part in its integrity, and has a breadth that extends through to retention, archiving and redundancy of data. It encapsulates auditing and tracking of data to be able to evidence integrity is being maintained against defined standards. It is related to, but separate from, data security, which also forges links through a dependency on data integrity to be able to support business continuity and data loss prevention.

Reflect on how data integrity features in your data strategy. Just like the other elements of data management, it may already be in train but it should be called out and referenced, with a clear view of where the organisation needs to get to in the period covered by the data strategy. Even if these activities are under way within the organisation, they should be incorporated into the data strategy, bringing coherence to the whole of data management in the wider context of how it enables data compliance and exploitation.

6.2.3.3.2 Data standards It is important to consider data standards within your data strategy. Whilst not necessarily called out explicitly in many of the models, data standards define the way you choose to operate within your organisation. Their role is to provide a common understanding, setting a standard all are expected to follow, enabling quality and integrity to be assessed from that basis. Without clearly defined and communicated data standards, each member of your organisation will have a view of what that standard is in their own mind, and you will find you are operating with many variations, making data governance an impossible task as each person will believe their interpretation to be correct.

Many organisations do not have data standards, or have something akin to these but have never documented them. This leads to confusion, as one interpretation of data entities and attributes differs from another, and so the way in which data is captured varies markedly. This carries a cost, through the daily effort in re-work that goes on at an individual level to transform the data to make it consistent before it can be used, as well as hindering the ability to bring data sets together through the lack of consistent data standards.

There are data standards published by type of activity as well as sectors. Just a few of the established versions include:

- ISO 55000 – asset management data and decision making – defines data as an asset, covers how data is there to meet stakeholder needs for information, highlights the data lifecycle and includes archiving and deletion, as well as the retention of data and document management.

- The FDA has established standards and a programme to enable organisations to align. The CBER-CDER[6] Data Standards Strategy provides a consistent methodology for pre- and post-market regulatory review to ensure safe and effective medical products are available to patients. The goals of the CBER-CDER Data Standards Program Action Plan are set out in Figure 6.5.

- Common Education Data Standards is a US-based model that creates a schema that easily identifies and standardises the educational organisations and relationship with others with clear naming conventions and metadata ready to be adopted by those within the sector. It is entirely voluntary to use, but its goal is to link and streamline the exchange of data across institutions and sectors.

Figure 6.5 CBER-CDER data standards strategy goals Source: USFDA Data Standards Program Action Plan https://fda.report/media/149624/Data_Standards_Program_Joint_Action_Plan_v5.1.pdf.

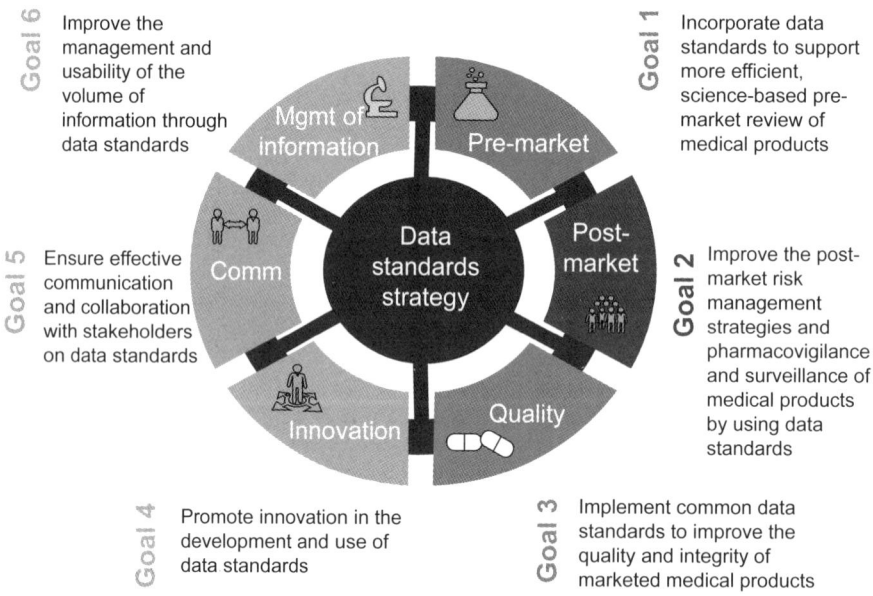

Goal 6 Improve the management and usability of the volume of information through data standards

Goal 1 Incorporate data standards to support more efficient, science-based pre-market review of medical products

Goal 5 Ensure effective communication and collaboration with stakeholders on data standards

Goal 2 Improve the post-market risk management strategies and pharmacovigilance and surveillance of medical products by using data standards

Goal 4 Promote innovation in the development and use of data standards

Goal 3 Implement common data standards to improve the quality and integrity of marketed medical products

Data standards are exceedingly important. For instance, if your organisation manufactures any physical products, there are almost certainly manufacturing data standards to be achieved to recognise they are appropriate for use. If those products are to conform to a consistent standard, such as AA batteries or type approval of a car or component, these standards are clearly articulated and industry-wide. Without data standards there would be a lack of consistency, and the cost of commonplace items would be significantly higher.

---

6   The Center for Biologics Evaluation and Research and the Center for Drug Evaluation and Research, both part of the FDA.

In 2020 the UK government established the Data Standards Authority, which consists of a multidisciplinary team drawn from a wide range of backgrounds in technology, strategy and policy. Working with experts across the wider public sector and devolved administrations across the UK, as well as academia and private sector organisations, the DSA identifies, improves and helps implement data standards that meet user needs.

It is important to establish what data standards your organisation is following, and the compliance to the standard. If you cannot find a standard, then there is probably a strong case for introducing one or more standards to drive greater efficiency in the organisation, further cementing the data strategy at the heart of making the organisation both data aware and conscious of the importance of the data strategy.

6.2.3.4 Data retention and compliance

One of the areas closely associated with data governance, as well as compliance, is the policy of the organisation towards data retention. In many jurisdictions, there are specified retention periods for various types of data but these may vary from one location to another, so if your organisation operates across boundaries and the data strategy has to support all parts of the organisation, it may be necessary to reflect differing compliance regimes in the data strategy.

Within the European Union, GDPR imposes the need for a data retention policy, covering the seven key GDPR principles:

1. Lawfulness, fairness and transparency.
2. Purpose limitation.
3. Data minimisation.
4. Accuracy.
5. Storage limitation.
6. Integrity and confidentiality.
7. Accountability.

Be aware of local regulations in the domain in which you are operating and, if yours is a global institution, how these differ by country and therefore the need for clarity in how these are complied with at a local level. Remember, basic concepts like the use and retention of data may differ, and you will be subject to local laws for data pertaining to that jurisdiction.

There are a growing number of GDPR-like data privacy laws established around the world, many of which have modelled changes based on GDPR. These are just some you might need to be aware of:

- Australia – the Privacy Amendment (Notifiable Data Breaches) to Australia's Privacy Act came into effect in 2018.

- Brazil – Lei Geral de Proteção de Dados, modelled on GDPR, came into effect in 2020.

- Canada – the Digital Charter Implementation Act has been, at the time of writing, proposed by the Canadian government and will reshape the Canadian privacy landscape through the introduction of the Consumer Privacy Protection Act to overhaul the existing Personal Information and Electronic Documents Act.

- Chile – in addition to amendments to Chile's constitution, a series of updates to Ley 19,628 (the legislation known as 'On Protection of Private Life') have been passed and current proposals are reflecting changes to bring it more into line with GDPR.

- China – at the end of 2020, the Personal Data Protection Law was released in draft form and impacts any organisation doing business in China, rather than just those operating via a physical presence in the country.

- India – the Personal Data Protection Bill 2019 has been progressing through the Indian parliamentary scrutiny process for some time but is expected to be debated post-committee stage via a final report in autumn 2021.

- Japan – the Act on Protection of Personal Information was amended to apply to both foreign and domestic companies in 2017, and has a 'reciprocal adequacy' agreement in place with the EU.

- New Zealand – the Privacy Act of 1993 was amended in 2020, though it is some way short of being as comprehensive as GDPR.

- South Africa – the Protection of Personal Information Act became law in 2020 and has some key differences to GDPR, not least the application of criminal charges.

- South Korea – privacy standards in South Korea have been well established, with the Personal Information Protection Act in law since 2011.

- Thailand – the Personal Data Protection Act was passed in 2019 but came into effect in 2021. It is similar to GDPR, but as with South Africa, criminal charges can apply.

- USA – the strictest, and most high profile, data privacy legislation is the California Consumer Privacy Act, which has some similarities with GDPR. Several states have followed California's lead in seeking to implement their own such legislation. Most interesting for those operating both sides of the Atlantic, the EU–US Privacy Shield framework was invalidated by the European Court of Justice due to surveillance fears and concerns over a lack of privacy standards in the US. Data transfers from the EU to the USA are typically using standard contractual clauses, non-negotiable legal contracts drawn up in the EU, until such time as a new accord can be reached.

In addition to the above, trading blocks such as the Organisation for Economic Co-operation and Development and Asia-Pacific Economic Cooperation have devised their own data privacy guidelines for cross-border data transfer. However, these guidelines tend to be less rigorous than those devised in country and so have little effect if trading with those nations who have adopted more stringent data privacy laws.

Do not be surprised if your investigations prior to developing the data strategy reveal there to be much more data out there than you were initially aware of. Organisations frequently store documents off-site, and the phrase 'out of sight, out of mind' is often very true when it comes to unstructured documents which may not have been recorded particularly well when sent off-site. You wouldn't be the first to find off-site storage belonging to the organisation that has no reference as to what documents are contained therein.

Seeking to get agreement to data retention periods sounds simple enough, but is often challenging, not least because different parts of the organisation may have different requirements of that data. This is where the data governance roles of data owner (the individual accountable for specific data, typically defined by domains such as finance, HR and so on) and data steward (who is responsible for implementing governance initiatives on behalf of the data owner and would usually be an individual with deep knowledge of that data domain) play a key part, identifying the stakeholders for data in the organisation and seeking to gain agreement to the retention policy for that data entity. Once established, of course, the rules need to be applied, which should also be borne in mind when defining the data strategy, as this will become a critical element of the implementation plan.

The final stage of the data lifecycle is to archive or, in most cases, destroy the data. In some (rare) cases, the data may not be destroyed due to the legal requirement to retain it or it being a matter for public record. However, most organisations can and should archive and subsequently delete data once it exceeds the data retention policy, and often will have an imperative to do so to remain compliant.

In some cases, systems may not enable hard deletion of records and this presents a significant challenge from a compliance point of view. This will be particularly so if those systems are relatively old and hence a soft deletion, in which the data is not visible to the user, may be the only option open to you. In such cases, there is a need to align your activity with that of the information risk community and IT systems architects to explore what their plans are to remediate this issue.

6.2.3.5 Open data
There is a growing trend towards transparency of data, making it more accessible to those outside the organisation where it is not specifically a competitive threat to do so. Open data standards are being developed rapidly to enable data to flow freely and to enable entrepreneurial organisations and individuals to access data from multiple sources to develop new applications.

There are many open data initiatives. I have listed just a few here (Table 6.1) but if you are interested to know more there are a number of groups you can engage with through the International Open Data Charter,[7] which works across governments and wider organisations worldwide to facilitate the sharing of knowledge of open data.

---

[7] https://opendatacharter.net/.

Table 6.1 Selected open data standards

Provider	Description
GovEx (the Centre for Government Excellence, Johns Hopkins University, USA)	Developing a list of civic data standards
Geothink (McGill University, Canada)	Project to enable municipal open data publishers to standardise data sets
European Data Portal (data.europa. eu) – joint venture with Johns Hopkins University and McGill University	The Open Data Standards Directory – over 60 open data standards
Open Data Institute	Developing an open data ecosystem with governments and organisations
Open Standards Board	UK government body to define open standards for data, technology and services
OpenActive	UK-based organisation providing open data standards for sport and physical activity
Open Data Standards	Develop Open Exposure Data Standard (OED) and Open Results Data Standard (ORD) to support Oasis loss modelling framework-based models in the reinsurance market

To enable the adoption of open data, you will almost certainly need to adopt a data classification approach to align the data governance effort with the sensitivity of that data, enabling it to be classified and accessed accordingly. Whilst this is potentially a low-level activity in itself, the trend towards a more open data landscape is gathering pace, and so this may well require an acknowledgement within the data strategy and a statement of intent and direction if it is something your organisation needs to embark upon.

6.2.3.6 Data acquisition

If your organisation is dependent upon data acquired from other organisations, such as credit reference agencies or other third-party service providers, then it would be appropriate to map out the acquisition strategy in the overall data strategy. This may not change in the period the data strategy covers, though with the increasing volumes of data in the world there are an ever more varied range of data sets that can be acquired, and so it is perhaps a timely opportunity to consider whether this innovation has created an opening to enhance your own data, or seize new business opportunities.

Setting out the current position, the value extracted from the data acquired and the current potential to be exploited enables all within the organisation to understand the value of the investment being made. This is particularly relevant if the data in question is key to the delivery of activity, and without it the activity may be hindered or not viable at all, just so there is clarity of understanding in retaining the investment through the period the data strategy covers.

6.2.3.7 Data systems

Whilst the data systems should be covered within an IT strategy produced elsewhere in your organisation, it is appropriate to cross-reference any significant changes or investments being made in new systems within the period covered by the data strategy. It is highly likely that there will be critical data migration tasks to be undertaken which will present opportunities to improve data quality (though it is depressingly common for organisations to make minimal efforts at enhancing data prior to it migrating, only to discover the significant investment in the new system is thoroughly undermined by the poor quality of data). Such instances should be called out in the data strategy and dependencies made across to the IT strategy.

6.2.3.8 Data capabilities

Depending on the current sophistication of data expertise within the organisation, the data strategy should highlight the current state and desirable future state of data capabilities within the organisation, and propose an approach to address this, either through training or recruitment. In many ways, a data capability assessment is as key to the organisation's success as the data maturity assessment, given one is identifying the steps needed to be taken and the other the means to be able to deliver these.

There are two levels: capability to deliver, and capability to utilise what is delivered. It is essential to establish the position of both, as these will either inhibit or enable your data strategy to realise its goals, and so there must be a clear focus on how any gaps will be resolved. It may require buying in expertise, either through recruitment or consulting routes (more a short-term expediency, as the expertise will need embedding in your organisation as soon as possible to be effective).

It is likely that you will need to specify how any gaps can be filled, as the nature of the specialism will probably mean that there is not an understanding as to how to resolve this within your organisation at the moment. There will also need to be consideration given to the potential to upskill your resources, as this is cheaper and has the benefit of building on the corporate knowledge those members of staff already have of your organisation. However, such an undertaking must not be done lightly, as it is equally a significant commitment from those colleagues who are willing to learn as it is for the organisation to invest in delivering training to them.

There is also a need to identify safe opportunities for staff who are either new to the organisation with relevant skills or being upskilled within the organisation to learn from experience, so it is important not to set them up to fail by taking on something too big or complex as their first opportunity to deploy those skills. Establishing confidence is key: the newcomers to the organisation feeling their way into it and establishing trusted networks will be a big part in making them effective quickly; the existing staff need to be seen to succeed and not likely to fail, as their newly acquired skills may be eroded if they are exposed in front of colleagues who may even be sceptical of their new-found capabilities.

6.2.4 Data exploitation

Now the foundations have been covered, assuming this data strategy has the broader definition of covering the entire information landscape, it is time to consider the exploitation of the data.

6.2.4.1 Reporting and management information

I mentioned in the previous section the confusion that arises from terms in this arena having different definitions, often causing a degree of complication through misinterpretation. MI or reporting – often the terms are used interchangeably in organisations – provide a backward look at what happened, tracking measures such as performance (how many stock items were sold last month), productivity (how many stock items were produced last month) and resources (how many days were lost last month due to absence, what was the return on investment last month).

What is the difference between MI and reporting? Again, it is largely preference and established practice within an organisation. MI is produced to enable decision making based on what has occurred, and underpins control and coordination of activities. It covers any business activity, so whilst the term 'finance MI' may be commonplace, MI does not have to be exclusively financial in nature. Without MI, organisations cannot report financial performance or compliance, or track sales or staff activities. It is therefore at the heart of any organisation wanting to know what is happening, whether by the minute, hour, day, week, month or even year, and typically is presented in the same format each month to ease the executive in spotting the key information of interest.

Reporting is a more generic term, and is confusing as MI is also a form of reporting. It can be used more colloquially to mean simple or routine reports, for example the quick insight generated by querying the system for basic information such as annual leave entitlement, stock levels for a particular item, staff in post at a specific grade or location – all things that the operational system can usually provide from its in-built reporting functionality without having to link numerous data sets and/or develop complex formulas to calculate the required information.

Whether you see benefit in having both terms in use in your organisation or not, it is likely that the genie is out of the bottle and these are already commonplace in the lexicon of the organisation. It may therefore be simpler, if you wish to avoid the terms being used as if synonymous, to try to differentiate along the lines above, in which reporting is low-level activity and not the calculated information generated as MI.

Many organisations will have an MI strategy, a coherent plan on how to use BI tools to deliver the outputs to run operational and financial activities. Assuming you are taking the track of creating a data strategy that encompasses the broader information landscape, the MI strategy would form a sub-strategy and hence be the more detailed view of what is to be delivered than is rightly positioned in the data strategy.

In addition, the MI strategy will dovetail with the IT strategy in terms of the BI tools, data warehousing or data lakes, data storage mechanisms to support the MI strategy and the data retention and integration strategies (increasingly, in a cloud computing environment, the traditional ways of integrating data are being superseded by new methodologies). There will also be overlap with the approach to information risk and security, along with data protection regulations, given the accessibility and retention policies play heavily into the reporting space.

The investment in a central repository, such as a data warehouse or lake, will be key to your ability to integrate data sets to support reporting. Whilst some organisations are able to avoid this sort of investment through deploying data virtualisation techniques, if your data is fragmented – especially if you have outsourced some of your activity and that data is managed by a third party on a system outside your organisation – then the integration of data is likely to require a means to bring these together, which is what a data warehouse or a data lake can do for you.

The benefits of taking extracts from multiple places and consolidating them in one place, using common keys and links to join data sets together, transforms the ability to deliver reporting in a consistent manner, opening up opportunities to build once and automate, thereby saving resources. It can also be very beneficial in opening up opportunities that would otherwise have been overlooked, as the first time data is linked together may reveal something which otherwise would have gone unnoticed in the organisation. It is such moments that deliver real value and accelerate the return on investment (ROI).

The use of maturity models has been referenced in other parts of the book, and one I particularly like – albeit one of the oldest, dating back to 2005 – is produced by an organisation formerly known as The Data Warehousing Institute, but now rebranded as Transforming Data With Intelligence (TDWI).[8] It has developed a number of maturity models, but the original BI maturity model was an effective way to assess progress of your organisation on its adoption of an investment in data warehouse technology to becoming intelligence-led. It assesses five key aspects of an investment in BI capabilities over six stages of maturity to determine how advanced your organisation has become in enabling greater exploitation of the information:

1. BI adoption curve – moving from a cost-based model to a strategic resource that drives the business and ultimately shapes the market. Low on this one and you are in the Japanese knotweed of spreadsheets. High, and yours has progressed to be a truly analytically driven organisation.

2. Local control versus enterprise standards – the balancing act between a devolved model with limited standards and a more strategic approach embedded in the organisation with greater clarity on standards to be followed. As progress is made along the six stages, the transition is from 'think local, resist global' to 'plan global, act local'.

3. BI usage – an initial early adopter approach, with power users exerting influence that shifts as the organisation utilises reports to drive more effective operations to be more empowered, with the capability extended more widely and becoming more customer-focused.

4. BI insight – shifting from a model of historic views of the data to drive a better awareness of issues within the organisation towards a more action-orientated approach, which ultimately exploits data nearer real time to optimise decisions, identify opportunities and embed such intelligence via models into core systems to lead to automated decision-making.

---

8   For further detail on the original 2005 TDWI data maturity model and other BI maturity models, this blog provides a helpful overview: James Serra, Business Intelligence Maturity Assessment. 2013. https://www.sqlservercentral.com/blogs/business-intelligence-maturity-assessment.

5. Business value and ROI – the transition from the initial investment, with limited exploitation to release value due to data integration challenges, to an enterprise resource with stable costs and a platform to be exploited through automation of decisions, insight leading to competitive advantage and a more outward perspective on the opportunities to drive the market.

6.2.4.2 Analytics

The exploitation of data is at its most advanced in the analytics arena, moving from the retrospective of what has happened to looking at what is likely to happen – predictive and prescriptive analytics. The goal of analytics is to shape the future and enable the organisation to either adapt to those situations it cannot influence, mitigating the impact and steering a course to minimise the effect, or to positively influence a future situation to the advantage of the organisation. Of course, this only works if the organisation has the maturity to comprehend the message and adapt, and this is the tricky balance so many organisations fail to achieve – they embark on wanting to exploit analytics, but are not prepared for the negative discoveries they find, as they have perceived only upsides.

In my first role, I was tasked with rebuilding a forecasting model that predicted the operational volumes and revenue for the organisation. It worked well for a number of months, and then suddenly indicated volumes were about to drop dramatically, plunging the company into a loss-making situation. The model, which had been heralded for its relative accuracy for many months, was now dismissed as flawed and inaccurate. However, in a matter of weeks volumes fell off a cliff as the recession of 1990 hit home, and the company was plunged into crisis. If only faith had been retained in the same model which had been in vogue weeks before, and time had been spent on preparation rather than continuing as if oblivious to what was coming.

In much the same way as a data maturity assessment can demonstrate how advanced the organisation is in its management of data, so there are analytics maturity models that can serve a similar purpose. Most consulting firms use these, and there are certainly versions, like the McKinsey maturity model on analytic capability and utilisation,[9] that are relatively easy to apply. Whilst these might be used in a less outwardly visible fashion than the data maturity assessment you undertake, it is worth exploring the maturity of the organisation in regards to becoming analytically driven.

The key to establish with the analytics maturity model when defining the data strategy is twofold: firstly, what capability you have to be able to deliver on the ambition in the data strategy (indeed, recruitment of analytics staff may be a part of the data strategy, if this is part of growing the capacity and capability); secondly, what the demand for analytics within the organisation is to be able to deploy this successfully.

9   G.R.M. Wood, Data & Analytics SIG: 'Data and Analytics the Key to Success & Growth', Organisational Maturity Survey (slide 12). 2016. https://www.slideshare.net/graemermwood/aiiadataanalyticsprojectexternal20160721.

In a lot of organisations, a few enlightened individuals recognise the potential of analytics to turn theirs into an insight-led organisation, utilising evidence and analytical skills to drive future outcomes. However, this may come unstuck if a similar demand does not exist across the whole organisation, such that the analytics capability is not well understood, it fails to gain traction and the organisation continues to operate as it always has – using intuition, repetition (and either failing or producing suboptimal outcomes) and flawed information garnered through asking the wrong question of poor-quality data.

I have often found myself being asked why, if these failings are so prevalent, more organisations don't fail or lose influence in their markets. Surely, there should be an almost Darwinian shift to those who do invest and exploit data effectively. My answer, unfortunately, is that the majority of companies still haven't truly found the sweet spot in analytics adoption to have really outperformed their competitors to fully evidence the significant differentiator that analytics brings, and, where this has occurred, companies hold dear the knowledge of the competitive advantage that the application of analytics provides, rather than be overt in publicising what they are doing that is making such a difference.

> I recall, many years ago, being prevented from presenting ground-breaking activity at conferences precisely because the organisation concerned did not want that sort of information leaking out to competitors.

In addition, just look at the vast majority of newer 'tech-based' companies and you will see that analytics is at the heart of the organisation's culture and strategy. This is why it is important for you to take the initiative, and challenge the organisation and its practices if there is scope to manoeuvre your organisation to be a leader and not a follower.

In terms of content, the analytics section of your data strategy will be guided by the maturity of the existing capability and appetite of the organisation to embrace it. There will be a temptation to leap ahead in this field to advanced analytics, but there are pitfalls in such an approach, not least the cultural embedding and data quality issues you are most likely to find. Keep a focus on what the goal of exploiting data through analytics is. It may be to increase profitability by focusing on the right blend of customers to generate more sales volume, expanding their product holding, driving cost out of processes by identifying ways to increase efficiency or a myriad of other things the organisation could look to achieve. It may also vary depending on business unit or function – whilst not endless, there is likely to be a lot of data, which in turn creates a lot of scope to deploy analytics.

I recommend a balance of opportunism – identifying where there are stand-alone activities that could result in 'quick wins' – mixed with a more pragmatic focus on getting the foundations laid to support a significant investment in analytics. The latter does not have to be seen as a constraint; there is plenty of value to be gained along the way, and the timescale for delivering the foundations can be as bullish as the organisation can afford, commit to and resource. You need to position it accordingly to retain the link in key stakeholders' minds that there is a need to invest in constructing the foundations to fully realise the greater ambition of the data strategy.

Bear in mind that the delivery of analytics early can increase its value, especially if it enables your organisation to be the first to spot and exploit an opportunity and so get first mover advantage.[10] In 2017 EY and Forbes identified through research[11] that only 7 per cent of organisations move fast in exploiting analytics, with 38 per cent of this group incorporating analytics into the design of business initiatives.

Figure 6.6 provides a good illustration of the key points to be reached on the journey to embedding analytics fully into the organisational DNA. Without achieving the steps along the way, regardless of how quickly these are achieved, progress will be illusory, as it is not building on the foundations of what went before. This is a continuum, and as such requires progression to make the gains stick.

As with the other sections of this chapter on content, I won't dwell too long on the specifics of analytics. Again, many highly regarded texts can be found that cover this in significant detail, and the bibliography of this book provides some I have found useful.

Remember that the content needs to be coherent for your audience, and this is a section with the potential to run away with advanced statistical terminology, making it daunting or forbidding to the reader. This is the opposite of what we are aiming to achieve.

6.2.4.3 Data science

Data science[12] is an oft-used term which is incorrectly applied more commonly than should be the case. Indeed, some would articulate data science and analytics to be one and the same, and from some of the descriptions applied to the former it is hard to distinguish it from the latter. For my purposes, I regard data science to be an extension of analytics that has embraced the exponential growth in computing power and intelligence to provide additional capabilities which broaden analytics into a programming environment much broader than that a traditional analytics team would provide. This incorporates machine learning, AI, deep learning and advanced coding, all of which utilise the power of computing alongside the algorithmic influences of statisticians.[13]

---

10 For an insight into companies that had first mover advantage, see D. Tyre, The First-Mover Advantage, Explained. 2018. https://blog.hubspot.com/sales/first-mover-advantage.

11 E. Maguire, Data & Advanced Analytics: High Stakes, High Rewards. Forbes. 2017. https://www.forbes.com/sites/data-and-analytics/2017/02/15/data-advanced-analytics-high-stakes-high-rewards-2/.

12 For a short but interesting background to the evolution of data science, see G. Press, A Very Short History of Data Science. 2013. https://www.forbes.com/sites/gilpress/2013/05/28/a-very-short-history-of-data-science/.

13 For a really insightful example of what data scientists are delivering in a range of organisations, see Hugo Bowne-Anderson, What Data Scientists Really Do, According to 35 Data Scientists. *Harvard Business Review*, 15 August 2018. https://hbr.org/2018/08/what-data-scientists-really-do-according-to-35-data-scientists.

Figure 6.6 FP&A strategy data maturity model to accelerate finance transformation J. Myers and A. Alhagi (2017).

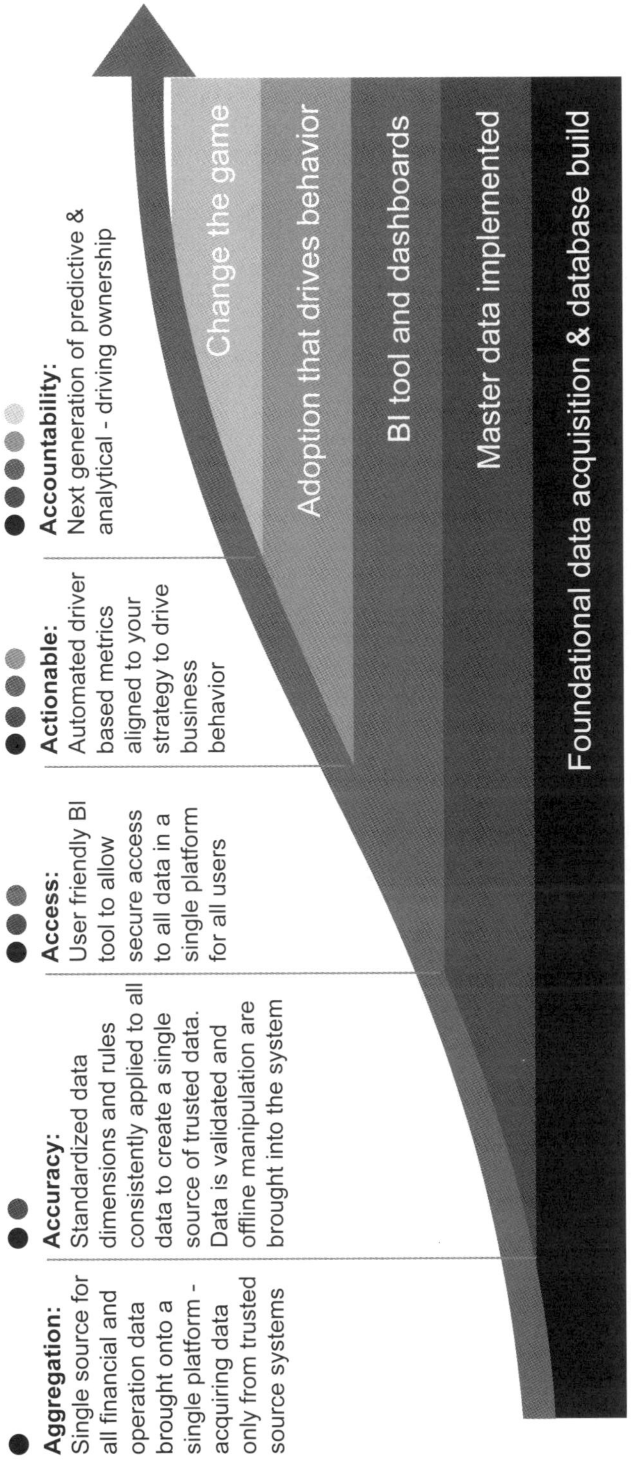

Aggregation:
Single source for all financial and operation data brought onto a single platform – acquiring data only from trusted source systems

Accuracy:
Standardized data dimensions and rules consistently applied to all data to create a single source of trusted data. Data is validated and offline manipulation are brought into the system

Access:
User friendly BI tool to allow secure access to all data in a single platform for all users

Actionable:
Automated driver based metrics aligned to your strategy to drive business behavior

Accountability:
Next generation of predictive & analytical – driving ownership

Change the game

Adoption that drives behavior

BI tool and dashboards

Master data implemented

Foundational data acquisition & database build

The field of data and analytics has never quite recovered from the marketing hype since the turn of the millennium that has unleashed a number of terms and phrases,[14] such as 'big data',[15] 'data is the new oil', 'open data' and 'data engineering', to name only a few. Those of us engaged within the data and analytics community would struggle to either define consistently or agree on whether these terms and phrases are of any value to us today. Indeed, my own experience has been that it has made the challenge of engaging with those eager to embrace what we can deliver harder by introducing more terminology which, in itself, creates a further barrier to simplifying and standardising our language to make it accessible. It is all the more important to recognise these terms do exist, but to use them cautiously, and with the caveat of providing as standardised a definition as possible of what is meant within the data strategy, if it is indeed necessary to incorporate them.

Should you include a section on data science in your data strategy? Increasingly, I would advocate that you should, even if this is nascent in your organisation's development, given the rate of growth of this discipline and the transformative effects it is having across all industries and the challenges it is posing to sectors which are being disrupted by it. If you are operating in one of those, data science should be part of your overall strategy, let alone data strategy, if you are to stay in business.

Examples of data science making significant headway proliferate across sectors, public and private alike. Indeed, there is plenty of discussion as to how data science is democratising data[16] in a way perhaps not seen previously, making major changes to our way of working (and living) that transcend not just the routine but the previously perceived complex. Radiography, for example, which required highly skilled practitioners who had undergone training over many years, is now realising higher accuracy rates from AI than the qualified radiographer. The application of AI and machine learning is also used in facial recognition, typically by law enforcement agencies across the world to identify individuals, behaviour traits and track criminals amongst large crowds, though there are significant ethical and accuracy concerns which have arisen, ranging from racial profiling to the infringement of human rights. Legal cases are beginning to identify instances in which the use of facial recognition and other AI applications are deemed unlawful due to privacy concerns and a lack of consent.

These are just two examples of radically different approaches which transform workplaces in a way we would not have envisaged a decade or two ago, but which provoke a growing disquiet over the advancement of technology and how it is balanced with the question of ethics. The advancement of data science is moving faster than the

---

14 Some terms and phrases were commonly used prior to 2000 – data mining and data warehousing being two examples from the preceding decades – but I would suggest the terminology has become less obvious and hence definitions increasingly diverse.

15 Francis X. Diebold, 'Big Data' Dynamic Factor Models for Macroeconomic Measurement and Forecasting. 8th World Congress of the Econometric Society, 2000. https://www.sas.upenn.edu/~fdiebold/papers/paper40/temp-wc.pdf.

16 This term has become increasingly commonplace. See Democratizing Data Science. https://news.mit.edu/2019/nonprogrammers-data-science-0115, and 4 Ways to Democratize Data Science in Your Organization. https://hbr.org/2021/03/4-ways-to-democratize-data-science-in-your-organization.

rate at which the ethical debate can keep pace, which is challenging, and there are many institutions seeking to provide guidance.[17, 18] However, this is a relentless challenge given the pace at which data science is moving, and so the ethical debate should also be referenced within your data strategy, to alert the reader to the challenges and to be prepared to engage – this is integral to the relationship your organisation has with its customers, consumers and stakeholders.

I would recommend, if this topic is pertinent to your organisation and therefore the data strategy, that you investigate further the direction of AI and machine learning and its impact on your organisation – even if you are not investing in this technology, you may find your competitors are, and this may put you at a significant disadvantage in the relatively near future if you are not prepared. It is also essential that you investigate the ethical dimension, and understand how this applies to your organisation, the sector in which you operate and the customers you engage with. The profile of the ethical concerns with this technology is growing, and your customers may well have concerns at any move your organisation makes to utilise it, so it is prudent and a key compliance step to communicate this element of your strategy proactively.

6.3 LOGICALLY STRUCTURING YOUR CONTENT

Establishing an understanding of what should be considered in your data strategy is clearly an early task to undertake in the process of determining the look and feel of the strategy. The maturity models mentioned in this chapter provide helpful context, a framework to build a consensus within your organisation to establish an agreed baseline, and focus minds on the aspiration and outcomes sought to be encapsulated in the data strategy; however, this needs a key thread to link the range of topics together into an easy to follow strategy document that the lay person can access and action.

As with so much in the world of data and analytics, what is needed is a story to cut through the detail that can seem to be forbidding to those who have little background or desire to explore too far – they just want to know the what, why, when and how. Of course, the data strategy alone isn't going to answer all of these, but it needs to 'sell' the vision and direction, such that the implementation plan is building on the positivity, bringing all parties together to make it happen.

Figure 6.7 shows how the steps outlined within this chapter build on one another to add value and intelligence and, as such, are not discrete islands of activity. The key to providing your content with a story is to build this narrative into a picture that flows seamlessly from one aspect of the strategy to the other. For many who work on a data strategy, this is one of the most challenging parts of delivering the strategy, as the flow is both obvious and also, ironically, difficult to describe without resorting to the same

---

17 Amongst many others, the Alan Turing Institute, the Institute and Faculty of Actuaries in conjunction with the Royal Statistical Society, and Harvard University have all devised frameworks for data science ethics in recognition of the need to provide some guidance.

18 A helpful framework for those conducting data science, which also incorporates ethics, is to be found in Sallie Ann Keller, Stephanie S. Shipp, Aaron D. Schroeder and Gizem Korkmaz, Doing Data Science: A Framework and Case Study. *Harvard Data Science Review*, 21 February 2020. https://hdsr.mitpress.mit.edu/pub/hnptx6lq/release/8.

Figure 6.7 The transition to an intelligent, data-driven organisation generating business value

Data ← Information ← Intelligence

Raw, fragmented data

Fragmented reporting using extracts

Data aware: catalogue and standards introduced

Coherent approach to MI/reporting with catalogue

Limited, ad hoc analysis using available data

Master data and governance implemented

Reporting using known data sources, KPIs supported by PIs

Diagnostic analytics, informing why event transpired

Quality data-integrity and assurance

Automated, controlled reporting with quality status

Predictive analytics, anticipating events to inform

Data recognised and valued as an asset

Descriptive analytics, dashboards and narrative to inform reporting

Prescriptive analytics, influencing events and outcomes

Insight and knowledge: determining the future to shape the medium-term (market/readiness)

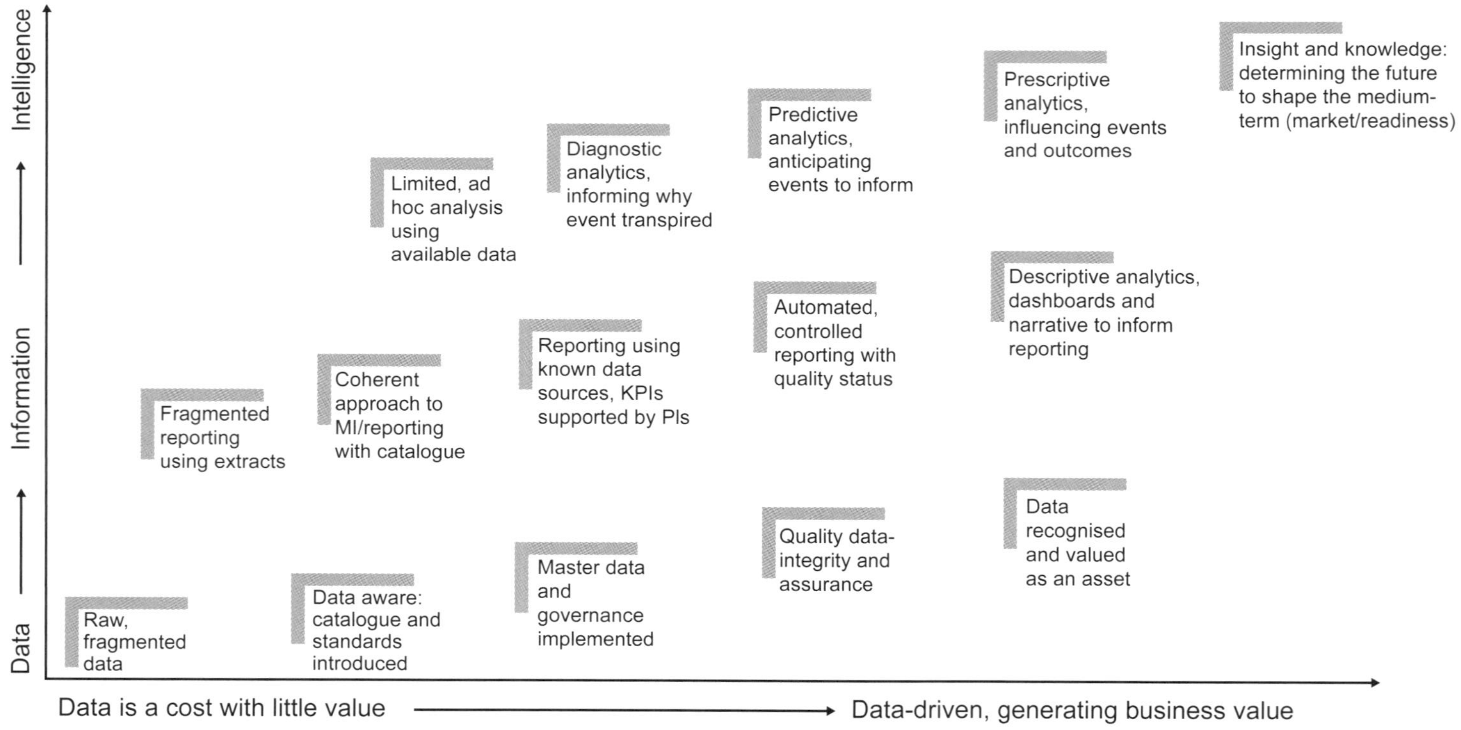

Data is a cost with little value → Data-driven, generating business value

words used to describe the content. It is an area where the analytical mindset has to converge with a creative partner to be able to describe, in whatever form it might take, how the series of interacting content blocks come together to deliver something recognisable and desirable to the wider organisation.

What is the risk of simply presenting the data strategy as a series of goals or statements of deliverables over a time period? To put it simply, unless you are in an organisation which is entirely data-driven or geared around data, most authors of a data strategy will discover that it is a hard 'sell' to be pushing any strategy, let alone one which is focused on data and its exploitation. An article in the *Journal of Management & Organization* in 2015[19] reported that an average of around 50 per cent of strategies fail, though it acknowledged that identifying failures in executing strategies is challenging.

The CLEAR acronym was provided earlier in this book to remind those embarking on data strategy definition of the essential building blocks to positioning the data strategy to ensure it remains relevant to all within the organisation. The challenge when structuring the content is to fit it to the CLEAR goals, with clarity and relevancy two of the key points to particularly bear in mind. If the final data strategy does not reflect the CLEAR principles, then you may find yourself making little progress despite devoting time and effort to it.

There are many ways the data strategy could be structured, and as with so many aspects of guiding the process of defining a data strategy, there is no 'one size fits all' solution. The maturity of the organisation, the drivers behind why a data strategy is being drafted in the first place, the sponsorship and wider alignment of the data strategy, not to mention the recognition of the need to change the organisation if the data strategy is likely to bear fruit, are all dependencies in the thinking required in approaching how to structure the strategy content. Nonetheless, there are some key principles to be considered.

Firstly, many strategies fail to reach execution because, in reality, they are not strategies at all.[20] This might sound obvious, but, as various studies have found, one of the commonest forms of failure is down to the strategy not being executable because it is an aspirational statement with no grounding on the rationale behind it or steps to achieve it. Therefore, do not fall into the trap of failing to set out your strategy, and remember to use CLEAR as a constant check.

Secondly, the strategy has to be relevant to all who are expected to read it, which should be a broad base across the organisation given that data touches all. It should be made accessible, interesting and informative – if the reader does not take something away with them having read the strategy, then nothing is going to change.

Thirdly, if the data strategy does not dovetail with the strategies already in place, especially the corporate strategy, then it is likely to be detached from the priorities of the wider organisation and therefore overlooked in terms of implementation.

---

19 Carlos J.F. Cândido and Sérgio P. Santos, Strategy Implementation: What Is the failure rate? *Journal of Management & Organization*, 21 (2), 237–262, 2015.

20 Freek Vermeulen, Many Strategies Fail Because They're Not Actually Strategies. *Harvard Business Review*. 2017.

Fourthly, and perhaps most alarming generally from a strategy perspective, a global study[21] conducted by Strategy&, the strategy consulting division of PwC, found only 8 per cent of company leaders were said to excel at both strategy and execution, with only 16 per cent said to excel at one or the other. Let me restate this, to reinforce the impact this is likely to have on what you are embarking on in defining and executing a data strategy – less than one in six company leaders excels at either strategy or its execution, yet you are about to embark on delivering both.

The task in getting the data strategy through the engagement and adoption phases to deliver benefits is one littered with failures in some of the largest organisations around the world. Do not underestimate the scale of the challenge, and consider wisely the choice of sponsor for the data strategy and those working with you to deliver it.

In making the data strategy accessible, interesting and informative, tell a compelling story. There are some great exponents of storytelling who can provide real insight into how to do this effectively, so I will keep it brief in this book and signpost for those who want to know more – hopefully, many of you, given how important this is to overcome the four hurdles above and more – to those who can provide the expertise in this critical area.

6.3.1 Strategy storytelling

The essence to devising a strategy story is to own it, by which I mean that you have to personalise your own understanding and develop the story to go with it. This is a collective effort, so if there are others who are part of the data strategy journey, they too must have the same level of understanding but, most importantly, be true to the story in telling it in their own way.

It may seem surprising to hear that personalisation is a key factor, as many will tell you to stick to a script and to avoid deviation from its core, but this is an artificial approach to enabling any leader to be true to themselves and their teams in retelling the story. Therefore it will be apparent to anyone who knows that leader that their story delivery is wooden or stilted, the words are not their own and they are fixated on the words to ensure they get every one of them delivered as written. It will be yet another corporate instruction to deliver this cascade and not to deviate from it, at which point it is hollow in its delivery and fools no one.

The essence is keeping the core messaging the same such that the key to it is retold time and time again, but each time with a delivery personalised to the individual giving it so it carries their passion and credibility to the audience.

Another aspect of storytelling the strategy is to balance the vision with reality. If the strategy is made to sound a walk in the park, then it is open to challenge on the basis of 'why haven't we done this already if it is so simple?' or 'is this truly aspirational or underplaying where we should be aiming for?'

---

21 Paul Leinwand, Cesare Mainardi and Art Kleiner, *Strategy That Works*. Boston, MA: Harvard Business Review Press, 2016.

In telling the story it is important to reflect on what could undermine the strategy or, at least, derail it in part, and you should be prepared to counter these potential points in advance of their being raised. In other words, demonstrate that there has been significant thinking that has gone into the strategy definition process and it has been challenged along the way. Reflect on what could go wrong, but also recognise that for those who have been in the organisation for some time there may be elements of revisiting past failures that those newer to the company (some of whom may have devised the strategy) are unaware of. By acknowledging that the strategy is going to tackle areas which may have failed previously but learn from the past, it recognises the history but importantly is embracing the future with experience behind the new approach.

There are different ways of delivering the strategy. One view is that the engagement of a larger audience in presenting and sharing the strategy is an effective way of bringing a collegiate mentality together, so all are immersed in the experience and get the opportunity to discuss, share anecdotes and views, and ultimately form a common bond and experience to take away a positive outlook to engage further.

There is also a view that the campfire approach, in which smaller groups gather to share the experience and participate in the discussion, is the way to go in building a strong bond and allegiances to take on to further groups. Successful engagement is likely to lead to informal discussions, whether gathered around the water cooler or coffee area or similar unofficial meeting spots, and if the data strategy programme team can participate in these in a relaxed way it helps bind people into the story through the sharing of updates, personal perspectives and anecdotes, bringing it to life.

In my experience, a blend of these approaches works, especially as some parts of the organisation may have more introverted or reflective personalities than others. Either way, it is a discussion, a story shared with contributions welcomed at an early stage, rather than a formulaic PowerPoint presentation with a tight script. These approaches can be supported by engagement groups, dropping into existing team meetings or other opportunities to keep the profile high, bearing in mind there is a need to have a story to tell and not all employees respond in the same way, so there may need to be some variation in trialling engagement.

The challenge with this is that the data strategy is fundamentally a document that needs to be supportive of the dissemination of it as a story. In that sense, the data strategy needs to provide the common core of a message to be delivered and so needs to read as such. If there is not a common core, then there is unlikely to be the level of consistency in the messaging required to keep everyone on board. However, the data strategy becomes the underpinning document that an audience can refer to having heard the delivery of the story rather than the story itself, as it is essential the audience relates to the data strategy content. You therefore need to work with your senior executive audience to frame the story based upon that core messaging and work with them until such time as they have fully bought into owning the data strategy. Achieve this, and you have a data strategy ready to navigate through the choppy waters where most strategies sink and can sail through to a successful implementation.

Further references on where to look for resources to help you shape your strategy story are in the bibliography.

6.3.2 Balancing vision and detail

There is always a temptation to provide more detail than is required – it is a flaw in so many data strategies that exist today, and one often a result of those most passionate about the subject being the author and so wishing to go a step further than is often needed. On the other hand, there are some data strategies in the public domain which are so light on detail that they are barely recognisable as strategies at all, rather falling foul of being visionary or aspirational statements with little grounding or foundation from which to build.

It is a tricky balance, but one which can be resolved by active engagement of a wider cross-section of those who know the audience and are able to advise in where best to pitch the content to make it land successfully. For credibility of the data strategy it needs to have sufficient basis to get agreement on where the starting point is, potentially a brief acknowledgement to some of the past that has led to that being the case, but is forward-focused with a positive message that sets a destiny and rationale. Throughout the drafting stage, iterate and review based on stakeholder feedback, utilising the connections to senior stakeholders to ensure they are aware that there is a data strategy coming, what it is shaping up to contain and how it aligns with the wider corporate goals. Do not forget to provide the means to develop a story from the core of the data strategy, so seek the opportunity to also gain a sense of how comfortable others are in how that story is shaping up to build understanding and familiarity.

As covered in the earlier chapters, remember that the audience for the data strategy is not those who are necessarily the architects of it. It must therefore be accessible and framed in a way that it aligns with the corporate strategy as a key enabler, so the linkage is obvious to all. A common failing is to expect the reader to make the links as if they are so obvious they do not need to be covered at all, when this is almost certainly not the case. Your stakeholders are likely to be busy, and if they have not seen a data strategy before may even disregard it as not relevant to them, unless the groundwork has been put in first to position it and then deliver on making it an essential read.

Be mindful as to what you are expecting to achieve. Those who are most effective at storytelling will paint a vision of where they are heading in a compelling way based upon providing the rationale for how this is achievable, so make sure that there is a vision of what the data strategy will enable that is markedly different at the end of its period, whether three, five or ten years (or any other variant). This is the core of the story, how it builds to gain buy-in to the series of objectives to be attained and how this impacts the organisation.

6.4 STRATEGY ALIGNMENT

I have referenced the need to align the existing strategies in the organisation with the data strategy, none more so than the corporate strategy which, if it has credibility within the organisation, will have a particular focus as it is likely to drive shareholder value and executive bonuses (for a private sector enterprise) as well as careers and credibility on being able to deliver on promises made. If you are seeking to make a data strategy a key partner in the strategies already at play in your organisation then you need to become a team player and align and acknowledge dependencies and, importantly, enablers in your data strategy to be embraced into the fold.

Clearly, the corporate strategy will be highly contextual and specific in nature to your organisation. It is therefore impossible to define how the data strategy might best be aligned, other than to give a few pointers as to areas you might like to consider incorporating into the data strategy.

6.4.1 Customer strategy

The nature of what constitutes a customer may differ markedly between organisations, and in some the notion of a customer may be rather more liberal than in others (for example, an individual or organisation being the recipient of services from a monopoly supplier – as may be the case in the public sector, or regulated industries). However, regardless of the type of organisation, what is common is that a service (or product) is provided in some shape or form to an end consumer, resulting in the customer having an experience which may be positive or negative, that creates a perception, regardless of the outcome. The degree of choice that the customer has may vary, and this may also lead to a difference in the quality of the experience based upon the resources or effort expended by the supplier.

It is essential that the data strategy recognises that it is performing a key role in enabling the organisation to manage its customer relationship more effectively, potentially resulting in a better customer experience. This may be through the provision of better MI to those making decisions to speed up the process, linking data together to provide a more holistic view of the customer, anticipating what the customer wants and tailoring a proposition accordingly; however this is achieved, data is at the heart of making it possible.

In addition, there will be a myriad of customer touchpoints with the organisation, and being able to capture these and ensure that the experience has been a positive one, learning from what engagement has taken place, is pivotal to enhancing the experience the next time. This involves capturing the data compliantly, linking it with other relevant data and turning this through analysis into meaningful insights that can be acted upon.

If improvements to the customer experience can be achieved through better-quality data, leading, in turn, to better-informed decisions, then the data strategy becomes a critical enabler to the corporate strategy.

6.4.2 Digital strategy

Increasingly, organisations are also developing digital strategies to enable customers to access services in an ever-expanding range of options and providing staff with the means to interact with customers through whatever channel is appropriate in a joined-up way. There is close alignment between the definition and implementation of digital capabilities and the data and analytics to underpin making these as effective as they can be. It would therefore be remiss not to link these two strategies if they both exist in the organisation, given the clear interdependencies. If new digital channels or capabilities are being implemented, then the data strategy should recognise the need to facilitate the support and data requirements necessary to make these work, in addition to determining how data can be extracted most effectively from new digital services to optimise analytics and so develop a better understanding of the customer.

6.4.3 Other strategies

Depending on the sophistication of the strategic planning capabilities in your organisation, there may be many other strategies that you may need to dock in with to align with the data strategy and identify opportunities to flag dependencies and enablers between the strategies. The following is a brief list, but is not necessarily exhaustive.

6.4.3.1 Marketing strategy

There will be significant demands for data and analytics support to a marketing strategy to deliver customer experience and determine key activities such as forecasting, pricing, channel strategies, targeting, optimisation strategies, customer propositions and next best activity for a customer, to name just a few. It is highly likely that a data and analytics capability will be working closely with marketing, given their dependency on data and analytics to drive engagement.

6.4.3.2 HR strategy

The relationship the organisation has with its own staff is directly related to data. Engagement of employees is directly correlated with customer satisfaction, and so it is probable that the HR team is a data-intensive environment to ensure its employees are being supported, managed and developed in a mutually beneficial way to drive optimisation from the HR budget and resources. This area has been a little behind in terms of the more sophisticated exploitation of data, focusing more on data capture and measurement historically, but this is certainly changing globally and becoming one of the functions with most to gain from becoming insight-led as the battle for talent in much of the world becomes more challenging.

6.4.3.3 Technology strategy

The organisation will almost certainly have some form of technology strategy given the constantly changing world of networking, hardware, software and IT consumables. The pace of change is moving faster, and lead times to change are now causing a degree of concern amongst the public as the nature of technological advances is seen to be potentially more invasive and discriminatory than at any time before.

In a 2019 survey conducted by Fujitsu,[22] 39 per cent of the UK public that were interviewed said they had less trust in organisations than they did five years ago, and a sizeable minority are resistant to adopting new technologies such as driverless cars, drone technology and cryptocurrencies. The same survey found that 58 per cent of business leaders had chosen not to adopt some technologies due to customer nervousness, citing data security perceptions and concerns about AI and quantum computing as two specific examples. Thirty-four per cent of leaders in manufacturing organisations highlighted employee resistance to technological change as their biggest concern.

22 Fujitsu, Driving a Trusted Future in a Radically Changing World. 2019. https://www.fujitsu.com/uk/imagesgig5/driving-a-trusted-future-research-report-uk.pdf.

The alignment between technology and data is obvious – one supports the other to capture data to be processed in operational environments and provides capabilities to exploit it – but the trend is increasingly converging, with AI, machine learning and data science increasingly utilising technological advances to drive data exploitation in more complex and sophisticated ways. The data strategy will therefore be both an enabler to the technology strategy and have dependencies on what it provides to manage and exploit data.

6.4.3.4 Finance, risk and compliance

There will be standards and policies in many organisations focused on finance – the risk approach and appetite and the compliance regime in which the organisation operates. There will be a data requirement to support these, but there will also be dependencies on the use of data to inform and shape approaches, and these will be either explicit in such standards and policies or specified in instructions to define processes and the use of data.

In addition, the compliance issues discussed in detail earlier in this book will need to be tracked via a data protection officer within your organisation, and evidence provided to demonstrate compliance and the processes underpinning this. This will also include adherence to the data privacy laws in those jurisdictions in which your organisation operates. The data strategy should reflect what is required to support finance, risk and compliance activities.

6.5 RELEVANCY IS KEY TO ENABLING EFFECTIVE ADOPTION

As highlighted in the CLEAR acronym in Chapter 2, it is essential to keep a strict focus on the audience for the data strategy. Chapter 4 also explained the need to compose the data strategy following the RAVE principles, and it is important to frame and define the content in as clear a way as possible to make the data strategy accessible to all. This combines the concept of storytelling with the need to focus on achieving the goals and waymarkers.

If there is one all too common a failing in data strategies, it is the temptation to make them too detailed through either straying into implementation activities or overplaying the content by providing too much information. The key is to recognise the level of information that needs to be imparted to make the data strategy coherent and likely to be endorsed, with as little information as is necessary to be able to make the point cogently. Brevity, and associated clarity in what needs to be achieved and why, is a winning formula in gaining senior executive sponsorship.

If you have followed the outline in this book so far, you will have ensured that your approach has been inclusive, iterative and tested along the way. This will provide an essential route to plotting the delicate balance between too little and too much information within the data strategy. It may sound obvious, but the reader will look at it through an individual lens, based upon their own perspective, role and personal experiences, and so no two individuals will arrive upon exactly the same interpretation of what the data strategy means – it is entirely contextual, based upon complexity that you will never be able to comprehend. Therefore, the data strategy has to be as clear and direct as possible. Remember, you want it to be endorsed, but more than that, to be the subject of campfire discussions across the organisation with the content being consistent, despite many flavours in how it is delivered.

So how do you ensure you strike the right balance?

There are several things you can do to ensure you are focused on what is needed to deliver a great data strategy.

6.5.1 Take on the implementation role

It may seem to contradict my advice throughout this book to this point, but take on the implementation role as you progress through the drafting stage. The acid test should be whether the data strategy is coherent enough to be picked up and delivered in the way you intended, recognising there will always be a degree of latitude required as events unfold and time informs what were assumptions made earlier.

It may be that you will be tasked with both the strategy definition and delivery phases, as is more than likely in smaller organisations with fewer resources to split these tasks apart. However, even if this is not the case, as the author of the data strategy you should be able to provide direction and consultation to those who do have implementation responsibilities. Therefore, you need to start to think about the practicalities of the implementation phase:

- What resources are you assuming will be devoted to implementation, both directly (coordinating the implementation activity) and indirectly (delivering or enabling parts of the strategy)?

- Is there funding required to deliver some elements of the strategy and, if so, is this secured, or linked in with another activity in which it is clearly understood and managed?

- What baseline have you used to start from, and has this been validated?

- What risks, assumptions, issues and dependencies (RAID) have you made, and are these documented?

- Who is sponsoring the implementation, and is that individual fully behind it, with the right governance in place to see it through?

- What authority has been delegated to you to drive this forward and to own the programme to drive the change?

- Have you provided clear evidence to underpin the baseline such that it could stand up to audit or other investigation should there be any queries raised through implementation?

- How front-end loaded is the implementation, and how is momentum from strategy approval to implementation maintained to keep up with the strategic objectives?

- How will progress be tracked and measured, to ensure there is clarity on how effective and successful the data strategy has proved to be?

- How will lessons learnt be captured through the implementation phase, such that the experience gained in delivery informs subsequent activity?

- What is the intent to keep the data strategy as a living document, rolling it forward a year at a time, and how will this be managed within the context of the implementation?

These questions represent only a small proportion of those likely to arise in the course of implementation, but they are a good starting point to challenge how thorough your data strategy is in being able to set a course for those tasked with implementation. Bear in mind my recommendation that the data strategy is kept relatively short, so inevitably it has to be high level, with sufficient guidance to lead those implementing it to know what was intended and the pace to be struck from the outset.

If you can challenge your own thinking through exercising a sufficient degree of distance and objectivity – easier to say than do – then swapping hats to consider how the above will be achieved is a valuable exercise to undertake as the data strategy begins to take shape. Invite others to do likewise who are involved in shaping the content, as it will inform their thinking and sharpen their content to frame it in a way that makes it clearer to implement.

6.5.2 Reflect on the waymarkers as guide rails

A key input to guide the implementation activity is the use of waymarkers through the data strategy. As discussed previously, the waymarkers serve as guide rails to inform the implementation and should not be a straightjacket to constrain decisions which need to be made at the time. However, the advantage of including waymarkers is the notion of pace, progress and delivery that they give to provide clarity and confidence in terms of outcomes, to both those signing off on the data strategy and those who implement it. Waymarkers also provide a means of assessing that the organisation has been able to maintain the assumed tempo that the data strategy has been devised upon.

As a result, there is significant importance in the clarity of the waymarkers to act as guide rails. If the waymarkers are unclear, it is likely that the data strategy will fail to maintain the rhythm required to deliver what it has stated due to a different interpretation or understanding. There is often a tendency to overstate the tempo rather than build in the contingency that will be required to accommodate other events or underestimation in the RAID timescales underpinning the data strategy.

Do review the waymarkers with a critical eye before finalising the draft data strategy, as they will almost certainly form the basis for the implementation plan and inform those who are leading the implementation as to what 'good' looks like to achieve delivery of the data strategy. Ask those who are providing input to the data strategy to review the waymarkers to ensure they are clear, in terms of specifics as to what is being delivered and the anticipated impact.

I would also recommend a review of the consistency of the waymarkers in terms of the links between those activities to be achieved (for instance, it would be a major oversight to have overlooked a critical dependency which comes via a later waymarker) and, in particular, the clarity of why those specific activities have been called out in the waymarker. It is likely that the rationale is the link between a corporate strategic objective and the data strategy, but it could also be a critical enabler which unblocks significant progress on a wider front across the data strategy.

Do make sure that the waymarkers are called out in a consistent way throughout the data strategy. It is often apparent that different hands have played a part in writing the data strategy and as a result the means to track progress (via waymarkers or any other recognition of what is to be delivered) is presented in different ways throughout, thus making it a challenge in its own right to piece together. If the waymarkers are to be successful, they need to be pulled through the text into either a specific section of the data strategy or as distinct elements of the content. This could be through a note at the end of each section, highlighting the waymarker in its own text box, for instance.

6.5.3 Develop your own story

As discussed earlier in this chapter, strategy storytelling will become a key part of the data strategy implementation. As the lead on the data strategy, you get to start the story, telling it in your own way to achieve the desired level of commitment through to approval. Start to develop your story with the team around you, the wider group you have consulted as SMEs in pulling together the data strategy content and those you work with closely who may not have been directly involved.

How you paint the picture of where the data strategy heads, its importance to the organisation and the vision of the future will all help shape understanding and advocacy. Test your story to see how it resonates with others and refine it based on feedback. Get others to play back their version of the story a day or two later, giving them time to reflect on what they heard. It will evolve, and you are not looking for repetition, rather that the message remains consistent at its core but is told in words that have meaning and commitment for that individual. We are aiming for individual storytelling of a common narrative: so long as the core remains true then it is achieving its purpose.

6.5.4 Steal with pride – learn from others who have delivered successful strategies

The task of devising a data strategy is a daunting one, especially if there is no precedent within your organisation. I am always surprised when I meet potential authors of a data strategy who have not looked at the evidence of others who have developed data strategies, as there are many accessible in the public domain via a basic internet search.

I structure my workshops to incorporate learning from others at the heart of the approach. It seems obvious to do this, but the value participants get from the experience of critiquing actual data strategies that are publicly accessible is the most useful part of those workshops. You should recognise that the process of developing a data strategy is broadly the same for anyone, regardless of the organisation or experience in doing so. For instance, we have the same activities to write about in our data strategies – we all undertake the basic premise of data capture, management and exploitation, albeit we do so in many different ways.

Therefore, the essence of the data strategy you are about to write should have commonalities with those you can access. Even better, those that are of a higher standard will also give you a sense of their baseline, culture and insight into their challenges – legacy data and/or system issues, proliferation of reporting leading to multiple versions of the same information, for example. Reflect on how you might construct your own review of a baseline to gain broad agreement as to where you are starting from.

If you are particularly impressed by a data strategy you come across, possibly one written a year or two ago, consider trying to reach out to the author to see how it has gone to learn from their experience. Many people welcome the opportunity to share experience, especially where it is proactively sought based on positive first impressions. However, tread carefully. As discussed in this book, most strategies fail to achieve a successful outcome, often falling at the implementation hurdle, so an impressive data strategy does not necessarily translate into a positive implementation story. Be prepared that this might be a sensitive topic, but if you can, learn from what prevented even the most favourably considered data strategy translating into delivery for that organisation, and apply your own approach.

6.5.5 Red team the final draft

A common practice in some organisations, and especially so amongst consultancy firms, is to 'red team' as you are approaching the completion of the final draft of your document. The practice is commonplace in procurement, security and military fields, but it can also be applied just as effectively to any situation in which a proposal is being delivered and there is a desire to test it as extensively as possible to ensure it can be enhanced to withstand the deepest scrutiny.

Creating a red team involves getting colleagues who have similar knowledge and expertise to those who would typically be faced with approving and also implementing the data strategy (though these could be run as two separate exercises, given the different nature of the challenge) to review the proposed final draft and provide as much challenge as they can to test those who have authored it on its content. This is meant to be an extensive process and one that is not to be undertaken lightly. Anyone chosen to participate on the red team is there to be as demanding as possible, with their goal to ensure they have left no stone unturned in trying to identify any weakness or oversight in the document.

This process can be a difficult one, so those who are there to represent the data strategy know they have to be ready for a challenging encounter in which they will feel grilled by those who are on the red team. However, it will ensure a better quality product which has higher integrity and clarity than if the data strategy were to be submitted without this input. It will also spot most of the likely errors and gaps in the data strategy that those who author the document perhaps miss, either through being too close to it or making an assumption that is not stated in the document.

If you have the means to take such an approach, it is a highly effective one to:

- improve the final draft before it is submitted for approval;
- identify the obvious weaknesses and bolster or change the draft prior to submission;

- highlight the way in which those who have to approve and/or implement the data strategy are likely to interpret it;

- give a sense of how ready the final draft is, to determine whether you are on track to meet the proposed submission date;

- clarify the take-away messages to ensure the priorities and tone of the data strategy set the implementation team on the right path;

- test the validity of the RAID and waymarkers to determine whether the basis for proceeding is correct and the tempo of delivery is realistic.

It is essential you prepare the team prior to the red team session. The whole point is to make it as challenging as possible to save time, reputation and credibility down the line. It is better to be put under this level of scrutiny in advance of publishing the data strategy than to find the issues later, when they are much harder to address and could call the whole basis of the data strategy into question.

6.6 TEN TO TAKE AWAY

In summary, the key points from this chapter are:

1. Always have someone within your team who can review the proposed content before a final review by an independent reviewer.

2. There are some common themes or topics you would typically expect to find in a data strategy: do consider whether you have got these covered in your approach.

3. The final data strategy is likely to be between 12 and 20 pages, but it is often easier to start with more and refine it to less than to aim for this from the outset.

4. Undertaking a data maturity assessment is an effective way to establish a common understanding of a baseline and to have a structured way to monitor progress. There are a number of models available that could be used.

5. Data governance, quality, integrity and standards are all essential components of data management, and so should be considered for inclusion in establishing your foundations.

6. Assessing capabilities within your organisation is important to identify any gaps which may hinder the implementation of the data strategy.

7. Strategy implementation is a high-risk activity; most fail. Therefore, be aware of the pitfalls and ensure you engage and communicate effectively with stakeholders. Strategy storytelling is a highly effective way to build understanding and momentum behind the data strategy as you transition into execution.

8. Strategy is visionary, so avoid too much detail. Align to other strategies within the organisation to make it coherent as to where the data strategy fits, particularly the corporate strategy.

9. Reflect on the implementation phase – the practicalities of funding, resources, responsibilities, sponsorship, timing, amongst others – to consider how the transition can be seamless. The data strategy, at the sign-off stage, should ensure these are known and agreed prior to implementation commencing.

10. Learn from other data strategies available in the public domain. These will help formulate your own thoughts as you determine the structure and content for your organisation, and review these in the context of the points in this book. You can learn a lot from doing some simple research in advance that can help guide your own approach.

7 COMMUNICATIONS, CULTURE AND CHANGE READINESS

'You can have brilliant ideas, but if you can't get them across, your ideas won't get you anywhere.'

Lee Iacocca[1]

Throughout the preceding chapters, reference has been made to the need to engage and manage stakeholders of all types through the data strategy definition process to ensure you have traction. This is essential to avoid developing the data strategy in a vacuum, the likely outcome of such a situation being confusion, resistance and ignorance of what the data strategy is, why it has been produced or where it fits in the wider purpose of the organisation. I have seen organisations where this has been the case, and it is not a good place in which to be – on the back foot, justifying your actions and the value the data strategy brings, defending why no one knew about it and a presumption that their teams have not been involved in its production.

Let's recap on some of the important ways that communication should have been managed throughout the data strategy definition phase before we get into readiness for the conclusion of drafting the data strategy, transitioning into formal sign-off.

In Chapter 2, the importance of understanding alignment to the corporate goals was addressed, highlighting the need to engage more widely with those who devised these and to explore how the data strategy should support the successful delivery of these goals. The concept of ownership of the data strategy was also explored, to understand the route to engage with those who are leaders in the organisation to get sponsorship and commitment to the data strategy at the right level. The CLEAR acronym highlighted the importance of stakeholder engagement as an integral part of leadership and to retain engagement with stakeholders to ensure relevancy.

Chapter 3 built on the scope and context of the data strategy to position it appropriately within the organisation and to frame how it contributes to, and is dependent on, other strategies and activities within the organisation. These need to be agreed with stakeholders so there is a clear mandate to operate that can open doors and also give credibility to your task.

Chapter 4 focused heavily on the role of stakeholders to ensure there is full under-standing of the stakeholder map you need to manage as you move ahead – those who contribute to the data strategy and are impacted by it need to buy in to the concept and approach, as well as those who will approve it. The PRIDE acronym acts as a good guide to ensure stakeholder management has been considered every step of the way to have a successful outcome and to review and iterate progress frequently.

---

1   *I Gotta Tell You: Speeches of Lee Iacocca*. Detroit, MI: Wayne State University Press, 1994.

Chapter 5 highlighted the role a route map needs to play in ensuring all parties are aligned and in agreement on the approach to be taken. It covered the need to keep the data strategy route map grounded, and to ensure that there is communication at all times to give confidence to those who will take the data strategy into implementation that they have got the right level of engagement with stakeholders from the outset.

Finally, Chapter 6 reviewed the need to balance ambition with keeping stakeholders onside in terms of relevance and being assured on feasibility in the delivery stage. The importance of clarity as to what the scope of the data strategy is, to avoid confusion or conflict with other activities, was outlined, whilst recognising the data strategy is not prescriptive in the detail needed to execute.

All of these steps are critical to have a high probability of a successful outcome when the data strategy is presented for approval and resources are assigned to commence implementation. This may sound like the end of the process, so what more could there possibly be to consider in communicating the data strategy in order to succeed?

In the first half of this book, I have sought to create a platform for you to be ready to succeed as you head to strategy implementation. It is a significant achievement if you have made it through to being ready to implement the data strategy, and I do not wish to diminish your success; many do not reach this point so you have already achieved what many others do not get to experience. Enjoy it. There has been a lot of effort in getting to this point and it is a time for recognition and reflection on how far you have come. However, we start to turn the corner from here, turning the strategy into reality through the implementation stage, and this is where the scale of shifting an entire organisation can become overwhelming without sufficient preparation to ensure you are ready for the next phase.

Before embarking on strategy implementation, communication needs to be providing a sound platform on which to build your drive to execute the data strategy. At this stage, the data strategy should be signed off, of course, so there will be a communication requirement to publicise this fact, recognise the sponsor and the programme lead, and the compelling reason why a data strategy is right for the organisation. This needs to recap the high-level points in the data strategy, so those who have not read it or been involved know what it entails, what it means for them and what the implementation approach will involve. You should use this as your reference point in the future, as it should act as a useful launch pad for your future activity.

This may be the first time you have implemented a strategy of any sort, or you may be an experienced hand at this who has plenty of scars to show from previous difficulties you have encountered in convincing those you work with that this is something they want to embrace. Either way, I hope to provide some steers as to what you might encounter, and how to be ready for it.

A big part of what lies ahead is navigating your way through the culture of the organisation, charting a course to a successful implementation programme. You will discover the change readiness of the organisation, and may have already established that either a lack of readiness or resistance to change will be a challenge that lies ahead in your preparation for implementation. There is a need to anticipate resistance and to engage proactively to find a way through it – your job is not to change the culture, but to work with it, find a way to embrace it and to ensure you are not be blocked or prevented from making progress in the implementation of the data strategy.

7.1 'CULTURE EATS STRATEGY FOR BREAKFAST'

Every organisation is different, and every function and every team are different within an organisation. It is fascinating to observe, as I have done through periods in my career delivering interim programmes in a variety of organisations, just how strong the 'local' culture can be and yet how intangible it is, as probably nothing will be documented to reflect that culture. Organisations have values, commitments, mission statements, visions and a plethora of other seemingly corporate messages that appear designed to say 'this is how it is round here', but the larger the organisation, the more fragmented and distanced these will often be in the reality of day-to-day operational activity.

Do not be surprised to find subtle differences in culture based upon location – even from one office to another in the same city – or function. A finance function will be very different in outlook, focus and therefore culture to a sales function, whilst an operations team will often be a tight unit focused on getting the job done with a distinct camaraderie compared to a marketing or other corporate support function that may be a group of experts and creatives who contribute as individuals to the team goal. Even subsidiaries within an organisation may be quite different, even though they may share branding, values and overall direction, simply because of history, product focus or their own perceived importance within the organisation. Certainly, investment banking arms of most financial institutions have historically felt very different places to their retail networks.

Most organisations would point towards a corporate culture – one that is enshrined in documents, intranets and items displayed prominently on office walls – to suggest that this is the culture of their organisation. In many cases, this passes for an aspiration, where the organisation aspires to be, but is likely unsure how to get the employees to fully buy in to this model. No matter how much training, reinforcement of messages from the top of the organisation or encouragement through the management chain, if it isn't what employees truly feel or recognise as their culture, then it is a false premise to base any expectation on a forced model of culture.

As a result, the corporate culture operates at a different level to the 'way we do things round here' culture, which is about established (but undocumented) norms and practices that have evolved and become established through habits, behaviours and precedence. The concept of having to 'fit in' with those around you leads to most people acquiescing to become part of the group, a tribal instinct to be accepted and not to stand out or challenge authority within the group.

> In the 2015 Deloitte Global Human Capital Trends report,[2] 87 per cent of leaders stated culture and employee engagement as a top organisational issue. This is regularly at the top of the stated reasons for programmatic failures worldwide, yet culture gets only a small fraction of the attention or resource needed to set about addressing this fundamental issue for virtually all organisations. It is the reason that there is a real need to address this when you embark on your challenge to define

2   Deloitte Global Human Capital Trends Report. 2015. https://www2.deloitte.com/content/dam/Deloitte/tr/Documents/human-capital/GlobalHumanCapitalTrends2015.pdf.

and implement a data strategy in your organisation. Do not be another statistic, caught by the culture and norms bear-trap that seems to engulf most programmes and strategic goals from realising more than a fraction of benefits, if any at all.

The importance of understanding both the corporate culture and the local norms in the teams you deal with cannot be overstated. This will make or break your strategy implementation, regardless of the level of support you have within parts of the organisation or the mandate you have to make it happen.

To illustrate the magnitude of failing to comprehend the pivotal role corporate culture and local norms take, I want to highlight how this can bring some of the most high profile of business activities to a disastrous outcome.

In 2005 two of the major telecommunications firms in the United States – Sprint and Nextel – merged, at a cost of $35 billion, fully integrating the technology and operations of the two organisations. Nextel had an entrepreneurial and aggressive operational style which conflicted with Sprint's top-down bureaucratic operational approach. The two cultures were fundamentally opposed, and yet this had not been factored in effectively to the merger implementation, resulting in the executives of the newly forged company being at odds and resenting their counterparts.[3] Within three years, Sprint Nextel announced a $29.7 billion write-down related to the merger. By 2010 Bloomberg ranked the Sprint Nextel merger as the third worst for shareholder value out of 100 of the biggest takeovers since 2005.

From the outset, there were clear differences. In December 2004, shortly after the merger was announced, the Nextel CEO, dressed down, had delivered a rallying cry to his managers which drew cheers when he declared 'Let's go stick it to Verizon.' He then introduced the Sprint CEO, attired in a suit, who delivered his expectations for the newly merged company via a PowerPoint presentation to a silent audience.

Mistrust grew due to the different styles of leadership, autonomy of decision making versus escalation at regular points, and it finally worsened through the inevitable competition for jobs between the two workforces as economies through de-duplicating posts dragged on. Nearly three years on, it was found that Sprint staff still socialised separately from those Nextel employees in the same location. Such is the divide in the corporate cultures and no one anticipated or sought to address it from the outset.

I have highlighted this case study not because the Sprint Nextel merger is a data strategy example, but to illustrate how important being aware of the corporate culture and local norms to ensure success. This was a merger which had been worked on at various levels within both organisations for some time, had both CEOs directly engaged, was one of the biggest mergers of the time but was clearly disastrous for both parties from early on.

---

3   K. Hart, No Cultural Merger At Sprint Nextel. *Washington Post*, 24 November 2007. www.washingtonpost.com/wp-dyn/content/article/2007/11/23/AR2007112301588_2.html.

So, what can be learnt from the case study above – one of the biggest failings in recent times in merging two large organisations? The corporate culture you are going to engage with will be prepared for the theory of what has been proposed, having been involved and party to the formulation of the data strategy as outlined through the preceding chapters. However, think about the stakeholder groups you are about to encounter and, in particular, their 'local' culture and the way in which they manage and exploit data. Use the network of contacts you have established throughout the data strategy definition process to gauge resistance to the future implementation and capture thoughts as to how to engage the audience – it will differ, depending on the function, leadership and nature of work undertaken, so do not rely on a 'one size fits all' communications strategy.

In my own experience, bringing together organisations is especially challenging. There are a number of things which are inevitably difficult to work through – duplication of senior roles, integration of teams, closure of offices, potential rationalisation of brands – but the biggest issue is the inherent cultures of those organisations and trying to integrate these.

In one instance, an organisation that had a strong process culture with a focus on investing in technology and people was acquired by a rival that had a low-cost approach and lesser systems and processes in place. Whilst the former had a stronger base from which to build and a workforce that was engaged in utilising the processes and systems, it was the low-cost acquirer that drove the way forward, such that the culture of that organisation pervaded in the enlarged organisation. This had a detrimental impact on data and its quality as the lack of process, historic asset data capture and systems integration led to the gains made in the acquired organisation being lost.

In another case, a subsidiary of an organisation that was acquired had recently invested in data and an outsourced technology solution that cemented its market leading position and provided a platform on which to move forward. The company making the acquisition had a rival solution, but one which had been discounted through the procurement exercise. The cultures of the organisations were rather different, due to scale and size, but the acquisition worked due to the initial period being relatively stable and both organisations remaining relatively unchanged. Over time, this would change, but it enabled the change to be more transitional, so that there was a gradual acceptance of how the cultures were realigned.

The quote used for this section of the book is attributed to Peter Drucker[4] and was used by Mark Fields, President of the Ford Motor Company, who had it on a wall in a conference room and further added: 'You can have the best plan in the world, and if the culture isn't going to let it happen, it's going to die on the vine.' People are now more aware of the impact of culture than ever before, though the subsequent limitations in

---

4   Though one of the most used quotes linking culture and strategy, there seems to be no evidence of Peter Drucker making this statement, and it was certainly used in a Giga Information Group headline in 2000, though the source remains uncertain.

strategies of all kinds fulfilling their potential demonstrates limited understanding of how to address it.

So, does culture eat strategy for breakfast? It does if you are not prepared for it, and find yourself on the plate rather than cooking the breakfast. However, there are ways to navigate around culture in your data strategy implementation, and some of these will be adaptable to your own organisation and the circumstances you find yourself in. There is more on culture later in this chapter.

Do not underestimate the challenge that culture will pose, ensure you have undertaken the appropriate preparation and be aware of the pitfalls to navigate your way around them.

7.2 BARRIERS TO CHANGE

The natural reaction of people is to resist and challenge change, often due to the element of familiarity, knowing what the way of doing things is, even if those approaches are not universally liked. Put this into a team environment and it multiplies, with many unwilling to subject their colleagues to the sort of upheaval many associate with change. It is also a fact that most organisations handle change ineffectively, which leads to either failure or suboptimal outcomes and a legacy of poorly initiated change due to it not being fully implemented as intended.

Resistance to change is not a new concept. Lawrence identified failing to understand resistance as a cause of failure in change programmes as long ago as 1969.[5] Yet, numerous reports over the last decade or so have consistently found around a 40–60 per cent failure rate in change programmes, with resistance to change consistently one of the top reasons given. In the 2016 Deloitte Global Human Capital Trends report,[6] only 19 per cent of respondents believed they had the 'right' culture to be able to adapt to or embrace change, which demonstrates that resistance to change, from a cultural perspective, is something that you should be prepared for. I would strongly recommend that you anticipate, and prepare for, such resistance if you are to get traction when introducing change in your organisation.

The forms of resistance to change will vary depending on the history of your organisation and its experience of seeking to implement change. We all dislike change – how many people tend to take the same route or train/bus to work, for instance, rather than a variety of routes or options to mix it up? – but the reasons are deeply embedded.

Resistance to change can be identified in a number of ways, and I have highlighted one of these from Zaltman and Duncan, which is structured on four commonly cited types of resistance, and dates back to 1977:[7]

---

5   P.R. Lawrence, How to Deal with Resistance to Change. *Harvard Business Review*, 1 January 1969.

6   Deloitte Global Human Capital Trends Report. 2016. https://www2.deloitte.com/content/dam/Deloitte/global/Documents/HumanCapital/gx-dup-global-human-capital-trends-2016.pdf.

7   G. Zaltman and R. Duncan, *Strategies for Planned Change.* New York: Wiley, 1977.

- organisation;
- culture;
- psychological;
- social.

7.2.1 Organisation

There are a series of organisational constraints to effective change being adopted that can prevent progress either individually or collectively. It is often the notion of power, or influence, which can give rise to a feeling of being threatened by the change that is proposed and will be exacerbated if the individual does not believe they have been fully engaged. Perceived lack of engagement can drive a negative response due to resentment or confusion as to why the individual has not been directly involved when others are. It can also apply the other way round, with those given influence seen to be exerting too much power over those without, leading to a level of resentment.

In many organisations, much of the workforce has low information literacy skills. They may have been given various software tools and expected to use them, but training may not have been provided to them in seeing data as anything other than a commodity – something you enter into a system simply to get a job done and move on. The lack of information literacy is something which holds back most organisations today, and is in danger of being the most divisive element of bold statements about seeking to become data-driven, evidence-based, insight-led or any other such term in popular use in the corporate world today. It needs to be part of your data strategy, either implicitly or explicitly depending on your organisation. I have found it refreshing to see information literacy skills increase in an organisation, through provision of the right training and support to staff across functions, and the power that such a multiplier has to move deriving information from data away from the domain of a handful of specialists.

There is a complex web of reasons as to why low information literacy is one of the biggest challenges in organisations today. For someone presenting a detailed Excel spreadsheet in many organisations today, there may still be a sense of that person being a 'data nerd' because they've successfully manipulated data, despite Excel probably being a core software product on every PC in the organisation. Earmarking those who are comfortable with data in this way makes it acceptable for those who are not in that group to feel mainstream, and that this somehow relieves them of the onus of doing something similar.

The rise of more software being made available to staff across the organisation is democratising data and empowering those able to learn to use these tools to exploit it for themselves. BI tools are becoming almost as common as Excel in organisations, and the expectation is shifting to people to be familiar with dashboards, visualisations and reports as a standard part of their role.

This breeds uncertainty and a perceived threat, and it may start to make junior staff more aware of key trends and issues than perhaps are those in senior roles themselves. It is the switch from knowledge by experience, in which time served and career progression equated to power within the organisation, to a democratised workforce that is able to derive information for itself and potentially be better informed. This makes some senior leaders feel threatened, challenged by those more familiar with exploiting data. Ironically, the solution is to be able to harness this, for making data-driven decisions at the relevant level leads to a better outcome much faster, which in turn reflects well on the senior leader.

The structure of the organisation can also be a barrier, either reinforcing silos or, conversely, forcing people to work together across the organisation from disparate parts, without having established trust and understanding in the working relations to make this an effective solution.

If there is a feeling that the organisation is imposing change top-down, but those at the top are not seen to be actively embracing it, then resentment can arise which is due to those implementing the change not being seen to act accordingly. Leading by doing what you expect of others is an important principle.

The climate for change is an important factor to be considered. If the rationale for change has not been clearly articulated and bought into by the whole organisation, then inevitably there will be resistance. It is essential to articulate clearly the need for change. It may not gain agreement in all parts of the organisation, but setting out the rationale enables people to understand the reason the organisation has chosen to embark on change. This has to be accompanied by an openness to change, clearly demonstrating at all levels that the organisation is committed to the change rather than being seen to say one thing but do another. The potential for change is about reaching agreement on the scale and scope of change required to deliver the end result. There is a fine line between ambition and realism of what can be achieved that needs to be fully appreciated to take people with the programme.

Lastly, the opportunity for technological change is often more challenging than it might at first appear. The appetite of the whole organisation to understand, accept and adopt technology universally is not always there – regardless of whether the systems are a fit for purpose – and a patchy adoption will usually cause more issues than failing to adopt at all. The resistance in this area may be a lack of understanding as to how the technology is to be used, a desire to stick with what was known and understood, or a lack of appreciation as to why the organisation needs to innovate. All of these can be overcome, but it does take concerted planning and effort.

7.2.2 Culture

The cultural challenge has been partly covered already within this chapter. There are typically four categories of cultural barriers:

- values and beliefs;
- cultural ethnocentrism;

- impact of change on the individual;
- cultural norms.

Values and beliefs can be exceedingly broad, encompassing everything from religious to secular, motivation and aspiration, as well as pride, which can take on a variety of forms. These tend to be very personal, not necessarily stated, but drive behaviours and establish individual norms which influence tolerance, acceptance and a collective response. These need to be understood to a degree, and the cultural journey should be navigated in an explorative manner that seeks to deliver change in a way which is least challenging to the individual, whilst recognising that there has to be a level of uniformity of approach in the spirit of fairness.

Cultural ethnocentrism can take many forms and is a highly divisive position, and so one to try to avoid at all costs. It can be stated as simply as 'our way is better than yours' and may be based on any number of different characteristics, from race, gender or religion through to socio-economic status, regional difference or the seniority within an organisation. It is important to consider how information is presented and the representation of groups throughout the change, involving or consulting with as wide a range of stakeholders as possible to avoid such conflict arising.

Change may be taken personally, almost as an assault on an individual perceiving that what they do is not good enough, when it might simply be a case of the new approach being better rather than the current method being flawed in any way. This may lead to defensiveness on the part of an influential individual, who wants to save face rather than be undermined in front of their peers or team. Of course, there is also the potential that the change may expose the failings of previous approaches and highlight weaknesses that the individual who seeks to save face should have spotted much earlier. This may indicate that the team is not well led or the influencer, perhaps a manager, has been coasting along rather than performing at a level to be expected. A root-cause analysis, for example, would almost certainly flush out such limitations. Therefore, it is necessary to be engaging in the adoption of the new approach, avoiding anything which suggests criticism of what preceded it, and to potentially give the individual or individuals who may be resistant an opportunity to champion the change and hence advocate others to follow.

Finally, implementing a change which conflicts with cultural norms is the biggest challenge of all. The change may be compelling, for all the right reasons, for the organisation as a whole, but may have a significant impact on the way a particular part of the organisation operates and breaks established norms. Even if those impacted recognise the wider benefit, it can be hard for them to accept the shift it requires, and it may require a significant sweetener to get those impacted to agree to the change. The change is likely to have to be compelling, such that there is a clear rationale for it to be for the good of the organisation, leading to the group affected recognising it is impractical for it to block the wider good.

7.2.3 Psychological

Psychological barriers can be particularly challenging, as they reside within individuals and may be deeply engrained. The challenge in overcoming these is to aim for a neutral position as a starting point to move the individuals into a space from which they can see positives. Often, trying to unpick the psychological barriers an individual might have in one go is just as likely to reinforce their resistance, as it is too big a step for many to contemplate and is reinforced by confirmation bias.

Perception is a common psychological barrier, operating in a number of ways. The individual may choose to be selective in what information is taken from a change to be able to focus on the negatives and dismiss the positives from their mind. This exacerbates the problem, as there is nothing constructive to build from and it reinforces the reasoning of the individual to resist the change. Perception may also result in two individuals having very different perspectives of the underlying problem, and be irreconcilable in reaching agreement on where the focus for change needs to be. Similarly, the perception may simply be down to interpretation, with two differing views taken as to what is to be achieved and why, leading to a confused and frustrating barrier to overcome. Finally, perception may be driven by the perceived favouritism of one person over another, without any understanding or clarification being provided.

There may be a feeling of deep comfort in the status quo, known as homeostasis. This may lead to the sort of inertia that makes it difficult to shift whole groups of people who do not want to change. Finding common ground, in which a level of comfort is maintained whilst adapting to elements of change, may be the best course to strike a conciliatory balance, although this may hinder the pace of change and may not be practicable.

The resistance to change may arise where there is a perception the change is undermining conformity – the way a profession may typically operate regardless of organisation, for example. This may be true: it may be that you are moving people along faster than they see other organisations with the same type of professionals moving – after all, change has to start somewhere! This doesn't necessarily mean that the change is wrong, but you need to recognise that it is breaking new ground and try to develop it with active engagement of those directly involved, otherwise you will find commitment levels drop and inertia retaining much of what you sought to replace.

The last psychological barrier is personality traits, and these can present an obstacle if they are in direct conflict with how the organisation is seeking to operate in the future. Rather like the earlier barriers which can cause an individual to fail to see the need to change, this one can be hard to shift other than to impose, especially if the change is driven by the traits being non-compliant or not acceptable in some way. It can be as hard as forcing individuals to accept whether the 'new' ways of working are for them, and it can be the prompt that leads to some individuals choosing to leave the organisation.

7.2.4 Social

Rather like personality traits, some of the social barriers to change can be deep rooted, albeit more as a collective than the psychological, which tend to be focused on the individual.

In some cases, group solidarity will be a collective force to resist change prompted by concerns over how members of that group will be affected. It is a difficult one to overcome unless you are willing to be open and engage the group and listen to their concerns. Focusing the effort on the specific concerns, rather than trying to answer a range of potential issues which are broader, enables progress to be made by channelling the resolution on those things that matter and demonstrating a listen, learn and act culture. Resistance may remain, but at a significantly reduced level, and you will have established a line of communication to the group, which is invaluable as a route to gauge response as you go.

The group you encounter may be very close and resistant to outsiders coming in to tell them how things are going to change, and for the better. This barrier is put up by a guild type of mentality in which no one outside the group understands what we do or how we do it, and hence has no place to preach change at us. The best way to approach this situation is to identify a way into the group to get representation and input into the design work you undertake ahead of implementation, and actively seek to engage on the basis of learning to be better informed. Finding a trusted insider to be willing to engage may prove challenging, but highly influential.

As highlighted earlier, conformity to norms is a characteristic of a tight-knit group. Understanding and being willing to comply with the established norms brings acceptance and kinship within the group, and it is hard to operate in many work environments whilst being an outsider. Challenging norms is a direct assault on the group, and it would be unwise to do so unless you are certain of your ground. As with most group situations, it is more effective to listen, learn and act based upon a greater understanding. An appreciation of the norms and the history that has led to their evolution will make it easier to comprehend how the change can best be implemented to accommodate or modify the norms rather than challenge them head on, with an awareness of how inflexible they might be.

There may be direct conflict between groups which has been simmering for some time or arisen recently due to a breakdown in cooperation or a feeling of a lack of understanding. Depending on how deep this goes, it may be impossible to reconcile the groups and you should identify how far you need to reach a common understanding to be able to proceed with your change. Operating in a form of neutrality, in which you can negotiate with both parties without undermining your own credibility, will put you in a position to find common ground that enables your change to proceed without being mired in the conflict yourself.

Finally, there is also a risk of group introspection in the way the group fail to see any need for change and are in denial that there is any flaw with their current approach. This may seem strange, even alarming, for an outsider trying to drive change and who believes that the evidence is compelling. However, without gaining trust and agreement to a need for change it is highly likely that this group will subvert any change by refusing to adopt new ways of working. It is imperative in such cases to bring someone who is sufficiently trusted by the group into an early discussion, as well as one from within the group who has credibility with their peers, and to work through the rationale as to why change is needed and the benefits of introducing the change. The combined impact of these two will provide the conviction and direction to the others, making it easier for you to achieve your goals.

7.2.5 Overcoming resistance to change

The US-based change management consultancy Prosci ran a webinar and captured eight categories of individual resistance to change from 350 responses.[8] These give a sense of the range of emotional constraints and fears you will need to overcome in the data strategy implementation:

- **Emotion** – Fear, loss, sadness, anger, anxiety, frustration, depression, focus on self.

- **Disengagement** – Silence, ignoring communications, indifference, apathy, low morale.

- **Work impact** – Reduced productivity/efficiency, non-compliance, absenteeism, mistakes.

- **Acting out** – Conflict, arguments, sabotage; overbearing, aggressive or passive-aggressive behavior.

- **Negativity** – Rumors/gossip, miscommunication, complaining, focus on problems, celebrating failure.

- **Avoidance** – Ignoring the change, reverting to old behaviours, workarounds, abdicating responsibilities.

- **Building barriers** – Excuses, counterapproaches, recruiting dissenters, secrecy, breakdown in trust.

- **Controlling** – Asking lots of questions, influencing outcomes, defending current state, using status.

There are a number of approaches to managing resistance to change. One of the oldest, and most widely used to this day, is a simple three-step process (unfreezing, changing and refreezing, discussed below) devised by Kurt Lewin[9] to navigate through the change process. It was created in 1947, which shows you how long organisational resistance to change has been with us and scholars have been researching to find answers, so do not think this is a new concept. This is why it is so important you are prepared to encounter resistance to change and know what to do when you identify it.

Lewin's change model forms a useful prompt to guide you through the process from start to finish, and has a simplicity about it that is easy to remember and follow. A key part of the theory is the refreezing stage (originally called freezing by Lewin), often referred to as 'making it stick'. The steps reinforce what the preceding chapters of this book and the next two chapters discuss, ensuring there is a consistent and clear approach every step of the way, but the concept of unfreeze and refreeze is a great way to think about the change you are seeking to achieve through the data strategy and its implementation.

The premise of the theory was, quite simply, to understand the rationale for change, to establish motivation for change to be generated before change can occur. This

---

8   Prosci Inc webinar. https://www.prosci.com/resources/articles/managing-resistance-to-change.

9   K. Lewin, Frontiers in Group Dynamics: Concept, Method and Reality in Social Science; Social Equilibria and Social Change – Understanding the Three Stages of Change. *Human Relations*, 1 (1–2), 5–41, 1947.

forms the initial stage, known as unfreezing, as it involves developing a compelling message as to why change is necessary. It is often the most challenging stage as it confronts convention, assessing beliefs, values, attitudes, behaviours and other aspects of the status quo that everyone is familiar with and might find comfortable, even it is recognised that it is not optimal. Unless change is seen to be needed, there will be continued resistance or, at best, passivity that leads to stagnation. There is a need to unfreeze in order to be able to progress.

Once uncertainty has been created through the unfreezing stage, the next stage is change. This is where uncertainty starts to bring a new clarity and a willingness to embrace an approach to set a new direction and participate proactively in change. This is what is sometimes referred to as the change curve, a means of bringing people with you on the journey to a new outcome. This stage is also where change becomes personal – what is in it for the individual to support this?

> The Herzberg model[10] of motivational behaviours is an interesting perspective on what motivates people and what the hygiene factors are that must be right but are not, in themselves, motivational.

The change stage requires communication, time and clarity of direction to demonstrate the benefits, and may take considerable effort, energy and commitment to navigate.

Finally, the refreezing (or freezing) stage. This is the final step in mobilising the changes once the commitment of the whole organisation is in place, and is essential to bake in the changes, otherwise there is a risk of reversion to old practices or a fragmented series of interpretations that lead to confusion and disarray in implementation. The impact is a zero-tolerance approach to diverging from the new norm, and evidence through measurement of the positive outcome of the changes made.

Bear in mind that resistance to change may appear at any time, at any stage. Whilst you can endeavour to try to address it from the outset, it is inevitable that there will be periodic concerns and misunderstandings as you go through implementation. It is essential to have tracking of resistance as a key strand of the communications activity, and the earlier it is picked up the greater the chance of resolving it quickly. Put in place a communications and continuity plan to ensure that there are ways you can mobilise to address any resistance early and locally to prevent it spreading further.

7.3 SPONSORSHIP

The preceding chapters have addressed the importance of gaining active sponsorship of the data strategy, which needs to be in place not only for the data strategy definition stage but also into implementation, as executive sponsorship will be key to getting

---

10 F. Herzberg, B. Mausner and B. Block Snyderman, B. *The Motivation To Work*, 2nd edn. New York: John Wiley, 1959.

organisation-wide traction. I want to explore the role of the sponsor and, in particular, the communication support you are likely to require from the sponsor.

You may not have any say in the choice of sponsor when embarking on the data strategy and seeking to gain executive-level support. There are often options as to who could perform this role, given data transcends functions, and assuming there is not a CDO (or similar) at board level in your organisation. There is also an element of the right sponsor being determined by the maturity of the organisation from a data perspective, as well as being the individual with most to gain and/or being most enthused about what you are seeking to achieve.

The key responsibilities of a sponsor are, broadly:

- Set clear direction and ensure there is clarity on the fit with the corporate strategy and direction to move the organisation forward.

- Ensure the programme to define and then implement the data strategy is effectively resourced and funded.

- Oversee that the programme is delivered to time, budget and agreed scope, prioritising where necessary to adapt or change through appropriate governance.

- Provide challenge to the programme as appropriate to ensure it remains on track and the focus is maintained, whilst keeping momentum and maintaining enthusiasm within the programme.

- Communicate, both within the programme and to external stakeholders, on high-level progress and priorities to ensure all are aware of the programme status and expectations to maintain progress.

- Be an executive champion and advocate of the programme to ensure its purpose is fully understood, commitment is maintained and visibility is retained; be prepared to hold difficult discussions with peers if obstacles cannot be overcome at the programme delivery level; be able to tailor communication and delivery style to each stakeholder that needs to be engaged and support the programme.

The sponsor needs to be slightly detached from the day-to-day delivery of the programme. In most cases, those leading the programme tend to have a strong functional reporting line to the sponsor, though many in the field of programme management would strongly recommend against this. They would suggest more of a contractual arrangement, in which the individual who leads on the definition and delivery has discretion to make day-to-day decisions and autonomy in the way the programme is run, and agrees how communication between the two will operate. This could be progress reports, a run through the risk matrix (see Chapter 9 for more information on risk management), or an escalation process with agreement on what the nature of things to escalate might be and when would be appropriate. There may be a temporary and more flexible reporting line, but it is entirely based on the programme itself rather than having to be from the area of the organisation that the sponsor represents.

There should also be agreement from the outset as to the frequency of meetings between the sponsor and the data strategy lead. It is essential that a sponsor gives you (whether you are managing the data strategy through definition and implementation, or just one phase of the overall end-to-end process) the space to operate and avoid getting too involved in the detail, otherwise it makes it difficult to lead the team around the task without being undermined in terms of decision making. This is a recipe for failure, as it will almost certainly diminish the value that the sponsor should be adding through peer networking and by providing direction, and limit the effectiveness of the team delivering the data strategy or its implementation through delays, confusion and, ultimately, the impact on morale.

One aspect of sponsorship to be wary of, however, is that in many large organisations all major programmes (and strategy would be one of those) have to have an executive sponsor. This can lead to senior executives sponsoring far more programmes than they have time to devote to them to support them effectively. If this sounds like your organisation, you need to find a way to ensure you make the demands on your sponsor as light, but effective, as possible to optimise the value you gain from their sponsorship. This is something you need to address up front, at the start of the engagement with the sponsor, and a well-organised programme is more likely to gain favour and effective input than one which is floundering and lacking clarity to make the best use of the executive sponsor.

Being clear, from the outset, what you can bring to make the life of the sponsor more focused on those aspects which you are not equipped to do on your own will be appreciated by your sponsor. You should seek guidance from your sponsor as to the time likely to be available to support your programme, which facilitates a discussion on how best this can be utilised to benefit you and the programme of work, and how they would like to check in on progress – reports, meetings and the like.

Depending on the type of organisation, you may wish to look at an extended network of executives to support or enhance the role of the sponsor. There may be other influencers – potentially at various levels in the organisation – that could be worth exploring to maximise the likelihood of success. For instance, if you have non-executive directors in your organisation, finding someone with a keen interest in strategy and/or data might be a good avenue to bring a different perspective to the executive board. It may be that there is someone who exerts greater influence than others in bringing members of the executive board together, who is seen to have a good eye for strategic decisions or to be simply a particularly effective communicator. This is not to undermine the sponsor, or to fragment accountability, but to widen channels of communication and engagement to assist the sponsor to drive the strategy.

Do not assume the obvious candidate to sponsor the data strategy is the right one. Understand as much as you can of the organisational politics and interests of the executive board, and test out your assumptions through the data strategy exploration stage before identifying your sponsor. Bear in mind too that a board member may not see the data strategy through definition and the implementation programme – this could be four years, for instance – before moving on, so do not put all the proverbial data eggs in the one basket. Ensure there is wider commitment at board level, to ensure continuity should there need to be a change of sponsor.

7.4 ORGANISATIONAL MATURITY

The maturity of the organisation is a major factor in how you structure the communications effort that will be an essential lever in getting your message across to the organisation throughout the data strategy process – from definition to execution. It is important that you assess and review the perception of the organisation's maturity, as this will be one of the bigger measures of success – how far you have you moved the dial in terms of organisational maturity.

The challenge you face will depend on the understanding and readiness of the organisation to embrace what you are seeking to achieve through the data strategy. If the organisational maturity is low, then there is a need to communicate progress in a way that is not only informative but also educational to provide the detail as to the difference it makes. By contrast, a more mature organisation may understand what is being described and just need the context of what it means by way of impact to help the organisation.

There are formal models to enable you to assess organisational maturity which look at benchmarks for process, quality, collaboration, knowledge, training and development, and change, amongst other things, depending on which model you choose to deploy. However, for the purposes of the data strategy, the requirement is less detailed and more based on the appetite and awareness of the organisation to embrace the data strategy. It can be, therefore, a more broad-brush assessment to determine how to pitch the activities you will undertake to ensure you get collaboration and appropriate engagement to achieve the outcome you are seeking.

You need to consider the purpose of the organisational maturity assessment. The data strategy will look at the data maturity assessment, which will give you an effective barometer of where the organisation sits and aspires to be. The focus of the organisational maturity assessment is based more on how to drive an engaged response through the communications you provide and where to pitch the materials so they land positively. Therefore, it is essential that you determine how communications can become a key enabler in maintaining engagement and visibility of the data strategy from its inception through to its implementation, and work for you to build interest and cooperation.

The organisation may have a formal corporate communications capability, in which case the data strategy implementation needs to be captured in their communications activity. The impact of communications needs to be considered in the widest of contexts too, as the data strategy itself may be seen to be a bit dry for those who are not necessarily able to link it to the impact it can and will have on the organisation. Therefore, you need to look for every opportunity to link in to the planned communications activity already being scoped, as well as that which lies ahead, to try to identify a way to weave in some core messaging about the impact the data strategy implementation will have on those activities in the future and how to get involved and/or learn more about the programme.

Integrating your messages into those which come from a wider range of programmes and senior leaders, and which have interest to a wider audience than you might be able to reach if creating a message focused solely on the data strategy implementation, will increase awareness and understanding. It will also link the core message, being delivered by someone elsewhere in the organisation, to your own, which will make it inherently endorsed by that individual.

The approach to communications may also indicate the maturity of the organisation and, indeed, how you can use communications to your advantage. In most organisations, communications is a team or function in its own right, or a dedicated communications team member is embedded in another function, such as HR, marketing or operations. The scale of the communications capability in the organisation will be indicative of the central coordination of a communications strategy that will have its own goals and programme attached to it. If your organisation has a minimal communications presence, your first task is to identify how information is communicated within your organisation. What is your own experience of receiving corporate messages, and who would be creating these if not a communications team?

The experience of others within the organisation in communicating strategy to the wider business will also give you some insight into how this has been approached and the perception of its effectiveness. Do not overlook learning from what others have done before; devising a data strategy is not a high-profile activity and so you need to use every tool in the box to be able to get your message across in a suitably engaging way that is likely to resonate with your colleagues.

If you are assisted at various points in the process of devising the data strategy by others from across the organisation, seek their input as to how they intend to engage on what they have been working on and what channels they are familiar with that are used within their own teams. As much as there may be formal ways of communicating, do not miss the opportunity to gain your own understanding of how things are cascaded through the local management chain within their function. It may be that there is an opportunity for you to address teams directly, presenting via team meetings or offsite to share your work with a wider audience.

Your sponsor should be able to guide you as to how best to promote the data strategy programme amongst their peers. Do set yourself the objective to make this as concise as possible, without leaving key information out, as this audience is likely to be inundated with material to read and digest, and so something well targeted that gets to the point quickly will go down well. Do not underestimate the challenge of writing something shorter but more focused. There is an art to being concise, complete and accurate, and it is unlikely your first iteration will succeed in this goal.

Do focus on the purpose of your communication. As I said at the start of this section, there may well be an educational purpose to your need to communicate, and so you need to set context and be clear on outcome and impact, as well as satisfying the key question of 'so what does it mean for me?' that will be in everyone's mind as they read it. If there is a need to provide the before and after perspective to demonstrate what has changed, then do not be afraid to do so, but be conscious that you are challenging the ways of operating that some of your audience might have been wedded to for some time, and so you may be inflaming resistance if you do not set this out in a constructive and empathetic way.

If you are outlining what change lies ahead, hearing of it through a remote communication is almost certainly not the best way to build trust, cooperation and engagement with the change you propose. Think about how you communicate, what you communicate and when you communicate to avoid creating more resistance to what is seen to be change by those affected.

Seek to create a feedback loop, whether through key contacts across different parts of the organisation or by actively engaging via team meetings or other such local groups. This will enable you to tailor your communications to land in the most effective way and also demonstrate that you are engaging with teams across the organisation rather than imposing something upon them. Building trust and understanding will pay back heavily as you progress through the data strategy programme, especially as you reach implementation and need to lean heavily on goodwill and clarity of understanding to succeed.

Remember to make these communication opportunities highly focused on the target audience, and digestible for those who possibly do not have the same technical background or understanding as you – avoid acronym overload and test your content out on someone outside your immediate team for a sense check. Keep it punchy and focused, getting your key points across in a way which is engaging. If you feel confident enough to do so (and possibly this is where you can lean for assistance on someone within the team you are briefing), pose questions which are relevant to the audience, highlight the benefits as you see them and try to get some level of engagement – feedback on whether this is heading in the right direction is invaluable to build credibility into your work and also ground it on tangible evidence collected from that stakeholder group, which will work well at the implementation stage. Do not forget the need for the emotional 'sell' alongside the hard analytical facts, if you are to overcome the psychological barriers to change. If you do not unfreeze then you will be unable to break the ice to deliver the change you need to achieve.

7.5 TRANSITIONING COMMUNICATIONS TO FOCUS ON THE DELIVERY OF THE DATA STRATEGY

The data strategy has been defined, submitted for approval and signed off to start the implementation. The communications process needs to be in full swing to keep the focus on the data strategy rather than lose sight of where the organisation has agreed it needs to head. The mobilisation of the communications activity has to pick up and keep the assorted loose threads of activity across the organisation suitably bound together to tell the story of how the implementation of the data strategy is progressing.

The first step needs to be the communication of the completion of definition and the seamless transition into execution – what does this look like, where are the priorities and what does it mean for me? The sponsor has a critical role to play here, as it is a big moment in the role that the individual plays in your organisation, stamping their credibility on this and ensuring that there is widespread acknowledgement this is a priority for the organisation. It is the achievement of a major milestone, and the start of a new phase, one which will demand more time and effort across the organisation than what has gone before. You need the big launch behind the implementation stage to ensure that the organisation does not take its eye off the ball and that you have a mandate to get resources from the whole organisation to support you through implementation.

Clearly the implementation plan will become a key artefact on which to build a formal communications plan to support it as it drives the focus, deliverables, milestones and benefits of what lies ahead. Identifying the key points around which the communications can be constructed enables a series of structured messages to be defined as anchor points, which provides opportunities to tailor localised messages relating to the impact and importance of changes within specific areas. These could be case studies, individual profiles in which those involved talk positively about the effect of the changes in their ways of working or experience of seeing the improvements realised, or more strategic pieces that outline the key activities ahead and the commitments to support those areas through the changes involved.

A regular stream of communications, to keep the organisation bound together in the enterprise of implementing the data strategy, is key to ensuring the momentum is maintained. Infrequent communication leads to a lack of visibility, resulting in it slipping from the focus of the wider organisation, and it becomes more of a challenge to gain support due to there being more of a feeling of upheaval than there would have been if the communications had been steady and constant.

> John Kotter, author and professor at Harvard Business School, says that most organisations under-communicate their vision for change by at least a factor of ten and suggests that communication has to be consistent with behaviour so that the entire organisation sees that the change is for real.[11] Do not think everyone hears, or believes, the first time you communicate. Thomas Smith devised a 20-step plan to get people to buy a product in 1885,[12] and whilst repetition may not need to be this extensive, do reflect that hearing a message and assigning it credibility may need multiple communication efforts delivered in different ways to make it stick.

Engage the communications team in what lies ahead and seek their guidance on what works, how you can co-develop the communications plan as an important stream within the data strategy implementation plan and get communications expertise aligned to this. They will have the experience of knowing what works within the organisation, the tone of messaging that is likely to hit the mark and the house style (if there is one) to be adopted in all communications issued through this programme. Understand the drumbeat of communications activity, align the frequency in your own activity to it and identify the opportunities to really focus in on the progress through implementation with some big success stories – remember, the success is the outcome, just don't forget to position the data strategy and its implementation as the key enabler behind it.

---

11 J.P. Kotter, *Leading Change*. Boston, MA: Harvard Business School Press, 1996.

12 T. Smith, *Successful Advertising: Its Secrets Explained*. London: Thomas Smith Agency, 1885.

The art of effective communications in relating positive change to the entire workforce is achieved through joining up the dots, linking activities from one part of the organisation through to another in a way that is measuring impact. The data strategy is meant to be making the organisation more effective in its management and exploitation of data, and therefore highlighting the benefits of unblocking a problem in one place and how it ripples through several other parts of the organisation starts to unlock the importance of data as a corporate asset that links everyone together. Join this up with the customer, the positive impact that it makes and the benefits that ensue, and the data strategy is beginning to become a rallying point for people to start to work together in a way that may be different to what has gone before.

Identify what else is in the corporate communications plan and be opportunistic. If you see an opportunity to get a line or sentence inserted into the core messaging then do so, as long as it is relevant. Keeping the data strategy implementation alive in the minds of the wider organisation is one of the key tasks within the implementation plan, otherwise it is quickly forgotten because of a lot of it operating in the background or not directly impacting some parts of the organisation at that time.

It is often overlooked that data is one of the few things that – on a day-to-day basis – binds the organisation together. For many organisations, data is seen to be more of a problem, or a constraint, than a true asset that generates value repeatedly and has application across the entire organisation. Creating communications around the commonality of data as an asset within the organisation positions it in a way that many may not have considered before. Therefore, following data through the corporate lifecycle of processes and decision points brings to life the importance of getting it right, and the consequences of getting it wrong.

> Filling in a field with an erroneous value may seem to have little impact to the person tasked with capturing that information – after all, that person never uses that field so what does it matter? However, understanding that the field drives billing, or the level of service that is provided, or the response time to queries all impact the customer and their experience. To the customer, the organisation is seen to be one entity; failings such as an inability to offer the right level of service are an indictment of the organisation and a reason to look elsewhere. To the person who fails to capture the data for that field, the impact may be some way down the line or not apparent at all, but bringing this to life through customer testimonials and other feedback will start to illustrate that data is a team game, and the weakest link in that team undermines the effort of the whole team.

Creating communications around examples such as that above is what makes a difference. It isn't the factual that engages people in the organisation; often it is the more emotional side of the story, explaining the value of data in a way that makes it a team game and, momentarily, breaks down the silos or the remit of the individual and brings everyone back to their common purpose – delivering a quality service to the customer.

One of the tasks, therefore, of the communications effort is to generate sufficient insight into the impact of the data strategy implementation to create interesting and engaging stories to enthral the workforce as a whole and to sell the benefits – as Lewin's change model illustrates. To do this requires a level of understanding of the organisation at large to know who the influencers and experts are within each part of the organisation – get these individuals on board and you are on track to get others to sit up and take notice. Explore the informal networks within the organisation, finding those who have a reputation for getting things done or who are seen to have influence through their expertise or longevity in the organisation. If you can win over some of these people you are well on track to get some compelling messages out that can really build traction behind your implementation programme.

Bear in mind that we all absorb and comprehend information in different ways, depending on format, messaging, big picture versus detail, or who we hear it from. Do not fall into the trap of assuming one size fits all. In my experience, sending everyone in the organisation an email, posting something on the intranet, even including a message for cascading via team meetings will all fail if you adopt a single communications strategy. Consider your audience, learn how they ingest information and talk to others who have seemingly succeeded in delivering strategic messages across the organisation as a whole. Don't be afraid to try things, use Agile to deploy the PDCA approach and refine on the basis of what you learn. Set out the bigger picture to ensure there is clarity on the context and purpose, but deliver the detail when useful to do so.

Whilst it is easy to be led by an internal communications team into fitting in to their preferred approach, do not be afraid to challenge if you have evidence it is unlikely to work for you, because of the nature of the messaging or the topic. After all, your data strategy is all about embedding the use of evidence, so build an understanding of how communication can work for you. It is a critical investment in the data strategy programme, and if you do not generate engagement or interest then your implementation is destined to fail, so do not skimp on getting the communications strand of your programme right.

In addition, identify those who are likely to be advocates and willing to support your initiative. Don't be afraid to issue a call to arms across key functions to get those individuals to come forward. Even if they are not influential to bring others along the journey with them, they will have insight into how these things tend to get done, the forums in which you need to engage, and the key messages needed to deliver support and engagement from those who are influential. In other words, do not be afraid to have too many contacts across the organisation. Identify what each person can bring to the communications effort and play to their strengths. Even if their only role is to help you navigate their part of the organisation, it serves a purpose. You need a lot of localised expertise to try to build momentum, and having people on the inside can only strengthen your knowledge and understanding.

7.6 TEN TO TAKE AWAY

The key themes to consider from this chapter are:

1. Culture and employee engagement are at the top of the list for programmatic failures worldwide, so do not underestimate this and prepare extensively for what you need to do to succeed.

2. Don't assume the 'corporate culture' is the way the organisation operates. In most cases the local culture pervades and there is a gap between the two – which could be the difference between your programme being dismissed as another central initiative and being embraced as something to engage with.

3. Resistance to change will take many forms, on a number of levels. Understand these and identify how you intend to tackle them in your organisation. This is not specific to your programme: it affects all change, so do not try to find solutions beyond doing what you need to achieve your goals.

4. Remember to unfreeze before embarking on change, and to freeze once more when the change has been delivered. In the middle lies change itself, the hardest and longest phase, but it is made easier if you run an effective preparatory (unfreeze) stage.

5. Sponsorship plays a critical role in your likelihood of success. Understand what you need from each other, have clearly defined boundaries and play to strengths. Provide the structure, information and clarity needed and the sponsor can drive the programme forward for you by influencing peers and removing blockers.

6. Assess the maturity of the organisation and reflect on how best to utilise communication to ensure information is aligned to enhancing understanding and generating goodwill towards your programme. Seek feedback to check in on how well messages are landing and adapt as necessary.

7. Build a communications strand into your implementation plan to ensure you align the two to optimise opportunities to promote the data strategy implementation and to make it an integral part of your programme.

8. Identify communication opportunities at every turn. The more you can integrate thinking on data strategy into the core of how the organisation works and key messaging, the greater the influence you can drive.

9. Do not be afraid to repeat messages, use multiple channels and gather learning as to what works well for different audiences. It is a common misconception that people pick things up from a single communication, and subtle differences to the angle of the communication can be effective in tailoring the message to specific groups.

10. Utilise local knowledge and expertise to support and supplement your communications drive. Credibility at a local level can bridge the gap between centralised communications and information of local interest.

8 EXECUTING THE STRATEGY – PART ONE: THE PLAN

'All you need is the plan, the road map, and the courage to press on to your destination.'

Earl Nightingale[1]

The data strategy has been drafted; the end is in sight ... or is it?

There have been references throughout this book to the focus being placed entirely on devising the data strategy, only to see it fail to materialise due to a lack of conviction, readiness, relevance or commitment to it by those you will depend on to see it into implementation. The goal of this chapter is to prepare you so you can avoid such an outcome, and see the fruits of your labours actually deliver some positive outcomes for your organisation.

I have seen organisations in which those who devise strategy hand over to others to drive implementation, as well as those in which the process of compiling the strategy and implementing it is done by the same person and/or team. I do not view one as better than the other, as there are pros and cons to both options and, in some organisations, it might necessitate the same individual owning all of the process.

However, I believe the successful evolution from a strategy defining team to a separate implementation team works best if there is a transition, with those who have defined the strategy on hand to advise on interpretation, baselines and key contacts and information, whilst those picking up the implementation work alongside the strategy definition team in the last weeks and months to get a handle on the organisational dynamics and commitment to seeing the data strategy come to life.

In 2013 *The Economist* provided some insight into the benefits of linking strategy formation with execution through their study into why good strategies fail.[2] This found that a third of respondents at the best executing organisations identified implementation as a strategic activity in itself with lessons learnt fed back into the process, compared to just 11 per cent at other organisations. In addition, 59 per cent of those organisations who were best at execution involved staff who set the high-level strategy in its implementation, compared to just 23 per cent elsewhere.

The intention of this chapter is to provide you with the tools and techniques you will need to navigate through the intent of the data strategy, bringing it to reality. It challenges on the mindset needed, which is a different one to that which has been pivotal to achieving

---

1   E. Nightingale, *The Strangest Secret* [spoken word – vinyl]. Nightingale-McHugh Company, 1956.

2   Economist Intelligence Unit, Why Good Strategies Fail: Lessons for the C-Suite. 2013. https://eiuperspectives.economist. com/strategy-leadership/why-good-strategies-fail.

the sign-off of the data strategy, and the approach to be taken, to provide you with an understanding of what can emerge as blockers and delays to a successful outcome. This chapter is focused on readiness for the implementation stage that you are about to encounter, ahead of the subsequent chapter which gives greater clarity on how the execution of the data strategy is delivered.

8.1 THE IMPORTANCE OF THE TRANSITION TO DATA STRATEGY EXECUTION

As the preceding chapter concluded, there are numerous factors to be taken into account in the transition to delivery. There are also many steps to consider to be sure that you are ready to meet the demands to mobilise the implementation of the data strategy. Bear in mind, when considering the resources that you need to succeed, how much of the work is embedded in the organisation today and the need to work with, rather than on top of, the existing priorities to fine tune or realign day-to-day activities. The key to progress is to find a way to have others embrace what you are seeking without it being seen to be an additional burden placed upon them – often the starting point if you ask people to engage and support an initiative. Consider how the request you are placing on them is either substitutional or enhancing what they already do, so there is something in it for them to want to engage with.

The start of the mobilisation phase in executing the strategy needs to be a fine balance between a bold statement of intent as to what is to be achieved and why, and a more modest focus on doing things better and smarter to deliver better outcomes for all – staff and customers alike. Remember the campfire stories: this is where you need to bring the many ways of delivering ostensibly the same story to engage radically different audiences in to play, taking the approach with the greatest chance of achieving engagement with each audience subset.

Mobilisation has become a little less trendy as an activity to be undertaken prior to commencing implementation than it was less than a decade ago. Certainly, the trend has been to make this little more than a token activity as the project or programme enters the delivery stage.[3] This overlooks the importance of the investment at the start of the implementation phase of any programme, and I have seen many instances where organisations have embarked on a course without considering the implications down the line and preparing for these in advance.

Time spent in preparation has been a constant in good practice, as two of the great leaders in American history are often quoted as saying:[4] Benjamin Franklin is said to have exclaimed 'By failing to prepare, you are preparing to fail,' whilst Abraham Lincoln is attributed with 'Give me six hours to chop down a tree and I will spend the first four sharpening the axe.' Whether mobilisation has been overlooked through the advent of formal methodologies such as Agile, which focus on artefacts, user stories or other ways of garnering background information, its importance has not diminished.

---

3   Project One, the management consulting firm, talk about the benefits of a full mobilisation approach in a blog post (https://projectone.com/blogs/mobilising-change-programme/) and as an article (https://projectone.com/mobilising-change-programmes-ive-started-so-ill-finish/).

4   These commonly used attributions are likely incorrect, however.

A very helpful short reminder as to what makes for an effective mobilisation stage was created by Malcolm Follos of Sensei UKE, in which he talks of five critical steps to take: ask and answer the question 'why bother?'; consider who to involve and select your core team carefully; plan the mobilisation session carefully; diverge and converge in sequence; and develop a project brief.[5] I will use these steps to some degree in this chapter, but as a common approach to embarking on a successful project, Follos's five tips are a sound basis to give your project every chance of a positive outcome.

Returning to the key theme of readiness to transition from strategy to execution, I find that too many data strategies have failed to give those responsible for implementation any guide as to where to start. The more effective data strategies may have some reference to goals – the better ones will have the waymarkers I talked about in Chapter 5 – but there is a need to make clear the baseline, assumptions and key drivers in the data strategy to stand any chance of the implementation starting off in the right place.

Think of the Tour de France, at this point: 21 stages of gruelling cycling over 23 stages, taking in mountain ranges, valleys and towns and cities across France (mostly). Yet how would it work if no one communicated where the start was to take place, the date it would commence or the route to be taken? Clearly, this would be an impossibility to manage as any event, let alone one so prestigious and internationally renowned, requires significant preparation well in advance along with logistical planning, which is the height of an effective mobilisation effort. Why would you or anyone else embarking on a three-year (or longer) implementation of a data strategy think they should operate with any less effort and expect success?

Referring back to Follos's five key tips, these can be applied just as effectively to a team planning ahead to the project that is the Tour de France as to the implementation of a data strategy in your organisation.

You are entering the operational phase. This entails: turning the data strategy into everyday language; incorporating it into the workplace as an extension, replacement or reinforcement of current activity; building a communications and evidence base to show progress; and retaining the confidence and backing of your key stakeholders.

An effective mobilisation is essential to ratify a commonly held understanding of the current landscape and a set of priorities to start to establish a sense of momentum that will ensure stakeholders remain committed. Rather like a pilot conducting pre-flight checks before taking to the skies, the mobilisation stage is an essential checkpoint to establish clarity, purpose and direction. If a plane fails mid-air, there is little chance of a positive outcome. If your strategy implementation gets off on the wrong foot, it will almost certainly be challenging to restore confidence, credibility and integrity, undermining the data strategy regardless of its merits.

---

5 Malcolm Follos, Sensei UKE. 9 October 2015. https://www.linkedin.com/pulse/mobilising-project-simple-checklist-follow-malcolm-follos/.

8.1.1 The pre-implementation review

Having established the premise of why the data strategy is needed, its relevance and importance to the organisation as the final stage in gaining approval from those who need to sign it off, commencing a pre-implementation review becomes the first integral step of the mobilisation phase. Cascading this knowledge to all who are to be involved, whether as part of an implementation effort or in the delivery of a component through everyday activity, through the campfire briefings gives the appropriate prominence to the implementation phase and its associated activities.

The implementation phase needs to plan out the detail of the data strategy, which inevitably involves adding further meaning and context to that which was considered in the drafting of the data strategy but was too detailed and peripheral for inclusion. This is why the link between those involved in the drafting of the data strategy and the implementation team is so important: the knowledge and understanding that bring life to the data strategy are held in the materials collated along the way or the heads of those who took part in countless discussions and gained context from so doing. Some of this will be documented, but the nuances and interpretation will best be gained from talking to those who translated the inputs to shape the outputs – the strategy team.

Depending on the organisation, the implementation plan may only need to define the year ahead rather than the full term of the data strategy. In a way, this is easier to do but also carries significant risks – the drafting of what can be achieved in the year ahead makes assumptions and sets dependencies for others to have to pick up, either in-year or in a later year, when these may be essential to the successful delivery of the data strategy. I would always advise at least sketching out the later years, even at a high level, to provide those who pick up the task of defining subsequent annualised implementation plans with the rationale for why decisions were made at the time.

It is all too easy to forget that the world of business undergoes constant change. The whole organisation therefore needs to be engaged with change for it to succeed. In an increasing number of organisations, there are dedicated teams that are called 'Change' or 'Transformation' that are detached from the rest of the organisation and centralise expertise in delivering such activity. The intent is to build deep skills and repeatable programme methodologies that increase the likelihood of success, but the challenge with this is that is makes it a specialist activity, and by implication not one the rest of the organisation can lead.

This is a dangerous path to take given much of the research quoted in this book shows that many programmes fail through a lack of engagement and resistance to change, and the best approach to resolving this is to engage at all levels and increase involvement. If this is the route taken by your organisation then guard against an 'ivory tower' risk of resistance through a 'not invented here' mindset, and ensure communications are inclusive and effective at all times.

To deliver change requires total organisational commitment and empowerment to achieve at all levels, which may be evolutionary. A global survey of strategy implementation found 51 per cent of middle managers resist strategic implementation initiatives,[6] and so progress has to be seen to be inclusive and evolutionary, even if it is more extensive in totality. There is a need to create positivity around the notion of change that the data strategy will bring.

A critical step in the pre-implementation review is to identify the waymarkers in the data strategy and plot these out. Hopefully, the dependencies will be aligned to the waymarkers to make it clear where they sit in the timeline, and when they need to deliver to enable the key outputs to be achieved on time. Indications of which functions are responsible, as well as those accountable, for the outcomes to be achieved should enable your implementation plan to be defined with these confirmed and assigned. A quick check on the baseline should ascertain whether the starting point has changed, though implementation should follow swiftly on from the data strategy having been signed off, so this should be a formality. However, engage widely, though quickly, to validate.

Discussions with those who devised the data strategy will inevitably identify opportunities for 'quick wins' in the first months of the implementation phase. The information picked up whilst compiling the data strategy will have encountered initiatives already under way which, through greater focus that the data strategy implementation phase can bring, can be accelerated and delivered sooner than would otherwise be the case. The strategy team will also have encountered those who are keen to engage and have either good ideas or work under way, but need some help in unblocking issues or building a head of steam to get momentum behind them. In many ways, these are the helpful equivalents of a 'cheat sheet' in providing the implementation phase with ready-made activities to get behind and build credibility in the data strategy implementation. Grab them with both hands: they will serve you well when, inevitably, there are trickier phases of the implementation ahead!

There is a need to review the risks, assumptions, issues and dependencies (RAID) captured in the process of compiling the data strategy, more of which will be discussed later in this chapter, focused particularly on the importance of assessing dependencies. Reassessing these and exploring them in more detail will provide the baseline for the commencement of the implementation. The data strategy has provided a high-level assessment of the RAID; it is the task of the pre-implementation review to establish further detail to quantify and qualify the RAID log to be the starting point for implementation.

It is highly likely that additions will be made to the RAID log as a result of the mobilisation phase, as the definition of the data strategy will have identified those which are significant enough to the strategy as a whole. Implementation will delve into a deeper level of understanding of the RAID to determine what needs to be factored in, enriching and enhancing the RAID to be more comprehensive in scope to manage and lead the implementation to achieve a successful outcome.

---

6   Bridges Business Consultancy Int Pte Ltd, What Drives Strategy Implementation? Top Line Findings. 2008.
    www.bridgesconsultancy.com/research-case-study/research/.

8.2 WHY DO DATA STRATEGY IMPLEMENTATIONS FAIL?

Whether specifically data strategies or strategies in general, the evidence suggests that most fail to transition successfully to the execution of the strategy. This may seem alarming and in many ways it is, given the amount of time, resource and effort which goes into producing strategies across organisations. Strategy has become central to the organisational psyche in most of the world, and academia has established specialist colleges and faculties focused on strategy, yet the inability to deliver on strategy has been overlooked far too long. Why is this?

Strategy has seemingly become a core activity of most management consulting firms. The major providers in this arena all have an array of expertise in a wide range of fields. Their expertise is founded, largely, on self-taught progression, as experts are created from within, and clients pay handsomely to tap into this knowledge.

Academia has turned strategy into something which can be taught through both graduate and postgraduate courses and provides academic rigour on how to apply strategic thinking and concepts that those management consulting firms have espoused as being insightful.

I am not dismissive of either management consulting firms or academia in terms of what they can bring to the strategy table. Indeed, many inputs to this book have been enhanced by the quality of research and thinking provided by both of these domains. However, I believe that strategy definition is the easy part when compared to the task of strategy implementation.

Strategy implementation is complex on so many levels it is hard to begin to describe its landscape. This is where the challenge is on the front line, knowing the organisation well enough to know how to be successful in navigating the often choppy waters to be encountered over a number of years.

Most senior executives are comfortable in the strategy space, and have reached their level of seniority through being able to command and control or set a vision with a degree of passion and confidence. Many are functional experts, comfortable in their own space and confident in leading in the adjacent spaces to bring enough of the workforce with them. Yet few have really practical experience in devising strategy and also having been responsible for strategy implementation. This is one of your biggest challenges in the steps that you have to take, as they will not have trodden the same path in terms of practical experience or be aware of the challenge of transitioning from one to the other to know how to do so successfully.

I referred previously to the research undertaken by Strategy& PwC which stated that only 8 per cent of company leaders were said to excel at both strategy and execution, in a global survey of 700 major organisations. More than one in three were classed as neutral or worse on both strategy and execution. This begs the question of how effective your organisation is in either of these spheres, given the gap amongst leaders in global organisations. It also exposes that the corporate strategy is just as likely to be either flawed or executed poorly, in the worst cases possibly both.

In their research for their book *The Balanced Scorecard* (1996), authors Robert Kaplan and David Norton found that 90 per cent of organisations fail to execute their strategies successfully.[7] This was the compelling case to introduce a balanced scorecard approach (a strategy-orientated performance management tool to align operational activity and financial performance to the corporate strategy through the use of lead and lag indicators) to focus on performance and measurement to achieve the subtitle of the book – *Translating Strategy into Action*. Subsequent research[8] suggests an improvement to just 67 per cent failing by 2016, but that is still two in three major organisations investing in strategy but failing to deliver on it.

To this day, the same concepts as found in the *Balanced Scorecard* apply: we should expect to measure the effectiveness of the implementation effort to deliver the strategy. Yet, most organisations struggle to articulate how to measure strategy implementation, often because the strategy fails to articulate targets, goals or anything measurable in the vision that is set to know when the objective has been achieved.

Many will argue that goals and objectives are too low level, the remit of the execution of the strategy rather than the strategy itself. However, without something tangible to anchor the aspiration it is akin to chasing rainbows – we can all see them but have little comprehension of where on the distant landscape they start or finish.

To add context through an example: an aspiration to be number two in a given market provides the measure, but it needs to be balanced with the strategy of how this is to be achieved, otherwise it is not a strategy.

If you recall from earlier in this book, the 5W1H concept should apply in the formation of the data strategy, articulating the detail to ensure the strategy has clarity on the direction to be taken, the choices to be made and the priorities to be followed. These need to be articulated in a way that makes it clear what is needed to deliver on the strategy, along with a framework in which to measure its achievement.

In an article by Sull, Homkes and Sull I can thoroughly recommend for those wishing to know more about failure to transition into executing a strategy effectively, the authors highlight a survey of more than 400 global CEOs that found executional excellence was the number one challenge facing corporate leaders in Asia, Europe and the United States, heading a list of some 80 issues, including innovation, geopolitical instability and top-line growth.[9] Just think about the importance of that message for a moment.

---

7   R.S. Kaplan and D.P. Norton, *The Balanced Scorecard: Translating Strategy into Action*. Boston, MA: Harvard Business Review Press, 1996.

8   Bridges Business Consultancy Int Pte Ltd, Strategy Implementation Survey. 2016. www.bridgesconsultancy.com/research-case-study/research/.

9   Donald Sull, Rebecca Homkes and Charles Sull, Why Strategy Execution Unravels – and What to Do About It. *Harvard Business Review*, March 2015. https://hbr.org/2015/03/why-strategy-execution-unravelsand-what-to-do-about-it.

Of all the issues facing them, over 400 global CEOs ranked executional excellence as the number one challenge, which is what you are seeking to achieve with potentially the first data strategy (or, harder still, a subsequent data strategy, following in the wake of a lack of executional excellence delivering any perceived value or traction from your predecessor).

In the same article there is the bold statement that, according to research conducted by Donald Sull some years previously, 'several widely held beliefs that managers hold about how to implement strategy are just plain wrong'. This provides the basis for five critical myths that were found and advice on how to replace these with a more accurate perspective to help managers effectively execute strategy.

The five critical myths they focused on were:

1. Execution equals alignment.
2. Execution means sticking to the plan.
3. Communication equals understanding.
4. A performance culture drives execution.
5. Execution should be driven from the top.

8.2.1 'Execution equals alignment'

There was a lack of cross-functional commitment – only 9 per cent of managers said they could rely on colleagues in other functions and units all the time, with half saying they could rely most of the time. This led to compensatory activity which undermined the whole execution process, further exacerbated relationships between functions, and caused slippage and, ultimately, performance failures. These are all at the heart of demonstrating that the strategy is being executed effectively, so their failure is inevitably going to impact on a successful outcome. Even those organisations that have effective performance management cultures (objective setting, goals and so on) fail to see such processes and systems through, with 80 per cent of managers saying they do not work well at all or most of the time. Twice as many managers highlighted the need for more structure in the processes to coordinate cross-functional activity as those who wanted more structure in the performance management through objectives.

8.2.2 'Execution means sticking to the plan'

Detailed route maps hindered progress, acting as a straightjacket to innovation, agility and adaptability, all of which are so key in the uncertainty that lies ahead. The majority of those questioned found a lack of resource alignment and agility in reallocation of resource to respond to a dynamic world one of the biggest constraints, resulting in organisations failing to realise opportunities or act rapidly enough to fast emerging threats.

Only 20 per cent of managers believed their organisations were effective in shifting resources across units to support strategic priorities. Worse still, only 11 per cent of managers thought their organisation had the financial and human resources needed to succeed in delivering all of the strategic priorities.

According to 80 per cent of managers, organisations were also inclined not to exit declining businesses or disinvest in failing initiatives soon enough. This distracts from the strategic intent, pulls resources away from those priorities (often disproportionately), and undermines confidence and credibility due to the perceived failure to resurrect what was beyond saving.

8.2.3 'Communication equals understanding'

Senior executives believed that relentlessly communicating strategy was key to success, but were often mistaken in how effective this was across the organisation. Only 55 per cent of middle managers surveyed in the research could name even one of the top five strategic objectives, despite 90 per cent claiming their leaders communicate the strategy frequently enough, which means the chances of onward communication being accurate or aligned to the strategy are low indeed. Just 16 per cent of frontline supervisors and team leaders were able to connect the corporate priorities to the strategy.

The myth is based on volume rather than value: in other words, say something frequently enough and it will be understood. Middle managers highlight the large number of corporate priorities and strategic initiatives four times more often than a lack of clear communications. The importance of ensuring understanding, rather than focusing on frequency, is the key here, which plays back into the importance of being able to track and measure the effectiveness of the communication being delivered.

8.2.4 'A performance culture drives execution'

The research found that the performance was being monitored, rather than the concept, with too narrow a focus being placed on outcomes. Broader abilities are required – agility, teamwork and ambition play a key role – yet these are all too frequently overlooked despite being essential to successful strategy execution.

In a changing environment, a willingness to try new approaches, collaborate across functions and be bold in decision making can all lead to failure in a way that is very visible, hence there is a reluctance to take such a path or to set ambitious goals when others play safe, hit their targets and reap the rewards. However, adopting a safety-first approach is more likely to constrain cross-functional collaboration and result in a failure to spot opportunities or react quickly enough to exploit them.

8.2.5 'Execution should be driven from the top'

This is related to the earlier example of the campfire strategy discussions. Concentrating authority and leadership with the CEO breeds a successful approach in the short term, as there is a focal point and drive, but this is where execution needs to operate at multiple layers of the organisation and will be constrained if it has to be managed through the senior hierarchy. Therefore, the concept of distributed leadership is essential to success, as this is where the fleet-footedness to respond opportunistically will arise and resources can be reallocated without recourse to senior leadership and a slow decision-making chain.

Distributed leaders exist at all levels in an organisation, whether middle managers, technical experts or others seen to carry authority and hold responsibility. Strategy is owned by the senior executive, who shoulders the responsibility for defining it, but their task is to support, guide and facilitate the execution of it at all levels of distributed leaders across the organisation. Unfortunately, all too often senior leaders are either failing to provide the structure to enable collaboration across functions or, worse still, are seen to be driving their own agendas at the top of the organisation rather than pulling together as an executive team.

8.2.6 Other evidence of leadership failings undermining strategy implementation

The findings in this report are not out of the norm. *The Economist* report cited above found that whilst 80 per cent of respondents regarded executing strategic initiatives as essential or very important for their organisations to be competitive over the next three years, 61 per cent stated that their organisation struggled to bridge the gap between strategy formulation and its day-to-day implementation. In the preceding three years, just 56 per cent of strategic initiatives had been successful. It concludes that those organisations that lack strategic alignment report weaker financial results than their peers.[10]

The rest of the report is equally damning of the failure of senior leadership to ensure strategy is effectively executed, finding broadly the same issues as Sull et al. – executives missing in action when it comes to providing guidance and facilitating delivery, and micromanaging the execution instead of providing the support and space to those better suited to driving the implementation activities. One additional area of concern is the lack of skills to successfully implement the strategy. Forty-one per cent of respondents agreed that their organisation provided sufficiently skilled staff to execute high-profile strategic initiatives, only 18 per cent could relate to their organisations hiring people with the necessary business skills or leadership talent to drive strategy implementation as a high priority, and just 11 per cent saw their organisations developing those skillsets amongst their existing executives.

In conclusion, *The Economist* identified 13 per cent of respondents benchmarked as well above average in strategy execution, and regarded these as best executors when comparing with all other respondents in terms of performance criteria.

The evidence is perhaps most stark when looking at alignment of strategy with the actual business model, with 51 per cent of those organisations found to be the best at execution having these aligned compared to just 8 per cent of other organisations.

If this is the canvas on which you are seeking to deliver a data strategy, possibly for the first time (maybe both for you and the organisation), then this is understandably daunting when the success rate is so low and the pitfalls so many and commonplace in organisations around the world. The steps in the remainder of this chapter seek to provide some clarity and guidance on how to navigate your way into delivery of the strategy, but this is – as so often the case – very much defined by your circumstances and organisational culture, so there is no 'one size fits all' approach. It is a case of picking up tips, learning about what to avoid and charting your own course to increase the likelihood of success.

---

10 Economist Intelligence Unit, Why Good Strategies Fail: Lessons for the C-Suite. 2013. https://eiuperspectives.economist. com/strategy-leadership/why-good-strategies-fail.

8.3 THE PLANNING CYCLE

Most established organisations will have a planning cycle, even if it is not evident to those who are not engaged with it. This will almost certainly be defined by the budgeting cycle, the financial year end for your organisation and the prioritisation of resources – human and financial – to enable the organisation to function and achieve its goals in the year ahead. As you can tell, the financial arm of your organisation will inevitably have a large say in the planning cycle process, so it is worth exploring how strategy works in the context of their view of the organisation, especially if you are approaching this area for the very first time. Remarkably, only 40 per cent of organisations link their budgets to their strategy,[11] which explains why so many strategic initiatives fail to materialise through a lack of funding, prioritisation or ability to commit resources.

The notion of planning itself defines a level of direction setting and resource allocation, along with an inherent prioritisation determining what is to be achieved. Whilst this may be as simple as an annual plan, there is a need to recognise that the short term will drive focus and decisions, not to mention reward and recognition in many cases, and so deviating from this will take a significant amount of effort to communicate the change of direction, realign priorities and convince the existing decision makers who are driving the behaviours at many levels in the organisation.

It is therefore imperative that you are fully versed in the annual plan, rationale, the timelines and the expected outcomes before embarking on any deviation – indeed, your ideas for the data strategy implementation plan may have already been considered, and it would be folly not to investigate this first to avoid repetition of what has already been discounted by those you now need to convince regarding the direction and content of the data strategy implementation plan.

However, a note of caution. Only 20 per cent of organisations review progress on strategy execution on a monthly basis (most only do so annually), and 47 per cent lack an effective measurement system for tracking the strategy implementation.[12] This suggests that there is a disconnect between the planning process, its implementation and the things an organisation chooses to track – what are usually termed key performance indicators (KPIs) but all too often are bloated to measure far more than what constitutes that which is key to the organisation. However, surely the definition of 'key' should be that which is linked to measuring the strategic initiatives through the strategy execution phase?

As highlighted earlier in this book, there may be a strategic time frame that the organisation operates to, and it is imperative that the data strategy is devised with this in mind. It makes more sense to connect the data strategy into the wider strategic landscape in your organisation, as failing to incorporate the same timings and, therefore, intent is more likely to cause the data strategy to be misaligned with the other strategies in play within the organisation. This will also determine the period of time that the data strategy needs to cover in the first instance to enable it to be devised to interconnect and align with supporting the corporate strategy.

---

11 J. De Flander and K. Schreurs, *The Strategy Execution Barometer*. Expanded edn. Enschede, The Netherlands: Performance Factory, 2012.

12 Bridges Business Consultancy Int Pte Ltd, Strategy Implementation Survey. 2016.

8.3.1 Waymarkers into milestones

Chapter 5 set the context of using waymarkers to guide the implementation plan. Waymarkers are guidelines to give the data strategy some context as to the intended course and pace of delivery but are not constraints or inflexible; their purpose is simply to assist in translating the breadth of the data strategy into something navigable and to give some insight into the intent of those who devised and delivered the strategy in the first place. This is particularly key if there is a transition to a different individual or team to implement the strategy to those who devised the strategy in the first place.

If waymarkers have been constructed in a comprehensive manner then they will also guide those implementing the data strategy through the complexities of the RAID that are embedded in the data strategy. Assuming these were checked and seen to be valid at the time the data strategy was approved – recognising the nature of a point in time being fraught with limited visibility of what lies ahead – then it would seem entirely rational that these should be the basis on which to build the implementation view of a RAID log to be managed, reviewed and enhanced through the subsequent implementation period.

The RAID log forms part of the suite of tools you need to keep track of the numerous variables you will need to be regularly apprised of and monitor throughout the implementation period. Of course, the environment you are working in is almost certainly going to change, which the data strategy is unlikely to predict, and hence you need to be adaptable and flexible in translating it into an implementation plan, and constantly review and revisit whether your assumptions are still valid. As W. Edwards Deming said: 'Two basic rules of life are: 1) Change is inevitable. 2) Everybody resists change.' Your challenge is to accept the first premise by taking the waymarkers and recognising the data strategy is not a fixed programme to be followed to the letter, whilst ensuring that the second rule does not apply to you, nor those you are collaborating with and dependent upon to ensure the implementation is a success.

The waymarkers identify deliverables or achievements at a point in time to give a sense of where the strategy expects to have reached, assuming the implementation goes well. They avoid the detail of what would typically be included in milestones – resources, dependencies and so on – and focus on a brief description of the outcome to be able to guide the implementation team. For example, a waymarker may include the following: 'data governance will have been established in half the organisation with quality metrics on all high-priority data attributes'. It is left to the implementation team to determine which half of the organisation, to define the high-priority data attributes with those who are SMEs in those data sets and to establish parameters against which to judge data quality. However, the waymarker has given an indication of the progress anticipated to be on track with the overall goals of the data strategy.

Distilling the waymarkers into key deliverables that form the milestones within your implementation plan is the first step to assigning roles and responsibilities in that plan, from which resources and timings can be assessed and confirmed as being achievable. This is the key point at which to determine the appetite and commitment across functions and business units for the collaboration needed to make the plan deliver the outcomes on which it is based. Up until this point, the waymarkers in the data strategy have been signposting what lies beyond, and whilst there is an inherent acknowledgement required to get behind these to reach agreement, this is still theoretical. Never forget, the time at which there is most scope for prevarication, procrastination and deviation from what has previously been agreed is the point at which this becomes real – when resources are being committed, objectives set and measures put in place.

If this sounds a little negative, just reflect on what the research demonstrates repeatedly. Strategy execution fails not through the lack of clarity, but a lack of will to work together when it becomes reality. Therefore, it is imperative that you are challenging and retain a healthy dose of scepticism on the commitments of those you need to pull together on this until you see the behaviours translate into positive, collaborative outcomes. This builds trust, not only in your resilience and determination to see the implementation plan through to successful delivery, but in those you will learn are willing to support your activity and enable you to succeed. Trust is the essence of collaboration, and will be needed throughout the implementation to remain on track to complete your goals.

The waymarkers should have been constructed to make them measurable, so breaking these into milestones in the implementation plan needs to be undertaken in a way which remains consistent with the intent as to how this was to be achieved. Do not lose measurability in defining the milestones, as these too need to evidence the progress made to demonstrate the success of the strategy execution. If you are seeking to have a budget assigned to your programme, then the waymarkers need to be specific enough through the measurability to outline an indicative budget, within a rough order of magnitude estimate. The implementation plans, along with the milestones, will fine-tune the budget needed to complete an activity over the annual planning time frame.

Finally, if the landscape does change to affect the pace, direction or feasibility of achieving what is set out in the data strategy, then do reflect this in your RAID log and capture the decision taken as a consequence and seek approval for this change of course. Failing to do so will risk undermining the integrity of the data strategy (one diversion will lead to another, which may be necessary, but could just as easily be a case of drifting from the original intent) and the credibility of your implementation of the data strategy. This reinforces why setting a data strategy as if the environment does not evolve, requiring the organisation to adapt, is a misplaced view that a strategy should endure. In most cases, the core principles of intent may remain valid, but it is the route to get there, as demonstrated by the waymarkers, which needs to be updated to reflect an emerging reality.

8.4 DEPENDENCIES – THE ICEBERG BENEATH YOUR IMPLEMENTATION PLAN!

The compilation of the data strategy will have captured many factors which are provided via the RAID log. As you start to think about the implementation of the data strategy, the review of the RAID log takes on significance, as this defines the understanding of the baseline position from which you are to commence implementation. I therefore recommend a thorough review and exploration of the contents, with a particular focus on the dependencies, as these are captured in the RAID log due to their importance for your future success.

Each dependency should highlight who owns it, why it is seen to be important to the data strategy, some context as to how the dependency is being managed and the timeline (and therefore the risk) to the effective implementation of the data strategy. Such dependencies could be programmatic – for instance, a programme to implement new technology that impacts on how data is to be managed – or managed in the context of business as usual.

Generally speaking, the latter are harder to track, simply because there might not be a focus on the activity at hand, and therefore the imperative to address it as quickly as the data strategy requires may be lacking and the reporting of progress might be a more time-intensive activity. However, it may actually be of benefit to the individual holding a dependency to be able to link it to something of greater focus, such as the implementation of the data strategy, simply to give it more visibility and hence elevate the need to resolve it beyond the level it is currently held. Either way, there is a need to ascertain the current position of all dependencies and decide how you wish to track these through your implementation plan.

In order to ensure that the dependencies are fully up to date, it is worth doing an audit of these to ascertain the current status to validate whether the position has changed as readiness for implementation comes into play (the same actually applies to risks, issues and assumptions). This forms a critical part of the pre-implementation review, and you should determine whether you wish to assume responsibility for some of these wider dependencies – such a course might be favourable if there is a lack of decisiveness or ownership that could hinder your progress otherwise.

Further, this is an opportunity to explore the full extent of the dependencies at large. Bear in mind that the current RAID log was collated in support of the data strategy, which had one eye to the need to implement it but was not focused on the detail. It is in the implementation that the essence of how strategy translates into the detailed activities to be undertaken that the majority of dependencies emerge, demonstrating that there is an importance to uncovering these before they become the iceberg on your chosen course.

To quote Dean Devlin, the American filmmaker: 'The Titanic hit the iceberg not because they could not see it coming but because they could not change direction.'[13] It is important that you have the time to change direction and to do so in the implementation phase, which requires agility underpinned by a detailed understanding of where those icebergs are, to be nimble enough to know their status and adapt accordingly.

You need to undertake an extensive review of the dependencies that have not yet been identified through the compilation of the data strategy and map these into your own initial version of the RAID log. It is essential that you create a capability to track these, getting updates on their progress and assessing the risk they pose to your success along the course of the implementation plan. It is also critical to make reference to these in your progress reporting, highlighting where these are likely to cause issues ahead of time, enabling others to lean in to support you in removing the blockages before they

---

13 In D. McNary, AFM: 'Independence Day' Producer Dean Devlin Celebrates Independence. *Variety*, 10 November 2013. https://variety.com/2013/film/news/afm-indepedence-day-producer-dean-devlin-celebrates-independence-1200812581/.

veer into your line of sight – remember, allowing the time to change course can be as important as resolving the dependency itself.

In some organisations, the management of dependencies is not as mature as it might be. This will be apparent if you discover that those activities on which you have a dependency are also essential to achieving goals in other programmes but are not being tracked as such. Remarkably, it is not uncommon for organisations to focus on risk management, possibly some issues tracking, but be weak on dependencies. This is often due to a lack of management across activities, with programmes and day-to-day activities managed in silos and dependencies known to individuals but not formally documented as such.

> I have found this to be the case in many organisations I have operated in and instituted a dependency tracking approach, which has increased the awareness and professionalism of those who were identified as critical to my programme through the deliverables they were accountable for.
>
> In one case, I took the lead midway through a global data programme which was one of 26 concurrent change programmes. One of the first tasks I undertook was to assess any dependencies amongst the other programmes. I was especially concerned to discover none of the other programmes were tracking my own, despite it being critical to them all as the key data source. This was exacerbated by a lack of a portfolio management approach to bring all programmes together.

In such cases, the only course of action might be to be open in what you are seeking to achieve through the implementation and actively engage parties from across the organisation to spot initiatives or activities which might have a bearing or influence on your own activity. Whilst this might sound laborious, it does have real benefits, as it gets the communication of your own activity known whilst also forging links across the organisation that might otherwise have been overlooked.

Whichever way you seek to capture and ratify dependencies, time spent in ensuring you have these under a level of control from the outset will serve you well as you enter implementation. Do not feel tempted to skimp, learning as you go. As the quote above demonstrates, time is as important a factor as knowing what lies ahead, and the combination of the two gives you a greater likelihood of success.

8.5 AGILITY AND FLEXIBILITY IN STRATEGY EXECUTION

One of the challenges in embarking on strategy execution is establishing the level of understanding of those who compiled the data strategy in the first instance as to the complexities of the world around them in order to comprehend the potential impact on the implementation of the data strategy. The process of defining a data strategy is often a long and complicated exercise, getting inputs and buy-in from a variety of teams across the organisation and plotting a course which, ostensibly, seems the right one to be heading for.

However, it is worth contemplating the level of knowledge those closest to the process of defining the data strategy can have of the rapidly evolving world around them and their desire to be constantly seeking to assess the 'what ifs' of the landscape in which the data strategy is set. For instance, we can all agree change is a constant, and one which will impact on the way an organisation collects, manages and exploits its data in the furtherance of its corporate objectives. How many of us within an organisation, particularly of some size and complexity, can have a comprehensive view of the way a market may change in the course of a year, let alone three, five or more years that the data strategy is set to reflect?

Aside from the seismic impact of coronavirus around the world, which has decimated some industries and yet seen others more profitable than at any time in living memory, there can be less obvious change that has ramifications for the data strategy. Consider a change in leadership within your own organisation, for example. This usually occurs due to the incumbent stepping down due to their retirement, ill health or seeking a break, being replaced or moving on, all of which have profound impacts on the future direction and priorities for the organisation and hence its data strategy. Certainly, if your organisation is a private sector organisation with aggressive shareholders or private equity funding, then a change in the CEO or chairman role can be driven by a change of tack, whether through acquisition, divestment or simply a reprioritisation of where focus is to be placed. All of these scenarios are data-heavy in the demands put on the organisation and the direction in which the data strategy will need to head.

Similarly, a change in your competitors' intentions can have profound implications for your own organisation, as can changes in the regulatory environment – most organisations, though, should have the right level of engagement to spot these coming, especially as they are rarely knee-jerk or instantaneous in implementation and may have included extensive consultation in advance.

The findings in the research undertaken by Sull et al. (2015) highlighted that most organisations do not adapt quickly enough to changing market conditions, with only 20 per cent of managers indicating that their organisations shifted people across business units to support strategy in such circumstances, and 30 per cent moving funding likewise. Agility is essential to spot opportunities for the organisation to reach a strategic outcome faster, smarter or more cheaply through being ready to act and seize the initiative, all the while continuing to meet the strategic intent.

The data strategy, just like the corporate strategy, will include activities needed to be undertaken to deliver successful outcomes, but does not preclude those tasked with its implementation from being opportunistic in spotting those initiatives which could lead to getting ahead in the delivery of the strategy. However, to do so requires alignment and the key factors of trust and collaboration to pull the resources together at the right time in the right way to achieve the right outcome. It is why smaller organisations, with more entrepreneurial focus and fewer lines of communication, can so often outsmart much larger organisations as they are prepared for, and ready to act on, any such initiatives swiftly to achieve significant gains.

At every step of the way, challenge the implementation team on how effective they are in opportunity spotting any activity that might enable the strategy to be delivered faster and better, regardless of the nature or size of your organisation. As Deming said, change is inevitable, so embrace it and be ready to be at the front of it rather than adjusting and coping through a lack of anticipation.

A good mantra is that a successful implementation team delivers the plan on time, to budget, achieving the targets set, whilst anticipating and handling change along the way. A great implementation team, on the other hand, exceeds the plan by identifying ways to deliver enduring progress smarter, faster and more cheaply than assumed within the plan, and explores the business landscape – internal and external – looking for ways to surpass what was expected to be delivered. Challenging the status quo, looking at risks and assumptions, and being willing to view things from a different perspective to realise opportunities which would otherwise have been missed are at the heart of operating at a fundamentally different level.

It is the blend of good programme implementation discipline with a zeal for innovation and exploration that is the differentiator between good and great implementation.

8.6 CAPABILITY ASSESSMENT

Research suggests that a constant failing in most organisations' efforts to execute strategy lies in the calibre of the people to deliver it. Yet, ironically, the one area that is assumed in almost all organisations is the expectation that all managers (regardless of level of seniority) have some inherent capability to execute strategy. This seems preposterous, as there is little or no formal training provided by most organisations to support this, and the evidence shows that there is limited expertise amongst managers to be able to hire this expertise in, which is why so many organisations turn to consulting firms to support this activity.

Given the direct link between strategy, delivery and corporate performance, it is still surprising how little credence organisations seem to give to preparing managers for this important role, yet the evidence suggests it has been like this for decades. Little appears to have changed in the way organisations tackle the implementation of strategy, and still the evidence shows a compelling case to address this if successful outcomes are to be achieved.

I have explored elsewhere in this book the dichotomy between the art of devising strategy and implementing it. However, neither of these disciplines are taught effectively in the vast majority of organisations, and often those tasked with devising the strategy are assumed to be just as skilled in its execution. Some organisations take it to a new level, creating a strategy function that is to some degree removed from the rest of the organisation, as if working in a specialism that has to bring every member of staff with them on a coherent journey is achievable by creating a hothouse of expertise, the strategy ivory tower, if you like, where only those capable of thinking strategically can be found.

My own experience has shown that organisations take a mixed approach to strategy formulation. These have ranged from the top-down board away-day sessions which provide a glorious vision of a future state with limited input from the ranks of expertise at their disposal, through to the more devolved or federated approach. In these, executives in business units or functions create a vision of what their own strategy might look like and a star chamber style approach[14] is adopted to work through how to blend these into something coherent.

There is also the more alarming approach that involves a lack of a 'real' strategy but instead some vaguely bold statements which set a vision but provide no clarity on what this means for the wider organisation or how to get there. One organisation had such bold strategic statements as 'to be the most efficient and effective organisation in the XXX market' without any comprehension of how to measure efficiency or effectiveness or even the concept of the market, which could be defined a number of ways, and no baseline to work from to know how efficient or effective it was today. The assumption, clearly, was that there was scope to improve, but no one knew what this meant in terms of closing a gap, the investment required to achieve this or how to benchmark it.

Therefore, in drafting the data strategy and embarking on its implementation, spare more than a thought for how to benchmark the current state and how you intend to measure ongoing progress to demonstrate success. This will be essential to retain buy-in and resources to maintain support.

I referred earlier in the book to the use of data maturity assessments as a key starting point on the strategy definition journey. It is important to explore the readiness of the organisation from a capability standpoint to implement the critical strands of the data strategy, identifying the need to upskill as part of the data strategy deliverables. As a prelude to moving into the strategy implementation phase, there is a need to review the findings of the data maturity assessment – which should form a key part of the overall tracking of progress of the data strategy through implementation – and to enhance it through a review of the readiness and capability of the organisation to enable the implementation to succeed. This may take the form of an employee skills audit or matrix to assess the capability in those parts of the organisation that are essential to success in a documented approach which can then be utilised to drive learning and development and identification of skills that are needed by the programme.

I have set out a checklist below for you to use in a pre-implementation review.

1. Construct a coherent implementation plan from the data strategy.

The first step is to consider how clear the data strategy is to be able to develop a clear implementation plan. This involves a review of the waymarkers (assuming these exist, of course), the timetable, the RAID log and the scale of commitment required to enable the organisation to meet the strategic timeline and ambition. Once this has been undertaken, it must be ratified by all stakeholders as part of a

---

14 A star chamber is a scrutiny board which challenges rigorously the thinking and decision-making process to test out how effective and optimal the proposal or outcome is likely to be. It usually consists of people with significant experience who have not been directly involved. It is named after the court that sat in the Old Palace of Westminster between the fifteenth and seventeenth centuries that was composed of judges and privy councillors.

pre-implementation checklist, to ensure the baseline position is fully understood and approved by those you will need to engage resources and support from. It will also be the trigger to determine the communications strategy to be followed, turning the implementation plan into a story to run alongside the data strategy vision that has already been developed. You now have the 'when', 'where' and 'how' to sit alongside the 'what' and the 'why' to complete the picture and enhance those campfire discussions with practical steps to be undertaken.

2. **Establish the maturity of the organisation to embrace and achieve the data strategy.**

The data maturity assessment will have identified the strengths and weaknesses of the organisation and had some input from all parts to have reached this conclusion. It should be a key artefact to be signed off within the data strategy, as this becomes an important element in the need to track progress and demonstrate the impact of change as it is implemented. The critical step to be undertaken at this point is to articulate, as clearly and simply as possible, what differentiates the next stage of maturity from the current position and to break this down to specific actions needed to evidence progress to the next level. Whilst this is usually an internal measure, it does have some merit in being conducted by a third party, to provide objectivity.

As the data maturity assessment highlights gaps, which hopefully should link clearly to the deliverables specified in the waymarkers, so there needs to be an assessment of the organisation's capability to fulfil those gaps. After all, if these capabilities were already within the organisation there is a perfectly reasonable argument to suggest these should have been addressed already, unless they were not deemed a priority previously (in which case, why has this been the case and what is so different now?) and were suppressed. It may be that there are gaps which require training and development of existing staff within the organisation, but there is just as likely a strong case for hiring expertise if that skillset is hard to develop without internal support, is too big a leap from the starting point or there is an urgency to make progress quickly that would benefit from acquiring those skills through recruitment.

This information gathering involved in reviewing the maturity of the organisation to be ready to embark on implementing the data strategy is perhaps the most focused activity to be undertaken. As such, it should be a key element of the pre-implementation review and be signed off as part of the commitment to deliver against the commitments that each part of the organisation needs to support – remember, strategic execution fails due to a lack of realism, commitment and collaboration across teams, so this is your opportunity to bring this to the fore in making it clear what you are expecting from senior leaders and to act as a reference point whenever resources are challenging to source.

If additional resources need to be hired, make sure there is clear accountability as to who will take the lead on this, when they are needed by and how these resources will be made available to support the implementation of the data strategy, and that there is an understanding of the core skills to be sought – I have seen organisations fail to appreciate the skillset being demanded within a role that is new to the organisation and so hire inappropriately. Finding an individual with unrelated skills to those you need to succeed will hinder the implementation more than having no one with those skills available.

3. Consider data and analytics capability.

There will inevitably be a high demand on those individuals in your organisation that undertake a variety of roles in data and analytics – assuming your organisation has these and it is not your single-handed task to be a jack of all trades. They will almost certainly have played a part in shaping the data strategy, so you probably have some insight as to their capability, experience and scale of ambition, but it is important that you embark on the implementation phase clear as to how resources are to be balanced between 'keeping the lights on' through the delivery of current activity (which may not, of course, be aligned to the direction of the data strategy, which is another issue you will need to address, as any activities that may need to be 'switched off' at some point will need the agreement of the stakeholders involved) and supporting the new activity that moves the organisation forward in delivering the data strategy.

In determining the capability of the organisation to deliver on the data strategy implementation, you will also need to consider the readiness of the data and analytics teams to support you as effectively as you will need. They will undertake a critical role in making the implementation a success, so it is essential that you do not compromise on capability in this critical area. In addition, these individuals must also carry the rest of the organisation with them and have confidence in their ability to deliver outcomes in conjunction with the wider teams across the organisation. Therefore, you may need to consider their effectiveness at engaging with the wider organisation and there may be a need for support to develop their confidence in this area.

Many analysts are comfortable operating in their own arena, but lack the ability to transcend the complexity of their world and translate it into language and stories that business leaders can comprehend and engage with. I recommend that you look for those who have the spark, the ability to be the go-between in the communication between analysts and the wider business, and harness that capability. I have developed many individuals in various organisations to perform this critical stakeholder management role, operating with a foot in each camp, building confidence and translating requirements. They are a minority, but I believe you will find people with the willingness to learn and be those translators; you just need to help by showing them the way to begin.

If you are not a data and analytics professional yourself, but are tasked with driving the data strategy implementation, then I would recommend getting an external assessment of the capabilities of the data and analytics resources at your disposal. It is relatively easy for those with years of experience in the field who have operated in complex environments as a leader to provide such assessments – I've done so in a number of organisations, as well as building teams from scratch. This provides an insight into the key resources you are about to depend upon to implement the data strategy, and for a modest investment will highlight where you have gaps or training needs that can then be tackled up front, before you are exposed by these in-flight.

8.7 AVOIDING STRATEGY PARALYSIS

'There are two fatal errors that keep great projects from coming to life:

1. Not finishing
2. Not starting'

Attributed to Buddha Gautama (c. 563–483 BCE)

This section could equally apply to many parts of this book, but I thought it fitted into this part as an important step in the readiness for strategy execution. There has been a logical structure throughout this book that might suggest that the process of defining a data strategy, structuring a communications approach and readying for implementation is a logical flow that moves seamlessly to a logical and rational conclusion – the delivery of a strategy and its successful implementation. If only life were so simple!

In reality, there is a stop-start nature to much of the work that underpins reaching readiness for implementation that is a fact of business life. As with every project, there is a planned approach to how the future will unfold that often falters within days, not through the lack of planning or thinking through the steps to be taken sufficiently but just because the unforeseen may happen and you have to adapt. Dwight D. Eisenhower is quoted as saying: 'In preparing for battle I have always found that plans are useless, but planning is indispensable.'[15] In other words, do not find yourself in an endless loop, refining the data strategy and readying for having to translate this into an implementation plan, constantly seeking ways to improve and amend the content. As General George S. Patton, renowned for his dislike of indecision, stated: 'A good plan, violently executed now, is better than a perfect plan next week.'[16]

This chapter has highlighted that the landscape around you is in constant change; there is every likelihood that you learnt something today that you did not know yesterday. However, the data strategy has to stand the test of several years, and so any expectation that planning accurately to within a week or a month makes all the difference is misplaced. It simply moves the goalposts to being more aware of some facts but conscious of yet more that you are not able to answer at that point in time.

In other words, there is no right time for the data strategy to be ready, other than the point at which you have mapped all the points to be captured in the RAID log, have sought inputs from all parts of the organisation and have the opportunity to engage senior leaders with the content you have refined to this point. In truth, no strategy is perfect – research has shown only 2 per cent of senior leaders were confident enough

---

[15] Richard M. Nixon, *Six Crises*. New York: Pocket Books, 1962.

[16] In G.S. Patton, *War as I Knew It*. Boston, MA: Houghton Mifflin, 1947.

to state that they expected to achieve at least 80 per cent of their strategy over the time frame it was due to deliver.[17]

Your goal is to minimise the risk of failure by providing a clear route map to achieve the strategic goals you have set and to provide the means to be able to measure progress reliably and easily. This is the point at which implementation takes over, and this is the phase which needs to be closer to the detail on a day-to-day basis to reflect whether the data strategy still holds true or needs further refinement based upon new observations and learning from what has been achieved so far. Uncertainty is unavoidable in the complex world we live in today, and to chase down every detail to try to mitigate it is largely a fool's errand. To quote Voltaire: 'Uncertainty is an uncomfortable position. But certainty is an absurd one.'[18]

The implementation plan will translate the data strategy into a series of defined deliverables to achieve, via milestones, the waymarkers you outline within the data strategy. The plan will iterate and evolve, shaped by what is known and a reflection on the changing nature of that which is contained in the RAID log and the priorities of the organisation. A highly experienced individual in the implementation of strategy will advise that there is little to be gained from trying to anticipate and prepare for every eventuality; these have to be addressed as they become known, otherwise there is little to be gained from what might never materialise in defining the data strategy.

Seek advice, get feedback, test drafts of the data strategy with those able to proffer an opinion as to how it might be received, but have the courage of your conviction to deliver a data strategy that is the best that you and your team (should there be one) can produce, and believe in the evidence you have gathered and the inputs you have gained from across the organisation to make this compelling to the senior leaders in your organisation. You know more about the detail within the data strategy than they will ever know: it is the alignment of your strategy with their conviction and appetite for change which will be put to the test. This cannot be addressed through constant review of the data strategy; it is to be hoped that your senior sponsor has acted as an effective supporter of your initiative at a peer group level to have prepared the ground, and you find a mutual meeting of minds, in which the data strategy is fully embraced with an appetite to see it delivered.

8.8 TEN TO TAKE AWAY

The important points to take away from this chapter are:

1. The most effective organisations at strategy execution treat implementation as a strategic activity, with the same people involved in both definition and execution.

2. The mobilisation phase of your data strategy implementation is critical to success. It enables detail to be gathered to ensure readiness to begin implementation, establishing the data strategy baseline, assumptions and key drivers.

---

17 Bridges Business Consultancy Int Pte Ltd, Strategy Implementation Survey. 2012. www.bridgesconsultancy.com/research-case-study/research/.

18 Letter to Frederick II of Prussia, 6 April 1767.

3. Review the RAID log at the start of mobilisation, with a strong focus on assessing the dependencies.

4. Senior leaders are not effective at both strategy and its execution, with more than one in three weak at either of these skills. Consider how the five myths of strategy execution fit with commonly held beliefs in your own organisation and prepare accordingly.

5. Assess the strategic alignment – both the corporate strategy and data strategy – against the actual business model to determine likelihood of success. Are you set to be one of the 13 per cent of organisations to be effective only half of the time, which in itself demonstrates the challenge of succeeding in strategy execution?

6. Convert waymarkers into milestones, defining the detail behind the deliverables and ensuring these are measurable.

7. Plan your course based on what you know about the dependencies that are ahead of you. Remember the Titanic analogy: it is about having sufficient time to adjust rather than simply seeing the iceberg lie ahead on your path.

8. Be agile. Flexibility is key: a great implementation team can exceed the plan through being smarter, faster and cheaper, and challenging the status quo to view things from a different perspective. Innovation and exploration, alongside good programme implementation discipline, are at the heart of a successful implementation.

9. Benchmark the capability of the organisation to deliver the data strategy. Evidence shows a lack of skills and capabilities to define and execute strategies in organisations worldwide, so do not assume your organisation is different. Use the data maturity assessment as a baseline and build a skills matrix to understand where capability lies and seek to utilise it.

10. Avoid strategy paralysis. There is never a period in which total knowledge is captured, so accept it is a world of change and embrace it. As Voltaire said, certainty is an absurd position. Utilise Agile, engage with your sponsor and gather facts as you go to refine the inputs that shape the plan and its deliverables.

9 EXECUTING THE STRATEGY – PART TWO: DELIVERY

'You have to be fast on your feet and adaptive or else a strategy is useless.'
Attributed to Charles de Gaulle

The data strategy is drafted and approved, and you have completed the mobilisation stage discussed in the preceding chapter. It is now time for action.

Mobilisation has given you the opportunity to review the continued relevance of the data strategy at a more detailed level, challenging the RAID log and enhancing it to provide the level of data you are going to need to be able to track an active RAID log as part of the implementation of the data strategy. Resources have been allocated (or, potentially, you know there are no other resources coming – still a certainty, even if a more challenging one!), timescales and priorities agreed, and now it is purely about delivering on the promise.

How you structure the implementation, whether as a programme or a loose arrangement of activities undertaken through other routes but tracked centrally, is entirely down to you, your organisation's preference and the resource you have to overlay formality over the strategy. Nevertheless, there are some practical tips and personal preferences I will share with you in this chapter, providing some guidance to the data strategy implementation path you choose.

9.1 ASSIGNING ROLES AND RESPONSIBILITIES

It is important to establish the roles people will play across the organisation as part of the delivery of the data strategy. The standard model used for some time in programme management is the RACI model, which identifies responsibility, accountability, those needing to be consulted and, finally, those to be informed. There are variations on this theme; I quite like the addition of support into the mix (those who will help and/or support those responsible), but it is a well-understood model and as such is probably familiar to some of your colleagues, if not to you yourself. See Figure 9.1.

I do not intend to cover in detail the thinking behind the usage of RACI (or RASCI) models as there are plenty of reference sources available should you wish to pursue this topic in more depth than space permits here. I shall instead provide a generic level of how you may wish to apply your RACI in the specific context of the data strategy and leave you to investigate other, broader, perspectives in the mass of literature on this topic.

Whilst the acronym leads with those responsible, it is perhaps more pertinent to start with who is accountable (A). Someone has ultimate accountability for the implementation of the data strategy. This may be your role, reporting in to a board or senior team to outline

Figure 9.1 RASCI D. Mann (2017) Working Well with Distributed Teams. Akoonu. https://www.akoonu.com/blog/working-well-with-distributed-teams/.

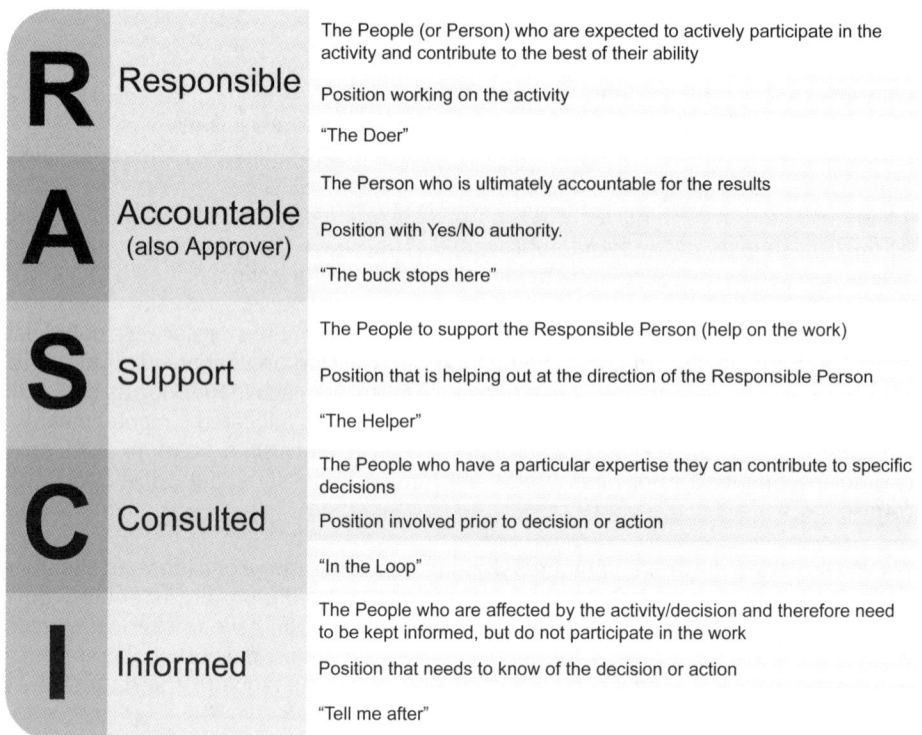

R	Responsible	The People (or Person) who are expected to actively participate in the activity and contribute to the best of their ability Position working on the activity "The Doer"
A	Accountable (also Approver)	The Person who is ultimately accountable for the results Position with Yes/No authority. "The buck stops here"
S	Support	The People to support the Responsible Person (help on the work) Position that is helping out at the direction of the Responsible Person "The Helper"
C	Consulted	The People who have a particular expertise they can contribute to specific decisions Position involved prior to decision or action "In the Loop"
I	Informed	The People who are affected by the activity/decision and therefore need to be kept informed, but do not participate in the work Position that needs to know of the decision or action "Tell me after"

and demonstrate progress, or that of a sponsor for the programme. Accountability should never be shared (unless a role is, of course, shared, such as a job share in which the role is managed carefully as one despite being undertaken by two). The point of accountability is that it is clear to all who has final say and determines direction and the corralling of resources to deliver that for which they are accountable.

It is feasible to have accountability split at a task level in multiple places, and this is actually quite common for large programmes such as the implementation of a data strategy. This entails a hierarchical approach, breaking down the project into a series of deliverables, each of which could have a set of tasks attached to it. In such a scenario, the accountability may be defined by groups of activities to be undertaken; it could even be accountability at a task level, though this tends to be unusual unless that task is so discrete and significant that it requires individual accountability.

Responsible (R) may concern any stage from the programme delivery owner, reporting in to a sponsor who is held accountable, or detailed tasks for which someone is responsible for delivery. Unlike accountability, the difference with responsibility is that there could be multiple people responsible for achieving a task if it involves a collaborative effort. Those responsible would be expected to track and report on progress regularly, as this is the step that helps guide the accountability in determining whether the programme is on target to deliver outcomes to intent, time and budget.

Those who are consulted (C) will be key agents in the delivery of tasks, whether individually or collectively. Their role is often to bring subject matter expertise, specialised input and alignment of activities to that which lies outside the programme, such as other programmes or business-as-usual activities which are undergoing changes and therefore need to be considered. They therefore perform a critical role in advising and guiding the programme to ensure there is integrity between the programme deliverables and those supporting the everyday running of the organisation. Whilst they are there to be consulted and to advise, it would be challenging to go against their opinion or recommendations without documenting and reaching agreement as to why the programme needs to do so. Therefore, the consulted can have more teeth in blocking the programme if it is not seen to be consistent with the wider direction, and so the term may not be as passive as perhaps it first sounds.

Finally, the informed (I) group will be a mixture of those who are impacted but not directly participating (they may have to work in a different way in the future as a result of the data strategy, but their views or opinions would be swept up by one or more individuals consulted on their behalf); those who have an interest in tracking your progress and therefore receive regular performance reporting (could be the board, or some group your sponsor is accountable to within the organisation); and those who have an interest that is peripheral unless the data strategy implementation strays into territory outside that which was initially considered (hence the importance of tracking changes throughout the programme). This could arise if there is a compliance issue that was unforeseen, resulting in those who were to be informed suddenly needing to be consulted, for instance.

The informed group is key to keep engaged, which is why the communications approach is so critical to get right throughout the implementation of the data strategy, otherwise there is a risk that the application of changes delivered via the implementation fails to land effectively through a lack of buy-in or simply low levels of awareness.

The addition of support (S) into the RACI provides a clear line of sight to those who can enable the successful implementation of the data strategy. This group will play a role in helping you deliver, whether through the provision of resources to support those who hold responsibility, the delivery of messaging via communications, or the tracking of progress via a structured programme management and financial control process. Capturing this additional area to assign supportive roles is vitally important to ensure those who need to work with the implementation programme know what is expected, when, why and how it is to be achieved. It also enables the responsible group to be aware as to whom they can turn to in order to achieve the desired outcome.

With a clear RACI (or RASCI) in hand, you should have a good understanding of not only what is to be delivered through your plan but also who is undertaking what roles to bring it to life. One simple, and relatively obvious, point – do not focus on named individuals per se, as there may well be changes in personnel in the life of the implementation plan, but capture roles that are essential to delivering on your plan and names of individuals currently in those roles as a secondary level input. You are seeking to fix the RACI within the organisation; do not come unstuck as people within your organisation come and go.

One final observation. The use of RACI within organisations does not mean that it is necessarily followed. This may seem a perverse statement: after all, the whole point is to assign roles and responsibilities. Often, it is the grey areas which cause issues, with people being too obsessed with what their responsibility is rather than being flexible and responsive to how they engage with others when such vagaries arise. Therefore, avoid making the RACI bureaucratic; it needs to be indicative but there is still no excuse for a lack of collaboration. A good idea is to link the responsibilities within the RACI in a value-added way, to demonstrate 'why' something should be done and to link it in a way similar to a value chain. This focuses the mind on completing end-to-end activities to release value, with the RACI acting as a guide to who plays what role in making it happen.

9.2 PLAN FOR ACTION, PREPARE FOR CHANGE

Operations keep the lights on, strategy provides a light at the end of the tunnel, but project management is the train engine that moves the organization forward.

Joy Gumz[1]

The implementation phase, once in action, will take the plan, defined through the mobilisation stage, and assign resources. At this point, the plan is communicated to all stakeholders to ensure that there is a thorough understanding of how, when and where the implementation will take place – the detail on what needs to be achieved by the organisation as a whole, and specific functions in particular. Bear in mind that the strategy may well have only touched a minority of staff in your organisation in its formulation, so the need to communicate the strategy takes on greater importance if you are to succeed in taking your colleagues with you.

It is highly likely that the implementation plan will focus in on greater detail in the months or year ahead, whilst sketching out in lesser detail the rest of the implementation of the data strategy. Do consider the validity of the waymarkers in determining the features in the first year as consideration will have been given in defining them as to the cadence to be expected in delivering the data strategy. If you know more detail such that it either changes the focus, accelerates or decelerates the pace or has new inputs which align with the core intent of the data strategy, then you should not feel a hostage to the waymarkers. However, these will have been a factor in the sign-off process, so you should communicate the need for change openly and vigorously, to ensure there is no confusion as to the rationale later.

This plays to one of the key themes that will be at the heart of project managing the implementation of the data strategy – change management. It is essential that there is a recognition of the likelihood of change throughout the implementation phase, and it is important to engage all parties openly on the need for (and approval of) change as well as clear lines of communication as to why change is required, the impact it has and the demand profile it now requires from others to meet the revised plan.

The significance of preparation in implementation planning was highlighted in the previous chapter, suitably referencing Abraham Lincoln's quote about preparation time for the axe to cut down the tree. If there is anything experienced programme managers

---

1   J. Gumz, *Risk on Complex Projects: A Case Study*. Newtown Square, PA: Project Management Institute, 2012.

will tell you about what made for successful programme delivery, one of their key messages would almost certainly be the need to focus your plan on what you intend to do, even if reality quickly becomes divergent from it. As Winston Churchill put it: 'Those who plan do better than those who do not plan even though they rarely stick to their plan.'

Therefore, familiarise yourself with the need to construct effective change management controls in your plan and to recognise that there will be divergence, whether that takes the shape of time, resources, focus or a mixture of all three. An inability to flex, make effective decisions and communicate those changes with clarity to all who need to be aware will result in your plan – and, thereby, the data strategy – failing almost as soon as it has started.

The first time you find a change needing to be implemented will be the opportunity for you to put your programme governance and controls to the test. I suggest you trial this prior to going live, as there is little to be gained from losing momentum through having to determine how to respond on the hoof and it will only lose time and confidence in your plan. Walking through the change management approach will check how effectively it engages those parties who need to know about the change, and establish how efficiently those areas are able to adapt to it to inform you as to the flexibility and adaptability your organisation has built within its DNA. You may well have a feel for this yourself, as it is one of those things that underpin the type of culture your organisation has, so whilst you might not be able to spot it via any documented evidence, you may have observed the inherent inertia or resistance to change on other activities you have been party to.

Change is inevitable; if your plan does not change then it is more likely that you are aloof from the challenges your organisation is facing than your environment being so stable that the implementation plan does not need to adapt and evolve. Unless you operate in a highly regulated, slow-moving sector – perhaps nuclear energy being one of the few examples – then your organisation will be buffeted by the winds of competition, compliance, economic stability, resource availability, sector changes, supplier delivery availability and pricing impacts; the list is almost endless, and applies equally to small businesses to those operating on a global scale.

The coronavirus pandemic has shown the fragility of our economies to factors outside our control that can have a global impact, regardless of size of business or sector in which you operate. Those who have been able to ride the storm and seen demand soar have had pressures in being able to source supply of raw materials and resource constraints, not to mention trading patterns which have been changeable on a regular basis that cannot be easily predicted. Many organisations with perishable goods in their supply chain have seen those assets disposed of due to an inability to trade. Whilst this has been an unusual event, at scale it shows the vulnerability of even the best-run organisations regardless of size.

I have stressed the likelihood of change, the importance of adaptability and the effectiveness of being able to take it in your stride as essential features for a successful outcome. I should add that if you find yourself having to diverge significantly from the underlying data strategy that you are tasked with implementing, there will be a trigger point at which that change is so great that the data strategy needs to be paused and consideration given to having to update it. This results in a reset of the implementation, as there are too many instances of strategies of all types no longer reflecting the reality of the implementation, and a confused outcome resulting due to a lack of common understanding and agreement on the direction being taken.

As Michael Porter said: 'Strategy must have continuity. It can't be constantly reinvented,' adding: 'continuity of strategic direction and continuous improvement in how you do things are absolutely consistent with each other. In fact, they're mutually reinforcing.'[2] Indeed, Masaaki Imai, regarded as the father of kaizen – defined as gradual, unending improvement, doing 'little things' better; setting, and achieving, ever higher standards – describes incremental change as a key part of continuous improvement. He says it is 'not a paradigm shift or invention, but slow and steady progress is the most innovative. It helps apply change easier, as well as giving the reins to the organization rather than having to respond to external forces.'[3]

You will also require some form of programme governance to track what you are achieving, assess progress versus the plan via metrics and bring the RACI to life to ensure there is the right engagement at all levels to keep things on track. This will be a critical window into the programme for your sponsor and/or those expecting you to deliver a successful implementation, but you should also treat it as a shop window to demonstrate the change you are making to the organisation. This chapter will cover the other key aspects of the governance you will require, but ensure you have representation across your stakeholders in the way you govern the implementation phase, as it is better to have all parties inside the tent focusing attention and effort collectively on the same objective than to have groups isolated, outside the governance but able to disrupt at a more senior level within your organisation.

9.3 CUSTOMER ENGAGEMENT

The theme of customer, or stakeholder, engagement has run throughout this book, so it should not come as a surprise to have it raise its head here, in this important chapter about the delivery of the data strategy.

The preceding section talked of the RACI (or RASCI, if you prefer) and aligning the implementation plan to the resources across the organisation. It is essential to consider the engagement across the organisation, as any data strategy needs total buy-in from all of it to succeed. There is not a single function within the organisation that operates in a vacuum without using data in some way, so this data strategy is for every function – it is neither optional nor limited in its application. You will need all parts to engage, and the more they do the more likely you are to succeed.

---

2   M.E. Porter, *Competitive Strategy: Techniques for Analyzing Industries and Competitors*. New York: Free Press, 1980.

3   M. Imai, *Kaizen: The Key to Japan's Competitive Success*. New York: McGraw-Hill, 1986.

9.3.1 Communications

Many of the communications challenges were covered in Chapter 7. However, in the context of customer engagement, with strategy execution the important factor is how to compete for communications space and deliver a compelling message that makes your colleagues take notice. This is what your focus needs to be on when you are devising your approach, and the constant refrain in your discussions with communications colleagues to ensure this is at the forefront of the messaging. It is essential to consider how you will deliver impact through communications rather than assume the act of communicating is, in itself, simply the answer.

Most organisations have far too much going on and, to put it bluntly, many messages from your communications function are likely to fail to land as well as hoped. This may be due to the sheer amount of noise in the organisation, making it difficult to comprehend how any of this comes together and what takes priority, or it might be that the communications are failing to reach the audience. I have experienced the latter, especially in those organisations that determine that the 'go to' place should be the intranet, or some social media type platform. That is not to say these platforms are not a good option, but do some analysis of the channels (it is a data strategy you are delivering, after all, so this should be familiar to you!) to assess effectiveness (measurement), breadth (coverage of the organisation using it) and frequency (how often they are accessed) to understand what they bring and how best to utilise them. A blended approach will almost certainly reap better rewards, especially if these are linked to drive a coherent story.

Often, those who are the most engaged will utilise the broadest range of channels to garner information, particularly within organisations that have multiple communication delivery routes available. This can lead to a sense that social media platforms are exceedingly popular due to the number of hits obtained, but actually it is a minority of the workforce using those channels disproportionately. Invariably, it is those who tend not to utilise the broad range of channels who are the hardest to reach but the ones you want to influence the most. This requires some creativity to identify how to get to the breadth of the organisation, and is where having local knowledge comes in very useful.

Wearing my analytics hat, it is disappointing (but maybe not surprising) how lacking the communications delivery is in terms of value-added metrics, counting hits (and usually not unique ones at that) or simply the fact that something 'is out there' as job done. I have to say I've worked in far more organisations with intranets which seem to have search engines designed to find what you don't want than those which do – the experience everyone expects is akin to an internet search, and the return of hundreds or thousands of hits in which nothing on the first two pages is even related to the search simply undermines the credibility of the intranet.

What does this mean for your communications strategy and customer engagement in this implementation stage? Simple: don't leave it to the communications team, take the bull by the horns and devise messaging for those who are connected to the programme to deliver. Remember the advice in the earlier chapters to get people aware and involved with the data strategy, the show and tells, the opportunistic seeking out of ways to embed your message alongside others and to weave a common thread, the strategy storytelling approach of Chapter 6. If you own the implementation, you own the communications. Remember what the RASCI indicated. You are supported by the communications team but you are accountable for this activity, so make it work.

Remember, too, we all learn and absorb information differently. It is quite likely that your organisation hasn't developed a sophisticated approach to communications in which it segments the channel, message, even the timing, based on what works best for the individual (this may be one of the goals of your data strategy in due course). As someone with some awareness of data and analytics, it should not surprise you to discover that we all like to listen and learn differently, so a 'one size fits all' approach is never going to work.

> Think about this carefully. Try to remember the last six to ten corporate messages you were told, set them down and try to identify the important 'takeaway' message in each. Do the same with some colleagues in different areas who should have had the same corporate messages. Compare notes. See how consistent they are, from whether you have the same list through to the detail of the takeaways in there. Invariably, you will discover differences and may not even have the same list – some messages will resonate for certain groups and completely pass others by, due to the brain filtering out those which do not seem to be relevant on the surface. Ask how the others received, or gathered, the information. Chances are there will be differences there too, even down to the opportunity to discuss and engage leaders on such things, to simply receiving these messages via a written update.

9.3.2 Employee engagement with the strategy implementation

De Bussy and Suprawan conducted a national study into which stakeholders had the greatest impact on corporate financial performance.[4] The coefficient for employees was 0.84, which left customers (0.36), suppliers (0.35), communities (0.32) and shareholders (0.08) in the distance. Whilst this research relates to a different field – financial performance – the findings would seem to hold true with regard to data strategy implementation too. Employees have to be engaged to drive the impact – if they are, then there is a clear association with driving successful outcomes.

Think about the governance you intend to put in place for the implementation of the data strategy. How do you want to ensure there is transparency, evidence and total commitment to your cause? In practice, this will demand that you make this everyone's business, something they want to participate in and influence in terms of the practical delivery steps. This will be onerous, challenging (having engaged stakeholders can be

---

4   N.M. De Bussy and L. Suprawan, Most Valuable Stakeholders: The Impact of Employee Orientation on Corporate Financial Performance. *Public Relations Review*, 38, 280–287, 2012. https://espace.curtin.edu.au/handle/20.500.11937/62193.

more of a handful than a seemingly passive organisation) and time-consuming, but it will bear fruit and achieve the best outcome through a really effective collaborative approach. You will need to be prepared, able to demonstrate progress and be in control of the narrative and direction, but be ready and willing to adapt and flex to achieve those outcomes you want. Getting there with all behind you, even if on the surface a little slower, and delivering something not quite what you had expected, is an achievement.

Having identified the key players to be involved in the governance group, ensure that there is clarity on how you expect them to communicate and the messaging to be delivered (and how this is defined and agreed by the group). Seek inputs across the group, and do not be afraid to abandon the 'one size fits all' flawed strategy – explore the reasons and the pitfalls of such an approach with the group and agree on the alternative, even if it is tailored to different areas of the organisation and takes advantage of some understanding of communications segmentation.

Many strategy implementations fail as the communications all but dry up, starting off with gusto and then turning into a trickle some months down the line, till there is no communication being issued at all. Whilst there is a risk of communicating with nothing to say, you do need to recognise that across the spectrum of the strategy implementation there are likely to be successes and progress to be reported, and often the art is ensuring you keep your programme front of mind through those periods when otherwise the stories might dry up. Remember, there will be communications of some sort in each part of the organisation on a daily basis; it is as much about seeking opportunities to align the work the implementation programme is doing as it is to have headline stories. Consider how you can devise links between such announcements into the strategy implementation, and support the relevant team members to make the most of such opportunities within their own functions.

Continuous engagement is essential if you are to keep the momentum behind the strategy implementation. It is the one of the highest causes of implementation failure,[5] and programmes are prone to over-elaborate the level of content required to enable communications to be released, which leads to delay and, when ready for release, too much information being issued to be absorbed effectively. Little and often – as often as possible – is the order of the day to keep progress at the forefront of minds and lines of communication going.

At every step of the strategy implementation, the impact on various parts of the organisation should be assessed and relevant communications drafted in conjunction with the key stakeholders representing those areas of the organisation. The programme implementation team should have key links into the relevant business areas, and be able to tailor messaging, spot opportunities to integrate messages and brief the appropriate people for onward dissemination of those messages.

---

[5] *Harvard Business Review* and Strativity Group identified 62 per cent, the highest rate of failure, was due to poor communications. Referenced in S. Percy, Why Do Change Programmes Fail? Forbes. 13 March 2019. https://www.forbes.com/sites/sallypercy/2019/03/13/why-do-change-programs-fail/#112e91872e48.

In my experience, there is always an angle to be found in linking data strategy to the communications activity within the organisation. However, I have also tended to utilise key messages within 'local' communications to reinforce elements of the data strategy implementation, rather than call them out specifically as data strategy deliverables. Putting the message into the localised context, in words that sound familiar to the audience receiving that message, increases the likelihood of adoption and support. It also binds the local leadership into the message they deliver, ensuring support for the data strategy implementation, which is key to your success.

9.3.3 Alignment with the corporate strategy

Clearly, the link between data strategy and the organisation's corporate strategy is integral to providing the important grounding and purpose behind the data strategy. This should be enshrined in the data strategy itself, but is an important communication message in its own right. Alignment between data strategy deliverables and the roles these play in enabling delivery of the corporate strategy should be clear for all, so the implementation plan needs to retain sight of these and track the wider impact as the implementation progresses.

Just as the data strategy needs to be flexible and have a coherent and integrated change management approach, so the corporate strategy should have adopted those same principles. Connecting the change management activities of both strategies is therefore essential to keep the alignment between the two strategies and to make sure that any change in the corporate strategy is assessed as early as possible (ideally, well in advance of the change being approved), and any dependencies or enablers reflected in the data strategy and how it plays into facilitating the strategic objectives of the organisation.

In the same way that the corporate strategy has been distilled into a series of divisional and functional objectives via an implementation plan, so the data strategy needs to find an alignment to reflect a similar construct. This is essential, as otherwise the practical alignment between the corporate strategy implementation and your own data strategy implementation will find a disconnect that will threaten to undermine the effectiveness of your implementation.

9.3.4 Retaining agility

The role of Agile in the process of defining and implementing the data strategy has been touched on at various points in this book. Much of the communications approach also fits well with an Agile approach, blending the milestones in the implementation plan with the opportunism of identifying how to communicate messages effectively alongside other plans to disseminate information across either part or all of the organisation.

As with any complex implementation programme over a longer time frame, the challenge of being able to keep messaging fresh and relevant becomes an issue, especially if the communication is not directly impacting those in receipt of the message. The importance of keeping the communications fresh and relevant is not unique to strategy implementation, but can be detached if it loses the sense of 'what does it mean for me?' in what is being disseminated. This is where the blend of Agile and local expertise in understanding the audience is so important.

There is always a risk with any programme implementation that the focus on milestones, the longer-term success and the overall intent of the strategy is too distant for some in the organisation to understand. I recommend taking a more thematic approach to turning the deliverables into use cases (rather than user stories), enabling your colleagues to understand the cause and effect of the change in the context of their work as the most effective way to get traction and retain it over a period of time.

> Use cases in an Agile context work well to describe functional behaviours in a flow of events that enable fine-tuning of the outcome, which is particularly suited to data strategy implementation, given there may be several ways to deliver a change to the benefit of the end user. The importance is to focus on value, and not spend too much time defining them to absolute levels of detail as they are indicative rather than a blueprint, and you will iterate the solution from the foundation of the original use case.

> Agile provides the means to deliver outputs and outcomes within a self-imposed constrained timescale that move things forward. There are a number of Agile approaches, and I particularly like the dynamic systems development method (DSDM) version as it is more project-based than many (Agile had its roots in software product development). However, there are many aspects of the Agile approach that can work and, if appropriate, I would suggest taking the best, or most pertinent, elements that these offer and defining a way of making it work for you (even if this is departing from the strict definitions of each model, it is being agile!). I have also operated using the Scrum approach, which is very team-focused and is simpler to operate due to being easier to explain and therefore quicker to adopt. Indeed, it is not uncommon to blend DSDM and Scrum as an approach, bringing the best of both together to get flexibility and effective stakeholder engagement as a key focus.

Agile is an approach which can be just as effective when deployed to your communications strategy. Identify the things to be achieved over a given period – I would suggest no longer than a month, possibly shorter – and devise the practical communications that deliver a message that tells your colleagues 'what it means for me' and also, if appropriate, what that means they need to do to help you keep moving things forward. Bringing them into the communication, making them feel some part of the delivery, will make for a more inclusive approach to sharing the burden and, consequently, the success, and the vast majority of us get a buzz from being part of a successful outcome.

Look for the key themes you want to feature through the month, start to build a range of use cases, communication pieces and briefings to share, and be prepared at the end of the month to review the progress made. As with all Agile activity, without the test and learn of what worked and what did not land as expected then you are likely to be in a cycle of repeating past mistakes. Improve, month on month, and you will start to build a following around engagement and getting actively involved with your communications approach, and sharing in the success of your implementation.

Share the measurement of your Agile communication sprints (a time-boxed period used within the Scrum methodology to deliver an agreed workload) as a key part of your overall progress. Don't forget, the measurement of a successful implementation is as much about overcoming those communication issues which hinder the majority of strategy implementations, so it should be one of your programme KPIs.

9.4 PROJECT TEAMS, A PMO AND THE DATA AND ANALYTICS FUNCTION

Inevitably, the data and analytics function (should you have one; if not it may be a collective of those with similar skills working informally across an organisation, or possibly just yourself as strategist, advocate and enabler) will play a key role in the definition and implementation of the data strategy. It is likely that many in such a function would have shaped the thinking of the data strategy and input to it along the way, possibly even helping with the final drafts. It is unlikely therefore that the data strategy implementation will come as a surprise.

The implementation will need a level of project coordination and tracking if it is to succeed. It is always a risk, once the strategy has been defined, that the daily activities of the organisation lead to the implementation of the strategy being lost, and so the organisation reverts back to a tactically driven approach, failing to achieve the things which move the organisation forward in a meaningful way. It is easy to spot such organisations: they tend to end up with numerous workarounds to key activities and a lack of design in how things work, and are then handicapped by major challenges such as technical debt – a dependency on systems which are no longer effective, compliant and/or supportable in delivering what the organisation needs.

The scale of the project team will need to align with the size and type of organisation you operate within. Some organisations will have these aspects already in place, a programme (or portfolio) management office (a PMO, or PfMO, if overseeing portfolio) that oversees all programmes within a portfolio. If either a PMO or PfMO is deployed to coordinate and direct the implementation, it is important that there is absolute clarity on all aspects of the data strategy, from the intent of the waymarkers, resources to be applied and from which parts of the organisation, the overall goals of the data strategy, the RACI (or RASCI) plus an understanding of the RAID log – they will need to utilise the latter two in their PMO planning.

To understand the complexity of what you are trying to do, consider the number of moving parts you have probably got within your data strategy. Data features in the work of every part of the organisation, whether capture, maintenance, use, manipulation, creation or storage to retain, through to deletion. The data strategy will therefore impact on everyone in the organisation as it is going to change some of the activities in the data lifecycle. You need to ensure everyone is playing their part in delivering whatever changes you are introducing over the course of the data strategy implementation, and that needs communication, understanding and buy-in to make it a reality, all of which needs to be tracked to identify it is happening and, more importantly, where it is not and why.

In the implementation of the data strategy, relatively small things can knock the whole programme sideways. If you find the organisation still capturing data inadequately, for instance, with missing or incorrect data, then it impacts the rest of the data lifecycle. One of the slightly frustrating aspects of having worked in the data and analytics space as long as I have is that the problems relating to data quality still persist despite effective technologies, increased awareness, greater resources in the data and analytics arena, and a myriad of articles written about the topic being available today. Indeed, we have more data today, and arguably it is less accurate in totality at a time when there is increasing demand to use it.

The project team may be a generic programme management function (if such a team exists) or may be left to you or someone similar who has had some influence in the design of the data strategy or is seen as an appropriate person to lead on its implementation. Either way, the task of the project lead is to quickly turn the data strategy, its waymarkers, RACI (or RASCI) and RAID log into an implementation plan with milestones, detailed deliverables, activity owners and the mechanism to track progress and measure success. This will need inputs from others, and some coordination to do so, which is where the PMO (or PfMO) comes into play to support the definition of the implementation plan in a way that can be tracked.

The PMO may undertake a number of activities, such as the following ten common examples:

- Governance – provision of support across the breadth of the implementation programme, capturing decisions and tracking actions to enable an effective governance regime to function.

- Performance management – delivery of reporting at all levels of the implementation programme to set standards. Proactive tracking of issues and assessment of current or future risk of performance failings with mitigation identified where possible.

- Planning – focused on milestones and tracking the plan to ensure deliverables are on course. Includes breaking down the plan into activities and ensuring these are tracked and aligned at all times to provide consistency and line of sight to any risks.

- Risk management – capture and maintenance of RAID logs and assessing scale of risks. Includes issues and dependencies, as well as tracking assumptions to ensure these remain valid. Evaluates RAID to determine escalation as appropriate.

- Human resources – ensures the resources are optimised to deliver the programme, identifies potential gaps and risks, and seeks to mitigate these through prioritisation and planning. Maintains the resource view of the implementation plan to track utilisation and need to roll on/off resources.

- Financial resources – oversight of budget, tracking progress and forecasting future spend based upon plan and commitments. Production of (at least) monthly reporting to senior stakeholders on tracking spend versus progress to flag whether on track.

- Supplier/stakeholder management – ensures third parties and other delivery arms within the organisation are aligned and delivering to plan, on time, to quality. Reporting performance wherever appropriate.

- Communications – oversight of communication plan, tracking deliverables and ensuring these align to the key messages the programme wants to provide to stakeholders. Manages sign-off processes and identification of opportunities to open new channels within the organisation.

- Quality control – provides a quality assurance function to ensure delivery meets requirements as captured and obtains sign-off. Undertakes benefits analysis in conjunction with stakeholders to ascertain these have met expectations, and conducts lessons learnt activities from such reviews.

- Document management – capture, cataloguing and availability of programme documentation. Ensures there is a consistent format to programme documentation.

Alongside the capability assessment, discussed in the previous chapter, there is a need to establish the capability of the data and analytics team to be more directly involved in driving the activity in the implementation plan, taking ownership and integrating into their own goals and objectives. How effective an approach this will be will depend on:

1. how skilled the data and analytics team are to step into this space;

2. their influence and reach within the organisation to drive this through;

3. their capacity to do so, given other work demands and priorities.

It is an ideal opportunity, should it be needed, to bring the data and analytics team (or community, in the absence of such a team) to the forefront of the organisation as all too often they operate in the background and lack the opportunity to exert influence on the organisation's thinking. This provides a great platform to be able to elevate their profile, demonstrate their wider business appreciation (assuming this is found to be the case through the capability assessment – not all data and analytics professionals possess contextual knowledge or the ability to apply it in a wider business environment) and see the impact that their work has in making a difference. In addition, it provides the opportunity to develop broader skills, whether those are in project management, benefits tracking and realisation or organisational understanding.

Just as the wider organisation may lack the information literacy skills that are essential to embed an intelligence-led approach to decision making, so the data and analytics team may lack the business awareness or depth of understanding to be truly effective in reaching in to drive change across the organisation. This is where finding those with the ability to bridge both of the groups is pivotal to a successful implementation. Without the business appreciation and comprehension of how the organisation operates, delivering change becomes a remote and, therefore, detached activity that lacks the necessary impact or the appropriate level of awareness across the organisation.

The capability assessment should have established how big a hill this is to climb and, indeed, this may be one of the earlier deliverables in your implementation programme, as the increased levels of awareness across the organisation are key to driving real change. If this is not tackled, then do not expect there to be any appetite to change to something unknown and potentially seen to be irrelevant. Resistance may be driven by fear of change, but it is as likely to be an indicator of failing to sell the benefits and importance of the change to those you need to influence. There will be change resistance but, equally, it may be just as much a failing to engage and inform.

> Do not assume everyone 'gets' the data strategy, communicate it effectively and with context for the various parties you need to engage, and prepare the ground for plenty of challenge on the case for change.

There is a strong case to be made to bring in data and analytics expertise into the lead roles in implementation delivery, and not just because of the subject matter expertise such individuals bring. The opportunity to see the end-to-end nature of the data strategy enabling the corporate strategy to succeed will enlighten those in the data and analytics function as to the impact of their work, but also the way in which it enables the execution of the ultimate outcome to deliver the objective. It is often the lack of opportunity to gain wider experience that holds back the influence of those data and analytics professionals within an organisation, yet they have insight and expertise not found elsewhere in the business to be able to define and deliver innovative solutions to business problems that may not otherwise be devised, let alone considered.

This is likely to require some additional skills within the data and analytics function, especially in operating as part of an implementation programme rather than simply as a contributor to it, so do bear this in mind when selecting those you wish to include. Make time to explain the benefits and opportunities this will bring, and the importance of being able to listen and learn to capture insight on business problems which the wider team could tackle – this is potentially bringing the data and analytics team nearer the frontline activities, which is where the biggest impact is often felt.

Extra skills the data and analytics function may need involve comprehending how Agile delivery methods operate to be an effective proponent of such techniques. I am a big advocate of utilising Agile in the approach to delivery in data and analytics, as I feel this provides rapid value to a customer, builds a level of understanding and sets expectations of needing to learn through delivery, given the answer to complex problems is often nigh on impossible to define through detailed requirements up front.

If the lead role in the data strategy implementation is taken on by the data and analytics function, utilising Agile methodologies, the awareness of programme management will increase within that function. It will also increase the way in which intelligence is used within a PMO/PfMO, given the skillset likely to be found amongst those in a data and analytics function, and support the coordination of managing the range of moving parts within the implementation phase. It will also give further opportunities to see how the wider organisation engages with information, to increase awareness of how future deliveries could be made easier to digest and act upon effectively without having to second-guess what the analysis indicates to be the right decision. Having subject matter expertise embedded in the implementation programme is also likely to keep a level of focus on the aims of the data strategy and an informed view on the impact of deviating from what was defined within the strategy.

The goal of having members of the analytics team involved directly in the implementation also presents an opportunity for those who might otherwise tend to be in the background to come to the fore and present their skills in a transformative way. It is a proactive approach, enabling the analyst to fulfil the role of being a change agent to link their work directly to the impact on decision making, increase their business awareness, enhance their stakeholder network and improve visibility of their capability to the wider organisation.

The impact of having clear benefits and being able to translate these into KPIs is covered elsewhere in this book. I do not propose to go into great detail on KPIs other than to suggest that the data and analytics function should probably have some ownership or oversight of how these are compiled and represented due to the nature of the implementation programme being focused on data strategy. The KPIs must be relevant and significant in what they measure whilst also being deliverable – do not define what cannot be reported due to a lack of data or a lack of clarity in their definition. There is little to be gained from defining KPIs which are, in themselves, riddled with quality and reliability issues, as this will only serve to undermine the implementation of the data strategy.

The data and analytics function will be an important delivery vehicle for the implementation programme, both in what it provides but also in the wider spectrum of contacts and insight within the organisation it may be able to provide. As such, the function is a critical dependency to the successful implementation of the data strategy and it will be essential that all the resources in this function are earmarked to support the implementation.

If resources prove to be constrained, then I would question the prioritisation process and the potential indicator this is alerting you to that the goalposts in the organisation may have moved, and the relevance of the data strategy implementation may have been lost or made redundant due to wider events taking priority. An effective implementation programme with strong leadership, sponsorship and an active PMO/PfMO should be able to spot this emerging long before it becomes an issue, and adapt and reflect in the programme accordingly.

The scale of the data and analytics function will reflect the maturity of the organisation and the level of investment it has made to date in this area. If you are just starting out on the journey, you may lack the depth of resources within the organisation and also be constrained on funding to bring in external expertise to assist. However, the data strategy covers the breadth of the information lifecycle, not just data management activities, and so needs to represent this in its implementation (see Figure 2.1). Many of the core data activities are critical enablers to those which exploit the data, and whilst it might be overplaying it to suggest that without the progress on the data front the exploitation activities would not be feasible, it is almost certainly the case that they would be highly suboptimal due to having to be repeated or having compromised actions which are undertaken due to the issues with the data. Do not lose sight of the nuances, the dependencies and the potential efficiency gains which, whilst they may be embedded in the data and analytics function, constrain or release resource to have a massive impact on what can be delivered to the wider organisation.

9.5 THE PRIORITISATION CHALLENGE

The implementation of the data strategy will need to be assigned to the relevant individuals and teams within the organisation based on the RACI (or RASCI) within the plan. However, those individuals and teams will have existing commitments and the anticipation of working towards future deliverables, so the engagement prior to confirming the implementation plan must determine the resources needed to commit to the data strategy deliverables. This leads on to a discussion regarding prioritisation.

Clearly, there is a strong likelihood that a proportion of the current workload will contribute in some way to the implementation of the data strategy – it is unlikely that the data strategy will start implementation with a major shift from the current approach, but if this is the intent, there is a need to be clear on this and make sure the communication process provides not only the rationale but also the implications on current activity and direction. Therefore, an initial assessment on the workload within teams, the direction in which they are heading, and the availability of the right resource – those with the relevant skills and knowledge – is a high priority for engagement at the start of the implementation phase.

The key lever to recall throughout the discovery stage at the start of implementation is the direct relationship between corporate strategy and the data strategy. The latter is a critical deliverable to make the corporate strategy a reality, either directly or indirectly. Understanding this is important when it comes to the prioritisation calls that lie ahead. All activities in the organisation should be selected on the basis that they are compatible with, and enabling, the corporate strategy to become reality. There are a few instances where this may not be quite so clear, such as compliance activity – unless your corporate strategy has some reference to effective governance or operating at a high level whilst remaining safe and legal – but these should also enable the data strategy implementation, as they are consistent with the foundational principles of sound data management practice.

Alignment to those activities which are clearly attributable to delivering the corporate strategy will bind the data strategy activities into the same reporting mechanisms and ensure the dependencies are tracked accordingly. This strengthens the importance of these activities being delivered, thus making the data strategy implementation more integrated and likely to reach a successful outcome.

Where there are activities which do not support the data strategy implementation, there is a need to investigate the ownership of such activities and the key drivers as to why these are consuming resources. If these are contradictory to the direction of the data strategy, or consuming key resources needed to move the data strategy implementation forward, then there is a case for exploring which of these takes priority.

The data strategy implementation, though effectively a programme in its own right, may find itself having to fight battles on several fronts across the organisation to align activities to deliver in the structured approach the implementation plan has devised. It is worth using the advanced planning that the waymarkers provide to define the milestones and deliverables, and to get these planned in as early as possible into priorities across the functions within the organisation.

A further challenge related to prioritisation is the competition for scarce resource, especially in data and analytics functions which are likely to be key to the successful implementation of the data strategy. The previous chapter highlighted the need to undertake a capability assessment, and, if this is done, it will highlight where challenges are likely to lie, enabling those leading on strategy implementation to plan ahead where pinch points are likely to occur.

These can be offset, of course, if the data strategy has the influence to increase capacity in areas where demand so clearly outstrips supply, but there is always a time lag in recruitment (from business case submission and approval through to advertising, hiring and having the individual start), followed by a period in which the successful applicant has to familiarise themselves with what has gone before and the nature and structure of the organisation, identify key networks and become truly productive. This could take most of the first year of the implementation plan to achieve, and so it would be wise to target any recruitment dependencies within the data strategy as early as possible to mitigate this potential constraint on progressing the strategy implementation.

The data strategy is an enabler of the wider corporate strategy and, therefore, for others to achieve their own goals. Therefore the other lever to use in the prioritisation challenge likely to be ahead of those leading the implementation is mobilising relevant stakeholders to apply pressure to increase the importance of implementation activities. If you are able to get those stakeholders driving the deliverables, recognising how they impact their own activities and contribute to the corporate strategy, then it is a powerful alliance to increase the likelihood of getting key activities prioritised.

The most effective way to get the data strategy implementation to succeed is to have stakeholders across the organisation taking ownership of various parts of it to ensure they have an active stake, rather than leaving it solely to an implementation team (or individual) to have to shoulder the load. I can speak from personal experience that the impact an active sponsor and motivated stakeholders have makes or breaks the successful implementation of the data strategy. It is well worth the investment in getting to the point at which those stakeholders are making the implementation happen, and the work of the implementation team becomes one of coordination, guidance and advising on details within the implementation activities.

Finally, understand the governance within your organisation. Prioritisation should be undertaken through some sort of approach which has a degree of formality behind it, with stakeholders assigned either as customers or functions to deliver the activity, timelines and resources agreed, and a clear understanding amongst all parties as to what success looks like as a result of delivering the activity. Being focused on the mechanics through which activities are agreed and resources assigned will become your focus throughout the implementation, so be prepared for the time it takes to fully engage with these groups, understand how they operate, and learn who is influential within them and how to get activity into the prioritisation process and achieve the right outcome. This will be your day-to-day way of operating in the months ahead, so get ready to become a master of the art of governance and prioritisation.

9.6 REQUIREMENTS

Just as the art of understanding the governance is important to appreciate how things get done within your organisation, so the need to be able to construct the activities within the implementation plan into requirements will be essential to get these through the governance and on to the work stack of relevant teams in the organisation.

Generally, organisations use a particular approach to capturing requirements, and there are several out there. If your organisation does not have a formalised approach to requirements gathering, this might be an opportune time to introduce something – a study by Stieglitz (2012) found over 70 per cent of failed projects were due to a lack of requirements gathering.[6] I am not intending to review the full range of requirements-gathering techniques, but I will reference a few I have found most common and/or useful that you might want to research further if you are keen to develop your knowledge in this particular area.

The collation of the requirements for data strategy implementation may involve one or more of the techniques listed below (or others not referenced here), but the process of wrapping up the information collated from these approaches tends to fall into one of two camps: user stories (sometimes called epics) and use cases, the cornerstone of the Agile methodology approach, or formal, documented requirements, which are the more traditional, waterfall-style of project approach.

I described use cases earlier in this chapter; user stories tend to capture the experience described by those specifying the need to be able to define what the outcome should achieve, feel like or deliver. They are relatively detailed, and are then used in the sprint and product backlog process of Agile to determine what will be delivered at the end of a sprint to the customer. They tend to be structured in a broadly common format, along the lines of:

> As a [job role], I want to achieve [define a goal] so that I realise the following benefit of/can do [the outcome/reason for the requirement].

In contrast, a documented requirement has historically supported a more conventional, or waterfall, approach which has a clearly defined expectation up front and then has the project or programme seek to deliver to that requirement. These requirements tend to be extremely detailed, given that they may be supporting a long-term activity to deliver an outcome or output some time off, and so have to provide that robustness to be able to operate to that sort of longevity.

---

6 C. Stieglitz, Beginning at the End: Requirements Gathering Lessons from a Flowchart Junkie. Paper presented at PMI® Global Congress 2012, North America, Vancouver, British Columbia, Canada. Newtown Square, PA: Project Management Institute, 2012.

Documented requirements have a breadth of detail encompassing all aspects – technical, functional, operational – and so tend to be created by those more closely associated with the technical detail who are focused on the delivery end of the activity, which can remove the level of engagement with the end stakeholder more closely associated with the user case. The nature of these requirements also makes changing them much harder, typically involving a detailed change process due to the impact across the breadth of activity over a longer time frame than the user case.

Both approaches have their place, and it is often quite clear as to which one to use, depending on the complexity, time to complete and the feasibility of adopting a more dynamically driven approach more closely associated with Agile.

There are some useful pointers in requirements gathering, regardless of the approach to capturing them:

- Establish goals and objectives early – ensure you capture all details and sign them off to align to why they are required.

- Document detailed notes – capture all stakeholder discussions as it may take more than one meeting to formulate the requirement.

- Share documentation – provide access to the requirement documentation as it takes shape to gather feedback. This will lead to a better end product and speed up sign-off.

- Ensure you engage all relevant stakeholders – it may seem that you have identified the key stakeholder for the requirement, but there may be others, including those who simply exert influence or can assist in promoting your activity. Without the buy-in of the wider group it may prove harder to garner full support and engagement – they may even block or delay progress – so do take a moment to assess if there are others who need to be involved.

- Capture and validate all assumptions – whilst an assumption may seem obvious to you, there is a risk that you may not be aware of a reason why it is flawed. State any assumptions and be prepared to work them through – generally, the less to be assumed the better.

Finally, some advice on how to engage stakeholders. It may be easy to gather the requirement; the stakeholder(s) may have a clear view on their need and benefits and be able to articulate it clearly. However, this is not always the case. A good approach to adopt is called active listening, which goes beyond what is said to comprehend the way it is said, the body language and the sentiment behind the words. Build trust and confidence, be as transparent as you can be, establish empathy, and comprehend the issue and its impact, and you are on a good footing to capture the requirement in a way likely to result in a positive outcome for your stakeholder and establish a good ongoing relationship.

9.6.1 Interviews

One-to-one discussions with customers, or key stakeholders, is a traditional but effective way of exploring the end goal – what is the outcome needed, and why – of the activity you are about to undertake. These can be extended to groups, if appropriate, but do be mindful that the larger the group the more influenced it can be by one or more individuals, and some may be less willing to speak up or be intimidated by others in the group.

Think about group dynamics. If you know a little about the likely participants do some research to assess the likely interaction of putting them together, and try to keep the group focused – having too much of a spread of interests can make it difficult to capture the breadth of inputs you receive or skew where the focus is, and therefore lead to unbalanced requirements emerging. Have a clear structure to the interviews, a line of questioning which provides a framework for all participants to follow the thread of the interview, and try to make sure everyone has their say – it is often wise to follow up individually after a group interview to ensure those who may have been less engaged or quieter have a second opportunity to participate and contribute.

Finally, prepare detailed outputs from the interviews to share with those who participated to ensure you have captured everything accurately and to provide an opportunity to embellish the information you gathered now there has been chance to reflect since the interview itself. It is surprising how few people do follow-up interviews in any way, and yet many who participate will continue to think and reflect on what they heard and evolve their thinking – remember, you may have caught them relatively cold on the day, and even sending information about the interview in advance may have remained in their inbox if they are awash with other priorities, so the quality time may be in that reflective period after the interview. Do not forget to ask: even if the individual does not suggest there were further reflections, there may be a nugget lurking in their mind which could be key to your success.

9.6.2 Focus groups

Not to be confused with wider group interviews, focus groups are a way of having (as the name suggests) focused discussions on a particular aspect or topic of the activity you are seeking to deliver, usually involving those who are recognised as the SMEs in their field within the organisation. These groups will be moderated by someone who leads the discussion, and so the SMEs are directed according to what the purpose of the focus group is to try to ensure a positive outcome, whereas an interview has greater steering by those who participate.

Typically, focus groups will be used to work through a more complex issue or where there are multiple stakeholders who all have to come together to contribute to a successful outcome. They are therefore a good approach to defining a requirement where there are multiple teams involved who all have to work together on a common goal, to try to avoid ambiguity or disagreement in the critical delivery phase.

9.6.3 Delphi technique

Similar in principle to focus groups but often used on a wider range of issues, the Delphi technique brings SMEs' knowledge to a particular issue or deliverable through a third-party facilitator. The SMEs will provide answers to a set of questions posed by the facilitator, often remotely, and once the facilitator has analysed the feedback it will be shared anonymously with the group as a whole, so the collective inputs can be seen by all SMEs. The answers may be similar or conflict, but the group reviews the content provided by the facilitator to work on a revised view based on the collective responses, and may do this a few times till a consensus is reached or the bar is raised through the benefit of the group of SMEs each contributing and stimulating fresh thinking or, at least, challenge to original thinking. Once the collective SMEs have reached an agreed point, or have converged to a broadly similar view, the facilitator structures the responses into a set of requirements.

9.6.4 Brainstorming

Brainstorming is a commonly used and well-known technique for a number of activities, including defining requirements. The key to a successful brainstorming session is the concept that there is no such thing as a bad idea: the focus is on gathering as many ideas as possible to capture for subsequent discussion. An effective brainstorming session is often recognised through the opportunity that all can contribute without critique in the process of idea generation, and sometimes the more way-out ideas can be the ones which are taken forward simply because, having been regarded as left field, on exploration they are found to open up opportunities well worth further investigation.

A well-run brainstorming session can deliver really innovative thinking that many other approaches would not create, due to more structured approaches being taken. Therefore, do not discount brainstorming if there is a need to introduce a more creative and exploratory approach to capture requirements; it can be highly effective at challenging the traditional approach and making others think differently.

9.6.5 Strawman approach (or prototyping)

In situations where the requirement can be difficult to articulate, or involve a series of decisions which could be time-consuming to work through, developing a strawman (also called a prototype) can be a very effective way of focusing the minds of a group of SMEs to critique and refine an initial proposal to shape a more developed approach. The benefit of this is that it gives a point of reference, or focus, to analyse something common to the group which would otherwise be difficult to define and so would be challenging to progress using a wider group.

The essence of the strawman is a starting point and it is quite feasible that the final solution may look totally different, or could end up very similar to the strawman. The point is that it does not matter: its purpose is solely to provide common ground on which to focus effort to improve, enhance or develop a solution which is better through using a common starting point developed by a much smaller group in the first instance (maybe 1–3 participants; the key is to have as few as reasonably necessary to develop the strawman). The requirements will be more robust having had the benefit of a common review point, and to have had clarity on the changes included to improve on the strawman.

9.6.6 Nominal group technique

This approach is a more rapid approach to identify a way to achieve an outcome, and is based on greater spontaneity than many others, so is often used in cases where time is short. Figure 9.2 demonstrates how it is undertaken, but essentially it works on a basis of individuals being brought together for this purpose, with no previous input or engagement, to share ideas and select the best through a voting process.

Figure 9.2 Nominal group technique Diagram courtesy of Shiv Shenoy, PM Exam Smartnotes (pmexamsmartnotes.com). S. Shenoy, How to Collect Requirements – Part 1. PM Exam Smartnotes https://www.pmexamsmartnotes.com/collect-requirements-process-tools-and-techniques-part-1-of-2/.

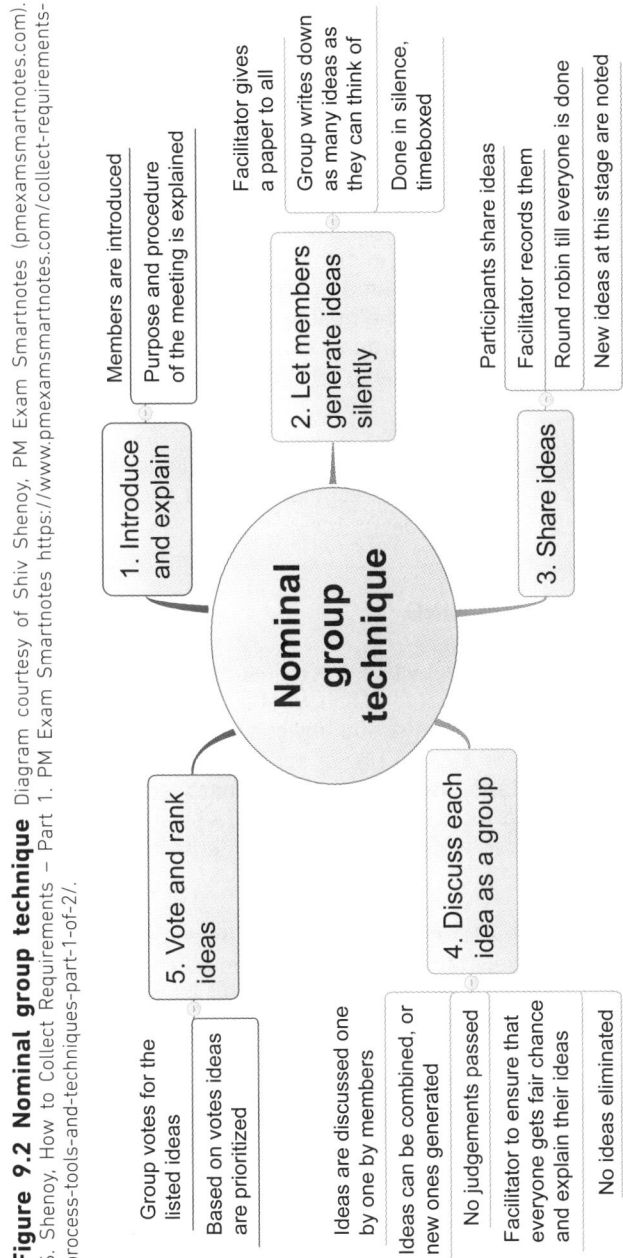

Nominal group technique

1. Introduce and explain
- Members are introduced
- Purpose and procedure of the meeting is explained

2. Let members generate ideas silently
- Facilitator gives a paper to all
- Group writes down as many ideas as they can think of
- Done in silence, timeboxed

3. Share ideas
- Participants share ideas
- Facilitator records them
- Round robin till everyone is done
- New ideas at this stage are noted

4. Discuss each idea as a group
- Ideas are discussed one by one by members
- Ideas can be combined, or new ones generated
- No judgements passed
- Facilitator to ensure that everyone gets fair chance and explain their ideas
- No ideas eliminated

5. Vote and rank ideas
- Group votes for the listed ideas
- Based on votes ideas are prioritized

9.6.7 Observation

This approach is effective in cases where those who are customers or key stakeholders of the requirement are not skilled in crafting requirements or lack the time to do so effectively. It involves someone with good observational skills working with the relevant area(s) to identify the problem, articulate the requirement and hence define success criteria in a structured way that can then be signed off by the customer. It usually involves an individual with good requirement capture skills to shadow key team members to observe the issue, build a complete picture (which may be complex in totality) and present in a way the customer can relate to the process that has led to the requirements as defined.

9.6.8 Document review

If there isn't an opportunity to engage with knowledgeable stakeholders, sometimes there is an approach which involves capturing information from documents to pull together a complete picture and form a requirement. This approach obviously has limitations, not least that it is only as good as the quality, relevancy and currency of the documents, and so may misrepresent reality due to failings in any of these areas. It also requires a breadth of documents to be able to form a complete enough picture, and ease of access to them.

In my experience, this is often a last resort due to the lack of stakeholder engagement and may be used as an input to some of the other techniques listed above rather than on its own.

9.7 BENEFITS DEFINITION AND TRACKING

Once the implementation plan defines the activities, the milestones and the resources required to achieve the outcome, it is essential to define what success looks like and to turn this into a measurable benefit. This might sound obvious, at least at a theoretical level, but in my experience the data strategies I have seen across a wide range of organisations worldwide are particularly weak in this area. There is also the rather academic debate over the accounting for benefits – is the data strategy an enabler for some other activity, especially those which are key components of the corporate strategy?

The difficulty with this debate is that it is largely futile. Without the enabler, the positive outcome realised elsewhere would likely fail to materialise, and as a result would be missed or possibly suboptimal at best. Therefore, the enabler is a clear contributor to the outcome, if not a direct outcome in itself.

The main impact of how your organisation tracks enablers is the visibility that they receive and hence the importance which is attached to their resourcing and delivery. Many organisations fail to track adequately the enablers and dependencies of a strategy implementation, which leads to periods of paralysis due to these bumps in the road becoming blockers or insurmountable obstacles. Tackling them only when they rear up in front of the organisation is costly, as the time it takes, resources needed and the delays caused far outweigh having a structured programme operating which ensures there is a smooth road ahead to ease the implementation journey.

> I find the best way to bring this to life, which is particularly apt given that strategy has its roots in warfare, is to outline the implications of marching forces across open ground unaware that there is a significant river in the distance without a bridge to enable the troops to cross. Reacting to the river only when it is in sight is probably just what the enemy were hoping for, and your forces are sitting ducks whilst the message is relayed to find engineers who can construct some sort of crossing whilst under heavy artillery. Having a map, knowledge and surveillance of what lies ahead, an advanced force of engineers able to construct the bridges in advance of your arrival and defend these makes for a faster and more effective assault, but needs priority to be given to supporting a front line of those who capture information and prepare the ground for what lies ahead.
>
> The same applies to your own data strategy implementation. Don't be caught cold, unaware of something which may derail your implementation; continue to do your homework and be several steps ahead of the main force delivering in the here and now. This means operating on multiple fronts, but it is worth it to avoid being stranded and exposed. In data strategy implementation terms, this may make the difference in retaining credibility and, with it, support from your stakeholders and maintaining momentum. As the phrase goes: 'By failing to prepare, you are preparing to fail.'[7]

The key to successful benefits definition is to identify the owner of the benefit and to ensure that that individual signs off the benefit as a first step to taking accountability for its delivery. The PMO team will continue to track these benefits, as they are integral to the successful implementation of the data strategy, even though the ownership of benefits may become fragmented. However, unless there is some accountability for the totality of the benefits to be realised – which may reside with the sponsor of the data strategy implementation, of course – there is a risk that the benefits will not manifest in the way intended and fail to deliver expected value. After all, the data strategy was devised as a whole and will have been designed to deliver optimal benefits in their entirety, and this would have been a key factor in the data strategy being signed off in the first place.

Finally, I would like to highlight the importance of transparency in the reporting of benefits to ensure those who are engaged in some capacity have assurance that they are contributing to the bigger prize of delivering change within their organisation. It is also a key factor in retaining support of your most influential stakeholders, and will also enable you to control the narrative on the progress of the implementation programme. Whilst it may not always be moving along as you might like, and there are bound to be twists and turns to deal with along the way, being open and honest about these will build trust that you are on top of implementation and managing the many strands which deliver the data strategy. Failure to do so will only lead to speculation, rumour

---

7   A saying often attributed to Benjamin Franklin, though there is no written evidence of his having uttered it.

and misinterpretation, all of which will suck energy from the implementation effort itself and may delay important approvals and resources being realised in a timely fashion.

Jeff Austin, the former Vice-President, Strategy Planning, at DuPont Pioneer said: 'Are we doing what we said we would be doing?'[8] and this is a useful prompt as you progress through the implementation journey. Keep in mind the intent, direction and impact the data strategy aimed to achieve and remain focused on the objectives, or goals, it set out to deliver. The data strategy was signed off as the direction the organisation wanted to commit itself to, and should be aligned to the corporate strategy. It is a useful – and simple – prompt to bear in mind to challenge the programme team and those around you focused on delivering it.

9.7.1 Non-financial benefits definition and tracking

A further area that can confuse the benefits definition from the outset is the question of those activities which result in non-financial outcomes but contribute to the overall goal. It is not necessarily that those involved in the implementation of the data strategy may not recognise the value of these activities, more a question of how to account for them in their contribution to the overall delivery.

The task to convert such non-financial benefits into something that can be tracked, and the impact assessed, is to convert these into something which can be inferred in a way that is easy to articulate and backed by clear evidence that the cause and effect have been quantified in some way.

Take employee engagement, for example: those who have to delve into the furthest reaches of the organisation looking for data and are hampered by the quality and timeliness of it when they find it, and then struggle to be able to repeat the exercise, will almost certainly find this a demotivating part of their role within the organisation. Improving that experience, making the data accessible, reliable, consistent and timely, would improve the effectiveness of that individual to focus their effort more on the task they are seeking to achieve, rather than spending the majority of their time in preparation and a minority in adding the value that the role is paid to achieve. This, in turn, may well lead to an increase in employee engagement, so the cause and effect can be related and a target of an improvement in employee engagement set and measured via KPIs.

There is also evidence that indicates an increase in employee engagement has a direct impact on customer satisfaction,[9] hence the indirect effect of making the performance of that individual employee increase is likely to be of benefit through to the customer experience. Richard Branson said: 'empowering and taking care of your staff is the best way to look after your customers and keep them coming back for more'.[10]

There is a handy seven-step process (Figure 9.3) which is a useful tool to define and measure both financial and non-financial benefits which is worth using as a prompt.

---

8 Economist Intelligence Unit, Why Good Strategies Fail: Lessons for the C-Suite. 2013. https://eiuperspectives.economist.com/strategy-leadership/why-good-strategies-fail.

9 See Institute of Customer Service, The Customer Knows. 2017. https://www.instituteofcustomerservice.com/product/the-customer-knows-how-employee-engagement-leads-to-greater-customer-satisfaction-and-loyalty/.

10 R. Branson, Like a Virgin: Secrets They Won't Teach You at Business School. London: Virgin, 2013.

Figure 9.3 Seven steps to legitimise, measure, and value financial and non-financial business benefits Copyright © 2020 by Marty Schmidt. Used with permission. https://www.business-case-analysis.com/business-benefit.html.

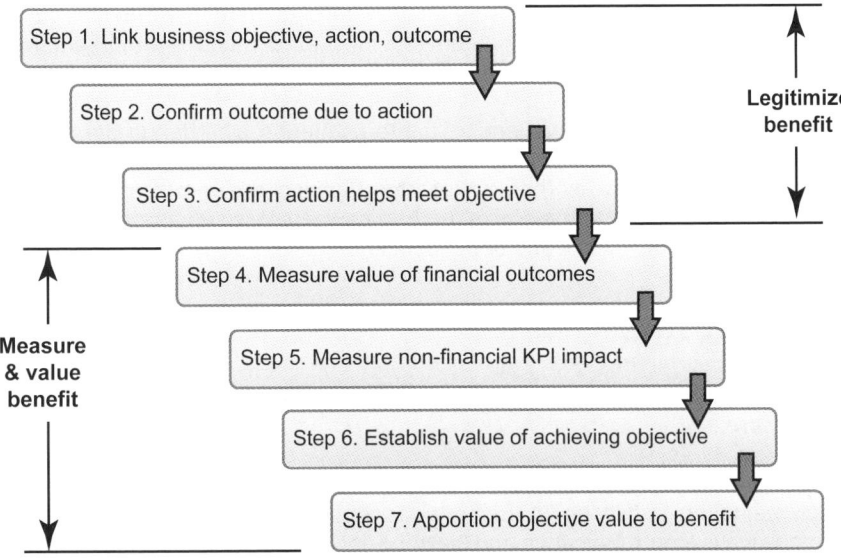

This gives a consistent approach to tracking business benefits and can be adapted to your own organisation. For instance, if you are in a not-for-profit environment, the value may be the opportunity cost of the action being taken which, in turn, is focused on optimising your decisions as to where business benefit is greatest for both your own organisation but also wider stakeholders you are there to serve.

9.7.2 Benefits dependency network

In the discipline of programme management, a process called benefits dependency network (BDN) is used to capture five critical pieces of information, all of which need to be tracked to be able to assess the benefit realised. The five categories are:

1. Objectives – the desired end state.

2. Benefits – the benefit to the organisation of the desired end state.

3. Outcomes – the specific aspects of the end state.

4. Projects – those activities to be undertaken to deliver outcomes.

5. Enablers – facilitators in the delivery of the projects and programmes, leading to the outcomes. These can be direct activities or indirect, contributing something which is an essential conduit or efficiency step to make delivery achievable faster or more effective (for example removing barriers or creating a new environment or process which reduces time and effort).

The value of adopting this type of approach is that it can be used for two directly related purposes. Read the BDN in the sequence outlined above and it provides the rationale for structuring the data strategy into projects and programmes to deliver outcomes, whilst recognising the key enablers needed to achieve these. Working backwards, it gives the purpose and structure to assure delivery through demonstrating the rigour of the approach in achieving effective outcomes, which in turn delivers the benefits and achieves the overall objective.

This is therefore a useful mechanism to use to challenge whether, in the context of a dynamic business environment, the approach from end to end is still relevant, and identify the impact of change on the whole, rather than just the immediate task at hand. It also provides visibility as to the critical path to navigate through a raft of activities to keep a focus on managing risks and dependencies.

9.8 TEN TO TAKE AWAY

This chapter has sought to set you on the path of strategy implementation. Key points to take away are:

1. Establish the roles and responsibilities at the start of your data strategy implementation. Utilise the RASCI model, as support will be vital to your programme in many ways (communication and learning, for example), and focus on the role as well as the person – people move on; you need the responsibility to remain with the post – whilst using it to guide delivery rather than create rigid boundaries.

2. Change is inevitable, so do not stick rigidly to the plan. Constant review is necessary, but if you find a need to diverge so far that it no longer relates to the data strategy as defined, you may need to redefine the data strategy. Do not lose sight of the link between the data strategy and its implementation.

3. You need to utilise communication as a key activity of the implementation programme, and to engage stakeholders at all levels in the organisation. Do not depend on a 'one size fits all' approach: there will be different challenges across the organisation and your success needs to align to those messages being delivered locally to drive the data strategy into their thinking. Employee engagement is a key element in determining your likely success.

4. Adopt an Agile approach to the data strategy implementation, especially communications. Break down your plan into a series of deliverables that fall within the month that you can wrap a series of communications around.

5. Build your programme team to harness a range of expertise. Incorporate skills in project coordination, data and analytics, local knowledge from various parts of the organisation and blend a cohesive capability to bring out the best of the team. Your ability to resource the team will be dependent on organisation size and commitment to the data strategy implementation, but seek to ensure there is a strong programme management office to oversee your own programme and the dependencies you are tracking elsewhere.

6. Undertake a capability assessment of the programme team at the outset to identify gaps and weaknesses and seek to address these through a variety of learning approaches.

7. Assess prioritisation within your implementation plan. The data strategy should align to the corporate strategy, which should assist in the process, but there are other constraints and challenges along the way, not least the availability of scarce resources. This may entail some negotiation or rephasing of the implementation plan.

8. Determine the appropriate governance to put in place to oversee the data strategy implementation. It is a key forum to raise visibility of the implementation programme, to determine prioritisation calls, and to seek to gain resources from key stakeholders who are therefore able to understand the need and timing of the request.

9. Utilise requirements gathering as part of the implementation programme. These may be captured via use cases or more formal documented requirements, but it is essential to get these signed off to ensure that deliverables within the data strategy implementation are aligned to what the organisation needs to be able to progress.

10. Ensure the implementation has clear links between its deliverables and benefits tracking to demonstrate the value the data strategy has delivered. Ensure that the benefits and requirements remain focused on the objectives, or goals, the data strategy defined.

10 FLEXIBILITY IN EXECUTION

'It is not the strongest of the species that survive, nor the most intelligent, but the one most responsive to change.'

Charles Darwin[1]

The previous chapters have outlined the key ingredients to achieving a successful outcome for your data strategy. It is not easy, but these are the steps to follow if you are going to do what many would contend is the hard part – turning strategy into successful execution. Strategy sets direction and execution plots the course, whilst adopting a dynamic, but aligned, approach to delivery is essential to achieving a successful outcome. So, you might ask, what does a further chapter that talks about flexibility in execution provide beyond what has been covered so far?

There are many reasons why the subject of this chapter is important, not least that you are not in control of the environment in which you operate. Many things can occur which impact your plan, and you are not necessarily in command of when or how they will manifest themselves, but it is important to anticipate that change is actually normality – it is a myth for most organisations that there is a constant in the environment in which they operate. In a speech delivered in Edinburgh in 1867, months before becoming prime minister, Benjamin Disraeli said: 'Change is inevitable. ... Change is constant.'[2]

An effective plan should not be a mould in which the execution has little scope to adapt. If this is the case, it will not survive long. The plan will have to flex to the challenges that arise, which could vary from resources having to be deployed elsewhere at short notice to solve an unforeseen and urgent task, or delays outside the control of the implementation team due to supplier issues, or a shift in priorities. The impact of these will vary widely, depending on the nature and length of time that they act as a distraction, but all will lead to a need to reset the plan in the context of what is the optimal way forward based on the new outlook for the programme.

It is likely that the impact of change will be felt more extensively where the nature of it is longer lasting or changes the direction of the organisation. It is important that data strategy execution is managed with a wider portfolio of programmes in large organisations, as this will provide important insight into changes that you need to be aware of. If the PMO (or similar) team is doing its job effectively, they should be tracking dependencies and benefits, and so be able to spot the implications of changes elsewhere on the data strategy implementation.

---

1   Attributed to C. Darwin, *On the Origin of Species by Means of Natural Selection*. London: John Murray, 1859.

2   B. Disraeli, Speech on Reform Bill of 1867, delivered in Edinburgh, 29 October 1867.

If you are operating within a smaller organisation, it is probably a case of keeping close contact with those who are privy to change occurring elsewhere which could have a bearing on your own plan. Your sponsor, for instance, should have access to the sort of information which could be essential for you to know to navigate your way around to keep your overall goals on track.

The risks of change are such that you should focus on capturing your dependencies as soon as you start work on defining your plan. These can range from the relatively obvious (risk of resources not being available to start the implementation) to the more esoteric (uncertainty in business demand which could place risk on technology investment being sustained throughout the planning period), but you should look at the wider impact such shifts could have on each key deliverable and manage them via a recognised risk management framework, and apply that technique to score and track the risk.

The changes that impact upon data strategy implementation could be short or long term. The response will vary, of course, but the approach to monitoring and tracking them should be the same. However, clearly the extent of the impact upon the implementation plan will determine the response. Depending on the assessment, it will likely result in a number of next steps:

- Determine if the nature or scale of the change is unavoidable, especially in the context of the impact upon the data strategy implementation. This is a tricky call to make, and one which will almost certainly need to be escalated to the sponsor if it is an organisation-wide change or requires the executive board to make the call.

- Assess options. Can the impact be mitigated by changes to timing within the implementation plan, realigning priorities or reassigning resources to lessen the effect on the programme? Is there a way to deliver part of the solution within the programme and return to complete it later in the programme? What is the impact of not doing the activity or task within the plan – does it have a material impact on the ability to deliver the data strategy? Provide options to the sponsor and agree the best course of action.

- Seek trade-offs. If the change is unavoidable, is there a way to find an alternative means to deliver the plan? For instance, if resources are no longer available, could you bring in external resources and gain funding to ensure you can remain on track? Is there a way to backfill resources being taken off the implementation of the data strategy through using alternatives, even if they need training to step up? These types of approach may have a consequence on the budget you are working to, but there may be a willingness to keep momentum and therefore a willingness to fund beyond the original budget if it ensures that progress is not stalled.

- Replan. The need to determine the revised approach will be informed by answers to the above, as appropriate, leading to some element of replanning. Whatever the outcome, there is a need to communicate this to all stakeholders and to reset the current status and projected outcome over the coming period. Do not forget to take the wider community with you. It is essential that there is understanding of what has led to the change and to retain confidence in the implementation programme – this is not due to programme failure, and it is important to retain credibility as well as maintain the morale of those involved in the delivery of the programme.

10.1 MANAGING THE IMPACT OF CHANGE

The change has been assessed, there is no alternative, and so you have to proceed with the implications to the implementation plan as you have assessed them. In part, this is a test of the agility of the implementation phase you are in, as you should have developed the appropriate mechanisms to track dependencies and assess the likelihood of the risk emerging. Of course, there may be things which you did not foresee when the plan was first approved, though an effective programme has dependency tracking built into it and so should spot new dependencies as they emerge – it is an ever-changing picture, and like radar on a ship, needs to be monitored continuously to see new threats or risks as they appear.

As we discovered earlier, the misapprehension that a successful implementation means sticking rigorously to the plan is a strong contender to lead to failure. Most organisations operate in a dynamic marketplace with a constantly changing landscape as each organisation seeks advantage over its competitors, the economy shifts and the customer makes choices. To think this has no impact on your data strategy implementation is clearly missing the point of why a data strategy is important to your organisation.

Referring back to the research conducted by Sull et al.,[3] some of the findings are stark in this space. They found that organisations do not adapt quickly enough to changing market conditions (see Figure 10.1) and miss opportunities through a lack of agility and pace of decision making. Whilst only 10 per cent of managers thought failing to adapt at all was the problem in strategy execution, it is the pace behind the agility which presents itself as the problem; 29 per cent of managers were able to seize fleeting opportunities

Figure 10.1 Organisations failing to adapt quickly enough to market conditions

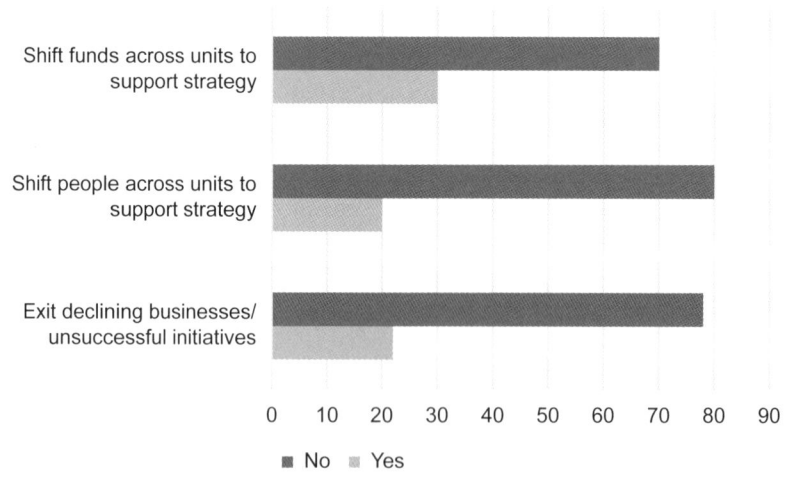

---

3   Donald Sull, Rebecca Homkes and Charles Sull, Why Strategy Execution Unravels – and What to Do About It. *Harvard Business Review*, March 2015. https://hbr.org/2015/03/why-strategy-execution-unravelsand-what-to-do-about-it.

or mitigate emerging threats, whilst 24 per cent believed their organisations reacted quickly but lost alignment with the corporate strategy.

Perhaps most damning of all, just 11 per cent of managers believed that all of the organisation's strategic priorities had the financial and human resources needed for success – indicating that nearly 90 per cent expected strategic priorities to fail for lack of resources. The key message in the research is that agility must be balanced with alignment, and the findings bear out the risks if this is not the case.

The need to manage change within the implementation phase requires strong stakeholder communications and clarity of messaging. The assessment of the change needs to be undertaken quickly, but reliably, as the message will convey the impact of the change both in terms of what will not be achieved and the consequence of replanning to try to mitigate the impact of the change and deliver what it is feasible to do so. Clearly, you must assess the relevance and impact of the change for each stakeholder. If a particular stakeholder or group is going to be impacted negatively, then there needs to be greater engagement, and discussions to explore how to strike a balance in the mitigation need to be put in place that might involve the stakeholder providing resources or funding to assist in finding a solution.

Of course, the impact of the change may not be prescriptive in terms of it having a direct effect on the implementation programme. There may be options to even out the impact on the plan that mitigate the effect but result in the burden being carried by several stakeholders. This will need a collective will to take a group approach to keeping things moving as a whole, and there may be wider dependencies upon the delivery of elements of your own implementation that then impact other programmes. All of this should be understood in advance, through an effective stakeholder assessment that identifies dependencies not only within your own implementation plan but those you are responsible for addressing in the implementation plans of others.

If you are able to work through the impact assessment and come up with options, then you may draw up recommendations to put before the stakeholder group. It is likely that the impact will analyse a number of considerations, including:

- wider dependencies (for instance, on other programmes or commitments) and the cost/benefit implications;
- opportunity cost of the delay (due to the alignment of activities as planned which would be lost through delay);
- resource availability at a future point if activities are delayed;
- sequencing implications of any reordering of the tasks to be undertaken.

There may need to be options that put different proposals in front of your stakeholders, with the consequences of these made abundantly clear so all parties are aware of what they would be signing up to. Clearly, this would also need to go through more formal governance via your sponsor too, but with stakeholder feedback to guide a preferred decision.

The prioritisation process is, therefore, a complex one. It has to incorporate:

- dependencies in both directions – those you have within your own programme and those you are carrying within other programmes;
- resource constraints;
- value-based judgements;
- delivery sequencing (there is no point moving something forward due to resource availability only to find it cannot progress due to a critical deliverable being planned for later delivery);
- material progress being demonstrable within your programme to avoid subsequent challenges on the evidence of delivery being strong enough.

It is a complex web to have to negotiate, so prepare yourself as best you can in the planning stage to have as much of this information to hand, so that you do not have to spend too much time collating it when you need it – at the point of having to implement this type of change, time will be of the essence and you will potentially be rushed into a decision.

The role of the sponsor is critical if and when you reach this point. The sponsor has not only potentially greater awareness of the wider political dimension as to what is driving the wider change decision, but also the network to be able to influence some of the audience you need to engage to enable you to gather all of your facts and get the right level of buy-in to the recommendations you put forward. The sponsor has to be party to the decisions to be reached, the implications and consequences, and be ready to fight your corner should there be any senior-level resistance to the proposed direction you intend to take. The sponsor might have to compromise, but if fully briefed on the background behind the proposed direction, then they can hold their own in finalising agreement on your behalf.

10.2 ASSESSING IMPACT OF CHANGE

This chapter has referred to the need to assess the impact of change on the data strategy implementation plan. The practical steps of doing this are a methodological approach to capturing all aspects of the change to ensure the bearing it will have on the implementation as a whole is fully comprehended, to enable you to make a decision fully cognisant of the totality of the impact. This forms a fundamental part of the programme management discipline, and so I do not intend to go into detail in this book when there are many other sources that provide more comprehensive coverage of this topic (see the bibliography at the end of this book for further references). However, I want to outline the basics, so you have a level of understanding should you need to do change impact assessments yourself for the first time.

You may have heard the term 'change control' within your organisation, and so may have experienced this for yourself without being fully aware of why or how this is undertaken. The process is simply trying to gather all aspects of the change and to manage it in a way that provides rigour to underpin a decision ultimately to be made based on the facts provided. It is relatively straightforward to do, though it may at times feel time-consuming to gather all the inputs before getting to a decision.

In the context of the data strategy implementation plan, change control is usually a five-step process:

1. Identify and capture/log the change.

2. Undertake an assessment of impact across the programme.

3. Recommend and agree a decision.

4. Implement the change.

5. Close and undertake change review (typically for larger changes, to learn from the process to improve subsequent instances).

The process is relatively clear; the challenge is usually identifying all stakeholders (step 2) to ensure all impacts are captured to be able to undertake this part of the process as extensively as necessary to progress to a decision. If you have to assess multiple options to identify which change is to be implemented, then this process can be accelerated by conducting the potential changes in parallel, especially if it involves a similar group of stakeholders being involved through each of the changes.

If the data strategy implementation has gone through a thorough review of key stakeholders at the outset, when the implementation is being planned, you should have a good understanding of who to engage in the change control process. If not, then this stage could be time-consuming in itself, which could have been avoided through earlier planning. Ideally, a stakeholder map or list is in place to support communications, as well as ownership or interests in part of the implementation plan, and there should be resources outlined in the plan that would guide you to the right areas to engage on those activities.

You may also find that those who you believe need to be engaged in making the decision, especially signing off on a recommendation, delegate it to others. If this is the case, then seek to make the implications of this clear – you are taking a delegate from them who is empowered to make decisions, otherwise that individual is of limited value to you.

10.2.1 Resources

The implementation plan will detail the resources – human and financial – assigned to deliver the outputs and when these are intended to be deployed. Any change to the plan will need to be impact-assessed, as it is more than likely that it will need to realign resources to those changes. Of course, it may not be feasible to switch human resources, due to other commitments, and the skillset required needs to be factored in if there is to be any proposed substitution of resource to cover those activities reassigned in the plan.

Operating in the data strategy space is a delicate balance, from marshalling scarce resources with specific data-related skills, on the one hand, to mobilising operational teams across the entire organisation to drive the outcomes needed, on the other. The interdependencies in this data ecosystem necessitate a complex web of activities to be delivered with relatively limited options to change sequencing. Ultimately it is likely that the dependencies between activities will lead to a constraint on further progress being possible, unless that critical activity is delivered.

It is, therefore, essential to know where the pinch points are in the plan for the most challenging skillsets you need, so you can do all you can to try to minimise the risk. Alongside this, explore what the options are for substituting those named within your plan with others within the organisation if necessary, and, if budgets to source additional resources are not totally out of the question, investigate the options to buy in the skills you require and identify what might be available – either through the contract, interim or consulting market. The latter, if the right person can be found, brings deep skills and experience, just not the depth of knowledge of the organisation that the employee would bring.

The financial resources available to deliver the implementation phase are likely to be impacted by any change. This may arise due to the replanning required, which no longer plots a logically sequenced approach but incurs additional costs through a less efficient order in which activities are delivered. It may require retaining resources for gaps between activities, otherwise they will be redirected, or the use of higher-cost resources (especially if resources need to be drafted in from outside the organisation). There is also the potential of delays incurring a rise in costs, whether through price rises for items such as software or hardware, or simply an increased cost base through moving between financial years.

It is important to explore the opportunities to accrue budget to offset some unforeseen delays or cost increases, especially if it is feasible to bring some of that into a current financial year rather than delay into the next year. Clearly, this will be guided by the finance function in your organisation, but if you are constrained to fixed budgets in-year to deliver the strategy implementation, then this is something you will need to consider if you are facing a shift of costs into a subsequent year.

If your funding is based upon achieving milestones in your implementation plan, then the risk is that the slippage in the plan through the change imposed upon it will have a greater bearing than would otherwise be the case. Whilst funding linked to milestones is more usually applied to externally delivered projects, it is increasingly a way to keep focus on the activities within and ensure there is a results mentality behind the strategy implementation, rather than a less focused course navigated through the delivery of the strategy. I am personally an advocate of such an approach – it provides a degree of certainty to those who are tasked with delivery and sets an expectation for those funding it, which guarantees alignment in the understanding of what is expected – but those things outside the immediate control of the implementation programme need to be spotted, impact-assessed and called out at the earliest opportunity to provide an early warning that the timeline is no longer achievable, enabling time to work through the consequences and agree a reset amenable to both parties.

10.3 CAPABILITY REASSESSMENT AND THE ROLE OF LEARNING AND DEVELOPMENT

Chapter 6 covered the importance of understanding the capability of the organisation and those within it at some length. It is important to comprehend the capability and readiness to embark on a data strategy from the outset, otherwise the expectation versus what is realistically achievable may differ and scupper the data strategy from the start. Similarly, it is essential to embark on the strategy implementation fully aware of the capabilities of the organisation to turn strategy into reality. Implementation is a different skillset to strategy development, and whilst it is not unheard of to find people skilled equally in these two capabilities, the need to have a team (whether formally or virtually) you can trust to deliver the implementation is critical to your likely success.

The evolving nature of implementation requires someone who is as comfortable dealing with ambiguity as they are marshalling granular detail into a comprehensive plan. Without the agility to adapt and flex to the unplanned and unforeseen that lies ahead, those in the implementation space will soon find their programme in difficulties, and ultimately those who lead in these situations have to be effective communicators to ensure those around them are equally comfortable with uncertainty and ambiguity.

The point of revisiting the topic of capabilities in this chapter is to highlight that there will inevitably be changes through the course of the strategy implementation. People move roles in an organisation, especially those with scarce skillsets and a proven track record of success in programme implementation, and will also potentially leave the organisation. Demands within the organisation may simply determine that someone within the implementation programme team is needed elsewhere and switch them out at relatively short notice.

10.3.1 Handling the risks of losing key members of the implementation programme team

In many respects, the more successful your programme is proving to be, the more attractive your team will become to others who are looking to staff programmes of their own or have challenges within their function that need someone to troubleshoot. Whilst this is a tremendous accolade to you and your programme, it is one of the greatest ironies that retaining a great team can become harder the more the profile of the programme is raised and recognised for being successful. Whilst a moment of pride and acknowledgement, in the short to medium term it is a big challenge.

Anyone who has operated for any time within a strategy implementation environment will become knowledgeable about the organisation, the strategy, the rationale for embarking on it and the direction the implementation is taking. Those in the team will build a strong rapport amongst themselves, but most importantly, with those stakeholders in the wider organisation that it is important to engage and keep motivated and positive towards the programme, in part because it opens doors to staff in that function and buys trust.

Losing this knowledge base inevitably causes a loss of momentum, no matter how effective the replacement may be or how quickly they can be *in situ*. The formalities – the background to the data strategy, what it is seeking to achieve and why, the implementation plan and the progress to date – can all be acquired relatively quickly; what is much harder to achieve is confidence in both the newly appointed individual who has to take over and the stakeholder group, and awareness of those nuances of what the colleagues you engage with really think, where they see their own role in the implementation and the level of their commitment (do not always assume what people tell you to be what they actually think about the work you are leading on) to what you are trying to achieve.

That individual is starting out for the first time but actually, from a stakeholder perspective, once again, building trust and having to grow a level of understanding because the implementation is already under way and is not going to stop to accommodate their need to learn quickly.

Think of it along the lines of competing in the Le Mans 24 hour motor race. The previous driver has been at the front of the pack, a clear leader and driving the race of their life – which is why they got hand-picked for promotion, a bigger opportunity or a career move. Rather suddenly, and abruptly, that leader has called ahead to say that on the next lap the car will be stopping at the pits and another driver needs to be found – a change which had not been anticipated so early in the race.

In the scramble to find an alternative – as it is unlikely you have a reserve driver already lined up ready to go so soon – whilst the car completes the current lap you have to alert people to the change about to be made, find a new driver and get that individual fully briefed on the car, the race, the tactics and conditions, and with the car heading for the pits the other cars go racing by whilst you enact the change. If you are lucky, the original driver may have a few words for the new driver whilst heading for the pits and then as they change places.

Your new driver, still getting familiar with the car, rejoins the race towards the back of the pack rather than the lead, and you have to support them in gaining confidence to tackle finding their way towards the front again, to re-establish that momentum you had worked so hard to build and lost in an instant. If the driver doesn't get familiar with the car quickly, they will not be working through the pack but risk being lapped by those who were behind only a lap or two ago.

This analogy demonstrates that the risk is known only from the point at which you have to deal with the uncertainty, but then you have to find a course which gets you back in the race and build the confidence of the new driver to try to make up the lost ground and get back to performing at a similar level to the previous driver.

It is often overlooked that at the start of an implementation there is an opportunity to undertake a period of mobilisation – identifying what needs to be done, refining the plan, and assigning resources and briefing those individuals accordingly. What is not considered, once the implementation is under way, is the impact of having to join midway through compared to the relative luxury of having the time for mobilisation. Of course, the benefit of joining part-way through is that the implementation has potentially been running long enough to gain a positive reputation, such that you join something with momentum, which had yet to be established at the outset.

Nonetheless, I think the challenge for those joining a programme and taking a leading role from someone who has built a strong reputation is always one which is daunting, and as the implementation lead something you need to consider – it is worth investing time in supporting your newcomer in whatever way enables them to achieve their own momentum for the greater good of the programme.

10.3.2 Learning and development

One area that programmes tend to lose sight of is the need to continue to invest in those who are undertaking leading roles within the implementation programme, who are also likely to need continuous development to keep their skills fresh and relevant to the tasks they are undertaking in your programme. They also need to consider their own career development and build their knowledge and skills to enhance their own career prospects.

The staff within the organisation will have been assessed, to some degree, in their capability to lead the data strategy implementation. It is essential that the findings of this activity are not lost at the outset of the implementation, as these will need to be factored in to the selection of the implementation team and to address the skills and/or capability gaps that have been identified at the earliest opportunity. I would recommend capturing this in a skills and capability matrix, so there is at least an understanding at a point in time to drive appropriate development. Ideally, this would then be updated, but clearly this is a significant overhead.

In the meantime, you need to consider how you operate most effectively given there are potential constraints in capability within the team, which might involve accelerating the learning by doubling up on resources so those needing to learn do so by shadowing someone within the team with the relevant experience. There is also the opportunity to take this further, using mentoring or coaching sessions with the team, using the skills and capabilities already within the team or possibly the wider organisation. You could also adopt a more project-team-based approach to delivery, utilising your resources to work in groups to collectively deliver on activities, rather than assigning each item to one or two members of the team. This spreads the risk and also accelerates the implementation team getting to know one another, building rapport and pooling skills to deliver as a group.

> Learning can take a variety of forms, and people tend to learn differently, so try to understand what works best for members of your team and provide appropriate opportunities.

Just as I have described the risk of losing some of the better members of your programme team, do not overlook that you may have talent within the team ready to make that step up, which of course mitigates some of the risk of losing programme knowledge. If you are running a programme which is going to last two to three years then you should be thinking about succession planning, risk mitigation plans and rotation of the team – often, moving people within the team to take on different elements enables them to keep learning, and constantly challenges the programme team to think out of the box in how to engage most effectively with the wider organisation to deliver a successful outcome.

You may well have some fantastic skills and capabilities within your programme team: if so, encourage the team to run knowledge-sharing sessions to upskill through pooling the team's capabilities. For those at an earlier stage in their career than some in the team, it is often these types of sessions that have the most impact, developing knowledge through seeing and then doing, reinforced by the approaches taken by more experienced members of the team. I can certainly remember moments in programmes I have been part of where I took away things I either observed or actively learnt from others in the team.

One of the ways you can build better links with the wider organisation is to actively seek opportunities to get members of functions across the organisation to talk through what they do and how they operate, and to give some insight into the specific skills and capabilities that underpin their work. It is often underrated how much satisfaction individuals get from being given the chance to talk with pride about what they do, especially if there is an attentive audience eagerly taking it in. Engaging in this way is often about building relationships on a one-to-one basis, establishing trust and respect for what one another brings to the organisation and getting the synergies from the collective effort. Of course, you may also find your next round of talented team members through such wider engagements, which also brings in fresh perspectives and diversity of backgrounds to the team.

Build in the need for learning and development into the programme. Do not regard it as something which is a luxury, as done well it will provide payback far greater than the time taken to undertake it.

10.3.3 Reassessing maturity through deploying new skills

The implementation of the data strategy should be measured by the data maturity assessment progression, amongst other KPIs. A key part of this is to focus effort on upskilling the organisation to be more mature in its understanding of data and the importance of becoming information literate (that is, most organisations and consultants talk of being data literate, but this usually misrepresents the goal which they are seeking, which is to be more intelligent in the acquisition and use of information, not the handling of raw data), and to be more insight-led to drive more evidence-based decision making.

The challenge, in trying to upskill an organisation, is how do you know it is sticking? Many organisations track the number of courses delivered and the hours accumulated undertaking e-learning or classroom teaching, or even rely on a simple post-course feedback sheet on the training provided before the individual has had the chance to put it to the test and demonstrate that they can now do things more effectively than was previously the case. This is auditing the activity has taken place, but is certainly not demonstrating value delivered through any assessment of impact achieved.

The various assessment models highlighted earlier in the book are designed to be able to measure progression and therefore assume that there will be some evidence beyond the audit style of approach to be able to demonstrate the difference. It may seem obvious, but very few organisations seem to have a methodical approach to conducting maturity assessments other than treating them as a point in time appraisal. This seems a rather haphazard and risky way to track whether one of the key elements of a data strategy has actually borne fruit and the organisation has made a fundamental shift in its ways of working.

As with any major deliverable within the implementation programme, there should be a strand of activities aligned to increasing the information literacy and proof of a shift to an evidence-based model of decision making. This should have a series of specific tasks to be delivered which, in turn, should have measurability to show how each contributes to the overall goal. This has to be rooted in practical evidence of progress, tracking how ways of working have changed to approach reaching a decision in a way the organisation would not have followed previously.

This can be hard to define, but it may be clearer if you take a discrete piece of work, either a project or a well-defined task undertaken within the organisation where you have a 'before' to act as a baseline, and have taken the relevant staff through the training to get them to approach it in a way that is putting into practice what the training has instructed. These examples become your case studies, those involved become your advocates and the evidence of progress becomes the momentum to build confidence that change will lead to a positive transformation for the organisation.

The maturity assessments provide detail behind the various steps and have rigour in how these are scored if applied correctly. It is therefore easy to identify the activities needed if the organisation is to progress to become more mature and the programme can structure itself to provide the means to achieve this. Of course, what the reassessment is seeking to evidence is that the learning has been applied rather than that the training has been provided, and so the implementation programme has to pursue the case beyond delivering information literacy to actually following this through into it becoming embedded practice. This is where stakeholder commitment, to provide the opportunities to demonstrate how powerful the change can be, is so critical to your success.

I will also refer back to Chapter 7 at this point. The art of being able to make progress in this area is as much about communication as providing the technical training. It needs commitment from the leadership that this is the direction the organisation is going, a reinforcement of the maturity assessment as a critical measure of success (some organisations embed the maturity assessment progress into objectives of managers to demonstrate this is not optional) and an ongoing drip-feed of success stories to demonstrate the benefits of shifting from the familiar to a new way of working. You need to ensure that you have the communications pipeline ready and the key messages from those who are influential to tell the story of why the change is needed and the impact it has made, and to call out those teams who have successfully embraced the new approach to give recognition.

10.3.4 Recruitment

The capability assessment undertaken at the data strategy definition stage will have highlighted where there are key gaps in the organisation to be able to transform to a new way of working. This could be down to a lack of knowledge, but it could just as easily be resistance to change. Without confronting these in the data strategy implementation the success of the programme will be undermined from the start.

Whilst learning and development is going to be a key weapon in the implementation armoury, there may well be a need for greater impetus from the start to get change moving. This could be through the implementation programme having a third party assist in its delivery, providing consulting support and expertise in getting change driven through an organisation similar to your own.

However, do remember that this will be a high cost to the implementation programme. You are likely to need to commit to the data strategy for a number of years, so building a dependency in a third party either leading or advising your programme may become a prop rather than supplementary, and make separation at the end of their engagement a significant risk to the endurance of the changes made or still to be achieved.

It might be that there are some key posts which require additional expertise or supplementary resources due to availability pressures impacting the amount of time that key stakeholders can provide to support your implementation. Consider whether hiring specific resource to cover these posts is a viable option, either as contractors or interim consultants, and whether they are backfilling to cover the current tasks for the individual in post or engaging with the programme on their behalf.

There may be posts which are either vacant or do not exist in the current organisation but which you identify as key to the data strategy being implemented. In the former case, take a look at the specification of the post in question and assess whether there is an opportunity to strengthen key inputs which you are likely to require in that post to be able to drive through the data strategy implementation.

You might be looking at how the current organisation is configured to build on the data strategy and, ultimately, to own it if there is not a logical place in the organisation for it to sit. Many organisations have introduced the CDO role, albeit with numerous variations as to what this post undertakes, from a specific focus on data to a broader brief to encompass its exploitation too. This is not to say that the CDO role should be tightly defined – many other roles with universally recognised titles have variations in responsibilities, not least finance, which can also incorporate loosely related activities such as procurement, risk, legal, audit and estates, whether in systems, unstructured data outside systems (for instance, offsite storage facilities) and the quality and accessibility of the data.

In some organisations, data is misleadingly put with the CIO on the grounds it resides in systems and so logically belongs to the CIO. Aside from the fact that not all data is in systems – unstructured data is often still paper-based, and keeping the document management companies providing offsite storage very comfortable in satisfying the insatiable demand that continues, despite talk of the paperless office for decades – the CIO controls very little data, providing the plumbing for the data to be contained and flow through but having no control over the staff within the organisation who enter and use the data. To get traction, data responsibility should sit with those who lead staff who generate and use the data, rather than those who provide the systems that host it.

Consider, as part of your data strategy and maturity, the readiness of your organisation to adopt a CDO role. It doesn't need to be titled as such, and many organisations operate with posts which have the same responsibilities you would expect a CDO to fulfil but with a different title (for example, chief analytics officer, head/vice-president/senior vice-president of data, chief data scientist). However, having a focal point at a high level of seniority for data and its exploitation is becoming increasingly commonplace in medium and large organisations and those operating in the public sector, and this is perhaps something you should consider in the data strategy (or its implementation) to ensure there is a senior role to take on leadership responsibilities for the strategy in the future.

There may be key roles that you need to add to your organisation to facilitate specific changes that the data strategy will introduce. For instance, if you are intending to commence a data governance programme it would be wise to seek to hire someone who has had experience in doing this in another organisation, ideally with similarities to your own in terms of the challenges you face (not necessarily the same sector – data and its governance are broadly the same – but preferably of similar scale and maturity). A plan to move into predictive analytics for the first time, for example, will require someone experienced in building that capability and engaging with stakeholders to define and/or demonstrate the art of the possible in what can be achieved, and then build a team to roll out that capability.

There may be a case to develop these skills in-house, particularly if there isn't the budget to recruit, but there is a steep learning curve to introduce these capabilities into the organisation if you have not done this before, especially as it will be new for all to comprehend and get behind within the organisation as a whole.

Therefore, the data strategy should identify what is required to achieve a successful implementation of the waymarkers and, if it doesn't, the implementation plan needs to specify these as critical dependencies and ensure appropriate budgets are assigned for recruitment and ongoing staff costs. It is also important to be pragmatic about the timescales to recruit and, if you need someone on board in advance of the approval and likely start date, to consider hiring a contractor, interim or consultant, to ensure the implementation plan does not stall.

10.4 COMMUNICATING CHANGE

The data strategy is a key agent of change within the organisation, transforming the way in which all staff within the organisation capture, maintain and use data. As Chapter 7 explained, much of the success of the data strategy implementation will depend on how effectively you are able to get the message across that the data strategy is something that impacts the whole organisation, rather than something distant for just the executive part of the organisation to think about.

The constant state of flux that many organisations experience in the fast-paced world we operate in will invariably lead to a degree of tacking and changing direction in the execution of the strategy. This is to be expected, but it also needs to be communicated. It is a factor of the human mind that we deal with change on a constant basis – things not turning out quite as we expected, unplanned-for changes that confront us in our daily lives, even the choices we make for dinner needing rethought if the store doesn't have the key ingredient or the restaurant no longer has that menu option available. Whilst these are commonplace in our lives, many people seem to regard work as a constant, doing the same thing routinely, and so change to this pattern becomes more significant than would be expected.

Of course, some react well to change and others positively thrive on it, and there is not a blanket rejection of change, otherwise we would not have change professionals in many of our organisations. However, even our most enthusiastic change professionals can, at times, overlook the resistance to change you may encounter. If you are leading a data strategy implementation, handling change resistance is going to be a key aspect of your role, so do not underestimate the extent of it and, more importantly, how changes to your implementation programme may be positioned as a failing of the programme when it isn't necessarily anything of the sort.

> The landscape of the organisation is important to consider when embarking on change. What has been the history of change in the recent past (up to the last decade, say), and how do staff refer to previous change programmes?
>
> In many organisations, the most animated discussions about change will be the 'remember the time when …' sort, as if change was being imposed and staff rallied round to resist the ill-thought-out ideas of the time. People often choose to remember what the low points of programmes were, the parts which did not land well and had to be dropped or redefined to get traction. It is remarkable how, if you explore such discussions with that group further to consider the positives or the overall intent of the programme, there will be tacit or reluctant acknowledgement that some of the programme was a success and may well have made a positive change, but it is the parts that went wrong that enter folklore.

The way you choose to implement the data strategy will almost certainly depend on the backdrop of your own organisation, the approach taken to strategic implementation programmes and the confidence to communicate boldly with the wider organisation on change. If your organisation is rather conservative in its approach, you may well have to work hard to create the oxygen to enable your implementation programme to breathe and get wider engagement in the organisation. By contrast, if your organisation is much bolder and confident in promoting change, then you will need to be alert as to how to seize this opportunity to engage with the wider organisation to make what you are doing relevant and of interest to them.

Assuming you are in a positive situation to build a coherent communications plan around your data strategy implementation, then you should be mindful that your direction may change and hence you need to provide some scope in your communication to set direction but not to box yourself in on the tactics used to get there. The communications need to be focused on the need for change, the direction of travel and the benefits of getting there, not the detail that will become a focal point if you are seen to keep changing the tactics within the implementation programme. Define the steps that lie immediately ahead in greater detail, where you have certainty, but not those which lie further ahead – this will lose focus for those reading it and blur the key messages you are trying to get across.

It is common for data strategy implementation to get lost in the wider scheme of transformational activity being undertaken within an organisation. This is particularly the case if there is a function or team that leads on data and analytics, which therefore makes the implementation seem like a 'business as usual' task for those in that team but not for wider consideration. This is completely flawed thinking, as data pervades the organisation: it is no exaggeration to say that organisations would not operate if it were not for data – how would we conduct transactions, know how to compile a product or service, assign resources, bill a customer, pay an employee and so on? – hence a data strategy is for all to understand and support its implementation.

I have found that many data initiatives fail in organisations due to three things: a lack of sponsorship and drive, limited executive commitment to achieve its goals or an inability to get the focus to make it important to get buy-in to change across the organisation. They have been trying to do the right thing, but trying to execute it in the wrong way.

Many of my peers across the data profession will be able to trade stories about the difference the three key elements above can make, regardless of how compelling the concept may be or the timing is right to execute. Back to the Le Mans analogy, no matter how great the driver, if the wider team is not committed to the same goals with the levels of intensity to make the execution of the race a success, then the driver alone cannot rescue the team from failing to win the race. Breaking down in the early stages of the race with engine trouble is not the fault of the driver or the original concept, but the issue is to be found in the preparation and commitment to ensuring successful execution.

Your challenge is to ensure you embark on the data strategy implementation cognisant of the importance of having the communications plan running as a key stream within your own plan, and to make sure it is resourced and has executive commitment throughout. Do not overpromise, nor delve into reams of detail, but keep the focus on why the programme is needed, what it is seeking to achieve, how it is being delivered and the part that you need each individual within the organisation to understand so that they are informed, ready and willing when called upon to play their part. Be as open as possible about the trajectory having to adapt but ensure that the core message remains the same, such that you demonstrate a degree of control over change that may be imposed on you and the programme, rather than being caught out unawares and having to make decisions as you go along. Whilst the latter may be the case from time to time – every complex programme has to deal with uncertainty, and it would be folly to think otherwise – it does not need to be evident in the communication delivered to the organisation at large.

Make the most of such uncertainty by turning it into an opportunity, and identify any benefit that accrues as a result. It is often the case that such unforeseen changes can yield positive outcomes, and whilst it might delay or impact some part of the programme at that time, there can often be unintended consequences that can be seized upon to deliver benefits which were not originally envisaged or to bring other activity forward in the plan that would otherwise have been much later.

If you have to adapt, look for what that brings in return. Even if this may be tenuous in your mind there is a positive story to be told and one which is focused on continuing to make progress – do not give the impression of stalling or losing your way. For instance, if you need to bring in expertise due to resources having to be realigned, look at the positives of bringing in knowledge and capabilities which were not originally anticipated, and the benefits of learning from what other organisations have done in this space. If you have to delay an activity due to a dependency slipping, then what does this enable instead to keep you moving forward, even if only at half the pace you had anticipated previously? In other words, retain control of the messaging to portray the positives about what you are doing and the difference you are making.

Should you feel that there is limited scope to communicate change within your organisation due to its risk-averse nature, the lack of communications expertise to give a clear message on change or the fear of 'they have heard it all before', then consider how you can share progress in a way which is not change-focused. This may seem a little odd, given the data strategy implementation is a change programme, but for many people change is a difficult thing to embrace as it often cannot give longer-term certainty for the individual to the intensity, or degree, they seek.

In such cases, the focus of communications has to be more subtle, highlighting collaborative activities that have led to something which can be viewed positively as a constructive use of time and resource to make things better for teams and individuals within the teams. This is much smaller in scale and ambition, but achieves much the same outcome – a willingness to work with the implementation team in a way which is more about driving local improvements with those directly involved, to enable those individuals to have input and potentially shape outcomes that they are satisfied will work and are happy to adopt.

If you think this sounds more like continuous improvement then I would not entirely disagree, other than to say that this is adopting those techniques in the context of a much larger planned series of activities that need to be implemented across the organisation. It feels rather more organic, getting people on board to work with you through building trust and a willingness to talk openly about frustrations and opportunities to do things better, and capturing this in a way that can be incorporated into your own approach to implementing the data strategy.

It does have a degree of stealth about it, as there is a plan behind the engagement model which is not necessarily shared as overtly as would be the case in an organisation more open to transformation than others, but it is also about overcoming fear and mistrust to be able to deliver change through engaging with those at the sharp end of activity so they buy in to it from the outset. Building trust in this way can be progressed into a more engaged model where the programme more proactively promotes what it wants to do to build on the initial successes, as it is about getting those who might be both most involved in any change and experience the greatest impact to feel they have a stake in its execution. In many ways, it is building advocacy from an initial position of suspicion, such that these individuals can be active promoters of this evolving approach to other groups who may have a similar mindset.

10.5 A DYNAMIC DATA STRATEGY

The earlier chapters of this book talked briefly about the strategy cycle within your organisation, and you may find that you are tied in with a fixed period the strategy is intended to cover. Whilst this provides certainty of direction to the executive members of the organisation, it is a relatively arbitrary way of working in most cases (there are exceptions, driven by the likes of regulatory compliance or contractual positions, where the timing is entirely beyond the organisation's control) and tends to bind the thinking to a period of time when strategy is an evolving activity – no organisation should stand still due to the complexities of the world in which it operates and the changing landscape that results from the impact of competitors, regulation, customer expectations and financial performance.

Historically, organisations have tended to work to fixed periods in defining strategy to ensure there was clarity for shareholders, regulators and the executive board to know what was intended to be achieved, and by when. It is often referred to as a 'plan then do' approach, in which the strategy is prescriptive and the execution purely tactical in conveying the strategy into delivery. Whilst this has served organisations relatively well, the dynamics of the modern world are making this not only less relevant but also too pedestrian for organisations to adapt to change. Decisions arise which will affect the strategic direction of organisations faster than ever before, and frequently these either disrupt the strategy or make it obsolete.

The case for moving to a more dynamic approach to strategy definition has been growing in recent years as the world becomes rather more challenging to operate in without some element of flexibility. Strategy has also become more fluid, less obsessed with needing to provide all the answers, and more focused on the direction and leaving the execution of the strategy more open to translation by those closest to the task at the time. The increased focus on techniques like Agile has led to a recognition that the prescription of the past is no longer practicable, and hence strategic execution is becoming much more a 'test and learn' model of adaptability, which enables those leading the charge on implementation to refine and repeat according to what has been learnt from the previous activity.

The other change is a more performance-based approach to strategy execution, seeking to measure what has been achieved in shorter windows rather than taking a longer-term view of whether the strategy has borne fruit. This demands a more responsive approach to strategy, as this lends itself to constant review of the implementation approach, and adaptation and evolution being applied to increase its effectiveness. It is important to stress that the measures need to apply at multiple levels in such a model, as the strategy still needs to be able to demonstrate its effect over a longer time frame to show the scale of what has been achieved from the original baseline, because a more granular level of performance will not necessarily present that bigger picture. This will also ensure that the performance in strategy execution is blended with the Agile iteration to retain its focus on the overall direction, and not lose sight of this for more opportunistic benefits in the short term which will detract from the bigger goal over a slightly longer horizon.

In terms of data strategy, I have been an advocate of adopting a rolling view rather than operating to fixed points of time throughout my career. I had a moment of clarity early on, when tasked with devising a ten-year strategy in an organisation that was embarking on taking a more strategic approach to its whole business than had previously been the case. I was leading a relatively new part of the larger business and had challenges in mapping out beyond a year; three years was a limit of realistic ambition given there were established competitors in a market still relatively new to us, and hence it was difficult to see how our recent arrival into that market would play out.

The ten-year vision was delivered, but there were two key components within it: a one-year strategy, which was easily transferable into an implementation plan, and a three-year strategy, which identified funding, people and product development needs to get to a point of greater maturity and, hence, stability, having passed the point of being a new entrant to the market. The ten-year strategy had the grand visionary statements that were little more than aspirational and was caveated with plenty of assumptions and forecasts that were inevitably lacking any robust evidence but were the best that could be produced at the time.

This demonstrated to me that, as someone with a keen interest in strategy, the situation you are operating within – often referred to as PESTLE, encompassing political, economic, sociological, technological, legal and environmental factors – defines the length of the viability of a strategy. For parts of the rest of the organisation, investment decisions were made on the strength of a ten-year projection of revenue based on likely demand, and whilst this might be questionable in the later years, without the view to a positive revenue outcome from the investment required, the project would likely have been curtailed or blocked.

Data strategy endures. It is not a business strategy in the sense of decisions needing to be made on what opportunities need to be grasped and where the organisation sees its future (expansion through organic growth, acquisition, stabilising or retrenching, for example). Data persists in organisations and hence needs appropriate controls and direction applied. This requires a data strategy to ensure the organisation remains compliant (or becomes compliant, of course), efficient in being able to access it and able to exploit it effectively. Therefore, there is a strong case to be made that data strategy needs to be a rolling strategy, conforming to the timelines imposed by the wider organisation but continuing to define its future as it goes.

How do you keep a data strategy relevant to the organisation? My own view is that it has to be dynamic, flexing to represent what the organisation needs to achieve whilst retaining a purpose and vision of how data can help make the organisation a more effective and efficient performer in a compliant and responsible manner.

I have encouraged those for whom I have delivered data strategy workshops to favour the concept of a three-year vision of what is to be achieved but to review annually, in order to keep it as a three-year direction of travel. Some suggest that a data strategy struggles to be of value if it goes beyond just a year, but I still harbour doubts that a data strategy covering a year is much more than an implementation plan.

If you operate in an organisation of complexity and scale, across multiple countries, or even one which is not used to change (or having a data strategy), a year is too short a time to demonstrate real impact to get an executive group to buy in to the change to be achieved. An effective data strategy should contain waymarkers that set out a vision of what will be achieved in a year, for those hungry for that level of immediacy. However, for many organisations, especially those early in their data strategy journey, there is so much to be done that real impact will be felt beyond the first year, which will be taken up with getting alignment, agreement and the infrastructure in place, along with the first series of pilots to demonstrate the art of the possible and whet the appetite for more to follow.

Establishing a three-year data strategy, reflecting on the impact of a completed year one to test and learn before setting the ambition for the new fourth year to be added to the rolling data strategy, will provide the opportunity to reassess and reset the ambition of the data strategy. As year two of the original data strategy becomes the next year in question, there is an opportunity to tighten some of the assumptions and expectations based upon the learning and experience gained within the implementation team.

One of the best-known approaches to iterative development is the concept of learning from experience, and what I am advocating here is to do just that – learn from your first year of strategy implementation, observe what went to plan and what did not, and adapt your approach and set your sights accordingly for the years ahead. A three-year data strategy should reflect that what has been discovered through the first year is valuable insight which must be used to revisit the data strategy in the context of the evidence gained.

It could be that the data strategy was not ambitious enough, progress and engagement has surpassed expectations and hence implementation has raced ahead, and so there is a need for a reset. Conversely, and possibly more likely, it might highlight that there has been more resistance than anticipated, the assumptions haven't necessarily played out as expected, and there has been less progress but a lot of learning about the nature of the organisation, the teams within it and the priorities assigned to the data strategy implementation. Either way, you have learnt something which now needs to be used as evidence to apply to the remaining years of the data strategy and to shape a new third year.

If you do not apply this evidence, then you are failing in one of the likely basic premises of the data strategy itself – a desire to be more evidence-based in decision making. You also run the risk of creating a split between the data strategy and the implementation plan, as it is likely that those leading on the latter are not about to repeat the same (possibly painful) mistakes again the following year and so will adapt the approach taken. It is essential to keep the data strategy and the implementation plan aligned, so if there is a risk of changing one but not the other it is a sign of drift and should be called out and dealt with immediately.

I recognise that the rolling view of the data strategy may not fit with the approach taken to strategy definition within your organisation. I also accept that having a dynamic approach, in which an annual review iterates the relevance and pace of the data strategy, may also be out of alignment with the way your organisation works. However, these things can be done either in partnership with those who control the strategy process or, if necessary, independently.

There is little to be gained from the data strategy seeking to be a realistic vision if you do not reflect potentially significant changes in the organisation or learning from the progress of the implementation (recognising the potential resistance to change could have been either over- or underplayed). There is also a risk of a lack of impetus or direction if you are almost at the end of the data strategy before defining what lies ahead. As I stated earlier, the data strategy is different to many other organisational strategies as it represents a continuum; data will always persist in the organisation, regardless of the direction the corporate strategy takes.

Therefore, I recommend operating a rolling and dynamic approach to data strategy definition, which in turn ensures a closer coupling between definition and execution – the lack of which, as stated earlier, is the biggest cause for the majority of strategies failing to deliver.

10.6 TEN TO TAKE AWAY

The key themes to take away from this chapter are:

1. Data strategy implementation needs to interlock with other change programmes or activities to ensure there is continued alignment, with a particular focus on any impact on your dependencies. Ensure you are tracking any wider activity that could have a bearing on the data strategy implementation.

2. Respond to changes with agility and flexibility, as an inability to adapt quickly enough is a known cause of implementation failure. Consider the impact on the implementation programme in terms of resources, dependencies and benefits.

3. Incorporate a change control process into the implementation of the data strategy and engage your stakeholder network appropriately to ensure there is an informed agreement to any changes to be made.

4. Consider the impact of the strategy implementation on resources – human and financial – to assess whether these can be addressed within the implementation programme or need to be escalated.

5. The implementation team will change over time and it is important to balance the risks of losing knowledge, continuity and personal relationships with the opportunity to bring in different perspectives and to keep the team energised. Plan for this as best you can: consider succession planning, broadening knowledge across the team and how to accelerate the integration of newcomers to the team.

6. Do not overlook the development of skills within the implementation team once the programme is up and running. Assess training needs, focus on how to ensure there is breadth of knowledge supplemented by the experience the programme can offer, and bring in others from those areas in which there is engagement on data strategy implementation to share experience. Allow time for learning and development in the programme.

7. Use maturity assessments to review progress through implementation. Information literacy will be key to making the shift underpinning the data strategy stick within the organisation, and needs to be embedded in the implementation programme as a key transformational deliverable.

8. Consider the resourcing available, and assess whether there is a need for additional resources – whether recruited permanently or as contractors or consultants – to enable the implementation to be delivered at the required pace and quality. The data strategy may be a conduit to defining a role of a CDO for the first time to provide a focal point for data management and exploitation in the future.

9. Build advocacy in the organisation as you communicate change. Bear resistance to change in mind; understand how change has been managed within your organisation to learn from experience. Build communications into your implementation plan and look to establish ways to share across the organisation and build some momentum to establish trust and understanding.

10. Explore the feasibility of running a dynamic, rolling data strategy to keep it moving forward and to review constantly and provide flexibility to accelerate or decelerate as appropriate. Ensure the implementation is focused on measurement to demonstrate the value the data strategy is delivering to the organisation.

11 ASSESSING VALUE IN DATA STRATEGY IMPLEMENTATION

'To me, ideas are worth nothing unless executed. They are just a multiplier.
Execution is worth millions.'

Derek Sivers[1]

Any investment in defining a data strategy and embarking on its implementation must be closely related to the value that such an activity is to bring to the organisation. If this is not uppermost in the minds of both those commissioning the data strategy and those tasked with defining and delivering it, then I would contend that it will lack focus, with an end product unlikely to gain wider traction or seem relevant to those you most need to engage.

This chapter focuses on the concept of value delivered through the data strategy and its implementation, how you demonstrate it through effective measurement and the importance of evaluating the programme to convey how the data strategy has achieved its goals which, through alignment, has enabled the corporate strategy to succeed.

I have known of instances in which an organisation has embarked on a data strategy because of having to address either a lack of compliance or an urgent need to meet compliance obligations. In reality, these instances did not lead to the development of a data strategy as discussed throughout this book. It is a reasonable question to ask whether this makes them any less a data strategy, and whilst there are clearly reasons why every organisation needs to be compliant in its management and exploitation of data, these reasons alone do not warrant a data strategy as the answer. I would suggest that a standard programmatic approach to compliance would be more effective than wrapping up compliance into a strategy (in other words, compliance should always be part of a data strategy, rather than the entirety of it).

There is, of course, nothing like a focus on an immediate crisis or compliance issue to drive attention to data! Therefore, it may be a case of not letting such a crisis 'go to waste', and addressing the immediate issue as a prompt to also cast the net wider, delivering a data strategy that turns adversity into a positive outcome.

One of the overriding reasons for any strategy failing is the danger of focusing solely on performance metrics, which track programmatic activity, such as spend, resources and timing. These are focused on the immediate or, more often, the historic, through MI

---

1   D. Sivers, *Anything You Want: 40 Lessons for a New Kind of Entrepreneur*. New York: Portfolio Books, 2015. The quotation is often attributed to Steve Jobs, though no source provides provenance.

and reporting which will tell you where you were a month or more ago by the time it is produced. Yet, without being able to measure the effectiveness of strategy execution, by which I mean the relevant transformation activities having been delivered and embedded, it is just as likely to be a failure.

It may seem obvious, but if you are delivering a strategy you are meant to be looking forward, driving change, and therefore performance measurement will only tell a small part of the impact that strategy implementation is having on your organisation. The optimal approach is to strike a balance between tracking the coordination of the programme, as measured via the performance metrics, in the short term and to align these with the impact of the change delivered, as measured over a period of time.

The essence of embarking on measuring impact is to have a clearly defined baseline. This may already exist, but in most organisations it does not. There will likely be performance reporting scattered like confetti in your organisation, and many individuals may be involved using a variety of tools to exploit one-off data sets sourced through contacts, which leads to a lack of consistency or quality of information produced. You need to be very clear in how you determine your baseline and get it approved and agreed on by those stakeholders who will later hold you to account for your progress. In some cases there will be such a paucity of data that there will be gaps, undermining your baseline. Ironically, this tells its own story. If you are unable to measure a baseline then there is clearly a significant issue with the data management in play in your organisation.

The first sign of progress is to be able to articulate where you start from, even if it takes some time to establish this fact. As John Foster Dulles, the former US senator, said: 'The measure of success is not whether you have a tough problem to deal with, but whether it is the same problem you had last year.'[2] In other words, be able to articulate the problems you are seeking to address with the strategy to be able to demonstrate your progress.

11.1 EVALUATION TO GENERATE MEASUREMENT IN DATA STRATEGY IMPLEMENTATION

As has been outlined above, the importance of measurement will become clear the further you get into the implementation of the data strategy. However, if you haven't defined, agreed and measured your baseline at the start, then you have missed one of the fundamentals of defining a data strategy.

Measurement should be a visible part of your data strategy, articulating the improvements you expect to deliver in the course of the implementation activity and being a key plank of your review discussions with your sponsor and senior stakeholders. If you have not defined your success criteria and how these will be evidenced through measurement, then it is highly likely that you are already operating to differing interpretations of what is going to be achieved through the data strategy implementation.

---

2 *Executives' Digest: Summaries of Timely Articles of Special Interest to Business Men.* Boston, MA: Baker Library at Harvard University, 1951.

It may seem complex to define success criteria before embarking on the data strategy, but I would suggest that you will have formed judgements based on some degree of evidence as to what to address, and when, in the data strategy. If not, then the data strategy is open to challenge as to what is driving the prioritisation and the return on investment the organisation can expect the implementation to generate. It is essential to build your measurement on evaluating improvement, in a way that can be evidenced, as opposed to being judgemental. The process is intended to be empirical, so think about where that evidence will be captured, stored and used to demonstrate progress.

The process of defining your success criteria, the options available to prioritise in terms of delivery, and the impact that the data strategy will have in terms of enablement and capability should all be factored in to the strategy definition phase and then refined in more detail at the implementation stage. Prior to commencing implementation, it is good practice to revisit the success criteria to evaluate whether these are still accurate, measurable and achievable in the time permitted. It is also recommended that you gain a final sign-off on the measures you are putting in place and enshrine these in the implementation programme reporting to ensure there is a tracker on progress.

The complexity of the measures will likely depend on the nature of the organisation, the scale of the programme and the way in which other strategic implementations report progress. If these are lacking, then you have a blank canvass to work with and can utilise good practice of others in your own approach.

Within UK government, there is a publication known as the Magenta Book[3] which is intended to guide the evaluation of policies, projects and programmes across government. Whilst this is intended for those who engage with, or operate within, government, many of the principles are equally applicable to strategy implementation measurement, especially in relation to the three evaluations – process, impact and value for money. It provides a coherent description of how to use these evaluation techniques to evidence progress against that which was anticipated, and so is a helpful guide for anyone new to evaluating delivery of a major programme, into which data strategy implementation would certainly fit.

A similar guide[4] produced by the New South Wales (NSW) government in Australia provides a very effective set of guidelines to be used to undertake programme evaluations (it also references the Magenta Book as one of its sources). Whilst aimed at those operating NSW government funded programmes, it clearly articulates how to undertake an evaluation of a programme, and I would recommend it for those keen to explore how this might be utilised to support a data strategy implementation programme evidencing successful outcomes. In 2013 the NSW government established, via its Treasury, the Centre for Program Evaluation, specifically to promote evidence-based decision making across the NSW government and to conduct evaluations of programmes using a consistent methodology.

---

3   HM Treasury, Magenta Book: Central Government Guidance on Evaluation. 2020. https://assets.publishing.service.gov.uk/government/uploads/system/uploads/attachment_data/file/879438/HMT_Magenta_Book.pdf.

4   NSW Government Department of Premier and Cabinet, NSW Government Program Evaluation Guidelines. 2016. https://arp.nsw.gov.au/assets/ars/f506555395/NSW-Government-Program-Evaluation-Guideline-January-2016_1.pdf.

11.1.1 Evaluation approaches

The balanced scorecard was originally designed by its founders, Robert Kaplan and David Norton,[5] as a management system for organisations to be able to manage their strategic implementation, based around four key themes at its heart.

- Financial – how the organisation should appear to shareholders so that the organisation can succeed financially. It focuses on bottom-line improvement, through measuring profitability and shareholder value.

- Customer – how the organisation expects to appear to customers in order to achieve its vision. This separates customer and market segments into those where it will seek to compete and its anticipated performance levels in those segments, whilst determining what approach to adopt in other segments (harvest or divest,[6] for example).

- Internal business – identifies how the processes within the organisation need to be refined or improved to excel and be able to meet shareholder and customer expectations. The focus is on those internal processes, core competencies and technologies that underpin customer needs.

- Innovation and learning – investigating the sustainability of the organisation's ability to change and adapt to meet evolving customer expectations and thereby achieve the organisation's vision. This involves a review of the entire infrastructure of the organisation needed to meet these objectives, and assesses the ability of the organisation to innovate, improve and learn, typically measured by new product launches and speed of response to change.

Core to the vision of the balanced scorecard is the importance of strategy mapping, aligning explicitly the cause and effect linkages that ensure outcomes are achieved through the alignment of initiatives and resources, tangible and intangible. Kaplan and Norton were clear that this is essential to be able to demonstrate value.

Mindful that their starting point had been the private sector, Kaplan and Norton adapted the model to make financial and customer factors equal in status in supporting the mission of a public sector organisation. Others have since altered this order and redefined or added to it to create variants which more closely relate to public sector and not-for-profit organisations, but all start with mission as the key driver.

Whilst the balanced scorecard is more typically used across the organisation, it is worth considering – especially if your organisation is using a balanced scorecard approach or a variant thereof – whether there are elements of the balanced scorecard that the data strategy implementation delivers. For instance, every one of the four key themes has

---

5   R.S. Kaplan and D.P. Norton, *The Balanced Scorecard: Translating Strategy into Action*. Boston, MA: Harvard Business Review Press, 1996.

6   Harvesting a customer would involve continuing to take revenue and profitability but not to increase investment; in other words, to make the return on past investment, hence the term harvest. Divesting a customer would be to reduce exposure, either in supporting that marketplace, investing in the customer or simply because the segment that customer is part of is no longer regarded as a core market.

a data dimension to it, and each will be enhanced by what you deliver through the data strategy implementation.

If your organisation does not follow the balanced scorecard, or has no desire to do so, I would still recommend considering it as a structured approach to aid your thinking in defining your outcomes and, thereby, the measurement to be used. It provides a structure that is focused on the organisation at large, as your data strategy should too, and therefore becomes an effective way to marshal your thinking into how you demonstrate real value to your senior stakeholders and sponsor to be able to reach through to those things which impact the bottom line, customer value or efficient delivery of services.

Two further commonly used methods of evaluation are the KAB model,[7] which assesses effectiveness in driving change in knowledge, attitude and behaviour, with each in turn more difficult to achieve than its predecessor, and the Fogg behaviour model (FBM), a design behaviour change model introduced by B.J. Fogg.[8] For those working in training organisations or learning environments, there is also Kirkpatrick's evaluation model,[9] which determines impact in terms of reaction, learning, behaviour and results, which I do not propose to cover in more detail here (I have provided a link in the footnote if you are interested in exploring it).

The KAB model is also referred to as a social cognition model, or knowledge, attitude and practice (KAP) model. It is used extensively in health education and is based on behavioural change being affected by knowledge and attitude. It is centred around knowledge, and the hypothesis that behaviour changes gradually, based on increasing knowledge leading to attitudinal change, which in turn impacts behaviour. Its core premise is that humans are rational, though of course we know that at times emotion or other triggers can overcome the rational, which can make the use of the KAB model challenging on occasions.

According to the FBM, behaviour is composed of three different factors: core motivators, simplicity factors (often referred to as ability) and a prompt. The concept is that an individual will succeed in behaviour change if they are motivated, have the ability to perform that behaviour and receive a prompt to do so. If the three do not converge then there will be no change. If you are interested to know more, then Dr Fogg provides a 'boot camp'[10] to share how to use the model to change behaviour.

Whatever evaluation approach is adopted, the evidence will usually be gathered via a combination of sources. There will be qualitative and quantitative data, observational data and trend data, which is gathered by the implementation team itself to infer enhancements to the way in which the organisation is operating. These may be

---

7   For further information I can recommend: P.G. Schrader and K.A. Lawless, The Knowledge, Attitudes, & Behaviors Approach: How to Evaluate Performance and Learning in Complex Environments. *Performance Improvement*, September 2004.

8   B.J. Fogg, A Behavior Model for Persuasive Design. Proceedings of the 4th International Conference in Persuasive Technology. 2009. https://doi.org/10.1145/1541948.1541999.

9   Kirkpatrick Partners, www.kirkpatrickpartners.com/our-philosophy/the-kirkpatrick-model.

10 www.behaviormodel.org.

the collation of observed, qualitative and quantitative data into a view which would otherwise fail to be interpreted in a way that demonstrates behavioural progression in the organisation.

Of course, there is also the external perspective to consider in all of the evaluation too. As well as the impact within the organisation, if the action taken drives improvements to the customer experience, these too should be captured. This may result in fewer customer queries being raised with the call centre or sales agents, greater retention through providing a more efficient service or a better understanding of customer needs through analytics, and being able to plot these in a way which was either suboptimal or not achievable previously.

There are other approaches which could have been used, but do consider the evaluation methods identified above, as they have a tangible impact on the bottom line or the brand image your organisation has. Most organisations exist to provide a service or product to the customer – regardless of private or public sector, not-for-profit or global conglomerate – and so this is the manifestation of your organisation becoming a more mature, data-led organisation that will likely start to differentiate itself from its competitors, in turn sparking innovation and a dialogue which might not have been present in the organisation previously.

11.1.2 Communicating measurement

Communicating the measures to be used, gaining agreement to their adoption and the data which underpins them is the first part of the communications process. Once this has been achieved, it is essential to establish the baseline, gain acceptance that this is the starting position (you may find there are as many versions of how this has been defined in the past as there are stakeholders, which is why defining the baseline and getting approval to targets is so key) and agree a production cycle of reporting.

Typically, measurement would be expected monthly but, in reality, progress within a month might be limited, especially on some of the bigger tasks which require significant mobilisation. Therefore, you may wish to report quarterly, or to even offer a hybrid of hard measures quarterly and a narrative-based progress report on a monthly basis, in which key deliverables can be called out supported by some key measures.

There could be some important elements that could act as lead indicators regarding the health of the implementation, such as the progress of dependencies elsewhere, the risk mitigation in advance having removed some potential barriers (for example, resource constraints which were forecast to constrain the pace of the implementation may have been resolved, enabling a faster pace to be achieved than forecast) or the necessity to do certain activities being removed from the programme (which could be due to an alternative approach being identified or these having been mistakenly understood to be essential when, in fact, they are not impacting the strategy implementation). These will enable further exploration to discover whether future milestones are on track or if there is some concern about how these are shaping up. I would encourage you to consider adding these, to give a sense of predicting future performance, as it might help mobilise additional support or focused activity to assist in bringing these back on plan if that is necessary.

As the strategy implementation gathers pace and there is more evidence to present, you may be confident that moving to a monthly reporting cycle based on harder measures is feasible, and I would encourage you to do so at the earliest opportunity. The more opportunities to raise the profile of the data strategy implementation, the more support you are likely to retain for it amongst your senior stakeholders.

Your organisation may already have an expectation as to the reporting frequency for strategic programmes such as the data strategy implementation, and so you may have to fit with the wider approach. However, do bear in mind that the data strategy implementation will almost certainly get off to a relatively slow start in terms of evidence of change due to the need to focus resource and potentially technology on delivering over several months. For this reason, quick wins showing clear results and benefits realised are to be sought to keep enthusiasm amongst stakeholders positive and to demonstrate progress, even if these are possibly quite tactical in nature.

In addition, do not forget those who are delivering the implementation of the data strategy. They will likely be working on part, rather than all, of the data strategy implementation and so will not necessarily be aware of the progress in totality. It is good for motivation, cross-programme communication and collaborative problem solving to have a joined-up approach to keeping the implementation team fully engaged and informed, and it enables them to have more rounded discussions with their stakeholders across the organisation.

11.2 BENEFITS REALISATION

'It is a central tenet of the Benefits Realisation Approach that benefits come only with change and, equally, change must be sustained by benefits. People must change how they think, manage and act in order to implement the Benefits Realisation Approach.' – John Thorp and Fujitsu Consulting's Center for Strategic Leadership[11]

A key measurement to use in data strategy implementation is tracking the benefits that have been realised through the implementation. The concept of benefits realisation is not a new one, yet many organisations struggle to articulate the benefits delivered by their programmes in a structured way.

Whilst the evaluation discussed above looks at the impact of the data strategy as a whole, benefits should be tracked throughout the delivery to demonstrate the success of the implementation. This will aid communication and retain confidence with your sponsor and stakeholders alike, and can then be presented in a way which makes a compelling case as to why the continued investment in the data strategy implementation is required.

---

11 John Thorp and Fujitsu Consulting Center for Strategic Leadership, *The Information Paradox*. Whitby, Canada: McGraw-Hill Ryerson, 2003.

Benefits realisation is closely related to the evaluation process as it seeks to achieve similar aims, and so the work will overlap and can be done in parallel so there is a consistent approach adopted. The key to benefits realisation is to identify, at a more detailed level, the actual benefits that are to be measured, via clearly defined monitoring processes, to enable the programme delivery to be tracked through to its conclusion and beyond, depending on how long a tail there is to the benefits being fully realised.

It is advantageous to start the process of defining these well in advance of implementation, ideally via the waymarkers within the data strategy itself, as these should articulate some of the benefits (not necessarily all, but the most significant should be included) and how these will be identifiable once delivered.

The similarities in benefits realisation and other forms of evaluation are the principle that they seek to establish whether the programme implementation has delivered what it set out to achieve. This may seem to be a statement of the obvious, but in many organisations the focus of performance measurement is fixated on whether the programme has run to schedule, met the requirements and delivered within budget. All of these could be achieved and yet the programme fails, as none of these realise the intent of the programme, which is to deliver the outcomes as fully realised benefits. It is often one of the sources of most frustration in organisations, as programmes diverge from reality, the deliverables remain theoretical due to an inability to adopt them or a failure to communicate how to transition to them, and a programme and sponsor declare success, yet nothing has actually been achieved.

The key to benefits realisation is to identify business owners of the benefits and hold them to account in terms of actually being able to achieve what the programme set out to deliver. This detaches the responsibility for benefits from being an introspective activity for the implementation or programme team and shifts the onus onto those who will need to materialise the benefit. It therefore brings operational responsibility into play and, in terms of a data strategy implementation, is critical to ensuring that changes and enhancements are fully embedded in the organisation in day-to-day operations.

The benefits realisation process should help inform a wider evaluation of the programme, demonstrating that the key aspects of the programme as set out have been achieved and subsequently adopted into business-as-usual activity.

There are a variety of ways in which benefits realisation and performance measurement can be tracked, and I have sought to provide a number of references within the bibliography for those wishing to explore this topic further, with guidance, plans and frameworks available via a number of organisations.

11.3 PERFORMANCE FRAMEWORKS

There are two commonly used performance frameworks in use, and both have their place and can co-exist as supporting measures quite effectively.[12] In short, the key differences are displayed in Table 11.1.

Table 11.1 Comparison of KPIs and OKRs

	KPIs	OKRs
Goals	Achievable	Ambitious and aspirational
Basis	Quantitative	Qualitative
Intent	Performance tool	Motivational tool
Focus	Outputs	Growth
Indicator	Lag	Lead
Purpose	Delivering success, often in business as usual/defined activities	Innovation, improvement, challenge

I shall cover the more common version first – KPIs – and then the less commonly used objectives and key results (OKRs).

11.3.1 KPIs

The term KPI is probably used in most organisations but is not always well understood. The reason for this is that most organisations fail to distinguish between the notion of a performance indicator from one which is a key performance indicator. These may sound to be largely the same but, if used correctly, makes a significant difference to your organisation and the way in which it operates its MI approach.

A KPI is a performance measure that demonstrates how effectively an organisation is achieving its critical objectives. They are used to track performance over a period of time to ensure the organisation is heading in the desired direction, and are quantifiable to guide whether activities need to be dialled up or down, resources adjusted or management resource focused on understanding what is in play that may be holding back the organisation. In many cases, KPIs are so well established that sectors have norms in the types of KPIs used, so universal have they become, and in some cases organisations may even know where they stand according to industry benchmarks on some KPIs. The important factor to determine is what constitutes a KPI in your organisation.

---

12 For a useful overview of KPIs and OKRs, this blog provides a brief comparison: J. Wishart, OKR vs KPI: What's the Difference Between OKRs and KPIs? 2021. https://www.rhythmsystems.com/blog/okrs-vs-kpis-whats-the-difference-infographic.

I have experienced organisations producing what are defined as KPIs that run to 100 pages or more each month, and yet I am still unable to find anyone who manages at the head of an organisation who is abreast of so many KPIs.

At one of the first conferences I ever attended, nearly 30 years ago, a wise individual stated that the best way to establish organisational KPIs was to ask the chief executive (or similar post in your own organisation) what keeps them awake at night in terms of the performance of the organisation. The presenter suggested, based on many years' experience, that the response would probably be between six and ten critical things that are top of the list of concerns, and for the more information-hungry CEO possibly a dozen. Those are your KPIs, he said, and anything else is background noise as far as that CEO is concerned.

I have to say that in my discussions with CEOs, this mantra has proved to be well founded, yet organisations convince themselves of the need to produce not only KPI reports in vast numbers but – until the more recent transition to electronically presented dashboards via more sophisticated MI tools becoming commonplace – churning out almost encyclopaedias of KPIs every month.

The KPI juggernaut has been misused and abused in too many organisations to the extent it has devalued the concept of KPIs. KPIs used well – the ten things that really matter to an organisation – can, in my experience, be a real galvanising force to get focus and attention put in those areas which really can make a difference. The rest is a distraction, there through some misplaced view that more adds value when actually it detracts through losing the focus from where it needs to be.

In addition, the important element in the KPI is not as such the data itself, but the quality of the narrative to add interpretation, context and accountability to the KPI. I find the narrative is often the area which gets left to the last minute or ignored completely, when a chart without a narrative is like a road sign without the place names – it advises of something happening but leaves those reviewing it in the dark as to why this is the case or what is being done about it. The true subject matter expertise in an organisation needs to earn its value through being able to support executive leaders by making the interpretation clear and the decision to be taken directed to the point in hand.

The importance of KPIs to the data strategy implementation will be the evidence they provide of the progress being made and the key decisions to be taken. Therefore, there should be little to report via KPIs – the status of the implementation may be a simple RAG status[13] on a dial – and a narrative statement demonstrating the impact of the implementation to date in driving the change the organisation signed up to in the data strategy.

---

13 A RAG (red, amber, green) status is a way to illustrate performance or progress, typically in project management and business reporting. Green would indicate the activity is on track, amber that there are concerns that are being managed but these represent a risk, whilst red indicates a project failing and in need of intervention or escalation.

The real focus in performance reporting is where the vast majority of reporting across the organisation should be – performance indicators (PIs). These should align to the objectives of individuals and teams, unlike OKRs, and should therefore be easy to track through the activities of both the implementation team and the wider organisation where the implementation impacts.

11.3.1.1 PIs

The elevation of performance measures into an avalanche of KPIs tends to mean that the concept of PIs has been lost on many organisations. The PIs will typically fall into two camps: those which contribute to the KPI, and are therefore essential to track to consolidate into the KPI, and those which are stand-alone, not in the top ten or thereabouts of critical things to measure but need tracking for operational reasons or to support decision making at a lower level in the organisation.

PIs are as important as KPIs, as without these the foundations of measuring performance would not hold together or be understood. Simply removing one letter does not mean they lack relevance or a place in the organisation: it is important to appreciate the role they play in enabling the smooth running of the organisation by tracking performance and, unlike the KPIs, the delegation of responsibility to track activity within the organisation, which provides much-needed bandwidth for the executive tier to focus on fewer things, with more time to devote to getting the big decisions right.

The data strategy implementation, therefore, functions via a range of PIs to steer the programme lead and sponsor in the right direction to ensure the top-level reporting is coordinated and aligned with the actual state of the implementation.

PIs should have a desired target, so there is clarity on where you wish to get to in a given time frame. If the indicator does not have a target, it is simply a metric that may provide some value in reporting status but does not add the value that a PI delivers in being able to track against a known goal. As a result, a PI should have objectivity through a quantitative assessment, along with a narrative to provide context in terms of progress. That measurement, aided by the narrative, should be informative of what is required to maintain or accelerate performance.

It is important to determine the appropriate PIs for the data strategy implementation to be able to track progress towards the milestones in the implementation plan. PIs should link with the delivery through to adoption of the data strategy as business-as-usual activity in the organisation, to ensure the full end-to-end activity is tracked. The PIs should be focused on what informs effective leadership in delivering the implementation programme and so should be enabling those within the programme to make the right decisions at the right time.

PIs will be a mix of lead and lag indicators, the former being measures of performance before the business or process result starts to follow a particular pattern or trend, whilst the latter measure performance after the business or process follows a pattern or trend and is used to confirm long-term trends. This enables change over time to be assessed through both aspects of measurement.

There will also be tracking of other routine metrics, such as budgets, resources, risks, issues and dependencies in addition to the PIs specific to the implementation deliverables, which of course form part of the effective governance of the data strategy implementation.

11.3.2 OKRs

One of the most effective ways to develop a performance framework to capture benefits is using a method known as objectives and key results (OKRs).[14] This is a particularly effective approach to adopt in an Agile environment where the setting of goals needs to be closely aligned to the strategic outcomes that matter most to the organisation. The OKR methodology was developed by Andy Grove at Intel in the 1960s, so has been around for some time, but has had a new lease of life following the publication of a book called *Measure What Matters* in 2017.[15] OKRs are now in use by Google, Amazon, Uber and Airbnb, amongst many others.

The smart element that OKRs bring is the specification of a way to measure achievement – the principle of OKRs is that they must be measurable, flexible, transparent and aspirational and operate outside the usual framework of performance or pay reviews. Most organisations track OKRs quarterly, to assess progress as measured by outcomes against their strategic goals.

The premise of OKRs is to keep objectives and results simple and flexible, ensuring they align with business goals and enterprise initiatives guided by regular reviews to assess progress during the quarter. The intent is to keep OKRs clear and accountable, as well as measurable, with between three and five objectives recommended at a high level that can each be tracked by three to five key measures. They should be ambitious goals, even uncomfortable, in challenging aspirations, making them stretch targets.

OKRs are measured between 0 and 1, or as a percentage between 0 and 100. The drive is to push on, to meet the stretch target but to regard success as anywhere between 70 and 100 per cent and failure as having achieved 30 per cent or less. Divorcing the OKRs from performance reviews enables those who are targeted to achieve them more ambitiously and with less concern about the impact of failure, leading to more innovative and experimental thinking being deployed to explore ways to achieve the desired outcome.

The rationale for quarterly measurement is that these are typically strategic goals, and therefore progress is expected to take longer than a single quarter to be achieved on any of the three to five objectives set.

The reason OKRs work well in a strategic sense is the link between an aspirational goal and the clarity of measurement. They also have an assigned owner, which provides an effective link to driving strategy implementation forward in a way which recognises that the desired outcome is to realise change within the organisation. The flexibility of OKRs – you are encouraged to ratchet up the target if it emerges that it can be obtained

---

14 This article provides a useful overview and starting point for further research: S.J. White, What is OKR? A Goal-Setting Framework for Thinking Big. 2018. https://www.cio.com/article/3302036/okr-objectives-and-key-results-defined.html.

15 J. Doerr, *Measure What Matters. OKRs: The Simple Idea that Drives 10x Growth*. New York: Portfolio Penguin Random House, 2018.

with confidence, potentially by at least 30 per cent further stretch – can enable the strategy implementation to be more dynamic and push on further than planned if the opportunity arises and the conditions are right to do so.

In terms of the format of OKRs, the objectives set the target for what you wish to achieve. In a strategic sense, this is the end point of the particular objective being defined, which may be one of the elements called out in a waymarker or a key milestone on the implementation plan. There are two types of objectives in the OKR methodology.

- Committed objectives – goals an individual, team or organisation has committed to achieve, regardless of wider events, that are suitably resourced with people, money and time to make them achievable. The committed objectives will be measurable in an unambiguous way.

- Aspirational objectives – may also be referred to as 'moonshots' as they are goals an individual, team or organisation aspires to get to and are typically where the organisation is pioneering or innovating and so cannot be absolutely certain in terms of approach, or even the resources needed to achieve them. As a result, the measurement will be uncertain and the quarterly reviews will potentially need to explore the learning gained, and reassess the direction to be taken and the goal definition.

The key results are often referred to as waypoints, or steps, along the way to demonstrate the progress being made in achieving the destination – the objective. Critically, key results should always measure outcomes, not outputs, since the focus is on the end result in terms of impact. This is central to why OKRs are used successfully in a host of organisations – it is the emphasis on measuring value-based results as opposed to activity-based results that differentiates the OKR methodology. It permits a level of licence to be taken in the way in which the result – the outcome – is achieved, enabling innovation, experimentation and an agile approach to be adopted that makes OKRs an empowering way for individuals and teams to work through challenges in an unconstrained manner to achieve success. This fosters collaboration whilst ensuring alignment of effort to work towards a common goal.

The challenge with using OKRs is to focus on just three to five objectives – sounds simple enough, but so many organisations follow the 'if it moves, track it' philosophy such that they can't see the wood for the trees. These are the strategic priorities for the organisation, even if they change periodically from one quarter to another, and so making significant progress on them will be moving the organisation forward at a greater pace than would otherwise be the case.

Similarly, these are not performance measures in the traditional sense of reviewing personal achievement, hence they have to be stretching, and likely unachievable – the moonshot as a destination should set your frame of reference. In the strategy implementation, these might be those areas of improvement within the organisation that involve having to try something for the first time – AI, for example, or other forms of advanced analytics to crack a wicked problem that has been challenging the organisation for some time. Hitting 70 per cent should be regarded as success, and so this needs to be embraced as aspirational and challenging to get the most inventive thinking applied by the team to solve the objective before them. These are not simply tasks; they are transformative challenges and must be measurable as value-based results.

It is also important to recognise that OKRs are aligning your organisation, and so their application to strategy implementation is ideally suited to their use. Therefore, consider how the objective is transformational, what the wider impact is on the organisation and how the result can be measured in terms of having delivered value through its adoption by the relevant part of the organisation on an enduring basis.

I would recommend regular reviews of OKRs – weekly or at least fortnightly, in a dynamic informal manner – to ensure progress is being driven throughout the team. If there is a strong case to adjust the OKRs within the quarter, then do so; otherwise consider a rebalancing or recasting of the result as part of the quarterly review. There is little point recognising the outcome either will be reached early – this is meant to be challenging, after all – or is unrealistic: progress needs to be made, and if this is unachievable it is better to reset than knowingly fail.

In the much more structured quarterly reviews (and potentially monthly meetings, depending on how you construct these) assess the confidence scores attached to each objective and the relevant measures. Utilising a traffic-light approach – in which red symbolises off-track; yellow, a need to monitor; and green, on-track – categorises progress against each measure. This will enable the group to reflect on where pressure points lie and the need for rebalancing or recasting the measure(s), and to flex either resources or the current approach to the objective.

11.4 EARNED VALUE

Some organisations have adopted the earned value management (EVM) approach to programme delivery, and so you may find your implementation programme needing to report according to this performance methodology.

The Association for Project Management (APM) defines earned value[16] as providing information which enables effective decision making by knowing: what has been achieved of the plan; what it has cost to achieve the planned work; if the work achieved is costing more or less than was planned; if the project is ahead of or behind the planned schedule.

EVM provides a detailed analysis of programme delivery based upon four key data elements to derive the assessment, namely:

- planned value (PV) – i.e. what we are going to do, the plan: the schedule for the expenditure of budgeted resources as necessary to meet project scope and schedule objectives;
- actual cost (AC) – i.e. what the work achieved actually cost;

---

16 Association for Project Management Special Interest Group, *Earned Value Management: APM Guidelines*. Princes Risborough: APM, 2014. https://www.apm.org.uk/media/31993/evmguide-no-print.pdf.

- earned value (EV) – i.e. what the amount of work achieved should have cost, according to the planned budget: the *earned value* for the work actually achieved;
- the estimate at completion of the project. This is the ACWP [actual cost of work performed] to date, plus the most knowledgeable estimate of remaining requirements, scope, schedule and cost.

Utilising the EVM methodology, it is easy to identify the progress of the programme in terms of the value delivered for the cost incurred and time spent. Therefore, it provides a focus on the value-add of the programme rather than the use of resources being as scheduled, for the value delivered is the true measure of effectiveness of a programme.

The EVM approach is highly effective but needs a significant amount of data and a highly structured approach to programme implementation through to delivery to be in place at all times to ensure the integrity of the data. It is therefore essential to undertake significant planning and effort to get EVM right, as trying to apply it retrospectively whilst a programme is in-flight is extremely challenging, as I know only too well – inevitably, data will not be constructed in a way to support EVM or is of poor quality or missing, undermining any effort to construct a historic view of EVM to build upon.

11.5 MATURITY ASSESSMENTS

The use of maturity assessments has been covered extensively elsewhere in this book. The point to be made here is that these are critical to the baselining efforts undertaken to support measurement and are high profile in their commissioning and delivery, which helps in providing a recognised input to the process of measuring data strategy implementation.

The assessments used are not a factor for consideration here; however, the importance of capturing the baseline and establishing a review process is clearly one that needs to be built into the measurement process.

There are various ways in which this can be undertaken, and there are benefits with each option to be considered, so it is entirely up to you, and the importance placed on independence of measurement by the organisation, how you proceed.

You may have undertaken the initial baselining of maturity internally, using the skills and knowledge within the organisation to deliver this. If so, you may be less concerned about maintaining the integrity of the process in reviewing progress – there is little to be gained by grade inflation, raising the scores on flimsy evidence to be able to claim progress if this has not actually been achieved. I would go so far as to suggest this is a waste of resources across the entire organisation, as it does not deliver improvement but takes up considerable time and effort for something which is clearly flawed. It is therefore important to be able to demonstrate that the process has been conducted with absolute rigour, even to the point of being a harsh judge on the evidence gathered and progress made, to satisfy all that any improvement in the score achieved in the maturity assessment process is demonstrable.

Of course, the alternative is to hire an external resource to deliver the maturity assessment and/or conduct the reviews using external help. If you do not have the capabilities in-house this might be the only option available to you, though I would strongly recommend upskilling the in-house team as soon as possible, so there is resource available within the implementation team who can direct and interpret what is needed in order to demonstrate progress in between assessments. The benefit of taking this approach is an element of objectivity, assuming the external assistance is not swayed by senior stakeholders to be lenient in their scoring. In such a case, I would question the integrity of the external support and challenge whether that individual or team is fit to conduct the assessment.

A further benefit of using external assistance is the wider perspective of other organisations undertaking the same maturity assessment approach to drive their own data strategy. This enables an element of benchmarking – depending on how willing other clients are to share experiences – and learning from what other organisations have done to drive improvements across their organisations. This can take some of the variability out of the process, utilising the experience of others to potentially fast-track improvements in your own organisation.

In some organisations, the maturity assessment is a key element of senior stakeholders' annual objectives, and hence the importance of having the integrity behind the review and scoring is increased due to there being a financial implication. Whilst this can be an effective means to drive attention, it may not drive the right behaviour, as it could lead to a focus on what drives the scoring, rather than what is the right thing for the organisation to achieve at that point in time. For instance, there could be a key infrastructural or behavioural activity needed to subsequently release value and as a result improve the scoring, but the score will not shift by placing the focus on the key enabler, despite this leading to progress later. Therefore some sort of governance around the prioritisation in such cases is needed to drive the appropriate corporate behaviours amongst stakeholders to focus on what is right for the organisation to enable it to make progress.

A key part of the assessment process is the debrief following the assessment. You should be made aware of the gaps that make each of the criteria fall short of the next level, enabling you to construct a programme within the implementation to remediate or address those gaps according to the prioritisation assigned to each of the criteria in terms of importance to the organisation. The benefit of the maturity assessment approach is the standardised methodology that makes it easier to construct a plan to work with it in readiness for the next scheduled assessment – I would recommend an annual assessment as part of the data strategy implementation.

11.6 DATA AS AN ASSET – REALISING VALUE

The business world is gradually waking up to the realisation that data is an asset, even if it is not recognised financially as one to stick on the asset register as an asset with a value. After all, most organisations operate through the medium of data exchange, trading information in the form of contracts, specifications and transactions, as well as holding internal data such as registers of employees, customers and suppliers. All of these are valuable to an organisation, and are fundamental to the ability to operate. Without a grip on your data, you are losing value every minute of every business day.

There is a view that data is the new oil, a phrase coined by Clive Humby back in 2006 which seems to have had a new lease of life in more recent years.[17] Whilst I understand the sentiment behind the quote, I tend to disagree, as data does not need to be captured in the same complex way as oil, which requires deep drilling to excavate it, often in hostile environments, but is made available much more readily for use to get the organisation operational.

I believe data is like water, essential to the running of any organisation, and without it there would be no organisation to speak of. It is renewable and simple in structure, yet easily degraded and diminished in value through a lack of cleanliness, and, if not managed carefully, can be destructive – just like flooding or a major leak can wreak havoc on a property, so can data if it is not managed compliantly or there is a breach. Like water, which is used extensively (for example, from manufacturing to our leisure and overall wellbeing), data is a truly versatile asset. We can use its immense flexibility to drive decisions and support risk assessments and meaningful engagement in the right way at the right time with our customers or key stakeholders. Therefore, data is the new water for me.

The lack of data being recognised as a key asset with a value has not deterred organisations being sold for premiums that belie the asset book value. This is particularly the case for those organisations that operate in a tech world in which knowledge of the customer and being able to manage a one-to-one relationship remotely and build customer loyalty is worth much more than the stock of the organisation.

Doug Laney has written a highly recommended book, *Infonomics*, focused specifically on how to monetise, manage and measure information as an asset and I recommend exploring this further if this topic is of interest to you.[18] The book is rich in information on 'how to monetise, manage and measure information', but there are some specific points I want to highlight here for you to consider in developing your data strategy and framing the execution of it in the right way to open the eyes of key stakeholders who may control or influence the decision as to whether to invest in a data strategy.

Laney notes how James Tobin, an American economist and Nobel laureate, developed a simple ratio known as 'Tobin's q' to understand the relationship between a company's market value and the replacement value of its tangible assets. Since reaching 0.4 in 1945, the ratio has more than doubled to be regularly above 1.0 in any given year. For those who have invested in what Gartner recognises as 'info-savvy' behaviour,[19] the ratio is nearly twice as much as the market average.

17 Michael Palmer, Data is the New Oil. https://ana.blogs.com/maestros/2006/11/data_is_the_new.html.

18 D.B. Laney, *Infonomics: How to Monetize, Manage, and Measure Information as an Asset for Competitive Advantage*. New York: Bibliomotion Inc, 2017.

19 Microsoft Links Into a Treasure Trove of Information. https://blogs.gartner.com/merv-adrian/2016/06/14/microsoft-links-into-a-treasure-trove-of-information/.

Further, the information-based organisations out there have a q value three times greater than the market average as they operate with fewer tangible assets and more focus on the customer.

A practical example of this is the initial public offering of Facebook, in 2012. With reportable assets of $6.6 billion and a predicted conservative post-IPO market capitalisation of $75 billion, the non-reportable assets were predominantly information assets. This translated to $81 per user account, and now exceeds $200 today.

Data has a value, without which an organisation is largely a shell, worthless and of limited appeal other than as a means of sweeping up fixed assets at a knock-down price. It is the lifeblood of an organisation, so whether you regard it as the water that is essential to life or the blood circulating around the body, without it our organisations are not functional.

It is well worth considering, as the data strategy is drafted, building in a perspective of monetising, managing and measuring data. You are seeking an investment in the core asset that enables your organisation to operate. It is more resilient than the people, processes or technology of your organisation, albeit it needs these three to breathe life into its value. If you consider the discussions that almost certainly take place within your organisation, particularly those which are asset-rich organisations, in terms of investment decisions, surely data warrants at least an equal footing in terms of asset management and investment. Without reflecting on an investment strategy, you are almost certainly diminishing the value of your biggest asset without even recognising it exists.

Many organisations have started out on the path to assign a value to data and to seek to manage the value in much the same way other assets have a level of control over managing their value. This is not an easy undertaking, and needs significant commitment from within your organisation. However, would it not be useful to appreciate how critical data is to your organisation, and to be able to wrap controls around it to ensure it has the investment needed to retain, or grow, its value?

I have often found myself debating the concept of allocating funding to data quality as less of an expense, more of an investment. As with any asset, the longer it is lacking investment, the more it will degrade and, depending on the volatility of the type of data, it may become worthless or even have negative value if inaccurate (for instance, failing compliance rules as well as preventing effective contact with your customer). Without being able to articulate value, the case for investment becomes subjective and easy to deflect, even if the implications are only at least partially understood.

For this reason, data quality programmes are often commenced as a reactionary plan to deal with non-compliance or to address an immediate issue (for example, the failure to integrate data into a new system because of inconsistencies in format or dates). This is to fundamentally misunderstand the importance of data, and to fail to recognise it as an asset – some even look at the cost of data quality as if it is money which will never be recouped, which is very short-sighted indeed. As with any asset, routine maintenance is required to keep it in good condition for its continued use, and investment in the quality of data will be repaid many times over.

As you progress through the data strategy definition, making the case to senior stakeholders and seeking to find a willing, committed sponsor, remember the importance of data as an asset in pitches to those who have the decision as to whether to invest or not. Consider the opportunity to move to a way of recognising the inherent value that your data brings to your organisation, seek to redefine the agenda in the way data is considered in your organisation, and identify ways in which you could begin to make data a recognised asset and managed as such alongside those other key assets the organisation recognises. If you can succeed, it will make your case not only stronger, but more enduring, changing the philosophy of your organisation to one potentially starting out on the journey to becoming a multiplier on Tobin's q ratio compared to its rivals.

It is also essential to keep a focus on data as an asset throughout the data strategy implementation. The potential to realise value through the delivery of key milestones is a powerful way in which to demonstrate the overall success of the data strategy implementation itself, and to bank those gains as you go. Recognising where data value can be realised may well determine some of the prioritisation calls you make as you set out the course of the implementation plan, and remember to build in the means to measure these gains and continue to track beyond the data strategy implementation.

If you find that the data strategy implementation does not realise the benefits you had expected, and as a consequence the measures are lower, explore why. It may be that there are changes required to the way in which data is exploited – in my experience, data is rarely allowed to take the straightest line to a decision; there are many hands that get in the way which leads to the data either being distorted or which results in delays, causing the data to be less effective at the time it is used (one of my favourite quotes is 'making the right decision at the wrong time', which reflects the impact of delaying a decision beyond what the data has the elasticity to cover, such that the data needs to be refreshed to be reliable for the intended decision to be made).

It is almost certainly the case that the data is only as good as the understanding that those looking to exploit it have in terms of its metadata – the information that describes it and clarifies its provenance. Of course, data is often dependent for quality on its capture, and the individual recording it in the first place, but this is another issue entirely. It is not uncommon to see the wrong data on which to base a decision used, and to create variations in the data through reworking the data into what an individual believes it should be, rather than trusting the data to be correct to begin with. The irony, of course, in this action is that the subjectivity of what the data should be fails to recognise the dynamic nature of data and the lack of repeatability in changing the data.

In one organisation, I recall the number of employees being changed several times over as the data was amalgamated and 'refined' by those who handled it prior to presentation to the executive. Unsurprisingly, queries about the data could never be acted upon because of the way in which it was manipulated through the process, yet this had been the case for several years, with no one seeming able or willing to grasp the fundamental data problem.

If you have the opportunity, look for ways to introduce the concept of data as an asset and assigning a value to it through the data strategy and its implementation. I am certain that this will be one of the biggest and most significant changes you can introduce into your organisation and, in many ways, can be done in a relatively low key way and yet deliver a very significant impact.

11.7 TEN TO TAKE AWAY

To summarise, here are ten things to take away from this chapter:

1. Avoid embarking on a data strategy solely for compliance reasons. This misses the importance of value and the asset that is inherent in data, which you need the organisation to focus on.

2. Be clear on the baseline at the start of the implementation phase and its calculation, as this needs to be followed through to demonstrate progress.

3. Establish key evaluation criteria to measure success of the implementation programme. An effective approach to consider is the Magenta Book produced by the UK government.

4. Identify benefits and track these throughout the implementation programme. These should be captured as part of the requirements process.

5. Implement a performance management approach to track programme delivery against a number of measures, consolidating these to support KPIs which will be of keen interest to your sponsor and executive stakeholders.

6. Consider use of OKRs as a way of making the performance measurement, due to its focus on results and therefore an effective way to establish credibility of the data strategy and its implementation.

7. Apply maturity assessments throughout the implementation as a means to track progress versus the baseline (assuming the maturity assessments were conducted prior to the implementation commencing).

8. Consider the governance and controls you might deploy to utilise maturity assessments (and other performance measures) to maximum effect.

9. Data is an asset, it is the new water – renewable, flexible, a key ingredient to so much of what we do.

10. Explore assigning value to data, it helps focus minds on the potential and importance to support the 'data as an asset' principle.

12 DATA STRATEGY: COMPLETING THE JOURNEY FROM DEFINITION TO EXECUTION

'The biggest challenge of making the evolution from a knowing culture to a learning culture ... is really not the cost. Initially, it largely ends up being imagination and inertia'.

Murli Buluswar[1]

This final chapter contains some key observations and insights that I wanted to share to conclude my thoughts on the wider responsibility you are undertaking in developing a data strategy and then executing it in your organisation, and some summary points that are here as reminders of some of the key points in earlier chapters.

12.1 CULTURE – IS YOUR STRATEGY HEADING FOR THE BREAKFAST PLATE?

I referred to culture at some length in Chapter 7. This is one of the most important factors to be aware of when embarking on any strategy effort, as it is probably the biggest challenge you will face and the hardest to articulate or embrace.

With the quote at the start of this chapter in mind, every organisation, in my experience, will have evolved a culture at its core that may not align with the corporate perspective of what the culture is thought to be. There may also be an external layer for wider consumption, particularly if there is an effective marketing operation that is building a brand and establishing what the brand stands for with its customers. Yet, this is different from an organisation's culture, which pervades every part of the organisation and has taken time to evolve and determine the type of belief system which exists.

Culture is not something that can be read in a corporate document (though many organisations will claim to have values, beliefs and other concepts that articulate the culture as the corporate centre wants it to be seen). It is intangible and can be challenging to comprehend to those on the outside looking in. Much of it is unspoken, a series of behavioural norms which are engrained in the fabric of the organisation and drive attitudes of employees to one another, management, change programmes and any external (to the group, as well as the organisation) effort to drive change that may be resisted simply because it 'isn't the way we do things around here'.

Efforts have been made to characterise culture, with varying degrees of success. Charles Handy identified four principal types of culture,[2] based on power, role, task and person, but these are categories in their own right. They are a route into understanding culture, rather than snugly fitting descriptors. Johnson, Whittington and Scholes[3] proposed a

---

1   M. Buluswar, How Companies Are Using Big Data and Analytics. 2016. https://www.mckinsey.com/business-functions/mckinsey-analytics/our-insights/how-companies-are-using-big-data-and-analytics.

2   Charles Handy, *Gods of Management: The Changing Work of Organisations*. London: Souvenir Press Ltd, 1978.

3   G. Johnson, R. Whittington and K Scholes, *Fundamentals of Strategy*. Hemel Hempstead: Pearson Education, 2012.

cultural web consisting of six interrelated elements in the work environment that feature in the organisational culture: stories; rituals and routines; symbols; organisational structure; control systems; and power structures. Together, they form the cultural paradigm and enable an assessment to be undertaken as to the existing culture in an organisation versus the one you would want to enable strategic goals to be achieved.

It is one thing to be able to assess culture – and even then this is subjective, based on trying to articulate and quantify the intangible – but quite another to change it. This requires the commitment of all parties to be willing to change, adopt different norms and become an organisation with a different belief set, and different values and behaviours. Many change programmes claim to have changed culture but are superficial, failing to supplant what was there before, and simply putting an additional veneer of corporate standards on top of it such that it drives the existing culture to be even more subversive. Do not be surprised to discover in some more traditional, long-standing organisations that some aspects of the culture date back to decisions taken 20 or more years ago, long before many of the existing workforce were there, based upon some form of perceived grievance that eroded trust and has been overlaid with a large dose of cynicism.

I would also add that any hint that you are seeking to change the culture will be unlikely to be well received. People like to have certainty, predictability and assurance, and if the culture is not to their liking, they will either leave or keep their head down to avoid rocking the boat. Of course, there are exceptions, particularly where strong characters can resist the pressures, challenges and tension that being at odds with other leaders brings, and they are comfortable being part of a small minority of like-minded individuals within the organisation.

Therefore, whilst there may be some who are willing to get behind your data strategy and see it through, many more will be in the shadows, either passively supportive or negative but not declaring themselves either way, to see how it copes with the onslaught of butting up against the culture. Inevitably a number will be vocal, critical, ready to explain why it will never work or that the change is not needed, or indeed the change is already under way so best to leave things alone (of course, there probably isn't any tangible change; it may simply be said to drive you away). This is why picking the right sponsor, getting the appropriate level of 'local' buy-in, and developing a resilient and well-informed team around you is so essential.

Returning to the opening quote, those who say that there is no reason to change do so as part of the knowing culture, certain that the decisions they made are the best available and resisting anyone from outside their team telling them otherwise. The transition from knowing to learning requires a level of humility to accept being told there is a better way; moreover, professional pride, concern at being undermined and potentially surplus to requirements, and reluctance to be seen to back something new which could easily fail are all reasons why the default can so often be resistance.

Yet learning in different environments is something which we have made a fundamental part of our own development. From being a small child, through school and the transition to the workplace, we are constantly learning, absorbing as much as we can, developing our own individual culture of norms, beliefs, values and expectations shaped by those around us. The transition to the workplace is a novel experience for many, working in an environment totally alien to us where we learn our craft and take on many of the cues from those we work with closest and the leadership we experience.

All of these things define us, our vision of the future, aspirations, interests, even our trust settings to know what to expect from colleagues, managers and those corporate messages that resonate. For most of us who make decisions, from the immediate transactional to the career-orientated strategic, it is a case of weighing up what we feel is right at the time and trusting instinct – supported by largely what we choose to hear from those we trust around us – to make a decision. Yet, as Buluswar states, we are seeking to unshackle the conscious choice (some might go so far as to say expectation) from knowing to continuous learning, to open up the mind to evidence which states there is a better option out there, regardless of what your intuition built over many years through countless experiences and numerous discussions with trusted others has instilled in your mind as the right course of action.

Many years ago, as marketing analytics gathered momentum and customer relationship management systems were gaining ground, I led a team which not only analysed its own customers in terms of profitability, loyalty and longer-term potential, but mapped this on to those customers of competitor organisations through using data from third-party providers. This led to some interesting insight as to which of these 'prospects' were the most appealing by overlaying them on our own customer base to reflect a prioritised list of who we might wish to target. Through this, we were able to develop a target list of those we wished to specifically focus our acquisition effort on and which of the prospects we didn't want to acquire at all.

The challenge with this was not the data, nor the capacity – we had also recently run an optimisation model to determine where, geographically, there was spare capacity to be able to acquire business without diminishing service levels – but the willingness of the sales teams to embrace an analytics-driven approach to customer acquisition. How could a central team who had never operated in a sales environment possibly know better than those who were sales professionals in a locality?

To prove the case, we were able to run two trials. One was based on providing a sample to sales teams in certain geographic areas that they committed to use alongside traditional techniques, whilst the other replaced the local sales list completely with the centrally provided list. Both were given a period of four to six weeks to determine the outcomes, from which a validation exercise would determine if it could be rolled out further.

Inside the four-week period, both reached the same conclusion. The central lists were seen to be gold dust, feeding prime targets to the sales teams and identifying prospects which, in many cases, were not necessarily under consideration locally. Not only that, but with a compelling message to drive switching (and the benefit of such a structured proactive approach being entirely novel at that time), appointments were on a multiplier of three to five times what would normally arise from localised activity, with conversions almost as effective.

> Within three months, the acquisition drive had to take a pause, as the sales teams had such a backlog of opportunities to close out that they could not set appointments soon enough to keep them engaged. So, the lesson of the exercise was to build trust, develop the confidence of those who thought they were being undermined by a group of outsiders and to let them learn by doing – the truly agile and collaborative approach to changing part of the culture in action – to overcome the initial inertia. The sales teams went from knowing to learning by doing, being engaged and part of the solution. Everybody gained in a way which retained control for all parties in the process, engendering trust.

The final point to make is that inertia in the face of change is often through a lack of understanding, which triggers a defensive response that materialises as resistance. Often, change can be uncomfortable, at least initially, due to changing practices or ways of approaching things, and the immediate impact may be more work, or things taking longer than was previously the case. All of these things build resistance. It needs the context – why make the change and what improves as a consequence – to give meaning to something that all can rally around. You need to be able to communicate this for the data strategy, providing context to win people over to achieve a common goal.

12.2 ARE YOU REALLY READY TO SAIL?

The quote at the start of this chapter highlights what, for many of you, will be the biggest challenge of all as you embark on defining and executing a data strategy in your organisation. I have navigated you through the challenges you will face, and aimed to prepare you for the breadth of experiences you will encounter as you plot a course and then set sail for the oceans with the crew on board the yacht. As with any analogy, it has limitations, but let me stick with the sailing theme a little longer.

Invariably, you would set sail with an end in mind, a distant port, perhaps, or a series of stopping-off points you are planning to make and have defined clearly in your mind. In preparation, you would plan a route, estimate time and make provisions accordingly, whilst recognising a need for contingency due to unforeseen things along the way and a need to be dynamic at all times. The data strategy is based on the conditions you observe, a distant goal to be achieved which aligns to the corporate strategy, and a series of waymarkers you have identified to get you there. You need a team around you to help define a data strategy with the quality of inputs from diverse parts of the organisation, as you do a crew with specific skillsets to ensure the yacht is shipshape and ready for the voyage, and an executive-level sponsor to help guide you, who in a major yachting race may well be the owner.

However, with the best planning in the world, once you set sail you are at the mercy of the weather, the yacht itself and the crew, not to mention the support staff on dry land who need to be in place to support as and when called upon. Your data strategy will follow similar vagaries in execution, being buffeted by the prevailing winds of other demands upon the organisation which could throw you off course or damage the sail itself. It will be exposed to scrutiny and challenge, in the same way the sun tests your crew, and it will face rough and choppy seas in deep water, which will prevail over your implementation at times where you find the organisation less than supportive in endorsing or enabling your programme to succeed.

Finally, the crew itself will show signs of weakness at times when under pressure, and at other times perform beyond your wildest expectations. Your implementation team will be no different, and you should prepare for emotional rollercoasters as these arise and anticipate that, at any time, a key person in your team could leave at short notice.

The reason I draw these parallels is that embarking on strategy definition and execution is one of the most uncertain things, in terms of an end-to-end activity, that you might ever embark upon. The window is long, much like a round-the-world yacht race, and the risks are great of failing to succeed.

I highlight this not to deter you from putting yourself into this position, but to ensure you are fully aware of the scale of the task you are undertaking. It is not for perfectionists, as you will have to make sacrifices along the way, face hard decisions regularly, feel isolated periodically and be operating in an environment in which the end product – the successes arising from the data strategy implementation – will be delivered by others. It is not for those who want to use this as a fast-track to bigger things; once you set sail you don't get to finish till the race is over, unless you walk away or are replaced in the role.

So why on earth would anyone put themselves into this position? Personally, I find the challenge of turning an organisation that has not really 'got' data fully into one which has data first and foremost in its thinking one of the most appealing and challenging things anyone with a data and/or analytics skillset could be charged with doing.

Consider those organisations that haven't 'got' it yet – to stick with the shipping theme – akin to the big cargo ships plying their trade around the world, stuck on a course from which they rarely deviate. It may surprise you that around 100 large ships are lost in an average year.[4] The giants can find themselves in a position unable to deal with challenging circumstances, failing to look ahead or use evidence available to them in a strategic sense; they can often be sunk, despite being established operators in their markets. Take Blockbuster, Polaroid, Pan Am, General Motors and Kodak, for example, all synonymous with being market leaders at a point in time that found themselves focused on the wrong things and overtaken by those more alert to the shifting market and customer expectations.

Being at the helm of the ship that is ready for the weather conditions ahead, able to resource and commit to whatever comes its way to make it through to the end goal: that is your opportunity, steering a course which will shape the future of the organisation.

Can you be the opportunist in the market, stealing a march on much larger, more established players as Netflix did, having been rebuffed by Blockbuster when it offered itself for sale just a decade before Blockbuster's collapse? Can you be the strategic leader who enables the organisation to reinvent itself and thus keep relevant, as IBM

---

4   J. Lang, How Many Ships Disappear Each Year? 2014. http://actuarialeye.com/2014/03/30/how-many-ships-disappear-each-year/.

has done through a huge acquisition strategy to shift its focus just at a time when it was ailing and at risk of corporate failure? Are you able to make your business one which continuously evolves through innovation, and not only keeps pace with the changing market but is able to influence it, such as Apple, spotting the business opportunities and designing products which reinvent the standard customers expect?

The one thing these organisations had in common was a forward outlook to where the market and customer demand was heading, focusing on where the organisation needed to be rather than resting on its laurels and unable to respond dynamically enough when the weather changed and agility was needed. That is not to say that these organisations did so without taking risks, and there are plenty of organisations that have either a great idea but an inability to execute it or simply the right idea at the wrong time. Having evidence – data – to hand is essential to being one of these organisations. Without it you are gambling on gut feel (though there is an informative book on the laws of chance I can recommend if you so desire[5]), with a likelihood that luck will run out at some point. Even the largest organisations can fail if you do not listen, learn and act upon what the data is telling you today, leading you towards tomorrow and predicting for the months ahead.

12.3 REVOLUTION VERSUS EVOLUTION – THE IMPLEMENTATION CHALLENGE

The nature of the change that the data strategy is to drive will be determined by the appetite and commitment of the organisation to change. It will also be shaped by the maturity of the organisation, with the maturity assessment process having identified and demonstrated where the gaps lie, and the resolve of the organisation to set its own pace and objectives to be achieved by the time of the next assessment.

There are two distinct approaches to strategy implementation which have fundamentally different ways of being managed – revolution versus evolution. I do not mean these terms in the sense of ripping everything apart versus retaining the status quo, more in reflection of the pace of implementation and therefore its approach.

The revolutionary approach is based on making the data strategy implementation the top priority of the organisation, and putting resource and commitment behind it to drive change at a faster pace than would otherwise be the case. It is an approach which seeks to get to the end result in as short a time as feasible, whilst also recognising it has to pull the strings of other related activities for it to be successful.

By contrast, the evolutionary approach is at a slower pace, with the data strategy implementation being one of a number of programmes within the organisation or having to be delivered at a pace which is less disruptive to the business-as-usual activities. The implementation will therefore take longer, be managed in conjunction with other programmes and activities, and need to track dependencies, risks and issues as it goes and be cognisant that there may be other priority calls from time to time that could

---

5   Robert Matthews, *Chancing It*. London: Profile Books, 2017.

cause delay. By contrast, it does enable those involved with the implementation to learn and contribute more effectively over time, developing the skills needed to ensure the results of the data strategy implementation are likely to endure.

There is a lot to be said for evolution in most cases, simply because it recognises that the data strategy in itself is not likely to be at the very top of the agenda for most organisations, even if it is recognised that it is important, and therefore the pace of change will need to grow over time but start off with a less ambitious cadence to it.

If there is an opportunity to embark on a more revolutionary approach, it will demand more resource, commitment and focus by some magnitude, but will, in the long run, almost certainly consume far less resource and investment. Working around the organisation, its priorities, potentially a shifting focus over time and other communications that may actually hinder progress (for instance, expediency may necessitate making a problem worse in the short term, or at least halt progress, and so actively setting a direction later for it to be upturned will be harder) will absorb a lot more energy, resource and hence investment, and take far longer to achieve.

The revolutionary approach could be a step change in pace. For instance, the UK government announced in 2021 its intention to kick-start a data revolution across the UK via the National Data Strategy. It is seeking to accelerate current activity through training 500 analysts in data and data science across the public sector by the end of 2021, hiring a CDO to have a cross-government remit to transform the use of data and drive efficiencies and improvements in public services, introducing primary legislation to boost smart data initiatives and a £2.6 million project to overcome barriers to data sharing and boost innovation in detecting data harm.

This is not to indicate that one approach is right: it is simply highlighting that the reality is most organisations are committed to evolution but at heart want progress to be more akin to revolution, which makes the task of implementation that much harder to achieve. It necessitates strong leadership in the implementation phase, keeping focus where it matters and ensuring those parts of the implementation programme which need to be maintained are not sacrificed to other priorities if at all possible.

The challenges of revolution and evolution are quite different, and so your task as the implementation lead will need to reflect the nature of the situation you are working to in the way you construct the programme and the tone of leadership you bring. It will also determine the approach you adopt in constructing your team, as an evolutionary approach involves working with and around other in-flight programmes and business-as-usual activities, whereas the revolutionary model is more driven and targeted, and hence has a greater focus on programme discipline to make other activities fit the programme.

If you have the opportunity to determine which approach to adopt – possibly a more likely scenario the smaller the organisation and the greater control you have over the implementation – then it would be wise to consider the benefits and potential pitfalls of each approach and assess which might be right for you. I have provided below a little more context on the scenarios in which revolution may be a more likely direction and the case for the evolutionary approach. Don't forget, whichever you choose, the importance of retaining alignment to the corporate strategy.

12.3.1 The case for revolution

There are situations in which a revolutionary approach to the data strategy and its implementation will be the right one to adopt. Whilst either approach can work, the revolutionary approach really comes into its own in the following situations.

- **Data-centric environments**, where a lot of the activity is constructed around data and so there is a greater awareness of, and integration with, the ways of working within the organisation – such cases will gain more value from a more decisive and direct approach to change in this space, and there is likely to be a greater level of commitment to cooperating with the changes needed to enhance current operations. These types of organisation will typically operate in an online or at least web-enabled model where the challenges with data and its utilisation are at the forefront of driving improvements. The impact is therefore more readily visible, which in turn will lead to a greater expectation arising from the data strategy implementation.

- **Acquisitions** – often the acquisition of one organisation by another will have a significant dependency on systems and data integration. Any delay in addressing these just continues to carry inefficiencies, resulting in a higher cost base and eradicating value through management time devoted to reconciling two organisations trying to operate as one. The process of identifying the work required to make systems and data align would typically start before the acquisition is completed; hence the data strategy will almost certainly need redrafting at pace to enable the implementation to adapt seamlessly to the strategic priority of handling the acquisition. This can also be an opportunity to accelerate existing plans or goals in the data strategy within the acquiring organisation, as it may unlock a lot of value to move on this more swiftly, applying such plans or goals to both organisations rather than just one.

- **Pace needed to address a compliance crisis** – the situation discussed in the opening chapters, in which compliance has highlighted gaps in data being controlled and managed in a satisfactory way and needs an urgent response, is a good example of an opportunity to adopt a more revolutionary approach to address more than simply the compliance issue. I have known organisations make a case to invest to be several steps ahead in the regulatory space to ensure that the resolution presented demonstrates more than a 'just enough' response to a compliance issue. This presents the opportunity to adopt a more revolutionary approach to the data strategy implementation, with the teeth of compliance as a helpful means of enforcement if needed.

- **Organisation in distress** – the worst situation, in some respects, in which to manage anything strategic. However, even if it requires a tactically focused approach to keep an organisation afloat, the opportunity to get traction and pace into an implementation is clear in an operationally challenging situation. Of course, the benefits of a revolutionary approach need to deliver in the short term, but the focus such a situation brings helps to prioritise effort and remove blockers very effectively.

- **Small organisations with a big appetite** – often, the pace can be driven harder in a smaller organisation which has fewer lines of decision making and can therefore see the merit of investing to progress as swiftly as possible. The more the data strategy implementation is linked to customer outcomes and/or financial returns, the greater the likelihood of success. In such an environment, there is likely to be a drive to 'get on with it', and whilst that brings its own challenges it can be rewarding and refreshing to have that backing.

12.3.2 The evolutionary approach

The evolutionary approach is typical of most data strategy implementations. This is just as acceptable a way of proceeding with the data strategy implementation, as it can be executed alongside other changes which are managed through a dependency on other activity, thus reducing the scale of the programme to be managed directly by the implementation team.

The evolutionary approach also gives greater flexibility to the programme, enabling it to work around those areas which are not ready or need further investigation, as well as providing more scope to test and learn through the implementation.

On the other hand, the challenge of the evolutionary approach is that there is more effort to coordinate activity. Dependencies will need to be managed across activities and there may be shifts in priorities or rates of progress elsewhere that may delay the pace of the data strategy implementation programme. The evolutionary approach will also have a lot of moving parts to consider, and this in turn presents a significant communications effort to keep these aligned and the messages consistent. In delivering through an evolutionary approach, it is critical to keep a clear focus on the direction you are heading by remaining aligned with the implementation plan, which is key to mitigate any risk of tangents or other diversions.

Of course, the evolutionary approach should become easier, if it is implemented well. The understanding of the organisation can grow and embrace what is required, the impact of change is visible as you go and the plan can flex to recognise pressures on resource to deliver the right result for the organisation. Indeed, if the evolutionary approach is successful, you may even find that it builds momentum to increase the pace, such that it begins to look more revolutionary in its pace and impact.

It is important to adopt a test and learn philosophy through the evolutionary approach, being able to conduct assessments and reviews within the implementation programme of what has worked well, what has been learnt and how to feed this in to the planning for what comes next. This is another benefit of the evolutionary approach, as it builds confidence in both stakeholders and programme team members, demonstrating that each activity is conducted in a way that learnt from the last and showing an appreciation for the feedback provided by those involved.

12.4 THE TRICKY TRIUMVIRATE – PRIORITISATION, DEPENDENCIES AND CAPABILITIES

Three aspects of the data strategy implementation will be ever-present in the way you manage the programme – prioritisation, dependencies and capabilities. Whilst these are not entirely in your control in the delivery of the implementation programme, they are a high priority for you to manage closely as they will all play a part in how successful your implementation will be.

In addition, there is an interplay between them. Depending on the priorities, it will focus which dependencies are a priority to track closely, and the capabilities you need to deliver the priorities. Should the dependencies slip, or capabilities be unavailable, a reprioritisation of the deliverables might be needed to accommodate what can be achieved as opposed to what it is desirable to deliver. The sponsor will also play a key role, as any shift from the priorities will need to be communicated so that there is a discussion as to whether this can be avoided. This could be through putting further focus on the availability of the critical capabilities (in other words, can these be released to your programme to make it achievable?), or the area responsible for the dependency being instructed to complete in the original timescales.

12.4.1 Prioritisation

In Chapter 9, the importance of prioritisation was discussed and highlighted as an inevitable challenge for anyone embarking on a data strategy programme, regardless of whether in the definition or implementation stage. This is clearly something which needs to be planned in to the approach you will take, as you do not want to be caught on the back foot, finding resources stretched or pulled in different directions, or blockers halting your progress with no alternative in mind. You need a clear understanding as to what constitutes your priorities within the implementation phase in particular, otherwise any traction gained can be just as easily lost.

The prioritisation may need to be fluid – as discussed previously, the organisation does not stand still, nor does it usually flex to suit your programme – so there will be a need to reprioritise and reassess the benefits to be accrued as these may change, depending on the circumstances driving the change. At the very least, changes to the running order or delays in implementation may affect the impact and/or the benefits to be realised and undermine the expected value to be delivered from the data strategy (unlikely if your prioritisation has been done effectively and it is not an unforeseen opportunity).

The key to prioritisation is balancing the focus on what I have termed here 'the tricky triumvirate'– dependencies and capabilities alongside prioritisation – due to the relationship of these factors with one another. For instance, you may need to delay due to the shift in availability of skilled resources that are scarce within the organisation, which, whilst a blow to the programme in the short term, is worth the wait as progressing without those resources involved would be suboptimal and lack credibility within the organisation. A change in a related programme that is due to release benefits for your own programme (for instance, a new system implementation, which you are dependent on to realise your master data management approach, may be delayed, leading to that part of the data strategy implementation work having to be mothballed or postponed) could realign your plan, shift deliverables and lead to releasing resources at one point but needing them back at another, which was not part of the original agreement with a particular part of your organisation.

More fundamentally, if the corporate strategy shifts, then you need to assess whether the data strategy needs to shift with it. This is a balance: there is clearly alignment between the two, but the importance of a change in corporate direction (maybe an unexpected opportunity to acquire a competitor has arisen, or to divest part of the organisation at an attractive price) means it should be considered in depth to assess whether you need to revise your own direction. A data strategy which no longer reflects the priorities of the organisation as a whole is doomed to fail, and likely to struggle to keep any momentum beyond the immediate term.

Prioritisation therefore is a fact of life in delivering any major programme and needs to be reviewed regularly – weekly as a routine check-in is not too much; monthly as a programmatic effort as a minimum, I would suggest, and should certainly involve ratification from your sponsor (the more engagement the better, as it ensures there is nothing on their radar which could catch you unawares). Remember to dock in with other programmes, tracking your own in conjunction with their priorities, asserting your interest in those things which represent dependencies and seeking confidence in timelines being met to build your own stakeholder confidence with your programme.

12.4.2 Dependencies

You should manage your dependencies as if they are as close to you as your key team members on the implementation team. A good programme manager will be able to recite the key dependencies, have a good feel for the current status, and be able to rest easy at night knowing these are being tracked and marshalled as if they were precious cargo. Anything less and you will be taken by surprise. In addition, you should manage them with a healthy degree of scepticism, anticipating shifts in delivery dates and being able to adapt your own activity almost instantly. Those responsible for delivering the dependencies should know you are on top of them as if you were personally responsible for their delivery, to ensure they attach the same importance to them as you do.

I recall one organisation where I was leading a change programme which, as it turned out, was one of about 26 global change programmes in play simultaneously. I had been drafted in to lead the programme which was a little over halfway through a three-year delivery cycle yet had struggled and delivered little so far. The scale of its importance only became apparent to me after a few months, as I sought to pin down a few dependencies I had uncovered and became aware of the much wider landscape of change programmes. These were not being managed at a portfolio level but simply as independent programmes.

It was remarkable to discover that the programme I was leading, in terms of cost the smallest of these programmes, was pivotal to virtually every other programme, yet none of them had my own programme on their dependency list, despite being entirely dependent on the data capability I was implementing. It led to a wholesale realignment of much bigger programmes to have to adjust to the new landscape I was tasked with bringing in, and the introduction of a new portfolio management approach to focus on dependencies between these programmes, amongst other things.

When you are building your implementation plan, bear in mind that you will most likely need to validate those dependencies which are made clear to you at the outset but almost certainly have to investigate how many more lurk in dark recesses of programmes and business-as-usual activities. The challenge will be to capture the information in anything like enough detail, but you have to play the role of the demanding customer in capturing this information, otherwise you will end up having to operate as the programme manager for more than just the data strategy implementation.

Keep attuned for new programmes, changes to ways of working and other activities that could cut across your implementation plan. I recommend sharing your plan widely with anyone receptive to listen: it may trigger thoughts or connections with those in other parts of your organisation you would not have thought to contact. It may also forge connections through its visibility, especially if your implementation team has subject matter expertise deployed into the implementation team, whether formally or informally, and create a local port of call to talk these things through in a more proactive way than being a centralised activity would.

12.4.3 Capabilities

Finally, in terms of the triumvirate, capabilities. The skills to move the data strategy forward in either definition or execution will depend entirely on the maturity of your organisation in the data arena. If you are embarking on this afresh, possibly the first person to define a data strategy in your organisation, then you may find willing 'amateurs' keen to join in, many of whom through sheer enthusiasm and a willingness to be part of something new bring a level of intensity to the programme. Just bear in mind that their capability will be low compared to the scale of the challenge you are undertaking, and no matter how much 'learning on the job' is a way to learn that suits some, the magnitude of what you are seeking to achieve – to transform the organisation into a different way of thinking and operating – is a bold task for anyone, let alone those with little experience.

You will find that the blend of experience and enthusiasm can be powerful in driving your programme forward, so consider whether you need to supplement your enthusiasts for a time with external resources that can bring a level of direction, focus and expertise to overcome the barriers you will face. If you are prepared to blend these within your programme, see how fast you can transition the knowledge and experience of others into your own team – do not become dependent on those outside your organisation, as this is a sure-fire way to end up with a data strategy that is unsustainable; you need that knowledge to reside and remain within your organisation.

If you have SMEs in your organisation who are willing to get behind the data strategy and drive it within their areas of expertise, then make the most of their networks, expertise and personal credibility. There is no substitute for having someone in your tent who is willing to be an early advocate: it will make the process of getting buy-in from their senior stakeholders all the easier.

I recommend you take a holistic yet pragmatic approach to corralling the tricky triumvirate together. It is worth reminding yourself, as you embark on data strategy implementation, that if you have a high degree of control over prioritisation within the programme, dependencies outside of it and locking capabilities around them both, you are in a strong position to be able to move forwards with a greater degree of confidence. It does not guarantee you success – nothing can – but it will probably help you sleep more easily at night.

12.5 EVALUATION AND MEASUREMENT

The preceding chapter highlighted the importance of evaluation and measurement as key disciplines along with benefits realisation in being able to manage the effectiveness of any programme. It is challenging to do so with a data strategy: the accounting practices in many organisations do not attribute benefits to those enablers which provide the means for another part of the organisation to declare success and claim those benefits as their own. However, there is a recognition that to deliver benefits there is often an upstream change programme required that either creates the right environment or delivers a capability for the benefits to be realised downstream.

As an example, the UK's Policing Vision 2025 led to the formation of the National Enabling Programme (NEP) by the National Police Chiefs Council to drive a consistent and efficient approach to digital enablement and data standards across the UK's separate police forces. The NEP delivers capability; it is for the individual police forces to realise the benefits from the improvements the digital investment is bringing.

Having an agreed approach to articulating benefits, evaluating the implementation programme and measuring activity is paramount to keeping stakeholders engaged and retaining confidence in the data strategy. To do this needs a clearly defined baseline, to confirm where you are starting from, and alignment as to what success looks like for your key senior stakeholders that your sponsor can sign up to and be held accountable for delivering. Without this, it is all too easy to lose sight of the progress that is being made and for funding or support to be drained away from the programme to those activities which have a higher profile.

The pre-implementation review (Chapter 8) is the opportunity to take a look at the way the programme will be structured to navigate into mobilising the programme. This would be an opportune time to assess your baseline and whether the starting point has shifted since the drafting of the data strategy, such that it leads to a reappraisal of the priorities or direction to be taken.

I would also recommend being as transparent and accessible as possible in publishing your progress via performance measurement, milestones achieved and benefits realised, to keep a high profile with your implementation programme. Assuming progress is being made, there is no substitute for making the news widely available in your organisation and supplementing this with positive endorsements from stakeholders and influencers across the organisation.

12.6 SPONSORSHIP, EXECUTIVE BUY-IN AND STAKEHOLDER MANAGEMENT

Throughout the book, reference has been made to stakeholder engagement. A data strategy will touch every part of the organisation – we are all data users in some form – and so it is impossible to develop a data strategy without engaging on the widest basis possible to get coherence and gain traction for the effort involved to turn strategy into implementation. Key to this is also the process of selecting the right sponsor.

The importance of ensuring a data strategy is understood from the outset cannot be overstated. Whilst in many organisations data is seen to be something that has always been done, the sad reality is that it is an asset that has been undervalued, underutilised and lacked investment in most organisations. The tide is definitely changing, but data has been overlooked as an asset class in its own right for far too long, and most organisations are not in a good place, whether legally, operationally or a combination of the two. The differentiator, in which data is clearly being taken seriously, can be seen when organisations in a competitive market start to operate in a markedly different way to their rivals due to the insight gained, which can lead to market dominance, increased profitability, acquisition of poorer performing rivals or a combination of the three. This can drive a major realignment of thinking in such a market, such that others need to catch up quickly to survive.

It is, therefore, vital that you get the right level of sponsorship and commitment from the outset. If you are hindered due to the sponsor not fully understanding, you will find yourself unable to get your message across in a compelling way. Similarly, if the sponsor is not fully committed to the programme, you will not have the executive influence you need should you encounter difficulties that need their engagement to address.

If the sponsor hasn't been selected – there is the possibility that the data strategy is driven from the executive group and has already assigned a sponsor – then make it your business to find the right sponsor, someone who understands the importance of data and is prepared to pitch to their peers on a subject which many of them might fail to find compelling at first, but which can be brought to life by the right person in the sponsor role.

You need to be really switched on to managing a stakeholder network. It is not enough to know who is in what post: you need to know what their data issues are and what could be done that would differentiate performance or compliance for them to make them sit up and take notice. It is a network, not simply a recognition of who sits on the executive board, as there will be influencers at all levels in the organisation. It is your business to know this and to flush these people out and get them engaged. The more effort you put into this from the outset, the easier the implementation activity will be. Build a wider network of interested parties in the data strategy and it makes your communication activity all the easier to land. Identify quick wins, major change opportunities and programmes already under way in their functional area and you are on course to build advocacy for your programme.

Many will say stakeholder engagement is distracting, is time-consuming and absorbs lots of effort. Each of these may apply, but all three will multiply in effect if you do not make the effort to drive it yourself, as you will be either herding cats to keep things aligned or completely out of the loop and last to know something which may be fundamental to the success of your programme. Invest the time, build the network and keep stakeholders engaged. It will be one of your wisest investments in the pre-implementation phase of your programme.

12.7 COMMUNICATIONS

Just as strategy execution requires an implementation plan, that plan will need a parallel stream of activity to communicate throughout the delivery of the data strategy. Prior to implementation, it will have been essential to keep stakeholders aligned and engaged to ensure you have their support when it comes to gaining sign-off of the data strategy, so this should be formalising the relationships and trust you have built up throughout that phase.

The key to successful communications is to understand your audience. In the same way any marketer will tell you that you need to tailor your message to meet client expectations and generate interest, you have the same challenge with the data strategy. It is essential that you understand your stakeholder network well enough to be able to tailor your message to be relevant and engaging, otherwise it will not register and your programme will lose visibility. Remember, a data strategy is for everyone within an organisation, so you have to find the key to make it appeal and generate continued interest.

There is a real risk, especially if you are defining or executing a data strategy within the role you currently undertake in the organisation, that the data strategy is seen as a business-as-usual activity. You might suggest that it is; any strategy is simply an evolution of an organisation and therefore the natural progression over a number of years mapped out for all to understand so they can deliver it. In some ways, this is true of a data strategy, but there is one notable difference. In most organisations there has not been such a focus on data to define a strategy around it, or previous attempts may have failed along the way. It is still a minority of organisations that have embraced a data strategy in a proactive, committed way to see it through and deliver on its impact. Therefore, the data strategy is much more akin to a major change programme, as it will likely seek to change the organisational culture, shift attitudes, realign priorities and break down silos, all of which are significant battles in their own right.

Therefore, it is essential that the data strategy communications effort is focused on driving forward, demonstrating the impact of change being delivered by being able to articulate what has been achieved, the vision of where the organisation is going, and the part each and every member of the organisation has to play in it – the message that data strategy implementation is not a spectator sport is one of the most powerful you will need to make if you are to really succeed in rallying change on any significant level within your organisation.

Communication is your lever to try to influence resistance to change on any organisation-wide level. Without effective communications you are simply setting yourself up to fail, as you need to project the voice of the implementation programme much further and wider than you and the team can do between you. Communicate too much and the programme loses credibility and is an irritant seeking to generate noise but little impact. Too little, and the programme is forgotten about or assumed to be failing. Getting it just right is an art, and the most effective way to succeed in this is to understand the communication routes open to you.

There are many layers to a communications approach to underpin the data strategy implementation. Indeed, the obvious are often the least effective, so balance the direct-from-the-programme messaging with what is delivered through other routes. By that, I mean that you will discover that within functional areas in your organisation there are communications plans and opportunities you may not have been aware of. For instance, that team awayday that the operations directorate is planning, when a significant proportion of the team come together, may be the ideal opportunity to do a 20 minute pitch to the group on data strategy and what it means for them. Make it engaging; if you are suitably prepared, then including time for a question and answer session may be a good way to get interaction and generate interest, especially if you have some supportive colleagues in that part of the organisation who could ask a few questions to get the ball rolling.

Try to get senior leaders and a few others involved; don't think you have to convey the message alone. As I have said a number of times in this book, recognise the importance of influencers within the group, the people who are recognised for talking sense and project credibility amongst their peers. Do not assume these are always the most senior people in attendance: there are bound to be individuals in that group who are seen to be wise heads or the rising stars that will do a great job for you in 'selling' your message in terms that the audience will lap up.

You will find other opportunities too, such as a CEO briefing to all leaders or staff within the organisation, where even a brief three- to five-minute mention of the data strategy shows that it clearly matters to the people at the top of the organisation. Your sponsor, too, should be proactive, finding opportunities to promote the data strategy and why it matters. If you can get each executive board member to do a short article in turn once a month, in the organisation's newsletter, on the intranet or via whatever other channel is available to you, then be prepared to provide the data strategy material relevant to their part of the organisation as well as the more corporate messages to be got across. Do not stifle their natural style of delivery; you want it to come across as genuine and personal to be most effective, as their people will spot if they are reading a script or using words that they would not normally use.

Review your dependencies, each of which presents a great opportunity to potentially jump on the back of communicating the delivery of that activity with a sideline of what it means in enabling your own implementation programme. In other words, do not pass up a good opportunity to weave your own messaging into the existing planned communications activity. It is often more effective to have the data strategy called out in connection with other newsworthy items than on its own, simply because the data strategy itself is an enabler and so aligns more effectively in partnership with a wider message.

If you are able to devote resource, or get resource assigned from a communications team within your organisation, then this is a sound investment, as it is understanding the nuances of the data strategy – its reach, impact and scale – that is important in maximising the opportunities to build a strong communications stream as part of your implementation plan. It is an investment, but one which will pay back in helping you gain traction and keep an enabling activity front of mind through spotting opportunities for linking to other news in the organisation.

12.8 ALIGNING AND EMBEDDING THE STRATEGIES

The data strategy should not live in a vacuum – it is an enabler to the organisation to reach its goals and beyond, realising what seemed aspirational much more efficiently through improvements to the corporate asset to which it probably has paid least attention: data. So long as your organisation has a corporate strategy, the data strategy is a key enabler to reach the goals through doing things smarter, utilising something which was always available to it but probably not seen in that light.

Of course, you may be working in a very advanced setting, one where data has always been seen to be at the forefront of differentiating your organisation from its competitors and driving innovation. If so, you are one of the lucky ones, as your task is probably to keep pushing the bounds of what can be achieved through innovation in data, and that is an exciting journey in its own right. If you are truly in the vanguard of thinking on data then you will know that data is already a differentiator, and you will be keenly seeking ways to keep your organisation several steps ahead of its competitors. If not, then just think how far you have to go before having to be so inventive, and how much there is to be gained from simply starting out with getting the basics right and building from there.

The data strategy should always align to the corporate strategy; anything else is either failing to comprehend how pivotal data is to the running of your organisation or destined to be seen to be irrelevant. If the corporate strategy is devoid of any understanding of what data can add, it may seem odd to tie yourself to something which has already marginalised data, and whilst the argument has some coherence it misses the one valuable lesson in getting buy-in to the data strategy – you have to work with the grain of supporting the organisation deliver its priorities, rather than use the data strategy as a Trojan Horse to undermine the corporate strategy and position something as 'better'.

Therefore, you need to be fully aware as to the content of the corporate strategy, its thinking, baseline and goals, to know what is involved in achieving the overarching objective set. This will inform you of the priorities as the executive board members of your organisation see them, the measures on which they are likely to be judged by either shareholders or other interested controlling parties and, therefore, the factor which will likely determine their future in the organisation. The corporate strategy is the key measure of the board's success in the eyes of those who pass judgement.

It is not enough to know the corporate strategy: you also need to comprehend the data that sits behind it. I don't just mean the data that has generated those impressive targets for the next three to five years, but the data which will be required to evidence performance. Where does it come from? How reliable is it? What are the decisions that underpin how that data is gathered and evaluated? You need to start to answer these questions if you are to be able to influence an executive board that your data strategy is entirely compatible, supportive and, in fact, an accelerator for their success. If you are able to get the organisation more focused on the data that matters, its quality and driving activity to exploit it more effectively, then you are almost certainly in the right territory to make the executive board succeed. Once you have done your homework, mapping this out to be able to demonstrate how the data strategy will enhance current performance, you are in a position to share this with the executive board and get its commitment.

I have talked at length in this book about the corporate strategy. This is deliberate, as any forward-thinking organisation will have a clearly articulated vision of where it is going, how it will focus efforts to get there and how it will evidence this over time to be able to claim success. Whether your organisation has realised it or not, it has just given you a blank canvas on which to draw up a data strategy that is essential for it to buy in to in order to increase its odds of victory.

However, as referenced in Chapter 6, there are likely to be many interlocking strategies already in play or in development within your organisation. By its very nature, data will almost certainly have a role to play in all of these to varying degrees, and, of course, the extent to which data is recognised as a key enabler in these other strategies is also a clear indicator of just how well data is understood within your own organisation.

It is important to review the other strategies as early as possible in the strategy definition phase. It is a question not simply of identifying what data-related activity sits in there, though of course this is a given, but also of figuring out what is missing. By that I mean what should be in there, either to accelerate the delivery of that particular strategy or to enable it to be achieved much more easily or effectively. Your data strategy drafting process will bring in other strategies from across the organisation. You should seek to identify opportunities to enhance those existing strategies through making your own commitments which, in turn, may become dependencies for other strategies subject to a redraft to recognise the need for an update.

As also discussed at some length earlier in this book, if you are new to defining strategies altogether or just new to the organisation in which you are doing this, do take the opportunity to gather insight from those who have drafted other strategies within the organisation to learn from them the levers of success, the pitfalls to avoid, the expectations within the organisation (could be length, style, structure or more general things such as timescales and route to turn definition into execution) and the key individuals to keep onside. The more advice you can obtain the better; it would be ill-advised to think that those other strategies are so different from yours that there is nothing to be gained from building a knowledge base and taking some friendly advice from those who have been in similar shoes to you yourself.

If you have time, do seek feedback on the update cycles of the other strategies and influence them with your own thinking as you progress through your own definition stage. If there are multiple strategies being worked on at a similar time, it would seem more compelling to link dependencies and themes overtly between them to ensure that, when it is time for review, they are seen to have been developed collaboratively and there is a level of coherence between them. Better to invest that time through the definition phase than to be pulled up on such connections being lacking when you come to present your first draft to the executive board. You may even want to link up your sponsors, so they too have a consistent message to project to the audience and appear aligned in their thinking.

12.9 BALANCING RISK

You will face challenges in developing the data strategy and then moving through to its execution; this is unlikely to be a surprise especially if you have read the book to this point. The key is how you manage the challenges you face, and how prepared you are for them to materialise and be dealt with.

I believe you have to take a measured approach to risk in defining and executing a data strategy. It is impossible to control all the variables. Within the programme itself, there will be occasions where it is likely to deviate from what you anticipated, but there are then so many factors outside the immediate control of the implementation programme that you will have to reassess many times in the course of delivering the data strategy.

Therefore, you need to manage your risk and work out what you are comfortable living with and those risks that need mitigating due to their nature or the significance they pose to the data strategy implementation. This is not to say that the balance you strike won't change: it probably will as you move into periods of greater certainty and those where the outlook seems very uncertain. However, you need to inform your team of the parameters you are willing to operate within and ensure they both accept the same level of risk and inform you at the earliest opportunity of any emerging risks that are outside those parameters.

There is a case for being prepared for risk and working through the detailed options to address it should various scenarios arise. However, this can consume a lot of effort and, inevitably, if the risk does not materialise it is of little value. Of course, being aware of potential risks and ready to respond as necessary is entirely sensible, and can put you on the front foot with the response you take swiftly which can mitigate the scale of impact. You must assess the risks, determine your parameters and then decide which risks you want to prepare contingency plans of varying levels of sophistication as your safeguard to being driven off course.

Some risks, as discussed in Chapter 10, are clearly more likely than others. For example, over a period of time, your team is likely to lose people who will have specialist knowledge and/or be experts in a particular line of the data strategy definition or execution. You should plan for such eventualities by having a form of succession planning in place, knowing how you would deal with having to shuffle resources or having natural deputies in place who could step up to provide continuity. If there is a lack of experience within the team, you can look to external sources of assistance, but you should only do so if you have a clear programme of how you intend to bring that knowledge in-house into the team around you, so you don't build an unhealthy dependency with a third party.

If you have the opportunity to influence risks in other programmes, especially when it comes to those activities which are your dependencies, recognise that these may not be the most pressing for those leading the programmes. That is where you need to be able to influence the weighting applied within the programme to reflect the risk to your own programme, otherwise you risk that such key deliverables are deprioritised through a lack of awareness of the wider impact. Of course, the same applies to your own implementation programme – you may be responsible for a key deliverable for another programme and so should balance your own risk assessment with those other programmes' perspective.

I would strongly recommend being open about the risks you are managing and report the status of them regularly, along with any issues flagged as red with the relevant mitigation actions on the register. It may be the case that those in senior roles within your organisation can assist in providing mitigation or alleviating the risk entirely by refocusing the activities they are responsible for, which those tasked with delivering the programme do not have the authority to do. By being open about your risk approach and reporting, you make it evident to all that there are activities which you are tracking but are not necessarily able to control, and you should assign where that ownership sits in the organisation so the accountability is clear.

12.10 PLAN FOR SUCCESS

Amongst the key messages I would wish you to take away from this book are the importance of planning and the approach you take to manage what I have referred to as waymarkers. The coherence of a plan through the implementation stage will be paramount to your success, and this needs to be the single source of truth when it comes to what you are seeking to deliver, by when, through which resources and to what end (in terms of what it achieves or enables).

Chapter 8 provided the key information to take away on the importance of the plan, and I would stress that the lack of this has been a recurring theme for the best part of two decades in organisations that have failed to turn strategy into execution. Without a plan that has the right elements to it, you are in danger of becoming another statistic!

The work to define the plan begins well in advance of mobilising the team to start on implementation. It takes research, piecing together the artefacts that led to the data strategy being defined and approved, recognising the baseline from which you are starting, deciding the priorities and practicalities of what to deliver when and why, and not least determining the right team to put in place to execute the data strategy. In essence, planning for success in advance of having a plan to go forward with.

There is a lot to comprehend in pulling your plan together, in particular the capabilities of the people around you who will take the data strategy into implementation, how you structure it as a programme and the criticality of aligning stakeholder engagement and effective communications to keep everyone focused. However, time well spent at this stage will pay back in the months and years ahead. Get it wrong now and you will repent throughout and be constantly on the back foot, having to respond to events that should have been foreseen, and identifying gaps and skill shortages that you needed to have spotted from the outset.

I do not want to give the impression that planning for a plan need take too long. Indeed, paralysis can often cause people to lose faith in the data strategy ever coming to fruition and there is a strong case to be made for striking whilst the iron is hot, as soon after getting approval from the executive board to embark on the data strategy implementation as time permits. However, there are ways and means of doing this without it needing to take an eternity, and it is essential that you create a sufficient window to give yourself the opportunity to set out as surefootedly as possible. As the saying goes, 'act in haste, repent at leisure'. It may be that there are quick wins you can deliver, elements of activity already in train that you can bring into your scope to create a sense of momentum, even the act of bringing the team together in an engaging way with the executive board can give a sense of progress or the programme at least taking shape.

Recognise the key programmes already in train within the organisation, or about to commence in the next 12 months, and align yourself with those shaping them to ensure you are on their radar. Identify as soon as possible those areas of common interest, how you can work together and how your plan can dovetail with theirs to ensure there is a level of integration of activity. Review the key priorities of the major stakeholders within the organisation to assess how you keep them on board and build confidence that your programme is focused on delivering outcomes that will have a major impact on what they are seeking to achieve. Every step you take, think about how you build an engaged community of interest, working with your colleagues to enable their priorities rather than cutting across them to deliver what to them become your priorities in preference to theirs.

Every stage of the process – from data strategy definition to execution – is challenging in so many ways. The pre-mobilisation phase of implementation, structuring your programme and having a clear plan is the one phase that you will struggle to revisit and determines your approach to implementation for a considerable period of time. Get it wrong, and you may struggle to recover. Fail to build confidence and establish trust at an executive level, and you will be in the spotlight as to whether you are the right person for the role and always struggling to assert control over the programme. It is the moment when you dive off the top springboard and it is important you do so on the right trajectory to avoid a painful crash into the water below. Get it right, and you are on course for top marks as you glide through the water gracefully!

12.11 THE NEXT WAVE

I explained in Chapter 10 the merits in having a dynamic data strategy. In some cases, this may not be feasible, but I am focused on where this is practicable, as I certainly think it desirable, if possible, in your organisation.

The concept of a rolling, or dynamic, data strategy is to build a view for the year beyond the original term the data strategy applies to, such that the period it covers remains the same throughout. This has the advantage of retaining the focus and commitment to the data strategy, rather than having to reinvent every three, five or whatever number of years the data strategy represents, and continuing to evolve the thinking through applying the learning as you go. It is a more agile way of working, rather than a waterfall style of approach where the data strategy comes to the end of its term and there is a whole process to justify a data strategy again, which is not the best use of time or effort.

Assuming you are working on a rolling basis, then you need to be thinking of the subsequent year to add long before getting to the end of the first year of the data strategy. Remember the effort involved to get all stakeholders engaged and bought into the content of the data strategy, and whilst you are approaching this extension from a position of having been through it with them once, you do need to recognise that it has to reflect the corporate strategic direction as well as their own aspirations.

Preparing for the next wave of the data strategy basically needs to capture input from the data strategy implementation that has delivered thus far to learn from the experience to date. This could be insight into the progress made in terms of deliverables, the barriers faced (particularly those not anticipated at the outset), the experience of managing dependencies or the commitment from the various stakeholders and their groups. It is also the opportunity to determine whether the anticipated pace in the first year was overambitious or not demanding enough, and whether you have the right resources in place to implement the data strategy effectively. In other words, you will have learnt a lot inside the first year to be able to inform the thinking to plan ahead.

You will also have gained a sense of impact on the corporate strategy, to know whether the focus of your activity is having the impact you had hoped to enable the corporate strategy to reap the benefit. This will have played a key role in determining the value the executive team in your organisation will have seen in the data strategy implementation, and may have given scope to commit further to the data strategy if the rewards are seen to be strong.

I discussed in Chapter 3 the importance of lessons learnt activities every step of the way through the implementation. These are variously called post-implementation reviews, after-action reviews or, in Agile parlance, sprint retrospectives, but all are forms of gathering evidence on what was intended to happen, the activity itself, and the outcome to assess and evaluate what can be adapted or improved in future strands of activity. These are important to you if you are planning to operate a dynamic data strategy, as they inform the design of the further year based upon practical experience.

The planning for the next wave to be added to the data strategy needs to take account of the fact that there might have had to be some reprioritisation of activities in the light of known events or factors which determined a change of plan. This is not an unusual occurrence, nor should you anticipate it to be a one-off. Flexibility is the name of the game when it comes to strategy implementation: it is much more likely to be a success if you operate with a degree of fluidity to recognise potential changing organisational drivers than if you are a hostage to your initial plan.

The mobilisation phase needs to assess the readiness for change, and this needs to be revisited at the start of each annual implementation plan (assuming you work to an annual timeline, of course). It would be a dangerous assumption to move from one year to the next on the basis that momentum is established, as it can be lost quicker than it can be gained, and the transition from one planning year to the next does carry risks of focus shifting elsewhere. Whilst subsequent mobilisation periods should be shorter and focused, they still add value to keep alignment to corporate goals and to revisit prioritisation decisions.

Delivering something which is not deemed a priority and overlooking something which would constitute a far greater benefit to the organisation is a risky strategy if you are to retain the confidence of your sponsor and executive group. Therefore, consideration of the planning assumptions in the data strategy for the remaining period of the original version, as well as the additional year, provides the opportunity to ensure the data strategy remains closely aligned to the executive priorities.

There are also numerous avenues to be pursued in drafting the additional year to be added to the data strategy. Those who were involved in the original drafting may have been involved with the implementation, and can therefore give an assessment of how it has turned out in practice compared to the expectations at the outset. There will also have been others involved in the data strategy definition stage, especially representing the wider organisation, and their feedback on how it has transpired and felt for them from a functional area of responsibility will be key to capture and learn from. There is also your sponsor, who will have a view on how the experience to date has landed, what can be improved, and whether the focus and delivery model is working to be able to sustain their sponsorship going forward. All of these need to be captured in preparing for the next wave.

The further you progress the data strategy, the skills and expertise required become more challenging to source. That is not to say that having the right capabilities is easy to begin with – this is often a stumbling block for many organisations, and especially those that are embarking on a data strategy for the first time – but the more the organisation moves into advanced exploitation of the data the harder it is to find those resources. You may therefore find that you need to bring in such skills from external parties, whether as consultants or interim management resources, to get you started and to provide the experience and knowledge to know how to begin framing the data strategy within your organisation. This comes at a cost, and so has to have a clear focus on what is to be achieved and the measures of success within the remit you are assigning them to fulfil. If not, then it can be high cost for little gain, which clearly undermines the credibility of the data strategy and its implementation.

Utilising resources from outside your organisation in a flexible approach enables the experience of such individuals be applied to build an internal team that is sustainable through having learnt what are the right skillsets to source for your needs. It is always a challenge to embark on a new line of activity within an organisation and to demonstrate the value-add it brings, but the essence of a successful implementation programme is that it should have brought the organisation along with you to be confident that this is the right move at the right time.

Planning for this shift in focus requires time and effort, and it is often hard to enable colleagues to comprehend the art of the possible. This is further reasoning for the value of bringing in skilled personnel to help you get this mobilised – the credibility that those expert resources bring at the outset to get a headwind of activity established and success behind them will make it easier for those who follow and are hired on a more permanent basis.

This assumes that bringing this talent in-house at this time is the right thing to do. It is also an opportune time to determine whether a need to branch out to hire scarce resources in a highly competitive market is the right option to take, and there are plenty of consulting firms that would offer partnering services through which they could take the resourcing headache away and deliver analytics or similar services to your organisation as an outsourced arrangement. Do bear in mind, however, that this activity is a critical differentiator for your organisation in the future and therefore you may deem this to be such critical intellectual property that you would prefer to retain a greater level of control by having an in-house team undertaking this activity.

Either way, the process of an ongoing review of skills and capabilities assessment should form a key part of your rolling strategy, as the initial work will need to evolve as the nature of the data strategy deliverables progresses. Therefore, the assessment will be a developing toolset, expanding as new capabilities are required and exploring the options on how to acquire these in the short and longer term – build, buy, hybrid for flexibility: all are options on the table to determine the best approach to establishing a capability to translate the data strategy into a successful implementation programme.

12.12 IS A DATA STRATEGY SIMILAR FOR ALL ORGANISATIONS?

One of the things that surprises me, and continues to be a perceived barrier to those of us who regard ourselves as data professionals, is the notion that 'my sector is different' and the belief that without prior experience in that sector the skills you bring are somehow worthless because of the lack of deep knowledge about the specific sector. There are pockets of activity where specialist data experience can be useful –analytics in the medical sector, for example, works to a slightly different model than most sectors. However, data is fundamentally generic across organisations – one byte is much the same as another, I was told in jest many years ago – and any organisation looking to develop a data strategy will have employees, customers (or users), transactions of some kind, financial metrics and other measures of business performance.

> I have had the benefit of working across around a dozen industry sectors in my career and can confidently state that the variety that has brought has enhanced my capability in my chosen profession, not diminished it. My challenge back to any organisation I've operated within when questioned at the outset how I can usefully exploit data in a sector in which I have little or no previous experience is always the same – I am surrounded by technical experts on the sector, but you have hired me as the only one with data expertise, so if I need technical input, I am blessed to have so many others to turn to.

Historically the public sector has been seen to operate on a completely different basis to the private sector. Whilst there are obvious differences – most public sector organisations are publicly funded, or at least have some central funding provided – the challenge with data is remarkably similar. Having split my career between public and private sector organisations, I can see that there are more similarities in challenges than there are differences.

> Twenty years ago, I met staff from HMRC who were working on pulling together a model to link activities at a citizen and business level, who were most interested in work I had recently undertaken at HSBC to build a single customer view. Two very different organisations, but with a common challenge – multiple systems, duplicated data that wasn't synchronised between core systems, a plethora of offline spreadsheets to link things together and an inability to report or exploit that data to drive out any meaning.

The appreciation of the importance of data has been one of the positives within the public sector in the UK over the last decade or so. In fact, some public sector organisations are now leading the way in certain sectors of activity and setting benchmarks for what 'good' looks like, such has been the transformation of centrally delivered services to the citizen via the internet.

It is a similar story in the not-for-profit sector. The learning and opportunity to deploy solutions implemented successfully elsewhere are still as valid; the constraint is simply the environment in which you operate, in particular the funding challenges. Some of the best innovation comes from such environments as it may be impossible to seek investment to buy a solution, and so the only course of action is to learn from others and invent your own approach to solving that problem. It is amazing how much can be achieved with so little when there is clarity of direction and a need to deliver to make a significant difference. Commitment and a 'can do' attitude can make up for a lot that 'politics' within a bigger organisation may stifle.

Finally, I want to reference those organisations operating in a highly regulated environment. It may be challenging to press ahead on a novel approach to data if there isn't the buy-in from the central regulatory body, which may well be encouraging greater uniformity of approach between organisations in that sector. The regulator therefore has to be seen in the same light as those key stakeholders who devised the corporate strategy and have been engaged from the outset to ensure there is an understanding as to how the data strategy impacts the ability to meet regulatory obligations.

Often, the regulator will be supportive if the data strategy delivers the potential of greater value to customers or a more efficient and effective delivery organisation at a lower cost. There may be a desire to encourage such ideas to be shared with rival organisations, but as the first mover there is a distinct advantage to setting the bar and being ready to meet it ahead of your rivals. If the regulated market has competition within it, then seizing the opportunity to differentiate and gain first mover advantage is one of the few ways to stand out from your competitors.

12.13 CASE STUDIES

When I deliver workshops on devising a data strategy, I utilise the data strategies already in the public domain to give an insight to the prospective author. This exercise tends to take a two-dimensional concept: considering the data strategy content for relevance and clarity to someone looking at it for the first time; and the ease with which any of the attendees believe they could translate the data strategy into execution. Without detailed knowledge of the organisation the attendees represent – its corporate strategy, goals and maturity – it is impossible for me to write a data strategy for them. Therefore, the workshop utilises the work of others to draw parallels with their own challenge of defining and executing a data strategy in their organisation.

An effective data strategy should outline clearly the current state of the organisation from a data perspective, highlighting the gaps in terms of the foundation layers of getting good-quality data into the right hands, and explaining the top priorities and timescales for delivering the data strategy.

The biggest challenge with most data strategies that are publicly accessible is that, by the very nature of being so, they tend to be published by public sector organisations and so give limited comprehension on those aspects which may differ and therefore be distinct in a private sector organisation. Nonetheless, the basic premise of a good structure with appropriate background to establish the baseline applies.

I ask teams to critique the data strategies I provide in terms of both positive and negative observations and find that this sharpens up the critical reasoning skills of the workshop attendees and starts to get them to think differently. The data strategies I choose are not necessarily exemplars, nor lacking in positive elements. I recognise that having delivered a data strategy, each of the authors of those I have utilised have succeeded in reaching the stage to be able to publish these in a public place for any interested party to view and pass judgement, which is an achievement in itself. I do not know how successful they have subsequently been in moving through the execution stage, and this is part of the challenge of the workshop – to consider the ease with which a participant could take over the reins and execute the data strategy before them.

The process of reflecting on them in a case-study approach enables those participating in the workshop to consider the key points I outline in this book and apply the approach I have proposed – see the Summary of Steps (Section 12.14) – to determine what they might have done differently. Of course, the elements which cannot be appreciated are the culture of the organisation, the resources available to define the data strategy or the expectations that were set at the outset of the process of defining the data strategy. In many ways, the constraints imposed – which could be direct or indirect, in so much as they may be physical constraints of resource, scope or budget as much as the cultural challenge to overcome – within the organisation are the very biggest challenge to comprehend and devise a way forward to either overcome or navigate around.

Links to the data strategies used in a recent workshop can be found via my website, where I maintain links to a variety of data strategies as I find and utilise them in my workshops.[6] The workshop was divided into six parts, each reflecting the approach I have taken here on defining and executing a data strategy. The attendees critiqued the data strategies to be able to identify some key points in each section, as identified below.

1. **Positioning and scope – ensure this is clear and engaging.**

- Participants identified that the background is important, to set context.

- There is a need to articulate the why, what and how in explaining the reasoning for defining a data strategy.

- There is a need to set a logical order to flow the scope through the data strategy.

- Goals – corporate and data strategy need to be clearly articulated.

- Define what 'data' and 'data strategy' mean in the context of the data strategy, so there is absolute clarity for all.

- If diagrams are included, ensure they are clear and articulate the point being made. Generally a positive thing if done well – helps those who can relate to a visual better than blocks of text.

---

6   https://www.datastrategists.com.

- Clarity is essential – a general point, avoiding jargon or assuming knowledge.
- Audience – ensure the data strategy is accessible to all staff.
- Ensure the vision of the data strategy is actionable, and there is clarity of how this is to be delivered.

2. **Audience and route map – pitch and targeting should be key. Set timescales and waymarkers.**

- Consider the audience: how does this relate to their goals?
- Clarity of the route map is often lacking, neither waymarkers or milestones to know what progress would look like.
- Delivery or implementation approach is unclear, to know how this would be translated into action.
- Use of case studies as an annex can help guide the reader, and bring context and meaning.
- One of the key quotes from the group: 'this data strategy is shorter, but seems longer, as it has more impact'.

3. **Content – be clear, have high-level direction and set strategy rather than execution.**

- A need to review the high level scope and structure, and the level of detail (often felt to be too much) and alignment to other strategies (not clear in the data strategy, so may be implicit, but this is a risky strategy in itself to let others imply links).
- Timing of deliverables unclear – no milestones, certainly no waymarkers, included to know expected pace or achievability of the data strategy.

4. **The plan – be focused on delivery, whilst mindful of dependencies, and ensure readiness.**

- A switch of mindsets; need to focus on planning cycles and establish dependencies.
- Agility – not clear on readiness to achieve goals to know how feasible the plan is, the way it is to be tackled or the flexibility to adapt through any contingency built in.
- Links to other strategies essential to know what is coming from where, and when, to track effectively.
- Plan should be more about reality, but potentially still visionary.

5. **Delivery and flexibility – focus on outcome, stakeholder engagement and benefits.**

- Unclear on what benefits are being tracked, how these would be tracked and what the evaluation criteria are.
- Communication – lack of clarity on how stakeholders will be engaged, and what communication strategies are being adopted in the delivery of the data strategy.
- Need to build in review points into the plan to flex the delivery; inevitably it will not go entirely as expected, so build in contingency to provide some options and identify those opportunities to reprioritise.

6. **Value – measure, assess, capture benefits as realised, and plan ahead.**

- Ensure the data strategy is relevant to all stakeholders to help them identify value.

- Review regularly, and update if necessary, to ensure value is being achieved.

- Focus on benefits realisation and how this is to be reported.

- Plan ahead, so change can be accommodated such that it does not diminish value being achieved.

12.14 SUMMARY OF STEPS – DATA STRATEGY: FROM DEFINITION TO EXECUTION

This section provides the process – reflected in the flow of chapters – that you should undertake to be able to define and execute a data strategy effectively (see Figures 12.1 and 12.2). There is a logic to the process, albeit that the process should have flexibility and agility to be able to refine and adapt based upon what is learnt over the course of following this process.

12.14.1 Data strategy – definition

1. **Positioning** – Start with positioning the data strategy. Why is it being commissioned and by whom, what do they understand a data strategy to be and what is driving this focus now? Unless you have the clarity as to why you are being asked to take the lead on defining a data strategy and, ultimately, what its purpose is, then you are likely to be second-guessing what is required and therefore likely to fail. Take the time to establish the rationale, key drivers, interested parties and expectations, and you have the foundations from which to work. There should be a coherent business case which defines the expected benefits of the data strategy.

2. **Readiness and scope** – Consider how ready the organisation is to embrace a data strategy. Establish some context, including how this aligns in the thinking to the corporate strategy, and the scope. Understand the timings, consider sponsorship (if not already determined for you) and assess the stakeholders – who they are and what they will want or expect.

3. **Definition** – Keep it simple and accessible for all. Set waymarkers and signpost the alignment with the corporate strategy. Identify resources to deliver and the impact of successful delivery for the organisation by reference to the baseline. Understand sign-off for delivery.

4. **Route map** – Check clarity of data strategy through an implementation lens, establish the timeline, and include waymarkers and measurement as critical elements. Ensure alignment of route map to stakeholder expectations and manage accordingly.

5. **Content, structure and alignment** – Review final content internally as well as externally. Aim for 12–20 pages, and reflect on simplicity and accessibility. Maturity assessments provide a recognisable baseline from which to plan and improve using a recognised structure. Assess capabilities, and ensure communication with stakeholders throughout to 'sell' the story focused on high-level direction across the organisation. Review readiness for implementation for smooth transition.

Figure 12.1 Data strategy definition process flow

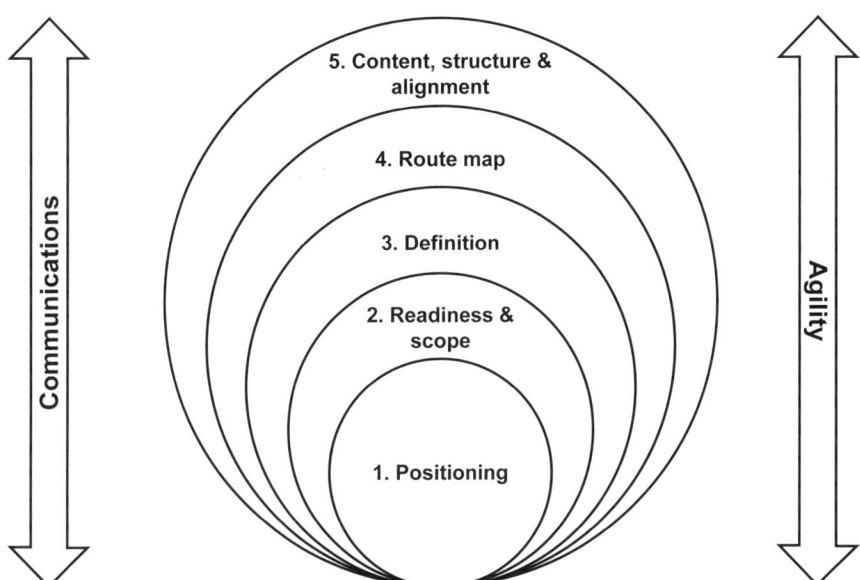

12.14.2 Data strategy – execution

1. **Communication, culture and change readiness** – Avoid culture eating your strategy for breakfast! Understand the 'local' culture, prepare for resistance to change and unfreeze before embarking on change, then freeze again. Cement your relationship with the sponsor, and ensure all communication channels are exploited. Integrate communications into the programme and be creative in spotting opportunities; don't be afraid to repeat messages. Utilise local knowledge to build credibility.

2. **Mobilisation and planning** – Have continuity in the transition from definition to execution, and establish a mobilisation phase to capture all relevant information pre-delivery. Ensure strategic alignment to the corporate strategy, and define milestones with detail and measures included. Plan in dependencies, and prepare to be agile and innovative. Benchmark capabilities for implementation but avoid strategy paralysis.

3. **Delivery** – Establish and communicate roles and responsibilities. Anticipate change to plan, but it is important to retain the link to data strategy as signed off. Utilise communications but be creative to secure employee engagement. Use Agile to deliver the plan in sprints, utilising the range of expertise in the programme team underpinned by a strong PMO. Ensure agreement to prioritisation, implement governance, and capture requirements and benefits to be tracked.

4. **Flexibility** – Align to other change programmes and keep tracking, especially dependencies. Be agile in responding to need to change, utilise a change control mechanism and review resource impact. Plan for change to the implementation team members, and develop their skills through the implementation. Use maturity

Figure 12.2 Data strategy execution process flow

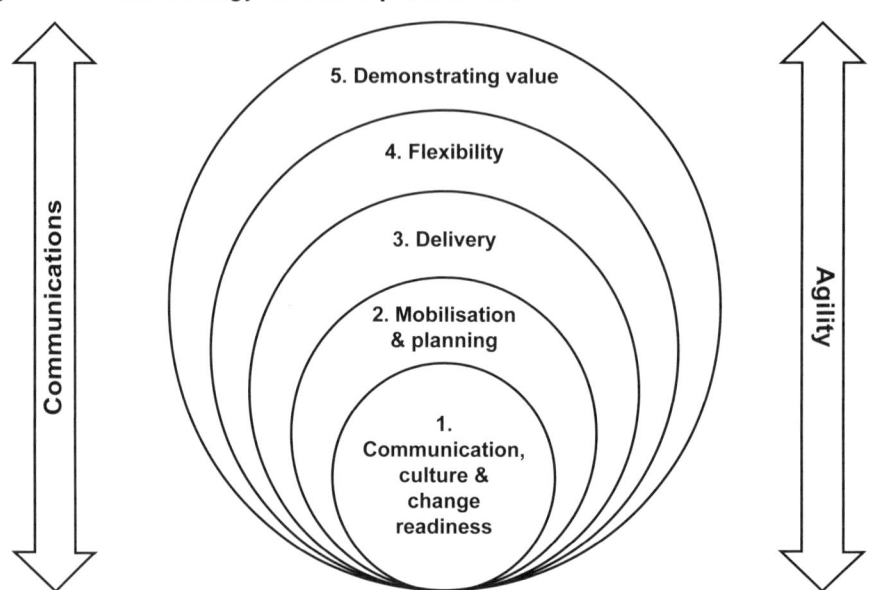

assessments to track progress against the baseline. Build advocacy in the organisation through the change. Explore opportunity for a rolling data strategy, and ensure value through implementation is clearly demonstrated.

5. **Demonstrating value** – Clarify the baseline to establish the ongoing measurement of the implementation programme. Establish key evaluation criteria, identify benefits to track and adopt a performance management approach. Incorporate maturity assessments to assess progress with appropriate governance and controls. Data is an asset – the new water: explore assigning value to it to focus on investment and maintenance in the asset.

12.15 SOME FINAL PERSONAL REFLECTIONS

There are a few observations I would like to share with you based upon my experience. I recognise that my experience is over a prolonged period of time, perhaps a period in which change in the workplace has been more dramatic than at any other time. As such, some of it may seem a bit dated, but I am a great believer that whilst the environment may change, the fundamentals – people and data – remain constant.

I began my working career delivering analytics and insight at a time in which the marketing team I was part of had one desktop computer between us. Whilst this was only the case for the first year or so, it gave me an incredible insight into how the advent of the PC so quickly changed the workplace and the decision-making process. Suddenly, everyone had the means to communicate, regardless of whether the individual they were communicating with was in the same office, busy doing other things or even remote from the office.

The immediacy of data had arrived, and with it the ability to process data in a way that was previously unimaginable. I built my first segmentation model using large sheets of paper stuck to a wall, a calculator and a lot of trial and error. The evolution of the thinking and calculations were there for all to see. Suddenly, I could do this faster, smarter and more reliably than ever before.

The organisation had bought into an early concept called an enterprise planning system, and whilst it took several years to deploy it successfully, it demonstrated to me how it brought together data from across functions so that it could be used commonly for the benefit of all. Once the technology worked, it demonstrated the failings of the data: not only the quality (and the gaps), but the different terminology that led to differing expectations of what that data represented – metadata, as it was called.

I reflect on this as the impact this had on my earliest dealings with data taught me that it was a universal language spoken with different dialects and different interpretations of terms. When people in organisations talk, they often use expressions that are known within the organisation and used commonly, such as acronyms. When we enter data into a system, we have to have the common understanding of what that field actually means – the metadata – to be able to enter data consistently. For instance, does address include postcode or not? If asked for forename and initials, does it include the first name initial or just those of middle names? This is the sort of confusion that leads to data inaccuracies, mismatches and so on.

When I started, these things were rarely defined, and unless we could establish a common vocabulary which had a consistency of meaning there would always be errors, not because the data was wrong, but because it wasn't being captured in any system with that consistent understanding and purpose in mind (the metadata).

In other words, a strategic view needed to be taken in order to gain maximum value from the potential to harness data across the entire organisation. It was not enough to be looking at it through a functional lens: if finance numbers did not accord with operations, then each would resort to their own numbers – talking their own language, if you will – and distrust and undermine the credibility of the other function. Further, from a sales and marketing perspective, the importance of understanding the customer was inextricably linked to being able to communicate in an increasingly technical way – they were improving their IT systems too, and so had expectations of their suppliers.

I was tasked with working with Honda at Swindon for a few weeks, understanding how they were applying a just-in-time approach to logistics, managing a supply chain to remove any inefficiency, and reducing waste in their processes to increase effectiveness and, ultimately, impact on the bottom line. It was fascinating to see at first hand the practices commonplace in Japan but still relatively alien to the UK, and to learn how data was at the heart of being able to operate in this way.

Some years later, I had the task of leading a single customer view programme for one of the UK banks. Integrating every customer record across more than 50 legacy systems that were never designed to be integrated into anything else demonstrated that the thinking of organisations had moved on, but the barriers were still very similar – poor data quality, gaps where data should have been captured, clear inaccuracies in data (especially date of birth, with the all too common problem of a default date in thousands of cases being traced back to an error in a previously badly implemented data integration project), to name just a few.

The bank had not appreciated at the outset the scale of data cleansing it was committing to in order to build a single customer view, but, to give it credit, saw the enormous benefit of delivering the project to enforce this being addressed, system by system. I was the first non-IT buyer of the data quality toolset then leading the market worldwide, which demonstrated how little the alignment of data with business owners had borne fruit at this stage. It was satisfying to realise that I was a pioneer in aligning data quality with business ownership, a concept which, whilst still not fully understood or implemented universally to this day, we now recognise as data governance. The notion of managing metadata, establishing data standards, meeting compliance obligations and, most importantly for me at the time, being able to exploit that data to enable the bank to outperform its competitors became the common currency of the organisation and a by-word for differentiating itself from rivals.

I recall these experiences as key drivers in what was a truly transformational period to be in data. The mobile phone had yet to become ubiquitous as a workplace tool at this early point in my career, and it was barely thought of as a sophisticated computer in its own right. I remember seeing a Blackberry for the first time, being shown how it could send and receive emails at a time when hardly anyone comprehended the notion of texting on a mobile phone, and how revolutionary it seemed to be able to receive emails other than whilst at a desk. Of course, this only expanded the data volumes further, and by this time call centres were becoming a very standard way to do business.

I had also been part of a new publishing operation within a small automotive organisation in the mid-1990s and, as a newcomer to the market, took advantage of developing a basic website to promote the publications to organisations around the world. We were delighted to get orders from Japan, Malaysia, South Korea, the USA, amongst others, all places we would never have been able to reach without a low-cost presence that anyone could access. It led to a number of automotive-related organisations in the publishing arena approaching us to act as agents, developing a network of geographically diverse businesses also promoting our products. As a result, our sales figures far exceeded our original expectations. Suddenly, with limited infrastructure or history, the organisation was competing against others with a longer history and brand as if we were equals.

I believe that data exploitation is bounded only by the knowledge we individually have and the constraints we therefore impose on what we do with it. There are plenty of organisations doing some really innovative data projects that shifts the way they tackle some of the biggest challenges they face to be transformational in the direction they are heading. There are some pioneering activities, but many organisations are still lagging behind when it comes to exploiting their data effectively.

In the first half of my career, I can claim to have been a pioneer in so much of what was achieved. None of this was inventing something from scratch; instead it was applying a number of activities or techniques collectively in a way that delivered something that had not been considered before or executed effectively. I look at my work today and the same applies – how can we take a number of things which are known and understood in their own right, but collectively achieve something which is transformational or delivering value that would otherwise fail to be realised.

When you embark on a data strategy, take a moment to think about the aspirations of the organisation and think outside the box. We are in a world awash with data – organisations have been deluged with what was termed 'big data' by marketing people out to invent a term for something many organisations already possessed but had made little use of – and the internet contains so much data it is often difficult to sort the wheat from the chaff.

Increasingly, any search for insight will produce as many positive as negative views on what is purportedly reality – the whole debate on coronavirus vaccines raging at the time of writing this book is evidence in itself of being able to use data in a way which confounds scientific sense in terms of a risk assessment and where the experts are losing the battle over the misinterpretation of data, whether innocently or maliciously. However, be bold, do not be timid in seizing the opportunity that defining a data strategy presents to you. It is your opportunity to demonstrate 'the art of the possible', to paint a picture that is visionary in what data could do for your organisation. You may be wary of setting high expectations, and that aspiration is fine so long as you have a clearly defined path to how you get there and, most importantly, the foundations that are essential for this to be deliverable.

A data strategy is an opportunity to say 'I know you say you want to achieve that, but what if we were able to go further, and achieve this?' It is your opportunity to bring data out from the shadows of the organisation. Let me bring this to life for you.

I mentioned earlier in the book that data is like water; it is renewable and a source of life for your organisation. In the UK a litre of water costs around one penny, and is therefore a commodity much like data in its raw form. Both water and data can degrade if not properly maintained and there is a need for constant review to ensure compliance with quality standards at every step to it reaching the end user. However, think about the value of water and the parallels with data increase. Champagne is 85 per cent water (albeit not straight from a domestic tap), so – whether it is the UK's favourite Moët & Chandon at £38 a bottle, or a Taste of Diamonds 2013 at £1.2 million – consider how much value has been added to that 85 per cent water content. Then think about the parallels with data, how data captured at minimal cost in the course of an interaction with a supplier, customer or other party can support decisions worth millions to your organisation.

This is why data strategy is important. You have the opportunity to distinguish your organisation, through its performance, as one of the pre-eminent champagne houses in your particular market. Every organisation has access to data; we all have the opportunity to collect and exploit it and do so securely, compliantly and effectively. It is a common denominator but is still a differentiator due to many organisations not seizing the opportunity to establish data as an asset and manage it accordingly to maximise its value. How do you do it better than anyone else, how does yours become the organisation that lifts itself above its peers and how are you seen as a top performer in the sector in which you operate? That is your opportunity, and that is your challenge.

12.16 TEN TO TAKE AWAY

This chapter has summarised the book as a whole, and highlighted some final thoughts. The final ten points to take away are less a repetition of points already made and referenced in the preceding chapters, and more advice in conclusion.

1. Reflect on the opening quote to this chapter. How much of what it says about the barriers being imagination and inertia is reflective of your own experience in your organisation, and where do you intend to start to challenge the culture? This is not a generic quote: it is directly about data and analytics, the subject of your data strategy, so it is likely reflective of your own organisation to some extent too – consider the culture of your organisation and baseline the starting point before embarking on an ambitious vision.

2. Are you going to change the culture or seek to get it to embrace what you are doing? Neither is easy, both present a challenge, but the tactics you adopt need to be clear. You cannot ignore culture, just as culture will not ignore what you are doing. Whether you are aware or not, culture is watching your every move, so bring it to the fore of your thinking, from strategy definition to execution.

3. Resilience is key. You may have a project team, or it may be a singular endeavour. Either way, there will be ups and downs in the programme, and you need to prepare for these and keep others motivated when there are days that don't go so well. Chart your course; recognise storms will arise and you may have to navigate your way differently from time to time to stay afloat. Don't lose sight of your destination, and make progress rapidly when conditions permit. There is no harm in getting ahead of the plan if conditions allow, just as it is not a sign of failure to use contingency or revisit some of the deliverables if necessary.

4. Consider the journey, your organisation and the implementation approach. Are you a revolutionary or more likely to succeed as an evolutionary? Recognise that this is entirely organisation dependent, potentially at a point in time, and choose accordingly. It may even be a combination, should you discover parts of the data strategy implementation need a more revolutionary approach due to the nature of the situation you find yourself in.

5. Keep a focus on prioritisation, dependencies and capabilities. These are three areas which may keep you awake at night if not managed tightly by using an integrated plan to keep a balance as you navigate. There are often creative ways in which you can adjust, often in the short term, so do not sacrifice the opportunity to do so through a dogmatic approach to the plan if it is likely to hinder you. Again, communication about these three is critical. Keep stakeholders informed, explain your reasoning and build their trust in your leadership.

6. Reflect on the pyramid of sponsor, senior executives and stakeholder engagement to secure buy-in. If you lose sight of these, even for a moment, you will undermine your programme. An effective sponsor can smooth the path, building consensus and winning over doubters through providing senior-level objectivity and credibility, so ensure you provide your sponsor with as much useful information that you can to provide backing to your programme.

7. Bring communications into the fold as a stream in itself within your programme. The evidence provided throughout this book has demonstrated that poor communication is one of the biggest causes of failure in strategy definition and execution, so don't become another statistic in the failed programme column. Identify as many opportunities as you can to use communications to your advantage, make the messaging about the core content where possible rather than calling out the data strategy specifically and build trust through using others' content. The more voices, the more routes to get the message across, the greater the chance of it landing.

8. Throughout the book the message of alignment with the corporate strategy has been stressed. It is an imperative to ground your data strategy in a common purpose that the corporate strategy should provide. Consider how your strategy aligns with other strategies within the organisation and what dependencies exist between the data strategy and others already out there. Build links, establish common goals and share messaging. There will be a greater chance of combined success by working together than each operating in a silo.

9. A strategy cannot be delivered without a plan; implementation needs coherence to bring together the moving parts in a structured approach that is coordinated and interlocking. Through the course of the strategy definition, you should have had a mind to how implementation would look, and in the implementation, you need a focus on delivery and managing dependencies. Make sure your plan is measurable, as your sponsor and senior executives will want evidence of progress and how implementation is delivering what they signed up to in the data strategy.

10. Finally, learn as you deliver. I am an advocate of rolling strategies, adjusting and reflecting as each year passes, using learning to adapt and evolve the strategy to suit business needs and the experience gained in strategy implementation. My experience tells me that the implementation rarely goes according to plan, and so it is feasible that progress may be slower than envisaged (though occasionally can be faster!) due to obstacles which were not foreseen at the outset or changes in direction or resource availability. Consider what has been achieved, what lies ahead and how the corporate goals are shaping up – is the data strategy still relevant and, if so, how can the data strategy implementation help the organisation reach its goals faster?

I would like to wish you well in your endeavour and to remind you that the course from start to finish on the data strategy journey is likely to be a challenging one, almost certainly not as you envisaged it at the outset. Do not lose faith, or feel like it is overwhelming and lose confidence, and do not become consumed by the number of moving parts, trying to keep your focus on too many things. Keep your eye on the goal and ensure you keep communicating. Recognise that there is a need to be agile in your approach and keep focused on where you are going and what have you learnt.

Each day in the world of data strategy is an opportunity to move forward and apply what you didn't know just a day, a week or a month ago. Do not fall into the trap of being driven by your own plan and fail to apply that learning, for it is the best guide you will ever have as to how your organisation is likely to react. Whilst past performance is no guarantee of future outcomes, in an organisation with a strong culture, a history of 'this is how we do things' and a low level of data maturity, it offers the most powerful insight you can have. Learn, adapt and avoid making the same mistakes – such repetition is likely to fatally undermine your credibility – and you will have every chance of keeping on the challenging path to using the data strategy as a key enabler of transforming your organisation and delivering the corporate goals.

Good luck with your next steps and I wish you well on the journey to a successful data strategy implementation!

GLOSSARY

Agile: An approach often used in project and programme management to time-box delivery activity in iterations, or short planned phases, to achieve incrementally the overall goal whilst retaining a focus on quality. It originated as the Agile Manifesto in 2001 following a group of like-minded individuals defining a different, lighter approach to software development. It is now used more extensively than just in software development, with a variety of forms – Scrum, dynamic systems development method (DSDM), XP, to name a few.

Artificial intelligence: Machine intelligence that uses systems to think and act to make decisions. There are numerous forms of artificial intelligence (AI), from what is termed 'weak AI' or artificial narrow intelligence (ANI), which is designed for a specific purpose and is most abundant today (for example Amazon's Alexa, or Apple's Siri); to artificial general intelligence (AGI), which has a self-aware consciousness to be able to solve problems, learn and plan for the future; to artificial super intelligence (ASI), which goes beyond the capacity of the human brain and is thought to be still at the theoretical stage in terms of active applications.

Benefits: A quantifiable improvement achieved from an activity to transform a situation via an input, which could be a programme or simply a series of tasks. Typically, benefits are identified in advance of an activity, so the progress can be monitored from an agreed baseline.

Big data: Significant and diverse data sets now being handled by many organisations – structured and unstructured – that are characterised by the 3 Vs: greater variety, velocity and volume. The explosion of internet-based data, whether social media or Internet of Things (IoT) applications, and the doubling of data available every two years[1] has led to the development of different ways to capture and process data, and two further Vs being added for consideration: value and veracity.

Business intelligence: An embracing term for the technologies, processes and architectural principles which enable an organisation to transform raw data into the appropriate outputs to make effective decisions based on insight and business performance, derived through the coherence that the whole suite of business intelligence activities provides.

---

1 J. Gantz and D. Reinsel, *Extracting Value from Chaos*. IDC Digital Universe study, 2011.

Change management: The use of structured processes to shift an organisation to a future state in which it delivers outcomes that achieve different, desired goals and has stakeholder engagement embedded within it. Typically, change management is people-focused, so it is closely aligned with culture.

Culture: The shared values, attitudes and characteristics of an organisation. These may be quite different to the published 'corporate' definition of the organisation's culture, evolving organically, and are shaped by events which define expectations, norms and beliefs over time. Whilst some of this may be documented, much of it will not be.

Data accessibility: The ease of gaining access to data within the organisation, recognising that controls may need to be in place for compliance purposes that restrict some access rights.

Data acquisition: The process of gaining data from other sources, including procurement of data from third party data providers. This may be to plug gaps in existing data sets or to enhance these data sets through the addition of data not available from within the organisation.

Data architecture: Models, policies, standards or rules that define how data is to be collected, stored, distributed, transformed and made accessible to relevant users to enable the achievement of business outcomes.

Data compliance: Ensuring data is captured, stored and made accessible in ways that conform to legislative and regulatory frameworks. These will include data privacy, data protection and data segregation, where appropriate.

Data exchange: The sending, and receipt, of data in a manner which enables it to be consumed in a structured format that prevents any loss or misinterpretation as a result of the process.

Data exploitation: The application of a range of tools and techniques to data to enable meaning and, therefore, value to be drawn from it. It is the interpretation and knowledge derived from data, and this ranges from the presentation of information via reporting, through analytics and insight to the world of artificial intelligence.

Data governance: The collective term that encompasses processes, roles, policies, standards and measures to manage and protect the data asset within an organisation. It includes people, process and technology, and is the key driver in ensuring data quality, compliance and integrity are maintained.

Data integration: The act of combining data from different sources into a single unified view within a system. It is often related to data migration, in which data is moved from one system to another, typically in the case of replacing systems, in which the final step is data integration.

Data lake: A centralised repository in which structured and unstructured data sets can be stored and accessed. This usually stores raw data in its native form, which differentiates it from other approaches (for example data warehouse), with the user manipulating data in the repository as required for the specific purpose for which it is needed. Due to the complexity involved, principal users tend to be data scientists and analysts who are comfortable dealing with large data sets held in an unstructured format, with the knowledge of how to integrate these for their immediate need.

Data maturity: An assessment of an organisation's sophistication in managing and exploiting the data it holds, and the extent to which data is used to underpin decision making across the organisation. This provides a clear methodology and measurement to track the progress an organisation is making in becoming more data mature.

Data modelling: A visual representation to illustrate connections between data within a system or across systems to enable coherence in understanding the data landscape. There are numerous types of data models which can be developed, each having its own purpose, with the logical data model determining how the data should be curated, and the physical data model representing the actual way data is held within a system.

Data quality: The multiple dimensions against which data can be assessed. Depending on what is relevant to the organisation, and the data attribute being assessed, these would typically reflect different levels of data quality maturity: completeness, validity, consistency, uniqueness, integrity, auditability, accuracy, precision, timeliness, relevance, reliability. Each of these will carry their own definitions as to what element of quality they seek to determine. Data quality can be difficult to specify, as it is often a question of how much you are prepared to invest to assure data is of quality due to its propensity (in many cases) to date and degrade if not maintained.

Data retention: Often referred to as records retention, the policies and processes for determining the period over which data is kept within the organisation. There is usually an organisational imperative that determines the retention period, but there must also be cognisance of compliance obligations. It covers not only data in active use, but that which is archived or 'soft' deleted on systems.

Data science: An extension of analytics that has embraced the exponential growth in computing power and intelligence to provide additional capabilities which broaden analytics into a programming environment much broader than that of a traditional analytics approach.

Data security: Specific controls, standard policies and procedures to protect data from a range of issues, including unauthorised access, accidental loss and destruction. The core elements are known as the CIA triad – confidentiality, integrity and availability.

Data standards: Documented agreements on representation, format, definition, structuring, tagging, transmission, manipulation, use and management of data.

Data transformation: The conversion of data from one format or structure to another. It is often part of a wider process known as extract, transform and load, which is commonly used in data warehouse design when data is recomposed in a format which is consistent for all incoming data sets being integrated into the warehouse.

Data virtualisation: The aggregation of real-time data, whether structured or unstructured, in-memory as an abstraction layer rather than a physical transfer of data. Unlike data warehousing that relies on extract-transform-load (ETL) processes, data virtualisation accesses data from source rather than processing it as an extract routine.

Data visualisation: The delivery of data, typically as information or other refined forms, in a visual and appealing way (such as charts, graphs or maps) to give greater insight or understanding to the recipient.

Data warehouse: Aggregated structured data from multiple sources integrated into a central repository to enable interrogation for reporting and analytics. Typically, this will hold historical data to provide trends and to reduce the burden of running queries on data held in operational/transactional systems.

Descriptive analytics: The process of providing information to illustrate *what* happened or is happening. It is also commonly referred to as reporting, or management information, as it provides a reliable way of processing breadth of data over a time series to report trends and performance.

Diagnostic analytics: An assessment of *why* something happened and, as such, a build on descriptive analytics. It seeks to establish the root cause of an event, using techniques such as probability, likelihood and distribution of outcomes to explore the data.

Evaluation: A systematic assessment of the design, implementation and outcomes of an intervention. It involves understanding how an intervention is being, or has been, implemented and what effects it has, for whom and why. It identifies what can be improved and estimates its overall impacts and cost-effectiveness.

Knowledge management: An integrated approach to the process of identifying, capturing, evaluating, retrieving and sharing information, from wherever sourced, and effectively using knowledge across an organisation to provide an information environment which can be accessed and exploited.

Machine learning: A branch of artificial intelligence focused on building applications that learn from data and improve their accuracy over time without being programmed to do so.

Master data management: The creation of a single master record for all critical business data, across internal and external data sources and applications. This information becomes a consistent, reliable source for an organisation, and has primacy over other data.

Metadata: A summarised definition of a data attribute. There are six types of metadata: descriptive metadata, which provides basic core information; structural metadata, relating to the nature of the data being described; preservation metadata, which enables it to be managed appropriately; provenance metadata, which provides data on its origins; use metadata, capturing how the data is used; and administrative metadata, which records any rules, restrictions or constraints on how data can be utilised.

Milestone: A point in a project (or programme) where specific outputs have been achieved on the project timeline. It may mark a shift in the project from one phase to another, or simply some significant achievement within the project that is clearly evident.

Open data: Data that is available to everyone to access, use and share. It must be licensed, permitting it to be used by anyone in any way they want, including transforming, combining and sharing it with others, even commercially.

Performance management: The methodologies, metrics, processes and systems used to monitor and manage the business performance of an enterprise. It can also be used to describe the performance of an employee within the organisation via a process of review with a manager.

Portfolio management: The selection, prioritisation and control of an organisation's programmes and projects, in line with its strategic objectives and capacity to deliver.

Predictive analytics: The use of advanced analytic techniques that leverage historical data to uncover real-time insights and to predict future events. The goal is to go beyond knowing what has happened to providing a best assessment of what will happen, and some sense of *when*.

Prescriptive analytics: Finding the best course of action in a scenario, given the available data, to influence *how* an organisation should be proactive in its actions. It is related to both descriptive analytics and predictive analytics, but emphasises actionable insights. Prescriptive analytics is the final step of the analytics continuum.

Programme management: A delivery mechanism to achieve change through the combination and coordination of a series of projects, or activities, that collectively contribute to the totality of the change and enable the delivery of the strategic objectives and direction of the organisation. Programme management is designed to guide the organisation through this dynamic environment, refining and refocusing as necessary along the way. Programmes are concerned with delivering outcomes, whereas projects are focused on outputs.

Project management: The coordinated means to structure a set of agreed activities with a definite start, middle and end to achieve the overall objective using a coherent and disciplined approach. Project management provides structure and control of the project environment so that the agreed activities will produce the right products or services to meet the customer's expectations.

Red team: The practice of rigorously challenging plans, policies, systems and assumptions by adopting an adversarial approach. A red team may be a contracted external party or an internal group that uses strategies to encourage an outsider perspective.

Requirements: The elicitation, analysis, specification and validation of requirements and constraints to a level that enables effective development and operations of new or changed software, systems, processes, products and services.

Risk management: The art and science of identifying, analysing and responding to risk factors throughout the life of a project and in the best interests of its objectives.

Route map: A high-level, easy-to-understand overview of the important elements of a programme (or project) plan. It provides a quick snapshot of the aims, important milestones, key deliverables, dependencies and possible risks.

Scrum: A process framework that is one of a number of methodologies to utilise an Agile approach, which involves breaking down activity into stages known as sprints. These are time-boxed periods in which the scope is agreed and optimised for the sprint window. A daily review is conducted to track progress and work through the deliverables collaboratively as a team, including a Scrum master and the product owner.

Stakeholder: Individuals and organisations who are actively involved in, or whose interests may be positively or negatively affected as a result of, the activity being undertaken.

Unstructured data: Data that is not in tabular or delimited format. Examples include natural language documents, email, speech, images and video. It is information that has not been specifically encoded for machines to process but rather authored by humans for humans to understand.

Use cases: The description of how an individual will utilise a system or process to accomplish a goal or a business objective. It is a common practice in software development and used extensively as part of Agile, but has become more widely used as a means to assist with process definition in organisations. It consists of an actor (the user), a system (or process) and a goal (which represents the desired outcome).

User stories: A way of capturing the experience described by those specifying the need to be able to define what the outcome should achieve, feel like or deliver. They are relatively detailed, and are then used in the sprint and product backlog process of Agile to determine what will be delivered at the end of a sprint to the customer. They tend to be structured in a broadly common format.

Waymarker: One of a series of signs used to mark out a route. In a strategy implementation context, the use of waymarkers is the logical approach to designate direction and an overarching indication of likely progress, rather than milestones, which provide more detailed definition.

BIBLIOGRAPHY

STRATEGY

Books

Aiken, P., Harbour, T., Kelly, E., Walsh, B., Walter, K. (2020) *The CDO Journey: Insights and Advice for Data Leaders*. Basking Ridge, NJ: Technics Publications

Ansoff, H.I. (1965) *Corporate Strategy: An Analytic Approach to Business Policy for Growth and Expansion*. London: McGraw-Hill

Brandenburger, A.M., Nalebuff, B.J. (1996) *Co-opetition*. New York: Currency Doubleday

Branson, R. (2013) *Like a Virgin: Secrets They Won't Teach You at Business School*. United London: Virgin

Carruthers, C., Jackson, P. (2017) *The Chief Data Officer's Playbook*. London: Facet Publishing

Chan Kim, W., Mauborgne, R. (2005) *Blue Ocean Strategy: How to Create Uncontested Market Space and Make the Competition Irrelevant*. Boston, MA: Harvard Business School Press

Chandler, A.D. (1962) *Strategy and Structure: Chapters in the History of Industrial Enterprise*. Boston, MA: MIT Press

Covey, S., McChesney, C., Huling, J. (2016) *The 4 Disciplines of Execution: Achieving Your Wildly Important Goals*. New York: Free Press

Davis, J.R., Frechette, H.M., Boswell, E.H. (2010) *Strategic Speed: Mobilize People, Accelerate Execution*. Boston, MA: Harvard Business Press

De Flander, J., Schreurs, K. (2012) *The Strategy Execution Barometer*. Expanded edition. Enschede, The Netherlands: Performance Factory

Drucker, P.F. (1954) *The Practice of Management*. New York: Harper & Row

Drucker, P.F. (1973) *Management: Tasks, Responsibilities, Practices*. New York: Harper & Row

Greenwald, B.C.N., Kahn, J. (2007) *Competition Demystified: A Radically Simplified Approach to Business Strategy*. New York: Portfolio

Hamel, G., Prahalad, C.K. (1994) *Competing for the Future*. Boston, MA: Harvard Business School Press

Hamel, G., Prahalad, C.K. (2010) *Strategic Intent*. Boston, MA: Harvard Business School Press

Hart, B.H.L. (1974). *Strategy*. New York: Penguin

Hiebeler, R., Kelly, T.B., Ketteman, C. (1998) *Best Practices: Building Your Business with Arthur Andersen's Global Best Practices*. New York: Simon & Schuster

Johnson, G., Scholes, K. (1993) *Exploring Corporate Strategy: Text and Cases*. Hemel Hempstead: Prentice Hall

Johnson, G., Whittington, R., Scholes, K. (2012) *Fundamentals of Strategy*. Harlow: Pearson Education

Kaplan, R., Norton, D. (2001) *The Strategy-Focused Organization: How Balanced Scorecard Companies Thrive in the New Business Environment*. Boston, MA: Harvard Business School Press

Lafley, A.G., Martin, R.L. (2013) *Playing to Win: How Strategy Really Works*. Boston, MA: Harvard Business Review Press

Leinwand, P., Mainardi, C.R. (2016). *Strategy That Works: How Winning Companies Close the Strategy-to-Execution Gap*. Boston, MA: Harvard Business Review Press

Marr, B. (2017) *Data Strategy: How to Profit from a World of Big Data, Analytics and the Internet of Things*. London: Kogan Page

McKeown, M. (2019) *The Strategy Book: How to Think and Act Strategically to Deliver Outstanding Results*. Harlow: Pearson Education

Mintzberg, H. (1994) *The Rise and Fall of Strategic Planning*. Hemel Hempstead: Prentice Hall

Mintzberg, H., Ahlstrand, B., Lampel, J. (2009) *Strategy Safari: A Guided Tour through the Wilds of Strategic Management*. Harlow: Pearson Education

Montgomery, C.A. (2012) *The Strategist: Be the Leader Your Business Needs*. New York: HarperCollins

Ohmae, K. (1982) *The Mind of the Strategist*. New York: McGraw-Hill

Osterwald, A., Pigneur, Y. (2010) *Business Model Generation*. Hoboken, NJ: Wiley

Porter, M. (1980) *Competitive Strategy: Techniques for Analyzing Industries and Competitors*. New York: Free Press

Rumelt, R. (2012). *Good Strategy, Bad Strategy: The Difference and Why It Matters*. London: Profile Books

Steiner, G. (1979) *Strategic Planning: What Every Manager Must Know*. New York: Free Press

Treacy, M., Wiersema, F.D. (1997) *The Discipline of Market Leaders: Choose Your Customers, Narrow Your Focus, Dominate Your Market*. Cambridge: Perseus Books

Tregoe, B., Zimmerman, J. (1980) *Top Management Strategy: What It Is and How to Make It Work*. New York: Simon & Schuster

Whittington, R. (1993) *What Is Strategy – and Does It Matter?* London: Routledge

Articles, online publications and reports

Bridges Business Consultancy Int Pte Ltd (2008) What Drives Strategy Implementation? Top Line Findings. www.bridgesconsultancy.com/research-case-study/research/

Bridges Business Consultancy Int Pte Ltd (2012) Strategy Implementation Survey. www.bridgesconsultancy.com/research-case-study/research/

Bridges Business Consultancy Int Pte Ltd (2016) Strategy Implementation Survey. www.bridgesconsultancy.com/research-case-study/research/

Buluswar, M. (2016) How Companies Are Using Big Data and Analytics. https://www.mckinsey.com/business-functions/mckinsey-analytics/our-insights/how-companies-are-using-big-data-and-analytics

Cândido, C.J.F., Santos, S.P. (2015) Strategy Implementation: What Is the Failure Rate? *Journal of Management & Organization*, 21 (2), 237–262

Curucci, R (2017), Executives Fail to Execute Strategy Because They're Too Internally Focused. *Harvard Business Review* (November)

DalleMule, L. and Davenport, T.H. (2017) What's Your Data Strategy? *Harvard Business Review* (May–June)

De Bussy, N.M., Suprawan, L. (2012) Most Valuable Stakeholders: The Impact of Employee Orientation on Corporate Financial Performance. *Public Relations Review* 38, 280–287. https://espace.curtin.edu.au/handle/20.500.11937/62193

De Flander, J. (2015) The Strategy Execution Barometer. The Performance Factory. https://jeroen-de-flander.com/wp-content/uploads/2015/08/Master-Class_Jeroen-De-Flander_Slides_f-1.pdf

Dontha, R. (2018) Data Strategy – What, Why, When, Who, Where. https://digitaltransformationpro.com/data-strategy-5ws/

Economist Intelligence Unit (2013) Why Good Strategies Fail: Lessons for the C-Suite. https://eiuperspectives.economist.com/strategy-leadership/why-good-strategies-fail_

Henderson, B.D. (1981) The Concept of Strategy. https://www.bcg.com/publications/1981/concept-of-strategy

Henderson, B.D. (1989) The Origin of Strategy. *Harvard Business Review* (November–December)

Horwath, B. (2020) The Origin of Strategy. https://www.strategyskills.com/the-origin-of-strategy/

Institute of Customer Service (2017) The Customer Knows. https://www.instituteofcustomerservice.com/product/the-customer-knows-how-employee-engagement-leads-to-greater-customer-satisfaction-and-loyalty/

Percy, S. (2019) Why Do Change Programs Fail? Forbes. https://www.forbes.com/sites/sallypercy/2019/03/13/why-do-change-programs-fail/#112e91872e48

Project One (n.d.) Mobilising Change Programmes – I've Started, So I'll Finish! https://projectone.com/mobilising-change-programmes-ive-started-so-ill-finish/

Sull, D., Homkes, R., Sull, C. (2015) Why Strategy Execution Unravels – and What to Do About It. *Harvard Business Review* (March). https://hbr.org/2015/03/why-strategy-execution-unravelsand-what-to-do-about-it

Vermeulen, F. (2017) Many Strategies Fail Because They're Not Actually Strategies. *Harvard Business Review*

DATA MANAGEMENT (INCLUDING GOVERNANCE, COMPLIANCE AND QUALITY)

Books

Batini, C., Scannapieco, M. (2006) *Data Quality Concepts, Methodologies and Techniques.* Heidelberg: Springer-Verlag

Chisholm, M.D. (2010) *Definitions in Information Management: A Guide to the Fundamental Semantic Metadata.* Canada: ByDesign Media

DAMA International, Data Management Association (2017) *DAMA-DMBOK2: Data Management Body of Knowledge.* United States: Technics Publications

Funk, J.D., Pipino, L.L., Wang, R.Y., Lee, Y.W. (2009) *Journey to Data Quality.* Cambridge, MA: MIT Press

Gordon, K. (2013) *Principles of Data Management.* Swindon: BCS

IT Governance Privacy Team (2020) *EU General Data Protection Regulation (GDPR): An Implementation and Compliance Guide.* Ely: ITGP

Kent, W., Hoberman, S. (2012) *Data and Reality: A Timeless Perspective on Perceiving and Managing Information in Our Imprecise World.* Basking Ridge, NJ: Technics Publications

Ladley, J. (2012) *Data Governance: How to Design, Deploy and Sustain an Effective Data Governance Program.* Burlington, MA: Morgan Kaufmann

Landoll, D.J. (2016) *Information Security Policies, Procedures, and Standards: A Practitioner's Reference.* Boca Raton, FL: Taylor & Francis

Loshin, D. (2010) *Master Data Management.* Burlington, MA: Morgan Kaufmann

McGilvray, D. (2008) *Executing Data Quality Projects: Ten Steps to Quality Data and Trusted Information.* Burlington, MA: Morgan Kaufmann

O'Keefe, K., O Brien, D. (2018) *Ethical Data and Information Management: Concepts, Tools and Methods.* London: Kogan Page

Olson, J.E. (2003) *Data Quality: The Accuracy Dimension.* Burlington, MA: Morgan Kaufmann

Redman, T.C. (1996) *Data Quality for the Information Age.* London: Artech House

Rhind, G.R. (2001) *Practical International Data Management: A Guide to Working with Global Names and Addresses.* Aldershot: Gower

Sadiq, S. (2013) *Handbook of Data Quality: Research and Practice.* Berlin Heidelberg: Springer-Verlag

Schwarzenbach, J., King, T. (2020) *Managing Data Quality: A Practical Guide.* Swindon: BCS

Seiner, R.S. (2014) *Non-Invasive Data Governance: The Path of Least Resistance and Greatest Success.* United States: Technics Publications

Smith, P., Edge, J., Wilkinson, D., Parry, S. (2016) *Crossing the Data Delta: Turn the Data You Have into the Information You Need.* United Kingdom: Entity Group Limited

Online publications and reports

Experian (2021) The Data Debate: A Forward View Of Key Trends for 2021 and Beyond (report). https://www.experian.co.uk/blogs/latest-thinking/data-quality/the-data-debate-a-forward-view-of-key-trends-for-2021-and-beyond/

Good Manufacturing Practice (GMP)/US Food and Drug Administration (FDA) (2020) 21 CFR Part 11 – ALCOA. https://www.fda.gov/drugs/pharmaceutical-quality-resources/current-good-manufacturing-practice-cgmp-regulations

Kauzlarich, T., Wertheimer, D., Heigel, J. (2014) Data Integrity's Central Role in Financial Compliance: Maintaining Regulatory Compliance with Dodd-Frank Rule 1.73. https://cdn2.hubspot.net/hub/293735/file-947400499-pdf/Documents/Sagence_Data_Integrity_Role_2014_MAY.pdf

Scriffignano, A. (2019) The Past, Present, and Future of Data (report). Dun & Bradstreet

US Federal Data Strategy (2020) Federal Data Strategy Data Governance Playbook. https://resources.data.gov/assets/documents/fds-data-governance-playbook.pdf

DATA MODELLING AND DESIGN

Books

Hernandez, M.J. (2013) *Database Design for Mere Mortals: A Hands-On Guide to Relational Database Design.* United States: Pearson Education

Inmon, W.I. (2005) *Building the Data Warehouse.* United States: Wiley

Inmon, W.I. (2016) *Data Lake Architecture: Designing the Data Lake and Avoiding the Garbage Dump.* United States: Technics Publications

Kimball, R., Ross, M. (2013) *The Data Warehouse Toolkit: The Definitive Guide to Dimensional Modeling.* United States: Wiley

Kleppmann, M. (2017) *Designing Data-Intensive Applications: The Big Ideas Behind Reliable, Scalable, and Maintainable Systems.* Japan: O'Reilly Media

Knifton, D. (2016) *The Data Model Toolkit: Simple Skills to Model The Real World.* United Kingdom: Paragon Publishing

Lemahieu, W., van den Broucke, S., Baesens, B. (2018) *Principles of Database Management: The Practical Guide to Storing, Managing and Analyzing Big and Small Data.* United Kingdom: Cambridge University Press

Sherman, R. (2014) *Business Intelligence Guidebook: From Data Integration to Analytics*. Netherlands: Elsevier Science

Silverston, L. (2001) *The Data Model Resource Book*, volume 2: *A Library of Universal Data Models by Industry Types*. New York: Wiley

Silverston, L. (2008) *The Data Model Resource Book*, volume 3: *Universal Patterns for Data Modeling*. New York: Wiley

Silverston, L., Simsion, G. (2001) *The Data Model Resource Book*, volume 1: *A Library of Universal Data Models for All Enterprises*. New York: Wiley

Online publications

Anderson, D. (2017) Data Model Design and Best Practices (Parts 1–4). Talend. https://www.talend.com/blog/2017/05/05/data-model-design-best-practices-part-1/

Kimball Group (2013) Dimensional Modeling Techniques. www.kimballgroup.com/wp-content/uploads/2013/08/2013.09-Kimball-Dimensional-Modeling-Techniques11.pdf

Milne, J. (2021) 6 Data Modeling Techniques for Better Business Intelligence. Klipfolio Labs. https://www.klipfolio.com/blog/6-Data-Modeling-Techniques

Tackels, D. The Definitive Guide to Data Modeling. Sigma Computing. https://www.sigmacomputing.com/blog/the-definitive-guide-to-data-modeling/

DATA MONETISATION/VALUE

Books

Aiken, P., Billings, J. (2013) *Monetizing Data Management: Finding the Value in your Organization's Most Important Asset*. Basking Ridge, NJ: Technics Publications

Laney, D.B. (2018) *Infonomics: How to Monetize, Manage, and Measure Information as an Asset for Competitive Advantage*. New York: Bibliomotion Inc.

Wells, A.R., Chiang, K.W. (2017) *Monetizing Your Data: A Guide to Turning Data into Profit-Driving Strategies and Solutions*. Hoboken, NJ: Wiley

Articles and online publications

Collins, V., Lanz, J. (2019) Managing Data as an Asset. *CPA Journal* (June). https://www.cpajournal.com/2019/06/24/managing-data-as-an-asset/

Moody, D.L., Walsh, P. (1999) Measuring the Value of Information: An Asset Valuation Approach. Seventh European Conference on Information Systems (ECIS '99). https://dblp.org/rec/conf/ecis/MoodyW99

PricewaterhouseCoopers (2019) Putting a Value on Data. https://www.pwc.co.uk/data-analytics/documents/putting-value-on-data.pdf

Short, J.E., Todd, S. (2017) What's Your Data Worth? *MIT Sloan Management Review* (Spring). https://sloanreview.mit.edu/article/whats-your-data-worth/

MANAGEMENT INFORMATION, REPORTING AND DATA VISUALISATION

Books

Aawar, W.A., Moutran, A. (2020) *PMP. Mastering the EVM: Earned Value Management.* United States: PMP Mastering Series

Association for Project Management Special Interest Group (2014) *Earned Value Management: APM Guidelines.* Princes Risborough: APM

Doerr, J. (2018) *Measure What Matters. OKRs: The Simple Idea that Drives 10x Growth.* New York: Portfolio Penguin Random House

Few, S. (2012) *Show Me the Numbers: Designing Tables and Graphs to Enlighten.* Burlingame, CA: Analytics Press

Gale, B.T., Bradley, T.G., Buzzell, R.D. (1987) *The PIMS Principles: Linking Strategy to Performance.* New York: Free Press

Healy, K. (2018) *Data Visualization: A Practical Introduction.* Princeton, NJ: Princeton University Press

Jeffrey, M. (2010) *Data-Driven Marketing: The 15 Metrics Everyone in Marketing Should Know.* Hoboken, NJ: Wiley

Kaplan, R.S., Norton, D.P. (1996) *The Balanced Scorecard: Translating Strategy into Action.* Boston, MA: Harvard Business Review Press

Kirk, A. (2019) *Data Visualisation: A Handbook for Data Driven Design.* London: SAGE Publications

Kirkpatrick, J.D., Kirkpatrick, W.K. (2016) *Kirkpatrick's Four Levels of Training Evaluation.* Alexandria, VA: ATD Press

Marr, B. (2012) *Key Performance Indicators: The 75 Measures Every Manager Needs to Know.* Harlow: Pearson Education

McCandless, D. (2014) *Knowledge Is Beautiful.* London: HarperCollins

Nussbaumer Knaflic, C. (2015) *Storytelling with Data: A Data Visualization Guide for Business Professionals.* Hoboken, NJ: Wiley

Parmenter, D. (2019) *Key Performance Indicators: Developing, Implementing, and Using Winning KPIs.* Hoboken, NJ: Wiley

Quagini, L., Tonchia, S. (2014) *Performance Measurement: Linking Balanced Scorecard to Business Intelligence.* Berlin: Springer-Verlag

Thorp, J. and Fujitsu Consulting Center for Strategic Leadership (2003) *The Information Paradox.* Whitby, Canada: McGraw-Hill Ryerson

Wexler, S., Shaffer, J., Cotgreave, A. (2017) *The Big Book of Dashboards: Visualizing Your Data Using Real-World Business Scenarios.* Hoboken, NJ: Wiley

Articles and online publications

Fogg, B.J. (2009) A Behavior Model for Persuasive Design. Proceedings of the 4th International Conference in Persuasive Technology. https://doi.org/10.1145/1541948.1541999

HM Treasury (2020) Magenta Book: Central Government Guidance on Evaluation. https:// assets.publishing.service.gov.uk/government/uploads/system/uploads/attachment_ data/file/879438/HMT_Magenta_Book.pdf

NSW Government Department of Premier and Cabinet (2016) NSW Government Program Evaluation Guidelines. https://arp.nsw.gov.au/assets/ars/f506555395/NSW-Government-Program-Evaluation-Guideline-January-2016_1.pdf

Schrader, P.G., Lawless, K.A. (2004) The Knowledge, Attitudes, & Behaviors Approach: How to Evaluate Performance and Learning in Complex Environments. *Performance Improvement* 43 (9), 8–15

Serra, J. (2013) Business Intelligence Maturity Assessment. https://www. sqlservercentral.com/blogs/business-intelligence-maturity-assessment

White, S.J. (2018) What is OKR? A Goal-Setting Framework for Thinking Big. https:// www.cio.com/article/3302036/okr-objectives-and-key-results-defined.html

Wishart, J. (2021) OKR vs KPI: What's the Difference Between OKRs and KPIs? https:// www.rhythmsystems.com/blog/okrs-vs-kpis-whats-the-difference-infographic

ANALYTICS

Books

Bari, A., Chaouchi, M., Jung, T. (2016) *Predictive Analytics for Dummies.* Hoboken, NJ: Wiley

Davenport, T.H., Morison, R., Harris, J.G. (2010) *Analytics at Work: Smarter Decisions, Better Results.* Boston, MA: Harvard Business Review Press

Dearborn, J. (2015) *Data Driven: How Performance Analytics Delivers Extraordinary Sales Results.* Hoboken, NJ: Wiley

Evans, J.R. (2016) *Business Analytics: Methods, Models, and Decisions.* Harlow: Pearson

Harris, J.G., Davenport, T.H. (2017). *Competing on Analytics: The New Science of Winning.* Boston, MA: Harvard Business Review Press

Levenson, A. (2016) *Strategic Analytics: Advancing Strategy Execution and Organizational Effectiveness.* Oakland, CA: Berrett-Koehler Publishers

Marr, B. (2015) *Big Data: Using SMART Big Data, Analytics and Metrics to Make Better Decisions and Improve Performance.* Chichester: Wiley

Marr, B. (2016) *Key Business Analytics: The 60+ Business Analysis Tools Every Manager Needs to Know.* Hemel Hempstead: FT Publishing International/Prentice Hall

Matthews, R. (2017) *Chancing It.* London: Profile Books

Nelson, G.S. (2018) *The Analytics Lifecycle Toolkit: A Practical Guide for an Effective Analytics Capability.* Hoboken, NJ: Wiley

Nguyen, T.H. (2016) *Leaders and Innovators: How Data-Driven Organizations Are Winning with Analytics.* Hoboken, NJ: Wiley

Tennent, J., Friend, G. (2011) *Guide to Business Modelling.* London: Wiley

Online publications

Accenture (2016) The 5As of Analytics Transformation: Embedding Analytics DNA into Business Decision Making. https://www.accenture.com/t20161201t011012z__w__/us-en/_acnmedia/pdf-33/accenture-analytics-the-5as-of-analytics-transformation.pdfla=en

Harvard Business Review Insight Report (2014) Predictive Analytics in Practice. *Harvard Business Review*. https://www.sas.com/content/dam/SAS/en_us/doc/whitepaper2/hbr-predictive-analytics-in-practice-107511.pdf

Olavsrud, T. (2020) Transforming Analytics into Business Impact. IDG Communications Ltd. https://www.cio.com/article/3572642/transforming-analytics-into-business-impact.html

Parks, R.F., Thambusamy, R. (2017) Understanding Business Analytics Success and Impact: A Qualitative Study. *Information Systems Education Journal* (*ISEDJ*) 15 (6) 43–55. https://files.eric.ed.gov/fulltext/EJ1151897.pdf

Stack, C., Westland, J. (2019) The Data and Analytics Leader: Your Competitive Advantage. https://www.spencerstuart.com/research-and-insight/the-data-and-analytics-leader

DATA SCIENCE, ARTIFICIAL INTELLIGENCE AND MACHINE LEARNING (INCLUDING ETHICS)

Books

Jagare, U. (2019) *Data Science Strategy for Dummies*. Hoboken, NJ: Wiley

Loukides, M., Mason, H., Patil, D.J. (2018) *Ethics and Data Science*. Sebastopol, CA: O'Reilly Media

Provost, F., Fawcett, T. (2013) *Data Science for Business: What You Need to Know about Data Mining and Data-Analytic Thinking*. Sebastopol, CA: O'Reilly Media

Ridge, E. (2014) *Guerrilla Analytics: A Practical Approach to Working with Data*. Burlington, MA: Morgan Kaufmann

Online publications

Bowne-Anderson, H. (2018) What Data Scientists Really Do, According to 35 Data Scientists. https://hbr.org/2018/08/what-data-scientists-really-do-according-to-35-data-scientists

Central Digital and Data Office (2020) Data Ethics Framework. https://www.gov.uk/government/publications/data-ethics-framework/data-ethics-framework-2020

Diebold, F.X. (2000) 'Big Data' Dynamic Factor Models for Macroeconomic Measurement and Forecasting. 8th World Congress of the Econometric Society. https://www.sas.upenn.edu/~fdiebold/papers/paper40/temp-wc.pdf

Fujitsu (2019) Driving a Trusted Future in a Radically Changing World. https://www.fujitsu.com/uk/imagesgig5/driving-a-trusted-future-research-report-uk.pdf

Hasselbalch, G. (2019) Making Sense of Data Ethics: The Powers behind the Data Ethics Debate in European Policymaking. *Internet Policy Review* 8(2). https://policyreview.info/articles/analysis/making-sense-data-ethics-powers-behind-data-ethics-debate-european-policymaking

Keller, S.A., Shipp, S.S., Schroeder, A.D., Korkmaz, G. (2020) Doing Data Science: A Framework and Case Study. https://hdsr.mitpress.mit.edu/pub/hnptx6lq/release/8

Press, G. (2013) A Very Short History of Data Science. Forbes. https://www.forbes.com/sites/gilpress/2013/05/28/a-very-short-history-of-data-science/

UK Statistics Authority (2021) Identifying Gaps, Opportunities and Priorities in the Applied Data Ethics Guidance Landscape. https://uksa.statisticsauthority.gov.uk/publication/identifying-gaps-opportunities-and-priorities-in-the-applied-data-ethics-guidance-landscape/

TRANSFORMATION AND CHANGE

Books

Anthony, S.D., Gilbert, C.K., Johnson, M.W. (2017) *Dual Transformation: How to Reposition Today's Business While Creating the Future*. Boston, MA: Harvard Business Review Press

Arora, A., Dahlstrom, P., Hjartar, K., Wunderlich, F. (2020) *Fast Times: How Digital Winners Set Direction, Learn and Adapt*. United States: Amazon Publishing

Herzberg, F., Mausner, B., Block Snyderman, B. (1959) *The Motivation to Work*. 2nd edn. New York: Wiley

Imai, M. (1986) *Kaizen: The Key to Japan's Competitive Success*. New York: McGraw-Hill

Kotter, J.P. (1996) *Leading Change*. Boston, MA: Harvard Business School Press

Kotter, J., Rathgeber, H. (2017) *Our Iceberg Is Melting: Changing and Succeeding under Any Conditions*. London: Pan Macmillan

Mascarenhas, O.A.J. (2011) *Business Transformation Strategies: The Strategic Leader as Innovation Manager*. New Delhi: SAGE Publications

Saldanha, T. (2019) *Why Digital Transformations Fail: The Surprising Disciplines of How to Take off and Stay Ahead*. Oakland, CA: Berrett-Koehler Publishers

Zaltman, G., Duncan, R. (1977) *Strategies for Planned Change*. New York: Wiley

Articles and online publications

Balogun, J., Hope Hailey, V., Cleaver, I. (2015) Landing Transformational Change: Closing the Gap between Theory and Practice. CIPD Research Report

Doty, E. (2016) Starting a Transformation? Don't Change Everything. *Strategy+business* (January)

Hultman, K. (2003) Managing Resistance to Change. *Encyclopedia of Information Systems*. https://www.academia.edu/595772/Managing_Resistance_to_Change

Kent, A., Lancefield, D., Reilly, K. (2018) The Four Building Blocks of Transformation: How to Lead the Disruption of Your Own Enterprise. *Strategy+business* (Winter, 93). https://www.strategy-business.com/article/The-Four-Building-Blocks-of-Transformation

Lawrence, P.R. (1969) How to Deal with Resistance to Change. *Harvard Business Review* (January)

Lewin, K. (1947) Frontiers in Group Dynamics: Concept, Method and Reality in Social Science; Social Equilibria and Social Change – Understanding the Three Stages of Change. *Human Relations* 1 (1–2) 5–41

Prosci Inc webinar (n.d.) Managing Resistance to Change Overview. https://www.prosci.com/resources/articles/managing-resistance-to-change

PROGRAMME MANAGEMENT (INCLUDING AGILE)

Books

Ashmore, S., Runyan, K. (2014) *Introduction to Agile Methods.* Upper Saddle River, NJ: Addison-Wesley Professional

Bennett, J., Bowen, J. (2018) *Agile Project Management: Step-by-Step Guide to Agile Project Management.* United States: CreateSpace Independent Publishing Platform

Lyngso, S. (2014) *Agile Strategy Management: Techniques for Continuous Alignment and Improvement.* Boca Raton, FL: Taylor & Francis

Measey, P. (2015) *Agile Foundations.* Swindon: BCS

Moran, A. (2016) *Managing Agile: Strategy, Implementation, Organisation and People.* Berlin: Springer

Richards, K., Office of Government Commerce (2007) *Agile Project Management: Running PRINCE2 Projects with DSDM Atern.* Norwich: The Stationery Office

Online publications

Alexander, M. (2018) Agile Project Management: 12 Key Principles, 4 Big Hurdles. IDG Communications Ltd. https://www.cio.com/article/3156998/agile-project-management-a-beginners-guide.html

Brocchi, C., Brown, B., Machado, J., Neiman, M. (2016) Using Agile to Accelerate Your Data Transformation. McKinsey & Co. https://www.mckinsey.com/business-functions/mckinsey-digital/our-insights/using-agile-to-accelerate-your-data-transformation

Denning, S. (2018) The 12 Stages of the Agile Transformation Journey. Forbes (4 November). https://www.forbes.com/sites/stevedenning/2018/11/04/the-twelve-stages-of-the-agile-transformation-journey/

Follos, M. (2015) Mobilising Projects: Simple Checklist to Follow. LinkedIn (9 October). https://www.linkedin.com/pulse/mobilising-project-simple-checklist-follow-malcolm-follos/

Franklin, M. (2018) Introduction to Agile Change Management. Agile Change Management Limited. https://agilechangemanagement.co.uk/wp-content/uploads/2018/10/Introduction-to-Agile-Change-Management-v1.0-1.pdf

MacKay, J. (2018) The Ultimate Guide to Implementing Agile Project Management (and Scrum). Planio. https://plan.io/blog/what-is-agile-project-management/

Stieglitz, C. (2012) Beginning at the End: Requirements Gathering Lessons from a Flowchart Junkie. Paper presented at PMI® Global Congress 2012, North America, Vancouver, British Columbia, Canada. Newtown Square, PA: Project Management Institute

LEADERSHIP, CULTURE AND STORYTELLING

Books

Biesenbach, R. (2018) *Unleash the Power of Storytelling: Win Hearts, Change Minds, Get Results*. Evanston, IL: Eastlawn Media

Callahan, S. (2016) *Putting Stories to Work: Mastering Business Storytelling*. Melbourne: Pepperberg Press

Coyle, D. (2019) *The Culture Code: The Secrets of Highly Successful Groups*. London: Penguin Random House

Dietz, K., Silverman, L. (2013) *Business Storytelling for Dummies*. Hoboken, NJ: Wiley

Duarte, N. (2010) *Resonate: Present Visual Stories that Transform Audiences*. Hoboken, NJ: Wiley

Handy, C.B. (1978) *Gods of Management: The Changing Work of Organisations*. London: Souvenir Press Ltd

Joyce, C. (2016) *Being an Agile Leader-Manager: Practical Skills to Handle People Challenges in Today's World of Work*. St Albans: Panoma Press

Kouzes, J.M., Posner, B.Z. (2017) *The Leadership Challenge: How to Make Extraordinary Things Happen in Organizations*. Hoboken, NJ: Wiley

Marquet, L.D. (2015) *Turn the Ship Around! A True Story of Turning Followers into Leaders*. United Kingdom: Penguin

Nixon, R.M. (1962) *Six Crises*. New York: A Cardinal Edition: Pocket Books

Pascal, B. (1657) *Lettres Provinciales*. London: Royston

Patton, G.S. (1947) *War as I Knew It*. Boston, MA: Houghton Mifflin

Simmons, A. (2019) *The Story Factor: Inspiration, Influence, and Persuasion through the Art of Storytelling*. New York: Basic Books

Sinek, S. (2011) *Start with Why: How Great Leaders Inspire Everyone to Take Action*. London: Portfolio/Penguin

Smith, T. (1885) *Successful Advertising: Its Secrets Explained*. London: Thomas Smith Agency

Vogl, C. (2020) *Storytelling for Leadership: Creating Authentic Connections*. Berkeley, CA: Apocryphile Press

Online publications

Deloitte (2015) Global Human Capital Trends Report. https://www2.deloitte.com/content/dam/Deloitte/tr/Documents/human-capital/GlobalHumanCapitalTrends2015.pdf

Deloitte (2016) Global Human Capital Trends Report. https://www2.deloitte.com/content/dam/Deloitte/global/Documents/HumanCapital/gx-dup-global-human-capital-trends-2016.pdf

Fuller, J.N., Green, J.C. (2005) The Leader's Role in Strategy. *Graziadio Business Review* 8 (2). https://gbr.pepperdine.edu/2010/08/the-leaders-role-in-strategy/

Hart, K. (2007). No Cultural Merger at Sprint Nextel. *Washington Post*, 24 November. www.washingtonpost.com/wp-dyn/content/article/2007/11/23/AR2007112301588_2.html

Herbinet, D., Carey A. (2017) Board Leadership in Corporate Culture: European Report 2017. Board Agenda and Mazars in association with INSEAD. https://www.mazars.com/content/download/914232/47476119/version//file/Board%20Leadership%20in%20Corporate%20Culture%20Report.pdf

Hsieh, T.Y., Yik, S. (2005) Leadership as the Starting Point of Strategy. McKinsey & Co. https://www.mckinsey.com/featured-insights/leadership/leadership-as-the-starting-point-of-strategy

Janicijevic, N. (2012) Organizational Culture and Strategy. *Ekonomika preduzeca* 60, 127–139. https://www.researchgate.net/publication/274025071_Organizational_culture_and_strategy

FURTHER READING

Data breach management

Davidoff, S. (2019) *Data Breaches: Crisis and Opportunity*. Boston, MA: Pearson Education

Data modelling and design

Gorelik, A. (2019) *The Enterprise Big Data Lake: Delivering the Promise of Big Data and Data Science*. Sebastopol, CA: O'Reilly Media

Hay, D.C. (2011) *Enterprise Model Patterns: Describing the World*. Bradley Beach, NJ: Technics Publications

Prakash, N., Prakash, D. (2018) *Data Warehouse Requirements Engineering: A Decision Based Approach*. Singapore: Springer Nature

Turkington, G., Deshpande, T., Karnath, S. (2016) *Hadoop: Data Processing and Modelling*. Birmingham: Packt Publishing

Data monetisation/value

Kumar, S. (2017) *Making Money out of Data: The Art and Science of Analytics*. United States: CreateSpace Independent Publishing Platform

Laxminarayan, R., Macauley, M.K. (eds) (2014) *The Value of Information: Methodological Frontiers and New Applications in Environment and Health*. Dordrecht: Springer Science & Business Media

Management information, reporting and data visualisation

Carroll, J. (2017) *Earned Value Management in Easy Steps: Keep Tabs on the Real Status of All Projects, including Agile Projects*. United Kingdom: In Easy Steps

Gray, D. (2019) *Objectives and Key Results (OKR) Leadership: How to Apply Silicon Valley's Secret Sauce to Your Career, Team or Organization*. United States: Action Learning Associates

Niven, P.R., Lamorte, B. (2016) *Objectives and Key Results: Driving Focus, Alignment, and Engagement with OKRs*. Germany: Wiley

Smith, B. (2016) *KPI Checklists*. United Kingdom: Metric Press

Analytics

Anandarajan, M., Hill, C., Nolan, T. (2018) *Practical Text Analytics: Maximizing the Value of Text Data*. Switzerland: Springer Nature

Covington, D. (2020) *Analytics & Probability: Data Science, Data Analysis and Predictive Analytics for Business & Risk Management, Statistics, Combinations, and Permutations for Business*. United States: Amazon Digital Services LLC - KDP Print

Spiegelhalter, D. (2019) *The Art of Statistics: Learning from Data*. India: Penguin Books

Verbeke, W., Baesens, B., Bravo, C. (2017) *Profit Driven Business Analytics: A Practitioner's Guide to Transforming Big Data into Added Value*. United States: Wiley

Data science, artificial intelligence and machine learning

Dignum, V. (2019) *Responsible Artificial Intelligence: How to Develop and Use AI in a Responsible Way*. Switzerland: Springer Nature

Godsey, B. (2017) *Think Like a Data Scientist: Tackle the Data Science Process Step-by-Step*. United States: Manning Publications

Kearns, M., Roth, A. (2020) *The Ethical Algorithm: The Science of Socially Aware Algorithm Design*. United Kingdom: Oxford University Press

Kelleher, J.D., MacNamee, B., D'Arcy, A. (2015). *Fundamentals of Machine Learning for Predictive Data Analytics: Algorithms, Worked Examples, and Case Studies*. United States: MIT Press

Prevos, P. (2019) *Principles of Strategic Data Science: Creating Value from Data, Big and Small*. Birmingham: Packt Publishing

Taddy, M. (2019) *Business Data Science: Combining Machine Learning and Economics to Optimize, Automate, and Accelerate Business Decisions*. United States: McGraw-Hill Education

Programme management

Harrin, E. (2013) *Shortcuts to Success: Project Management in the Real World*. Swindon: BCS

Rigby, D., Berez, S., Elk, S. (2019) *Doing Agile Right: Transformation without Chaos*. Boston, MA: Harvard Business Review Press

Stellman, A., Greene, J. (2017) *Head First Agile: A Brain-Friendly Guide to Agile Principles, Ideas, and Real-World Practices*. Sebastopol, CA: O'Reilly Media

Todaro, D. (2019) *The Epic Guide to Agile: More Business Value on a Predictable Schedule with Scrum*. North Hampton, NH: R9 Publishing

Leadership, culture and storytelling

Brown, B. (2018) *Dare to Lead: Brave Work. Tough Conversations. Whole Hearts*. London: Vermilion

Moller, C. (2020) *The Rise of the Agile Leader: Can You Make the Shift?* Prominence Publishing

Putter, B. (2020) *Own Your Culture: How to Define, Embed and Manage your Company Culture*. United Kingdom: CCF Publishing

INDEX

Note: Page locators in **bold** refer to tables; those in *italics* refer to figures.